D1384164

The CELEBRATION HYMNAL

SONGS AND HYMNS FOR WORSHIP

Containing Scriptures from
New International Version
New American Standard Bible
The New King James Version

This hymnal is available in two editions: One has Scripture readings
from *The King James Version of the Holy Bible*;
the second contains readings taken from three translations: *New International Version*,
New American Standard Bible and *The New King James Version*.

All musical selections from this hymnal have been fully orchestrated.
Part books and score are available for any size ensemble.

WORD MUSIC / INTEGRITY MUSIC

Foreword

Our *song* is the one thing we most commonly enjoy amid the broad diversity of our Christian traditions. We meet in different types of buildings on every continent; we set our tempo at varied paces, our tone at varied levels. But we all still meet on the common ground of *song*—and often intersect at the precise point of even singing the same *songs*! But I wonder if we all realize how central our *song* is to the release of God's divine power *within, among* and *through* us—the many-membered body of Christ's living Church.

Song may not be listed as one of the gifts of the Holy Spirit, but it is certainly one of His mightiest means of ministry. There is a "life-begetting" power in music that's born of His anointing. It's found in its dual potential for "life"—both in respect to life's *birthing* power and its *breakthrough* qualities. Millions have been born again as God's Word has come to them through music! And how many millions more have experienced the *broken chains* of bondage to doubt or fear as they lifted their voices in praiseful *song*? The Church thrills and thrives, multiplies and advances on a Holy Spirit breeze of blessing that we simply call *song*.

For this reason, the book you have in hand may be called more of a "seeder" than a songbook—more a "weapon" than a hymnal—for its pages are laden with an awesome potential. When breathed upon by the Holy Spirit, and born upon the lips of devotion in praise, the *songs* in this book become an explosive force. Here are *songs*—filled with life and liberty, waiting to break forth with grace and glory. This is an entirely biblical proposition, for God's Word clearly reveals:

> Song is the *climate* in which God Himself works in His
> most glorious ways as Creator—Job 38:4-7
> Song is the *companion* means by which we are taught
> to see the Word of God enriched in its workings
> within our lives, in practice and purity—Colossians 3:16-17
> Song is the *conduit* by which the soul's night of darkness
> is ignited with hope and deliverance—Job 35:10; Psalm 32:6-7
> Song is the *claim* of the barren, by which God says we may
> entertain and expect fruitfulness—Isaiah 54:1
> Song is the *conquering* instrument available when we are
> outnumbered by circumstance—2 Chronicles 20:21-22

The secret of *song* is the Church's most distinctive resource, not because music is more powerful than the Word or the Spirit, but because *song* is a means by which both can become so joyously conjoined—by ALL the people of the Lord!

The Celebration Hymnal has been planned, prepared and published with this in mind. There have been two primary goals targeted: (1) to provide new possibilities for expanded praise, and (2) to assure rich dimensions of substance in worship.

First you will find an unprecedented resource of themed series of *songs* which have proved to bring a blend and a flow in praise that brings rejoicing to gatherings of believers! This is no ordinary hymnal: It is a marvelous collection of musical resources, conceived and arranged in ways that fulfill a call to creativity which Jesus Himself issued:

> He said to them, "Every teacher instructed in the Kingdom of heaven is like a householder who brings both new things and old out of his treasure-store." Matthew 13:52

Don't just *sing* from this book—strategize with it! The abundance of worship resources is the fruit of a pursuit: These are strategic means to revitalize, energize and maximize the possibilities of some of the richest music of all time—from *today* and from *yesterday*.

Second, be assured that nothing here is offered in the socially causal sense of *celebration*. All sensitive souls know that *high praise* is more than noise, and that *joyous worship* is more than foot-tapping. So, expect to find depth and dimension here—a richness in content that bypasses the superficial, and moves toward the significant. These pages contain spiritual resources designed to bring all who want to worship God toward a genuine entry into His presence—to bow before our awesome, living and loving Father!

> He is the *Founder* of our Song, so it's to Him we come!
> His Son is the *Foundation* of our Song, so it's Him we praise!
> His Spirit is the *Fountain* of our Song, so we drink of Him!

May *The Celebration Hymnal* be an instrument in your hand to assist you to new planes of praise, and unto new wonders in worship.

Jack W. Hayford

---

*L*ET THE WORD OF CHRIST
DWELL IN YOU RICHLY
AS YOU TEACH AND ADMONISH ONE ANOTHER

WITH ALL WISDOM, AND AS YOU

SING PSALMS, HYMNS AND SPIRITUAL SONGS

WITH GRATITUDE IN YOUR HEARTS TO GOD.

AND WHATEVER YOU DO, WHETHER IN WORD OR DEED,

DO IT IN THE NAME OF THE LORD JESUS,

GIVING THANKS TO GOD THE FATHER

THROUGH HIM.

COLOSSIANS 3:16-17 (NIV)

Acknowledgments

SENIOR EDITOR
Tom Fettke

ASSOCIATE EDITORS
Ken Barker – Hymnal
Camp Kirkland – Instrumental Hymnal

EXECUTIVE PROJECT MANAGER
Jim Gibson

EXECUTIVE COMMITTEE
Tom Fettke – Chairman, Don Cason, Michael Coleman, Jim Gibson, David Guthrie,
Tom Hartley, Camp Kirkland, Don Moen

THEOLOGICAL CONSULTANT AND SCRIPTURE EDITOR
Dr. Kenneth L. Barker

HYMNAL CONSULTANTS
Todd Bell, Jack Hayford, Randy Kettering, Marty Nystrom, David Ritter,
J. Daniel Smith, Jim Whitmire, Steve Williamson

INSTRUMENTAL CONSULTANTS
John Gage, Richard Kingsmore, Scott Revo, David Winkler

GENERAL ADVISORY BOARD
Greg Allen, George Baldwin, Laurey Berteig, Wendell Boertje, Dan Burgess, Harry
Causey, Martene Craig, Bob Deal, Sue Farrar, Paul Ferrin, John Gustafson, O.D. Hall,
Doug Holck, Dr. Steve Holcomb, Stan Jantz, Tim Mayfield, Dwayne McLuhan,
Ken Parker, Marty Parks, Dr. Dave Randlett, Bill Rayborn, Gary Rhodes, Jim Watson

ADMINISTRATIVE STAFF
Connie Jarrell, Pat Mishler

PRODUCTION CONSULTANTS
Charlotte Collier, Ernie Couch, Karla Graul, Nan Gurley, Tom Hartley, Doug Holck,
Peter Kobe, David McDonald, Phil Rhoten, Dr. Terry C. Terry

PRODUCTION ASSISTANTS
Editorial – Sheldon Curry, Sarah Huffman, David McDonald, Penny Schaeffer
Administration – Monica Visser, Don Mayes

COPYRIGHT ADMINISTRATION
Debra Mayes, Sheila Crocker

LOGO DESIGN
The Puckett Group, Pollei Design

MUSIC TYPOGRAPHY
Carl Seal Music Typography, Inc. – Hymnal
Kyle Hill Music Production Services – Orchestrations

WORD RECORDS AND MUSIC
Roland Lundy, President; Don Cason, Vice President and General Manager;
David Guthrie, Vice President of Print Music

INTEGRITY MUSIC
Michael Coleman, President and CEO; Don Moen, Executive Vice President and
Creative Director

*The Publishers gratefully acknowledge permission received from other publishers,
organizations and individuals to reprint texts, music and arrangements contained in this book.*

Preface

To offer worship and praise to the triune God in song is not an optional activity for believers! Throughout Scripture, God's people are invited, encouraged, exhorted—indeed commanded to raise hearts and voices in thankful and joyful praise to the Creator, Redeemer, Sustainer.

As publishers of *The Celebration Hymnal*, we take seriously this imperative and have made it our goal to create a hymnal which, in every way possible, aids worshipers in bringing their best sacrifice of praise to the One who is worthy. At the dawn of a new century and a new millennium, we rejoice in the privilege of presenting a worship resource intended to equip The Body of Christ with excellent and varied tools for meaningful worship.

Upon these pages you will find classic hymns of the church, beloved gospel songs, well-known inspirational songs, as well as contemporary praise and worship songs, all woven together with the thread of Scripture. In other words, you will find the tools for "blended worship." As more and more churches grow in their appreciation and use of both foundational hymns of the faith and newer praise and worship songs, worshipers are experiencing a vital, blended congregational expression. This "blended worship," increasingly manifest in nearly every denomination, is a guiding force behind the design of this hymnal. *The Celebration Hymnal* has been created for churches who cherish their rich heritage, while eagerly welcoming the future.

Ultimately, the usefulness of a hymnal for corporate worship hinges on two major factors: song selection and practical features. We trust you will find *The Celebration Hymnal* to be both unique and commendable in both critical areas. Selections were included in the compilation on the basis of their textual integrity, musical interest, utility in worship, and universal usage by today's evangelical church. As a nondenominational, multi-publisher resource, the compilation was influenced solely by the requirement to provide congregations with the strongest possible collection of songs and hymns.

Unique and thoughtful features abound throughout *The Celebration Hymnal*. There are, in fact, too many to enumerate here. They include creative musical material such as modulations within and between songs, descants, last stanza settings, and segues. Innovative organizational features include the sequencing of songs according to their worship objective, with, for example, songs and hymns to "Exalt the Lord" placed together. Over fifty thematic worship sequences unite song and Scripture in an unbroken flow of worship, with all needed transitional material included. The section entitled "The Family at Worship" is an important innovation. The material here has been carefully chosen and crafted for use by children, youth and adults—together in worship. It has also been our goal to elevate the role of Scripture in relationship to the music. No longer relegated to the back of the book as seldom-used or rigid "responsive readings," Scripture now appears throughout the volume, to be used creatively and interactively with songs of the same theme or topic. The entire hymnal is fully orchestrated for church orchestras and smaller instrumental groups.

The creation of a project of this magnitude requires the prolonged and focused commitment of a veritable army of talented and dedicated individuals. *The Celebration Hymnal* has been blessed by the efforts of a remarkable array of uncommonly gifted contributors. It has been our sincere honor as publishers to labor side-by-side with such qualified and respected leader/servants, each passionately pursuing a commitment to excellence before God. Though space prohibits us from properly thanking each one, our deep gratitude and admiration goes to each person listed on the Acknowledgments Page who gave so much to this ambitious undertaking. In particular, we must recognize the clear vision and the tireless efforts of Senior Editor Tom Fettke. Without compromise, Tom unswervingly guided a collaborative effort which stands as a loving tribute to the Maker of Music, our God most Holy. Tom was ably assisted by Instrumental Editor Camp Kirkland, who continues to set new standards of excellence in instrumental resources, and by biblical scholar Dr. Kenneth Barker, who, as Scripture Editor has ensured accuracy and integrity in the integration of God's Word into *The Celebration Hymnal*. Executive Project Manager Jim Gibson skillfully directed the complex administrative process, and the expert editorial assistance of Ken Barker was essential to the project's success. Lastly, the insightful, informed guidance so graciously provided by the Consultants and Advisory Board members has made a lasting and important contribution. *The Celebration Hymnal* could not have been created without their committed involvement, and we are truly grateful.

It is our prayer that *The Celebration Hymnal* be a tool God uses to deepen your worship, energize your praise, enrich your fellowship, and bring honor and glory to Him!

The Publishers

Table of Contents

1 Praise, My Soul, the King of Heaven

Praise the Lord, O my soul, and forget not all His benefits. Psalm 103:2

Unison

1. Praise, my soul, the King of heav-en; To His feet your trib-ute bring. Ran-somed, healed, re-stored, for-giv-en, Ev-er-more His prais-es sing. Al-le-lu-ia! Al-le-lu-ia! Praise the ev-er-last-ing King!
2. Praise Him for His grace and fa-vor To our fa-thers in dis-tress; Praise Him, still the same as ev-er, Slow to chide and swift to bless. Al-le-lu-ia! Al-le-lu-ia! Glo-rious in His faith-ful-ness!
3. Fa-ther-like, He tends and spares us; Well our fee-ble frame He knows. In His hands He gent-ly bears us, Res-cues us from all our foes. Al-le-lu-ia! Al-le-lu-ia! Wide-ly yet His mer-cy flows.
4. An-gels in the height, a-dore Him; You be-hold Him face to face. Saints tri-um-phant, bow be-fore Him; Gath-ered in from ev-ery race. Al-le-lu-ia! Al-le-lu-ia! Praise with us the God of grace!

TEXT: Henry F. Lyte; based on Psalm 103
MUSIC: Mark Andrews
Alternate tune: REGENT SQUARE at No. 403

ANDREWS
8.7.8.7.8.7.

Holy God, We Praise Thy Name 2

I will exalt You, my God the King; I will praise Your name for ever and ever. Psalm 145:1

1. Ho - ly God, we praise Thy name; Lord of all, we
2. Hark, the glad ce - les - tial hymn An - gel choirs a -
3. Ho - ly Fa - ther, ho - ly Son, Ho - ly Spir - it:

bow be - fore Thee; All on earth Thy scep - ter claim;
bove are rais - ing; Cher - u - bim and ser - a - phim
Three we name Thee While in es - sence on - ly one;

All in heav'n a - bove a - dore Thee. In - fi - nite Thy
In un - ceas - ing cho - rus prais - ing; Fill the heav'ns with
Un - di - vid - ed God we claim Thee, And a - dor - ing,

vast do - main; Ev - er - last - ing is Thy reign.
sweet ac - cord: Ho - ly, ho - ly, ho - ly Lord.
bend the knee While we sing our praise to Thee.

TEXT: Ignaz Franz; translated by Clarence A. Walworth
MUSIC: *Katholisches Gesangbuch*, 1774

GROSSER GOTT
7.8.7.8.7.7.

3 Holy, Holy, Holy! Lord God Almighty

Holy, holy, holy is the Lord God Almighty, who was, and is, and is to come. Revelation 4:8

1. Ho - ly, ho - ly, ho - ly! Lord God Al - might - y!
2. Ho - ly, ho - ly, ho - ly! all the saints a - dore Thee,
3. Ho - ly, ho - ly, ho - ly! tho' the dark - ness hide Thee,
4. Ho - ly, ho - ly, ho - ly! Lord God Al - might - y!

Ear - ly in the morn - ing our song shall rise to Thee.
Cast - ing down their gold - en crowns a - round the glass - y sea.
Tho' the eye of sin - ful man Thy glo - ry may not see.
All Thy works shall praise Thy name in earth, and sky, and sea.

Ho - ly, ho - ly, ho - ly! mer - ci - ful and might - y!
Cher - u - bim and ser - a - phim fall - ing down be - fore Thee,
On - ly Thou art ho - ly– there is none be - side Thee,
Ho - ly, ho - ly, ho - ly! mer - ci - ful and might - y!

God in three Per - sons, bless - ed Trin - i - ty!
Which wert, and art, and ev - er - more shalt be.
Per - fect in pow'r, in love, in pu - ri - ty.
God in three Per - sons, bless - ed Trin - i - ty!

TEXT: Reginald Heber
MUSIC: John B. Dykes; Last stanza setting
and Choral ending by Camp Kirkland

NICAEA
11.12.12.10.

4 Praise the Savior

Praise His glorious grace, which He has freely given us in the One He loves. Ephesians 1:6

1. Praise the Savior, ye who know Him! Who can tell how much we owe Him?
2. Jesus is the name that charms us, He for conflict fits and arms us;
3. Keep us, Lord, O keep us cleaving To Thyself, and still believing,
4. Then we shall be where we would be, Then we shall be what we should be;

Gladly let us render to Him All we are and have.
Nothing moves and nothing harms us While we trust in Him.
Till the hour of our receiving Promised joys with Thee.
Things that are not now, nor could be, Soon shall be our own.

Optional segue to "I Sing Praises."
No transition is needed.

TEXT: Thomas Kelly
MUSIC: Traditional German melody

ACCLAIM
8.8.8.5.

5 I Sing Praises

I will praise You among the nations, O Lord; I will sing praises to Your name. Psalm 18:49

1. I sing praises to Your name, O Lord, Praises to Your name, O
2. I give glory to Your name, O Lord, Glory to Your name, O

Lord; For Your name is great and greatly to be praised.
Lord; For Your name is great and greatly to be praised.

TEXT: Terry MacAlmon
MUSIC: Terry MacAlmon

I SING PRAISES
Irregular meter

6 There Is No Name So Sweet on Earth

Give Him the name Jesus, because He will save His people from their sins. Matthew 1:21

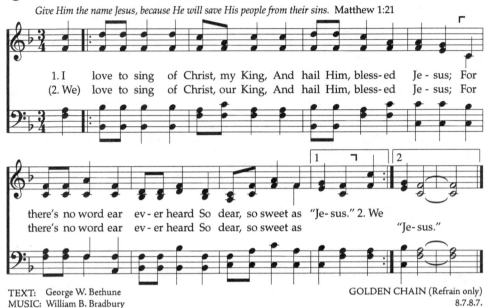

1. I love to sing of Christ, my King, And hail Him, bless-ed Je-sus; For
(2. We) love to sing of Christ, our King, And hail Him, bless-ed Je-sus; For

there's no word ear ev-er heard So dear, so sweet as "Je-sus." 2. We
there's no word ear ev-er heard So dear, so sweet as "Je-sus."

TEXT: George W. Bethune
MUSIC: William B. Bradbury

GOLDEN CHAIN (Refrain only)
8.7.8.7.

7 PRAISE THE ALMIGHTY KING

A Worship Sequence

Come, Thou Almighty King; stanzas 1,2,4
Glorify Thy Name; stanzas 1,2
Majesty
Suggested stanzas have been marked with an arrow: ➤

WORSHIP LEADER Yours, O Lord, is the greatness and the power
and the glory and the majesty and the splendor,
for everything in heaven and earth is Yours.

EVERYONE **We give You thanks, and praise Your glorious name!**

WORSHIP LEADER Yours, O Lord, is the kingdom; You are exalted as Head over all!
Wealth and honor come from You; You are the ruler of all things.

EVERYONE **We give You thanks, and praise Your glorious name!**

WORSHIP LEADER In Your hands are strength and power
to exalt and give strength to all.

EVERYONE **Now, our God, we give You thanks,
and praise Your glorious name!**

from 1 Chronicles 29:11-13 (NIV)

Optional introduction to "Come, Thou Almighty King"

Come, Thou Almighty King 8

The Lord is the great God, the great King. Psalm 95:3

1. Come, Thou Al - might - y King, Help us Thy name to sing; Help us to praise. Fa - ther all - glo - ri - ous, O'er all vic - to - ri - ous, Come, and reign o - ver us, An - cient of Days.
2. Come, Thou In - car - nate Word, Gird on Thy might - y sword; Our prayer at - tend. Come, and Thy peo - ple bless, And give Thy word suc - cess. Spir - it of ho - li - ness, On us de - scend.
3. Come, Ho - ly Com - fort - er, Thy sa - cred wit - ness bear In this glad hour. Thou, who al - might - y art, Now rule in ev - ery heart And ne'er from us de - part, Spir - it of pow'r.
4. To Thee, great One in Three, E - ter - nal prais - es be, Hence ev - er - more; Thy sov - 'reign maj - es - ty May we in glo - ry see, And to e - ter - ni - ty Love and a - dore.

TEXT: Anonymous
MUSIC: Felice de Giardini

ITALIAN HYMN
6.6.4.6.6.6.4.

Optional transition to
"Glorify Thy Name"

f same tempo   decresc.   rit.

9 Glorify Thy Name

Father, glorify Your name! John 12:28

1. Fa - ther, we love You, we wor - ship and a - dore You,
2. Je - sus, we love You, we wor - ship and a - dore You,
3. Spir - it, we love You, we wor - ship and a - dore You,

Glo - ri - fy Thy name in all the earth. Glo - ri - fy Thy name,

Glo - ri - fy Thy name, Glo - ri - fy Thy name in all the earth.

Optional segue to "Majesty."
No transition is needed.

TEXT: Donna Adkins
MUSIC: Donna Adkins

GLORIFY THY NAME
Irregular meter

10 Majesty

Yours, O Lord, is the greatness and the power and the glory and the majesty. 1 Chronicles 29:11

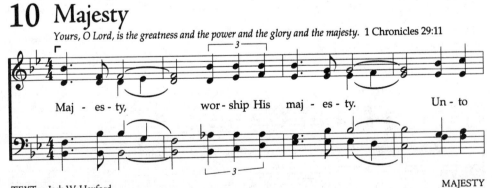

Maj - es - ty, wor - ship His maj - es - ty. Un - to

TEXT: Jack W. Hayford
MUSIC: Jack W. Hayford; arranged by Eugene Thomas

MAJESTY
Irregular meter

Je - sus be all glo - ry, hon - or, and praise. Maj - es - ty, king - dom au - thor - i - ty Flow from His throne un - to His own; His an - them raise. So ex - alt, lift up on high the name of Je - sus. Mag - ni - fy, come glo - ri - fy Christ Je - sus, the King. Maj - es - ty, wor - ship His maj - es - ty— Je - sus who died, now glo - ri - fied, King of all kings.

*Cued notes optional for a few choir sopranos.

The end of PRAISE THE ALMIGHTY KING - A Worship Sequence

11 Come, Thou Fount of Every Blessing

The blessing of the Lord brings wealth. Proverbs 10:22

1. Come, Thou Fount of ev-ery bless-ing, Tune my heart to sing Thy grace;
2. Hith-er-to Thy love has blest me; Thou hast bro't me to this place;
3. O to grace how great a debt-or Dai-ly I'm con-strained to be!

Streams of mer-cy, nev-er ceas-ing, Call for songs of loud-est praise.
And I know Thy hand will bring me Safe-ly home by Thy good grace.
Let Thy good-ness, like a fet-ter, Bind my wan-d'ring heart to Thee:

Teach me some me-lo-dious son-net, Sung by flam-ing tongues a-bove;
Je-sus sought me when a strang-er, Wan-d'ring from the fold of God;
Prone to wan-der, Lord, I feel it, Prone to leave the God I love;

Praise His name— I'm fixed up-on it— Name of God's re-deem-ing love.
He, to res-cue me from dan-ger, Bo't me with His pre-cious blood.
Here's my heart, O take and seal it; Seal it for Thy courts a-bove.

TEXT: Robert Robinson; adapted by Margaret Clarkson
MUSIC: Traditional American melody; John Wyeth's *Repository of Sacred Music,* 1813
Last stanza setting and Choral ending by Carl Seal

NETTLETON
8.7.8.7.D

Optional last stanza setting
Unison

3. O to grace how great a debt-or Dai-ly I'm con-strained to be! Let Thy good-ness, like a fet - ter, Bind my wan- d'ring heart to Thee: Prone to wan - der, Lord, I feel it, Prone to leave the God I love; Here's my heart, O take and seal it; Seal it for Thy courts a - bove.

Optional choral ending

Here's my heart, O take and seal it; Seal it for Thy courts a - bove.

12 Praise Him! Praise Him!

You are worthy and with Your blood You purchased for God members of every nation. Revelation 5:9

1. Praise Him! Praise Him! Je-sus, our bless-ed Re-deem-er! Sing, O earth, His
2. Praise Him! Praise Him! Je-sus, our bless-ed Re-deem-er! For our sins He
3. Praise Him! Praise Him! Je-sus, our bless-ed Re-deem-er! Heav'n-ly por-tals

won-der-ful love pro-claim! Hail Him! Hail Him! high-est arch-an-gels in glo-ry;
suf-fered, and bled, and died. He, our Rock, our Hope of e-ter-nal sal-va-tion—
loud with ho-san-nas ring! Je-sus, Sav-ior, reign-eth for-ev-er and ev-er.

Strength and hon-or give to His ho-ly name! Like a shep-herd,
Hail Him! Hail Him! Je-sus, the Cru-ci-fied. Sound His prais-es!
Crown Him! Crown Him! Proph-et, and Priest, and King! Christ is com-ing,

Je-sus will guard His chil-dren; In His arms He car-ries them all day long.
Je-sus, who bore our sor-rows; Love un-bound-ed, won-der-ful, deep, and strong!
o-ver the world vic-to-rious; Pow'r and glo-ry un-to the Lord be-long!

Refrain

Praise Him! Praise Him! tell of His ex-cel-lent great-ness;

TEXT: Fanny J. Crosby
MUSIC: Chester G. Allen

JOYFUL SONG
Irregular meter

Praise Him! Praise Him! ev - er in joy - ful song!

Sing Hallelujah, Praise the Lord! 13

Sing the glory of His name; make His praise glorious! Psalm 66:2

1. Sing hal - le - lu - jah, praise the Lord! Sing with a cheer - ful voice;
2. There we for all e - ter - ni - ty shall join th'an - gel - ic praise;

Ex - alt our God with one ac - cord, and in His name re - joice.
And songs in per - fect har - mo - ny to God, our Sav - ior, raise.

Ne'er cease to sing, O ran - somed host, praise Fa - ther, Son, and Ho - ly Ghost,
He has re - deemed us by His blood, and made us kings and priests to God;

rit. 2nd verse   2nd verse: slowly

Un - til in realms of end - less light your prais - es shall u - nite.
For us, for us the Lamb was slain! Praise ye the Lord! A - men.

2nd verse: slowly

TEXT: John Swertner
MUSIC: John Christian Bechler

BECHLER
8.6.8.6.8.8.8.6.

14 NAME ABOVE ALL NAMES
A Worship Sequence

No Other Name
All Hail the Power of Jesus' Name; stanzas 1,3,4
Suggested stanzas have been marked with an arrow: ➤

WORSHIP LEADER

God has promised He will never leave us or forsake us.
In Christ, God revealed His faithfulness to us from the beginning of time:

PASTOR OR WORSHIP LEADER

In Genesis Jesus is the Ram at Abraham's altar
In Exodus He's the Passover Lamb
In Leviticus He's the High Priest
In Numbers He's the Cloud by day and Pillar of Fire by night
In Deuteronomy He's the City of our refuge
In Joshua He's the Scarlet Thread out Rahab's window
In Judges He is our Judge
In Ruth He is our Kinsman Redeemer
In 1st and 2nd Samuel He's our Trusted Prophet
And in Kings and Chronicles He's our Reigning King
In Ezra He's our Faithful Scribe
In Nehemiah He's the Rebuilder of everything that is broken
And in Esther He is the Mordecai sitting faithful at the gate
In Job He's our Redeemer that ever liveth
In Psalms He is my Shepherd and I shall not want
In Proverbs and Ecclesiastes He's our Wisdom
And in the Song of Solomon He's the Beautiful Bridegroom
In Isaiah He's the Suffering Servant
In Jeremiah and Lamentations it is Jesus that is the Weeping Prophet
In Ezekiel He's the Wonderful Four-Faced Man
And in Daniel He is the Fourth Man in the midst of a fiery furnace
In Hosea He is my Love that is forever faithful
In Joel He baptizes us with the Holy Spirit
In Amos He's our Burden Bearer
In Obadiah our Savior
And in Jonah He is the Great Foreign Missionary that takes
the Word of God into all the world
In Micah He is the Messenger with beautiful feet
In Nahum He is the Avenger
In Habakkuk He is the Watchman that is ever praying for revival
In Zephaniah He is the Lord mighty to save
In Haggai He is the Restorer of our lost heritage
In Zechariah He is our Fountain
And in Malachi He is the Sun of Righteousness with healing in His wings

In Matthew Thou art the Christ, the Son of the Living God
In Mark He is the Miracle Worker
In Luke He's the Son of Man
And in John He is the Door by which every one of us must enter
In Acts He is the Shining Light that appears to Saul on the road to Damascus
In Romans He is our Justifier
In 1st Corinthians our Resurrection
In 2nd Corinthians our Sin Bearer
In Galatians He redeems us from the law
In Ephesians He is our Unsearchable Riches
In Philippians He supplies our every need
And in Colossians He's the Fullness of the Godhead Bodily
In 1st and 2nd Thessalonians He is our Soon Coming King
In 1st and 2nd Timothy He is the Mediator between God and man
(Begin music underscore)
In Titus He is our Blessed Hope
In Philemon He is a Friend that sticks closer than a brother
And in Hebrews He's the Blood of the Everlasting Covenant
In James it is the Lord that heals the sick
In 1st and 2nd Peter He is the Chief Shepherd
In 1st, 2nd and 3rd John it is Jesus who has the tenderness of love
In Jude He is the Lord coming with 10,000 saints
And in Revelation, lift up your eyes, Church, for your redemption draweth nigh;
He is our King of kings and Lord of lords.

Optional underscore and introduction to "No Other Name"

*"Name above All Names" underscore
by Camp Kirkland and Tom Fettke

Segue to "No Other Name"

15 No Other Name

God gave Him the name that is above every name. Philippians 2:9

No oth - er name but the name of Je - sus, No oth - er

name but the name of the Lord; No oth - er name but the name of

Last time to Coda

Je - sus Is wor - thy of glo - ry, And wor - thy of hon - or, And

1
wor - thy of pow - er and all praise. No oth - er praise.
2
praise. His

TEXT: Robert Gay
MUSIC: Robert Gay

NO OTHER NAME
Irregular meter

name is ex-alt-ed   far a-bove the earth; His name   is high a-bove the

heav-ens.   His name is ex-alt-ed   far   a-bove   the earth; Give

glo-ry   and hon-or   and praise un-to His name.

D. S. al Coda   CODA

No oth-er   wor - thy of pow-er and all   praise.

*If desired, you may use measures 10 forward of the "Name above All Names"
underscore as an introduction to "No Other Name"

Optional transition to
"All Hail the Power of Jesus' Name"

f   rit.

16 All Hail the Power of Jesus' Name

Every tongue confess that Jesus Christ is Lord. Philippians 2:11

1. All hail the pow'r of Je - sus' name! Let an - gels pros-trate
2. Ye cho - sen seed of Is - rael's race, Ye ran- somed from the
3. Let ev - ery kin - dred, ev - ery tribe On this ter - res - trial
4. O that with yon - der sa - cred throng We at His feet may

fall, Let an - gels pros-trate fall; Bring forth the roy - al di - a -
fall, Ye ran - somed from the fall; Hail Him who saves you by His
ball, On this ter - res - trial ball; To Him all maj - es - ty as -
fall, We at His feet may fall! We'll join the ev - er - last - ing

dem, And crown
grace,
cribe, And crown Him, crown Him, crown Him, crown Him,
song,

Him,

crown

crown Him, crown Him, crown Him, And crown Him Lord of all.

Him,

TEXT: Edward Perronet; adapted by John Rippon
MUSIC: James Ellor; Descant and Choral ending by Camp Kirkland

DIADEM
C.M. with Refrain

The end of NAME ABOVE ALL NAMES - A Worship Sequence

17 Our Great Savior

Our great God and Savior, Jesus Christ, gave Himself for us. Titus 2:13-14

1. Je - sus! what a Friend for sin - ners! Je - sus! Lov - er of my soul;
2. Je - sus! what a Strength in weak - ness! Let me hide my - self in Him;
3. Je - sus! what a Help in sor - row! While the bil - lows o'er me roll,
4. Je - sus! what a Guide and Keep - er! While the tem - pest still is high,
5. Je - sus! I do now re - ceive Him, More than all in Him I find;

Friends may fail me, foes as - sail me, He, my Sav - ior, makes me whole.
Tempt - ed, tried, and some - times fail - ing, He, my Strength, my vic - t'ry wins.
E - ven when my heart is break - ing, He, my Com - fort, helps my soul.
Storms a - bout me, night o'er - takes me, He, my Pi - lot, hears my cry.
He hath grant - ed me for - give - ness, I am His, and He is mine.

Refrain

Hal - le - lu - jah! what a Sav - ior! Hal - le - lu - jah! what a Friend!

Sav - ing, help - ing, keep - ing, lov - ing, He is with me to the end.

TEXT: J. Wilbur Chapman
MUSIC: Rowland H. Prichard; arranged by Robert Harkness;
Choral ending by Ken Barker
A lower setting may be found at No. 309

HYFRYDOL
8.7.8.7.D.

Optional choral ending

Hal - le - lu - jah! what a Sav - ior! Hal - le - lu - jah!

Let's Just Praise the Lord 18

Lift up your hands and praise the Lord. Psalm 134:2

Let's just praise the Lord! Praise the Lord! Let's just

lift our hearts to heav - en and praise the Lord;

Let's just praise the Lord! Praise the Lord! Let's just

lift our hearts to heav - en and praise the Lord!

TEXT: Gloria Gaither and William J. Gaither
MUSIC: William J. Gaither

LET'S JUST PRAISE THE LORD
Irregular meter

19

SING HIS PRAISE
A Worship Sequence

Let There Be Glory and Honor and Praises
O for a Thousand Tongues to Sing; stanzas 1,2,3,5
Suggested stanzas have been marked with an arrow: ➤

WORSHIP LEADER	I will praise You, O Lord, with my whole heart; I will be glad and rejoice in You.
EVERYONE	**I will sing praise to Your name, O Most High.**
WORSHIP LEADER	You are my God,
EVERYONE	**And I will praise You.**
WORSHIP LEADER	You are my God,
EVERYONE	**And I will exalt You.**
WORSHIP LEADER	I have trusted in Your mercy;
EVERYONE	**My heart shall rejoice in Your salvation.**
WORSHIP LEADER	I will praise the name of God with a song, and will magnify Him with thanksgiving.

from Psalms 9:1-2; 118:28; 13:5; 69:30 (NKJV)

Optional introduction to
"Let There Be Glory and Honor and Praises"

20 Let There Be Glory and Honor and Praises

Worship the Lord in the splendor of His holiness. Psalm 29:2

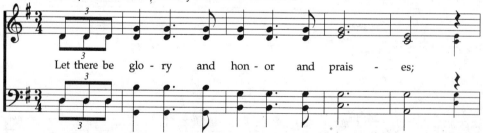

Let there be glo - ry and hon - or and prais - es;

TEXT: James and Elizabeth Greenelsh
MUSIC: James and Elizabeth Greenelsh

LET THERE BE GLORY
Irregular meter

Optional segue to "O for a Thousand Tongues to Sing"

21 O for a Thousand Tongues to Sing

My tongue will speak of Your praises all day long. Psalm 35:28

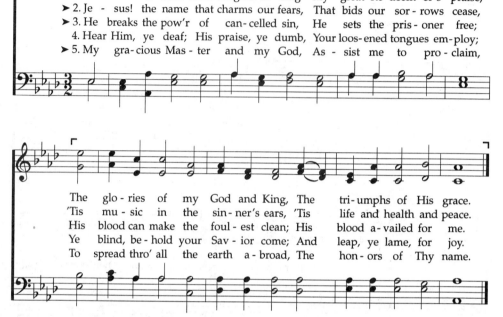

► 1. O for a thou-sand tongues to sing My great Re-deem-er's praise,
► 2. Je - sus! the name that charms our fears, That bids our sor - rows cease,
► 3. He breaks the pow'r of can-celled sin, He sets the pris - oner free;
4. Hear Him, ye deaf; His praise, ye dumb, Your loos-ened tongues em-ploy;
► 5. My gra-cious Mas - ter and my God, As - sist me to pro - claim,

The glo - ries of my God and King, The tri-umphs of His grace.
'Tis mu - sic in the sin-ner's ears, 'Tis life and health and peace.
His blood can make the foul - est clean; His blood a-vailed for me.
Ye blind, be-hold your Sav - ior come; And leap, ye lame, for joy.
To spread thro' all the earth a-broad, The hon - ors of Thy name.

TEXT: Charles Wesley
MUSIC: Carl G. Gläzer; arranged by Lowell Mason;
Last stanza setting and Choral ending by Tom Fettke

AZMON
C.M.

A lower setting may be found at No. 221

Optional last stanza setting

Unison

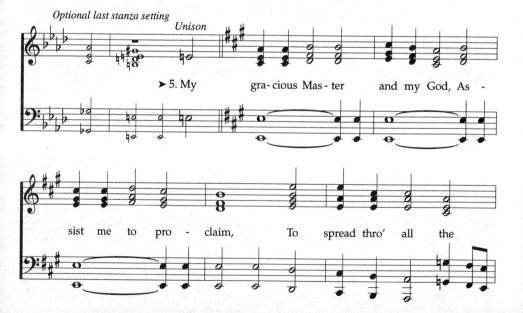

► 5. My gra-cious Mas - ter and my God, As -

sist me to pro - claim, To spread thro' all the

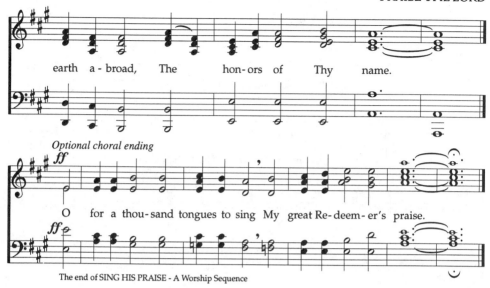

earth a-broad, The hon-ors of Thy name.

Optional choral ending

O for a thou-sand tongues to sing My great Re-deem-er's praise.

The end of SING HIS PRAISE - A Worship Sequence

Praise the Name of Jesus 22

The Lord is my rock, my fortress, and my deliverer. Psalm 18:2

Praise the name of Je - sus, Praise the name of Je - sus.

He's my Rock, He's my For - tress, He's my De - liv-er-er, In

Him will I trust. Praise the name of Je - sus.

TEXT: Roy Hicks, Jr.
MUSIC: Roy Hicks, Jr.

HICKS
Irregular meter

23 The God of Abraham Praise

Abraham was strengthened in his faith and gave glory to God. Romans 4:20

1. The God of A-br'ham praise, Who reigns en-throned a-bove,
2. He by Him-self hath sworn; We on His oath de-pend.
3. The God who reigns on high The great arch-an-gels sing,
4. The whole tri-um-phant host Give thanks to God on high;

The An-cient of e-ter-nal days And God of love.
We shall, on ea-gles' wings up-borne, To heav'n as-cend.
And "Ho-ly, ho-ly, ho-ly," cry, "Al-might-y King!"
"Hail, Fa-ther, Son and Ho-ly Ghost!" They ev-er cry.

Je-ho-vah, great I AM, By earth and heav'n con-fessed:
We shall be-hold His face; We shall His pow'r a-dore,
Who was and is the same And ev-er-more shall be:
Hail, A-br'ham's God and mine! With heav'n our songs we raise:

We bow and bless the sa-cred name For-ev-er blest.
And sing the won-ders of His grace For-ev-er-more.
E-ter-nal Fa-ther, great I AM, We wor-ship Thee.
All might and maj-es-ty are Thine And end-less praise.

TEXT: Thomas Olivers; based on Hebrew *Yigdal* of Daniel Ben Judah
MUSIC: Traditional Hebrew melody; adapted by Meyer Lyon

LEONI
6.6.8.4.D.

PRAISE HIM WITH YOUR HEART 24

from Psalm 9 (NIV)

WORSHIP LEADER
I will praise You, O Lord, with all my heart;

EVERYONE
I will tell of all Your wonders.

WORSHIP LEADER
I will be glad and rejoice in You;

EVERYONE
I will sing praise to Your name, O Most High.

WORSHIP LEADER
The Lord reigns forever;
He has established His throne for judgment.

MEN
He will judge the world in righteousness;
He will govern the peoples with justice.

WOMEN
The Lord is a refuge for the oppressed,
A stronghold in times of trouble.

EVERYONE
Those who know Your name will trust in You,
For You, Lord, have never forsaken those who seek You.

WORSHIP LEADER
Sing praises to the Lord, enthroned in Zion;
Proclaim among the nations what He has done.
Sing praise to the Lord.

EVERYONE
We sing praise to the Lord.

SHOUT WITH JOY TO GOD! 25

from Psalm 66:1-5 (NIV)

WORSHIP LEADER
Shout with joy to God, all the earth!
Sing to the glory of His name;
Offer Him glory and praise!

EVERYONE
Father, we give You glory and praise!

WORSHIP LEADER
Say to God, "How awesome are Your deeds!"

EVERYONE
Father, how awesome are Your deeds!

WORSHIP LEADER
All the earth bows down to You;
They sing praise to Your name.

EVERYONE
We sing praise to Your name.

26   THE LORD IS WORTHY OF PRAISE

from Psalm 145 (NIV)

WORSHIP LEADER
I will exalt You, my God, the King!
I will praise Your name for ever and ever.

EVERYONE
Great is the Lord and most worthy of praise;
His greatness no one can fathom.

WORSHIP LEADER
One generation will commend Your works to another;
They will tell of Your mighty acts.

EVERYONE
Great is the Lord and most worthy of praise;
His greatness no one can fathom.

WORSHIP LEADER
Your kingdom is an everlasting kingdom,
and Your dominion endures through all generations.

EVERYONE
Great is the Lord and most worthy of praise;
His greatness no one can fathom.

WORSHIP LEADER
The Lord is faithful to all His promises and loving toward all He has made.
The Lord upholds all those who fall and lifts up all who are bowed down.

EVERYONE
Great is the Lord and most worthy of praise;
His greatness no one can fathom.

WORSHIP LEADER
The Lord is righteous in all His ways and loving toward all He has made. The
Lord is near to all who call on Him, to all who call on Him in truth.

EVERYONE
Great is the Lord and most worthy of praise;
His greatness no one can fathom.

WORSHIP LEADER
My mouth will speak in praise of the Lord.

EVERYONE
Let every creature praise His holy name for ever and ever.

27   SING PRAISES TO HIS NAME

from Psalm 135:1, 3 (NKJV)

WORSHIP LEADER
Praise the Lord.

EVERYONE
Praise the Lord.

WORSHIP LEADER
Praise Him, O you servants of the Lord!

EVERYONE
Praise the Lord, for the Lord is good;
We will sing praises to His name, for it is pleasant.

At the Name of Jesus 28

Every knee should bow and every tongue confess that Jesus Christ is Lord. Philippians 2:10-11

BERRY
Irregular meter

29 Begin, My Tongue, Some Heavenly Theme

My tongue will tell of Your righteous acts all day long. Psalm 71:24

1. Be - gin, my tongue, some heav'n-ly theme And speak some bound-less thing:
2. Tell of His won - drous faith - ful - ness And sound His pow'r a - broad;
3. His ver - y word of grace is strong As that which built the skies;
4. O might I hear Thy heav'n-ly tongue But whis - per, "Thou art mine!"

The might - y works or might - ier name Of our e - ter - nal King.
Sing the sweet prom - ise of His grace, The love and truth of God.
The voice that rolls the stars a - long Speaks all the prom - is - es.
Those gen - tle words shall raise my song To notes al - most di - vine.

TEXT: Isaac Watts
MUSIC: William Croft

ST. ANNE
C.M.

30 EXALT THE LORD

A Worship Sequence

I Exalt Thee
Be Exalted, O God

WORSHIP LEADER

I will praise You, O Lord, among the nations;
I will sing of You among the peoples.
For great is Your love, reaching to the heavens;
Your faithfulness reaches to the skies.
Be exalted, O God, above the heavens;
Let Your glory be over all the earth.

from Psalm 57:9-11 (NIV)

Optional introduction to "I Exalt Thee"

mf

I Exalt Thee 31

You are exalted far above all gods. Psalm 97:9

For Thou, O Lord, art high a-bove all the earth;

Thou art ex-alt-ed far a-bove all gods.

For Thou, O bove all gods.

Harmony optional

I ex-alt Thee, I ex-alt Thee, I ex-alt Thee,

O Lord. I ex- Lord.

Optional transition to "Be Exalted, O God"

TEXT: Pete Sanchez, Jr.; based on Psalm 97:9
MUSIC: Pete Sanchez, Jr.

I EXALT THEE
Irregular meter

32 Be Exalted, O God

Great is Your love. Be exalted, O God, above the heavens. Psalm 57:10-11

I will give thanks to Thee, O Lord, a-mong the peo-ple. I will sing prais-es to Thee a-mong the na-tions. For Thy stead-fast love is great, is great to the heav-ens; And Thy faith-ful-ness, Thy faith-ful-ness to the clouds. Be ex-

TEXT: Brent Chambers; based on Psalm 57:9-11
MUSIC: Brent Chambers

BE EXALTED
Irregular meter

alt - ed, O God, a - bove the heav - ens; Let Thy

glo - ry be o - ver all the earth. Be ex -

alt - ed, O God, a - bove the heav - ens; Let Thy

glo - ry be o - ver all the earth.

Optional choral ending

Be ex - alt - ed, O God; be ex - alt - ed, O God!

The end of EXALT THE LORD - A Worship Sequence

33 Immortal, Invisible, God Only Wise

Now to the King eternal, immortal, invisible, the only God, be honor. 1 Timothy 1:17

1. Im - mor - tal, in - vis - i - ble, God on - ly wise,
2. Un - rest - ing, un - hast - ing, and si - lent as light,
3. To all, life Thou giv - est— to both great and small;
4. Great Fa - ther of glo - ry, pure Fa - ther of light,

In light in - ac - ces - si - ble hid from our eyes.
Nor want - ing, nor wast - ing, Thou rul - est in might;
In all life Thou liv - est— the true life of all.
Thine an - gels a - dore Thee, all veil - ing their sight;

Most bless - ed, most glo - rious, the An - cient of Days,
Thy jus - tice, like moun - tains, high soar - ing a - bove
Thy wis - dom so bound - less, Thy mer - cy so free,
All praise we would ren - der— O help us to see

Al - might - y, vic - to - rious— Thy great name we praise.
Thy clouds, which are foun - tains of good - ness and love.
E - ter - nal Thy good - ness for naught chang - eth Thee.
'Tis on - ly the splen - dor of light hid - eth Thee!

TEXT: Walter Chalmers Smith; based on 1 Timothy 1:17
MUSIC: Traditional Welsh Hymn melody
from John Roberts' *Canaidau y Cyssegr*, 1839

ST. DENIO
11.11.11.11.

He Is Lord 34

Every knee should bow and every tongue confess that Jesus Christ is Lord. Philippians 2:10-11

He is Lord,   He is Lord!   He is ris-en from the dead and He is   Lord!

Ev-ery knee shall bow, ev-ery tongue con-fess that Je-sus Christ is Lord.

Optional repeat setting

He   is   Lord,   He is Lord!   He is ris-en from the

dead and He is   Lord!   Ev-ery knee shall bow, ev-ery tongue con-fess that

Optional extended or choral ending   rit.

Je-sus Christ is Lord.   Je-sus Christ is   Lord!

TEXT: Based on Philippians 2:10-11
MUSIC: Traditional; arranged by Tom Fettke

HE IS LORD
Irregular meter

35 Hallelujah! Our God Reigns

Hallelujah! Our Lord God Almighty reigns. Let us rejoice and give Him glory! Revelation 19:6-7

Hal - le - lu - jah! For the Lord, our God, the Al - might - y reigns.

Hal - le - lu - jah! For the Lord, our God, the Al - might - y reigns.

Let us re - joice and be glad, and give the glo - ry un - to Him.

Hal - le - lu - jah! For the Lord, our God, the Al - might - y reigns.

TEXT: Dale Garratt
MUSIC: Dale Garratt

GARRATT
Irregular meter

Optional transition to "He Is Exalted"

A short, but definite break should occur after the last note of "Hallelujah! Our God Reigns" before proceeding to transition.

He Is Exalted 36

Yours, O Lord, is the kingdom; You are exalted as head over all. 1 Chronicles 29:11

He is ex-alt-ed, the King is ex-alt-ed on high; I will praise Him.

He is ex-alt-ed, for-ev-er ex-alt-ed, and I will praise His

name! He is the Lord; for-ev-er His truth shall

reign. Heav-en and earth re-joice in His ho-ly name.

He is ex-alt-ed, the King is ex-alt-ed on high.

TEXT: Twila Paris
MUSIC: Twila Paris

HE IS EXALTED
Irregular meter

37 You Are Crowned with Many Crowns

On His head are many crowns. Revelation 19:12

You are crowned with man - y crowns and rule all things in

righ - teous - ness. You are crowned with man - y crowns, up - hold - ing

all things by Your Word. You rule in pow - er and reign in

glo - ry! You are the Lord of heav - en and earth!

You are Lord of all. You are Lord of

TEXT: John Sellers
MUSIC: John Sellers

YOU ARE CROWNED
Irregular meter

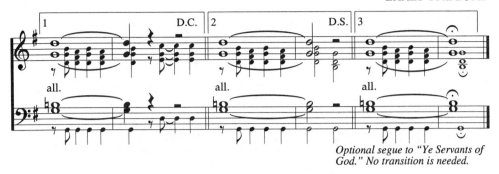

all.   all.   all.

Optional segue to "Ye Servants of God." No transition is needed.

Ye Servants of God 38

Salvation belongs to our God, who sits on the throne, and to the Lamb. Revelation 7:10

1. Ye ser-vants of God, your Mas-ter pro-claim, And pub-lish a-broad His won-der-ful name; The name, all-vic-to-rious, of Je-sus ex-tol: His king-dom is glo-rious, He rules o-ver all.

2. God rul-eth on high, al-might-y to save, And still He is nigh, His pres-ence we have; The great con-gre-ga-tion His tri-umph shall sing, As-crib-ing sal-va-tion to Je-sus, our King.

3. "Sal-va-tion to God, who sits on the throne!" Let all cry a-loud, and hon-or the Son; The prais-es of Je-sus the an-gels pro-claim, Fall down on their fac-es and wor-ship the Lamb.

4. Then let us a-dore, and give Him His right— All glo-ry and pow'r, all wis-dom and might, All hon-or and bless-ing, with an-gels a-bove, And thanks nev-er-ceas-ing, and in-fi-nite love.

TEXT: Charles Wesley
MUSIC: William Croft

HANOVER
10.10.11.11.

39 Hallelujah Chorus

Hallelujah! For our Lord God Almighty reigns. Revelation 19:6

Hal - le - lu - jah! Hal - le - lu - jah! Hal - le - lu - jah! Hal - le - lu - jah! Hal - le - lu - jah!

Hal - le - lu - jah! Hal - le - lu - jah! Hal - le - lu - jah! Hal - le - lu - jah! Hal - le - lu - jah!

For the Lord God om - nip - o - tent reign - eth. Hal - le - lu - jah! Hal - le - lu - jah! Hal - le -

lu - jah! Hal - le - lu - jah! For the Lord God om - nip - o - tent reign - eth. Hal - le -

This vocal score is complete and uniform with most editions.

TEXT: George Frederick Handel
MUSIC: George Frederick Handel; from *Messiah*

HALLELUJAH CHORUS
Irregular meter

EXALT THE LORD

EXALT THE LORD

40 You Are My God

You are my Lord; apart from You I have no good thing. Psalm 16:2

You are my God, You are my King, You are my Mas-ter,
my ev-ery-thing. You are my Lord, that's why I sing to You,
"Hal-le-lu-jah. Hal-le-lu-jah!"

Optional segue to "Lift High the Lord, Our Banner."
No transition is needed. 𝅗𝅥 = 𝅘𝅥 at about the same tempo.

TEXT: Macon Delavan
MUSIC: Macon Delavan

YOU ARE MY GOD
Irregular meter

41 Lift High the Lord, Our Banner

Sing joyfully to the Lord; it is fitting for the upright to praise Him. Psalm 33:1

Lift high the Lord, our Ban-ner. Lift high the Lord, Je-sus King.
Lift high the Lord, our Ban-ner. Lift high your praise to Him sing.

TEXT: Macon Delavan
MUSIC: Macon Delavan

LIFT HIGH
Irregular meter

42 CROWN HIM LORD OF ALL

A Worship Sequence

All Hail the Power of Jesus' Name; stanzas 1,3,4
Crown Him King of Kings
Crown Him with Many Crowns; stanzas 1,3,4
Suggested stanzas have been marked with an arrow: ➤

WORSHIP LEADER
He is the image of the invisible God, the firstborn over all creation. For by Him
all things were created: things in heaven and on earth, visible and invisible,
whether thrones or powers or rulers or authorities; all things were created by
Him and for Him.

EVERYONE
He is King of kings and Lord of lords!

WORSHIP LEADER
He is before all things, and in Him all things hold together. And He is the head
of the body, the church; He is the beginning and the firstborn from among the
dead, so that in everything He might have the supremacy.

EVERYONE
He is King of kings and Lord of lords!

WORSHIP LEADER
Therefore God exalted Him to the highest place and gave Him the name that is
above every name.

EVERYONE
He is King of kings and Lord of lords!

WORSHIP LEADER
At the name of Jesus every knee should bow, in heaven and on earth and
under the earth.

EVERYONE
He is King of kings and Lord of lords!

WORSHIP LEADER
And every tongue confess that Jesus Christ is Lord to the glory of God the
Father.

EVERYONE
HE IS KING OF KINGS AND LORD OF LORDS!

from Colossians 1:15-18; Philippians 2:9-11; Revelation 19:16 (NIV)

Optional introduction to
"All Hail the Power of Jesus' Name"

f

All Hail the Power of Jesus' Name 43

God gave Him the name that is above every name. Jesus Christ is Lord. Philippians 2:9-11

1. All hail the pow'r of Jesus' name! Let angels prostrate
2. Ye chosen seed of Israel's race, Ye ransomed from the
3. Let every kindred, every tribe On this terrestrial
4. O that with yonder sacred throng We at His feet may

fall; Bring forth the royal diadem, And crown Him
fall, Hail Him who saves you by His grace, And crown Him
ball, To Him all majesty ascribe, And crown Him
fall! We'll join the everlasting song, And crown Him

Lord of all; Bring forth the royal diadem, And
Lord of all; Hail Him who saves you by His grace, And
Lord of all; To Him all majesty ascribe, And
Lord of all; We'll join the everlasting song, And

Optional transition to
"Crown Him King of Kings"

crown Him Lord of all!
crown Him Lord of all!
crown Him Lord of all!
crown Him Lord of all!

rit.

TEXT: Edward Perronet; altered by John Rippon
MUSIC: Oliver Holden

CORONATION
C.M. with Repeats

44 Crown Him King of Kings

He has this name written: KING OF KINGS AND LORD OF LORDS. Revelation 19:16

Crown Him King of kings; Crown Him Lord of lords.

Won-der-ful, Coun-sel-or, the Might-y God;

Em-man-u-el, God is with us, And

He shall reign, He shall reign, He shall reign for-ev-er-more.

TEXT: Sharon Damazio
MUSIC: Sharon Damazio

CROWN HIM
Irregular meter

Optional repeat setting

8vb

Crown Him King of kings; Crown Him Lord of lords.

Won - der - ful, Coun - sel - or, the Might - y God;

Em - man - u - el, God is with us, And

Cued notes optional for choir sopranos

He shall reign, He shall reign, He shall reign for - ev - er - more.

*Optional segue to
"Crown Him with Many Crowns."
No transition is needed.*

45 Crown Him with Many Crowns

His eyes are like blazing fire, and on His head are many crowns. Revelation 19:12

▶ 1. Crown Him with man - y crowns, The Lamb up - on His throne.
2. Crown Him the Lord of love! Be - hold His hands and side–
▶ 3. Crown Him the Lord of life! Who tri - umphed o'er the grave;
▶ 4. Crown Him the Lord of heav'n! One with the Fa - ther known,

Hark! how the heav'n - ly an - them drowns All mu - sic but its own!
Rich wounds, yet vis - i - ble a - bove, In beau - ty glo - ri - fied.
Who rose vic - to - rious in the strife For those He came to save.
One with the Spir - it thro' Him giv'n From yon - der glo - rious throne.

A - wake, my soul, and sing Of Him who died for thee, And
All hail, Re - deem - er, hail! For Thou hast died for me: Thy
His glo - ries now we sing, Who died and rose on high, Who
To Thee be end - less praise, For Thou for us hast died. Be

hail Him as thy match - less King Thro' all e - ter - ni - ty.
praise and glo - ry shall not fail Thro' - out e - ter - ni - ty.
died e - ter - nal life to bring And lives that death may die.
Thou, O Lord, thro' end - less days A - dored and mag - ni - fied!

TEXT: Matthew Bridges, stanzas 1,2,4; Godfrey Thring, stanza 3
MUSIC: George J. Elvey; Arrangement and Choral ending by William David Young

DIADEMATA
S.M.D.

Optional last stanza setting   Broader

rit. 4. Crown Him the Lord of heav'n! One with the Fa - ther

known, One with the Spir - it thro' Him giv'n From yon - der glo - rious

throne. To Thee be end - less praise, For Thou for us hast died. Be

Thou, O Lord, thro' end - less days A - dored and mag - ni - fied!

Optional choral ending

ff

He shall reign, He shall reign, He shall reign for - ev - er - more. Crown Him!

ff

The end of CROWN HIM LORD OF ALL - A Worship Sequence

46 Sing unto the Lord

Sing to the Lord a new song; sing to the Lord, all the earth. Psalm 96:1

1. Sing un-to the Lord a new song, Let His prais - es fill the
2. Sing un-to the Lord a new song, For He loves to hear our

tem - ple. He is the King of kings and the Lord of lords.
prais - es. Let all of cre-a - tion sing, "Glo-ry to our God!"

1. Bow down be-fore Him.
2. Bow down be - fore Him.

Hal - le - lu - jah! Glo - ry to

God. Hal - le - lu - jah!

TEXT: Leon Patillo
MUSIC: Leon Patillo

PATILLO
Irregular meter

Glo - ry to God. God.

Jesus, Lord to Me 47

In your hearts set apart Christ as Lord. 1 Peter 3:15

Je - sus, Je - sus, Lord to me. Mas - ter, Sav - ior, Prince of Peace!

Rul - er of my heart to - day, Je - sus, Lord to me.

Optional repeat setting

Je - sus, Je - sus, Lord to me. Mas - ter, Sav - ior, Prince of

Peace! Rul - er of my heart to - day, Je - sus, Lord to me.

TEXT: Greg Nelson and Gary McSpadden
MUSIC: Greg Nelson and Gary McSpadden

JESUS, LORD TO ME
7.7.7.5.

48 Mighty Is Our God

You are worthy to receive glory and honor and power, for You created all things. Revelation 4:11

TEXT: Eugene Greco, Gerrit Gustafson, Don Moen
MUSIC: Eugene Greco, Gerrit Gustafson, Don Moen

MIGHTY IS OUR GOD
Irregular meter

EXALTED ABOVE THE HEAVENS 49

from Psalm 57 (NIV)

WORSHIP LEADER
Have mercy on me, O God, have mercy on me,
for in You my soul takes refuge.
I will take refuge in the shadow of Your wings until the disaster has passed.

EVERYONE
Have mercy on me, O God, have mercy on me.

WORSHIP LEADER
I cry out to God Most High, who fulfills His purpose for me.
He sends from heaven and saves me, rebuking those who hotly pursue me;
God sends His love and His faithfulness.

EVERYONE
Have mercy on me, O God, have mercy on me.

WORSHIP LEADER
I am in the midst of lions; I lie among ravenous beasts–
men whose teeth are spears and arrows, whose tongues are sharp swords.

EVERYONE
Have mercy on me, O God, have mercy on me.

WORSHIP LEADER
Be exalted, O God, above the heavens;

EVERYONE
Let Your glory be over all the earth.

WORSHIP LEADER
They spread a net for my feet– I was bowed down in distress.
They dug a pit in my path– but they have fallen into it themselves.

EVERYONE
Be exalted, O God, above the heavens; let Your glory be over all the earth.

WORSHIP LEADER
My heart is steadfast, O God, my heart is steadfast; I will sing and make music.
Awake, my soul! Awake, harp and lyre! I will awaken the dawn.

EVERYONE
Be exalted, O God, above the heavens; let Your glory be over all the earth.

WORSHIP LEADER
I will praise You, O Lord, among the nations;

MEN
I will sing of You among the peoples.

WORSHIP LEADER
For great is Your love, reaching to the heavens;

WOMEN
Your faithfulness reaches to the skies.

EVERYONE
Be exalted, O God, above the heavens; let Your glory be over all the earth.

50 GOD HIGHLY EXALTED HIM

from Philippians 2:1-11 (NASB)

WORSHIP LEADER
If therefore there is any encouragement in Christ,
if there is any consolation of love,

WOMEN
If there is any fellowship of the Spirit, if any affection and compassion,

WORSHIP LEADER
Make my joy complete by being of the same mind, maintaining the
same love, united in spirit, intent on one purpose.

MEN
**Do nothing from selfishness or empty conceit, but with humility of mind,
let each of you regard one another as more important than himself.**

WORSHIP LEADER
Do not merely look out for your own personal interests, but also for the
interests of others.

WOMEN
Have this attitude in yourselves, which was also in Christ Jesus—

WORSHIP LEADER
Who, although He existed in the form of God, did not regard equality
with God a thing to be grasped;

MEN
**But emptied Himself, taking the form of a bond-servant, and being
made in the likeness of men.**

WORSHIP LEADER
And being found in appearance as a man, He humbled Himself by
becoming obedient to the point of death, even death on the cross.

WOMEN
**Therefore also God highly exalted Him, and bestowed on Him the
name which is above every name,**

WORSHIP LEADER
That at the name of Jesus every knee should bow, of those who are in
heaven, and on earth, and under the earth,

EVERYONE
**And that every tongue should confess that Jesus Christ is Lord, to
the glory of God the Father.**

51 GOD IS HOLY

from Psalm 99:5, 9 (NIV)

WORSHIP LEADER
Exalt the Lord our God and worship at His footstool;

EVERYONE
He is holy.

WORSHIP LEADER
Exalt the Lord our God and worship at His holy mountain;

EVERYONE
For the Lord our God is holy.

Blessed Be the Name 52

Praise be to His glorious name forever. Psalm 72:19

1. O for a thou-sand tongues to sing– Bless-ed be the name of the Lord!
2. Je - sus, the name that charms our fears– Bless-ed be the name of the Lord!
3. He breaks the pow'r of can - celled sin– Bless-ed be the name of the Lord!
4. I nev - er shall for-get that day– Bless-ed be the name of the Lord!

The glo - ries of my God and King– Bless-ed be the name of the Lord!
'Tis mu - sic in the sin - ner's ears– Bless-ed be the name of the Lord!
His blood can make the foul - est clean– Bless-ed be the name of the Lord!
When Je - sus washed my sins a - way– Bless-ed be the name of the Lord!

Refrain

Bless-ed be the name, bless-ed be the name; Bless-ed be the name of the Lord!

Bless-ed be the name, bless-ed be the name; Bless-ed be the name of the Lord!

TEXT: Charles Wesley; Ralph E. Hudson, Refrain
MUSIC: Anonymous; arranged by Ralph E. Hudson
and William J. Kirkpatrick

BLESSED BE THE NAME
L.M. with Refrain

53 GREAT THINGS HE HAS DONE
A Worship Sequence

My Tribute
Bless His Holy Name
To God Be the Glory; stanzas 1,3
Suggested stanzas have been marked with an arrow: ➤

WORSHIP LEADER
Bless the Lord, O my soul;
And all that is within me, bless His holy name!
Bless the Lord, O my soul, and forget not all His benefits:
Who forgives all your iniquities,
Who heals all your diseases,
Who redeems your life from destruction,
And crowns you with lovingkindness and tender mercies.

from Psalm 103:1-4 (NKJV)

Optional introduction to "My Tribute"

54 My Tribute
How can I repay the Lord for all His goodness to me? Psalm 116:12

To God be the glo - ry, To God be the glo - ry, To God be the glo - ry for the things He has done. With His blood He has saved me; With His pow'r He has raised me. To

TEXT: Andraé Crouch
MUSIC: Andraé Crouch

MY TRIBUTE
Irregular meter

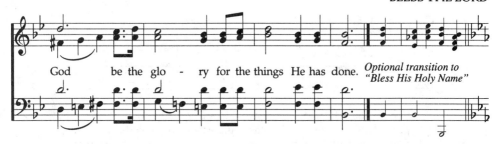

God be the glo - ry for the things He has done.

Optional transition to
"Bless His Holy Name"

Bless His Holy Name 55

Praise the Lord, O my soul; all my inmost being, praise His holy name. Psalm 103:1

Bless the Lord, O my soul, and all that is with - in me, bless His ho -

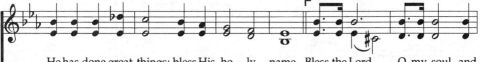

ly name. He has done great things, He has done great things,

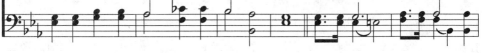

He has done great things; bless His ho - ly name. Bless the Lord, O my soul, and

all that is with - in me, bless His ho - ly name.

Optional transition to
"To God Be the Glory"

TEXT: Andraé Crouch
MUSIC: Andraé Crouch

BLESS HIS HOLY NAME
Irregular meter

56 To God Be the Glory

The Lord has done great things for us, and we are filled with joy. Psalm 126:3

1. To God be the glo-ry— great things He hath done! So loved He the
2. O per-fect re-demp-tion, the pur-chase of blood— To ev-ery be-
3. Great things He hath taught us; great things He hath done, And great our re-

world that He gave us His Son, Who yield- ed His life an a-
liev- er, the prom-ise of God. The vil- est of-fend- er who
joic- ing thro' Je-sus, the Son. But pur- er and high- er and

tone- ment for sin And o- pened the life- gate that all may go in.
tru- ly be-lieves, That mo- ment from Je- sus a par- don re- ceives.
great- er will be Our won- der, our trans-port, when Je- sus we see.

Refrain

Praise the Lord! Praise the Lord! Let the earth hear His voice! Praise the Lord!

Praise the Lord! Let the peo- ple re- joice! O come to the Fa- ther thro'

TEXT: Fanny J. Crosby
MUSIC: William H. Doane; Arrangement and Descant by Doug Holck

TO GOD BE THE GLORY
11.11.11.11. with Refrain

Je - sus, the Son, And give Him the glo - ry– great things He hath done!

Optional repeat refrain setting
Optional descant

Praise the Lord! Let the earth hear His voice!

Praise the Lord! Praise the Lord! Let the earth hear His voice! Praise the

Praise the Lord! Let the peo-ple re - joice! Come to the Fa - ther thro'

Lord! Praise the Lord! Let the peo-ple re - joice! O come to the Fa - ther thro'

rit.

Je - sus, the Son, And give Him the glo - ry– great things He hath done!

rit.

Je - sus, the Son, And give Him the glo - ry– great things He hath done!

The end of GREAT THINGS HE HAS DONE - A Worship Sequence

57 Sing unto the Lord

Sing to the Lord a new song; sing to the Lord, all the earth. Psalm 96:1

Unison

Sing un-to the Lord a new song, Sing un-to the Lord all the earth.

Sing un-to the Lord a new song, Sing un-to the Lord all the earth.

earth. For God is great and great-ly to be praised.

God is great and great-ly to be praised! O

sing un-to the Lord a new song, Sing un-to the Lord all the earth.

TEXT: Becky Fender
MUSIC: Becky Fender

FENDER
Irregular meter

Sing un-to the Lord a new song, Sing un-to the Lord all the earth.

Optional segue to "Bless the Lord, O My Soul." No transition is needed.

Bless the Lord, O My Soul 58

Praise the Lord, O my soul; all my inmost being, praise His holy name. Psalm 103:1

Bless the Lord, O my soul; Bless the Lord, O my soul;

And all that is with - in me bless His ho - ly name.

Optional repeat setting

Bless the Lord, O my soul; Bless the Lord, O my

soul; And all that is with - in me bless His ho - ly name.

TEXT: Author unknown; based on Psalm 103:1
MUSIC: Composer unknown

BLESS THE LORD
Irregular meter

59 Our God Is Lifted Up

I saw the Lord seated on a throne, high and exalted. Isaiah 6:1

Our God is lift-ed up midst the shouts of joy, Our God is lift-ed up

in the sound-ing of the trum - pets; Our God is lift-ed up midst the

shouts of joy— Shout joy-ful-ly un-to our God, Shout joy-ful-ly un-to our

God. Our God. Let the trum-pets make a joy - ful noise, Let us

clap our hands and praise our God; For our God is lift - ed up, Our

TEXT: Tim Smith
MUSIC: Tim Smith

OUR GOD IS LIFTED UP
Irregular meter

BLESS THE LORD

God is lift-ed up, Our God is lift-ed up on high.

Optional extended ending

Our God is lift-ed up, Our God is lift-ed up, Our

1 *Repeat as many times as desired* **2**

God is lift-ed up on high. Our high.

Bless God 60

Come and see what God has done. Psalm 66:5

Bless God for all He's done! Bless God for Christ, His Son!
voice in u-ni-ty, One voice of praise to Thee, With

1 **2**

Let us mag-ni-fy Him for He's ho-ly, ho-ly! One
hearts of love and wor-ship we will sing, "Bless God!"

TEXT: Carman and John Rosasco
MUSIC: Carman and John Rosasco

BLESS GOD
Irregular meter

61 BLESS THE LORD YOUR GOD

A Worship Sequence

Blessed Be the Lord God Almighty
All Creatures of Our God and King; stanzas 1,2,5
Suggested stanzas have been marked with an arrow: ➤

WORSHIP LEADER
Stand up and bless the Lord your God forever and ever!

EVERYONE
Blessed be Your glorious name,
Which is exalted above all blessing and praise!

WORSHIP LEADER
You alone are the Lord;
You have made heaven, the heaven of heavens, with all their host,
The earth and everything on it, the seas and all that is in them,
And You preserve them all.
The host of heaven worships You.

EVERYONE
Blessed be Your glorious name,
Which is exalted above all blessing and praise!

from Nehemiah 9:5-6 (NKJV)

Optional introduction to "Blessed Be the Lord God Almighty"

62 Blessed Be the Lord God Almighty

Holy, holy, holy is the Lord God Almighty, who was, and is, and is to come. Revelation 4:8

Fa-ther in heav-en, how we love You; We lift Your name in all the earth. May Your king-dom be es-tab-lished in our prais-es, As Your

TEXT: Bob Fitts
MUSIC: Bob Fitts

LORD GOD ALMIGHTY
Irregular meter

BLESS THE LORD

63 All Creatures of Our God and King

Praise the Lord, all His works everywhere in His dominion. Psalm 103:22

1. All crea-tures of our God and King, Lift up your voice and with us sing
2. Thou rush-ing wind that art so strong, Ye clouds that sail in heav'n a - long,
3. Thou flow-ing wa-ter, pure and clear, Make mu-sic for Thy Lord to hear,
4. And all ye men of ten-der heart, For - giv-ing oth-ers, take your part,
5. Let all things their Cre-a-tor bless, And wor-ship Him in hum-ble-ness,

Al - le - lu - ia! Al - le - lu - ia! Thou burn-ing sun with gold-en beam,
O praise Him! Al - le - lu - ia! Thou ris - ing morn, in praise re - joice;
Al - le - lu - ia! Al - le - lu - ia! Thou fire so mas-ter - ful and bright,
O sing ye! Al - le - lu - ia! Ye who long pain and sor - row bear,
O praise Him! Al - le - lu - ia! Praise, praise the Fa-ther, praise the Son,

Thou sil - ver moon with soft - er gleam, O praise Him! O praise Him!
Ye lights of eve - ning, find a voice, O praise Him! O praise Him!
Thou giv - est man both warmth and light, O praise Him! O praise Him!
Praise God and on Him cast your care, O praise Him! O praise Him!
And praise the Spir - it, Three in One, O praise Him! O praise Him!

Optional last stanza setting

Al - le - lu - ia, al - le - lu - ia, al - le - lu - ia!

TEXT: St. Francis of Assisi; translated by William H. Draper
MUSIC: *Geistliche Kirchengesänge*, Cologne, 1623; harmonized by Ralph Vaughan Williams;
Last stanza setting and Choral ending by Ken Barker
A higher setting may be found at No. 112

LASST UNS ERFREUEN
L.M. with Alleluias

The end of BLESS THE LORD YOUR GOD - A Worship Sequence

64 Blessed Be the Name of the Lord

Praise be to His glorious name forever. Psalm 72:19

Bless-ed be the name of the Lord, He is wor-thy to be praised and a - dored;

So we lift up ho - ly hands in one ac - cord, Sing-ing, "Bless-ed be the name,

bless-ed be the name, Bless-ed be the name of the Lord!"

TEXT: Don Moen
MUSIC: Don Moen

BLESSED
Irregular meter

65 Stand Up and Bless the Lord

Stand up and praise the Lord your God. Nehemiah 9:5

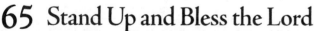

1. Stand up and bless the Lord, Ye peo - ple of His choice;
2. Though high a - bove all praise, A - bove all bless - ing high,
3. O for the liv - ing flame, From His own al - tar brought,
4. God is our strength and song, And His sal - va - tion ours;
5. Stand up and bless the Lord, The Lord your God a - dore;

TEXT: James Montgomery
MUSIC: Aaron Williams

ST. THOMAS
S.M.

A lower setting may be found at No. 405

Stand up and bless the Lord your God With heart and soul and voice.
Who would not fear His ho - ly name, And laud and mag - ni - fy?
To touch our lips, our minds in - spire, And wing to heav'n our thought.
Then be His love in Christ pro-claimed With all our ran-somed pow'rs.
Stand up and bless His glo - rious name Hence-forth for - ev - er - more.

Optional segue to "I Will Celebrate."
No transition is needed.

I Will Celebrate 66

Sing to the Lord a new song, for He has done marvelous things. Psalm 98:1

Part I Unison

I will cel - e - brate, Sing un - to the Lord;

I will sing to Him a new song.

Part II

I will praise Him, For He has tri - umphed vic -

1

- to-rious- ly.

2

He has tri - umphed vic - to-rious-ly.

*May be sung as a 2-part round

TEXT: Linda Duvall
MUSIC: Linda Duvall

DUVALL
Irregular meter

67 I Will Bless the Lord

Every day I will praise You and extol Your name for ever and ever. Psalm 145:2

I will bless the Lord and give Him glo - ry. O I will bless His name and give Him glo - ry. The Lord is gra-cious and mer - ci - ful, Great in kind-ness and good to all. The Lord is

TEXT: Frank Hernandez
MUSIC: Frank Hernandez

HERNANDEZ
Irregular meter

68 We Praise Thee, O God, Our Redeemer

You, O Lord, are our Father, our Redeemer from of old. Isaiah 63:16

1. We praise Thee, O God, our Re - deem - er, Cre - a - tor;
2. We wor - ship Thee, God of our fa - thers, we bless Thee;
3. With voic - es u - nit - ed our prais - es we of - fer,

In grate - ful de - vo - tion our trib - ute we bring.
Thro' life's storm and tem - pest our guide Thou hast been.
And glad - ly our songs of true wor - ship we raise.

We lay it be - fore Thee; we kneel and a - dore Thee;
When per - ils o'er - take us, Thou wilt not for - sake us,
Thy strong arm will guide us; our God is be - side us.

We bless Thy ho - ly name, glad prais - es we sing.
And with Thy help, O Lord, life's bat - tles we win.
To Thee, our great Re - deem - er, for - ev - er be praise.

TEXT: Julia Cady Cory
MUSIC: Netherlands folk song; arranged by Edward Kremser;
        Last stanza setting and Choral ending by Bruce Greer

KREMSER
12.11.12.11.

Optional last stanza setting

Unison

rit.   3. With

69 Holy, Holy

You alone are holy. All nations will worship before You. Revelation 15:4

1. Ho - ly, ho - ly, ho - ly, ho - ly, Ho - ly, ho - ly,
2. Gra - cious Fa - ther, gra - cious Fa - ther, We're so blest to be Your
3. Pre - cious Je - sus, pre - cious Je - sus, We're so glad that You've re -
4. Ho - ly Spir - it, Ho - ly Spir - it, Come and fill our hearts a -
5. Hal - le - lu - jah, hal - le - lu - jah, Hal - le - lu - jah,

Lord God Al - might - y; And we lift our hearts be - fore You as a
chil - dren, gra - cious Fa - ther; And we lift our heads be - fore You as a
deemed us, pre - cious Je - sus; And we lift our hands be - fore You as a
new, Ho - ly Spir - it; And we lift our voice be - fore You as a
hal - le - lu - jah; And we lift our hearts be - fore You as a

to - ken of our love, Ho - ly, ho - ly, ho - ly, ho - ly.
to - ken of our love, Gra - cious Fa - ther, gra - cious Fa - ther.
to - ken of our love, Pre - cious Je - sus, pre - cious Je - sus.
to - ken of our love, Ho - ly Spir - it, Ho - ly Spir - it.
to - ken of our love, Hal - le - lu - jah, hal - le - lu - jah.

TEXT: Jimmy Owens
MUSIC: Jimmy Owens

HOLY, HOLY
Irregular meter

Optional last stanza setting   a tempo

rit.   5. Hal - le - lu - jah, hal - le - lu - jah, Hal - le -

lu - jah, hal - le - lu - jah; And we lift our hearts be-fore You as a

to-ken of our love, Hal - le - lu-jah, hal - le - lu - jah.

Optional transition to
"A Perfect Heart"

A Perfect Heart 70

I will give you a new heart and put a new spirit in you. Ezekiel 36:26

Bless the Lord who reigns in beau - ty; Bless the Lord
bless the Lord bless the Lord

who reigns in wis - dom and with pow'r. Bless the Lord
bless the Lord

who reigns my life with so much love, He can make a per-fect heart.

TEXT: Dony McGuire and Reba Rambo
MUSIC: Dony McGuire and Reba Rambo

A PERFECT HEART
Irregular meter

71 BLESS THE LORD, O MY SOUL

from Psalm 103 (NKJV)

WORSHIP LEADER
Bless the Lord, O my soul; and all that is within me, bless His holy name!

EVERYONE
Bless the Lord, O my soul, and forget not all His benefits:

MEN
Bless the Lord, O my soul, who forgives all your iniquities, who heals all your diseases, who redeems your life from destruction, who crowns you with lovingkindness and tender mercies;

WOMEN
Bless the Lord, O my soul, who satisfies your mouth with good things, so that your youth is renewed like the eagle's.

WORSHIP LEADER
The Lord is merciful and gracious, slow to anger, and abounding in mercy.

MEN
He has not dealt with us according to our sins, nor punished us according to our iniquities.

WOMEN
Bless the Lord, O my soul; for as the heavens are high above the earth, so great is His mercy toward those who fear Him.

EVERYONE
Bless the Lord, O my soul. As far as the east is from the west, so far has He removed our transgressions from us.

MEN
As a father pities his children, so the Lord pities those who fear Him.

WOMEN
For He knows our frame; He remembers that we are dust.

WORSHIP LEADER
As for man, his days are like grass; as a flower of the field, so he flourishes.
For the wind passes over it, and it is gone, and its place remembers it no more.

EVERYONE
But the mercy of the Lord is from everlasting to everlasting.

WORSHIP LEADER
The Lord has established His throne in heaven, and His kingdom rules over all.
Bless the Lord.

EVERYONE
Bless the Lord, O my soul. Bless the Lord!

72 I WILL SING PRAISE

from Psalm 104:33, 35b (NKJV)

WORSHIP LEADER
I will sing to the Lord as long as I live;
I will sing praise to my God while I have my being.
Bless the Lord, O my soul! Praise the Lord!

EVERYONE
Bless the Lord, O my soul!
Praise the Lord!

PRAISE AND BLESS THE LORD 73

from Psalm 146 (NIV)

WORSHIP LEADER
Praise the Lord.

EVERYONE
Praise the Lord, O my soul.

WORSHIP LEADER
I will praise the Lord all my life.

EVERYONE
I will sing praise to my God as long as I live.

WORSHIP LEADER
Do not put your trust in princes, in mortal men, who cannot save.
When their spirit departs, they return to the ground; on that very day
their plans come to nothing.

WOMEN
**Blessed is he whose help is the God of Jacob, whose hope is in
the Lord his God, the Maker of heaven and earth, the sea, and
everything in them.**

MEN
**The Lord remains faithful forever. He upholds the cause of the
oppressed and gives food to the hungry.**

WORSHIP LEADER
The Lord sets prisoners free.

EVERYONE
The Lord gives sight to the blind.

WORSHIP LEADER
The Lord lifts up those who are bowed down.

EVERYONE
The Lord loves the righteous.

WORSHIP LEADER
The Lord watches over the alien and sustains the fatherless and the
widow, but He frustrates the ways of the wicked.

EVERYONE
The Lord, your God, reigns forever.

WORSHIP LEADER
Praise the Lord!

EVERYONE
Praise the Lord, O my soul.

WORSHIP LEADER
I will praise the Lord all my life;

EVERYONE
I will sing praise to my God as long as I live.
Praise and bless the Lord!

74 Holy Is He

Exalt the Lord our God and worship at His footstool; He is holy. Psalm 99:5

HOLY IS HE
Irregular meter

TEXT: Claire Cloninger
MUSIC: David T. Clydesdale

Holy Is the Lord 75

Holy, holy, holy is the Lord God Almighty, who was, and is, and is to come. Revelation 4:8

TEXT: Traditional
MUSIC: Franz Schubert

HOLY IS THE LORD
6.5.6.5.D.

76 Jesus Is the Sweetest Name I Know

Jesus Christ is the same yesterday and today and forever. Hebrews 13:8

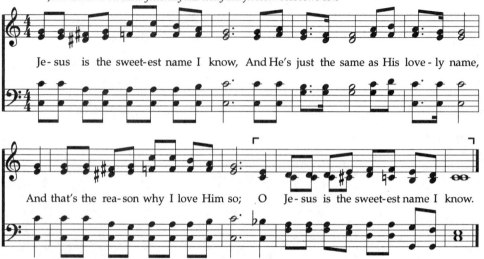

Je-sus is the sweet-est name I know, And He's just the same as His love-ly name,

And that's the rea-son why I love Him so; O Je-sus is the sweet-est name I know.

TEXT: Lela Long
MUSIC: Lela Long

SWEETEST NAME (Refrain only)
9.10.10.10.

---

77 WORTHY OF LOVE AND PRAISE
A Worship Sequence

I Love You, Lord
My Jesus, I Love Thee; stanzas 1,2,4
Suggested stanzas have been marked with an arrow: ➤

WORSHIP LEADER

Now, my God, may Your eyes be open and Your
ears attentive to the prayers offered in this place.
I love You, O Lord, my strength.
The Lord is my rock, my fortress and my deliverer.
I call to the Lord, who is worthy of praise.

from 2 Chronicles 6:40; Psalm 18:1-3 (NIV)

78 I Love You, Lord

I love You, O Lord, my strength. Psalm 18:1

I love You, Lord, and I lift my voice To wor-ship

TEXT: Laurie Klein
MUSIC: Laurie Klein

I LOVE YOU, LORD
Irregular meter

You, O my soul, re - joice! Take joy, my King, in

what You hear: May it be a sweet, sweet sound in Your ear.

Optional repeat setting

I love You, Lord, and I lift my voice To

wor - ship You, O my soul, re - joice! Take joy, my King, in

what You hear: May it be a sweet, sweet sound in Your ear.

Optional segue to "My Jesus, I Love Thee."
No transition is needed.

79 My Jesus, I Love Thee

We love because He first loved us. 1 John 4:19

1. My Je - sus, I love Thee; I know Thou art mine. For Thee all the
2. I love Thee be - cause Thou hast first lov - ed me And pur - chased my
3. I'll love Thee in life; I will love Thee in death And praise Thee as
4. In man - sions of glo - ry and end - less de - light, I'll ev - er a-

fol - lies of sin I re - sign. My gra - cious Re - deem - er, my
par - don on Cal - va - ry's tree. I love Thee for wear - ing the
long as Thou lend - est me breath. And say when the death - dew lies
dore Thee in heav - en so bright. I'll sing with the glit - ter - ing

Sav - ior art Thou: If ev - er I loved Thee, my Je - sus, 'tis now.
thorns on Thy brow: If ev - er I loved Thee, my Je - sus, 'tis now.
cold on my brow, "If ev - er I loved Thee, my Je - sus, 'tis now."
crown on my brow, "If ev - er I loved Thee, my Je - sus, 'tis now."

TEXT: William R. Featherston
MUSIC: Adoniram J. Gordon; Descant and Choral ending by William David Young

GORDON
11.11.11.11.

Optional last stanza setting

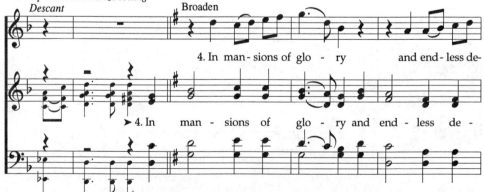

Descant

Broaden

4. In man - sions of glo - ry and end - less de-

4. In man - sions of glo - ry and end - less de-

The end of WORTHY OF LOVE AND PRAISE - A Worship Sequence

80 I Stand in Awe

Stand in awe of God. Ecclesiastes 5:7

You are beau-ti-ful be-yond de-scrip-tion, Too mar-vel-ous for words; Too won-der-ful for com-pre-hen-sion, Like noth-ing ev-er seen or heard. Who can grasp Your in-fi-nite wis-dom? Who can fath-om the depth of Your love? You are beau-ti-ful be-yond de-scrip-tion, maj-es-ty en-throned a-bove. And I

TEXT: Mark Altrogge
MUSIC: Mark Altrogge

I STAND IN AWE
Irregular meter

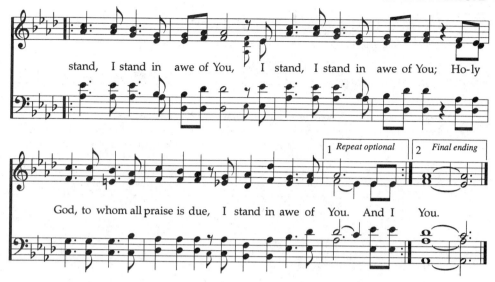

stand, I stand in awe of You, I stand, I stand in awe of You; Ho-ly

God, to whom all praise is due, I stand in awe of You. And I You.

1 *Repeat optional* 2 *Final ending*

Abba Father **81**

You received the Spirit of sonship. And by Him we cry, "Abba, Father." Romans 8:15

1. "Ab - ba Fa - ther, Ab - ba Fa - ther," Deep with-
2. Fa - ther, Fa - ther, Je - ho - vah Sham - mah, You are the

in my soul I cry. Ab - ba Fa - ther,
One who's stand-ing near.

Ab - ba Fa - ther, I will nev - er cease to love You.

TEXT: Steve Fry
MUSIC: Steve Fry; arranged by David Allen

ABBA FATHER
Irregular meter

82 Praise the Lord! Ye Heavens, Adore Him

Praise the Lord from the heavens. Praise the Lord from the earth. Psalm 148:1, 7

1. Praise the Lord! ye heav'ns, a - dore Him; Praise Him, an - gels, in the height.
2. Praise the Lord! for He is glo - rious; Nev - er shall His prom - ise fail.
3. Wor - ship, hon - or, glo - ry, bless - ing, Lord, we of - fer un - to Thee.

Sun and moon, re - joice be - fore Him; Praise Him, all ye stars of light.
God hath made His saints vic - to - rious; Sin and death shall not pre - vail.
Young and old, Thy praise ex - press - ing, In glad hom - age bend the knee.

Praise the Lord! for He hath spo - ken; Worlds His might - y voice o - beyed.
Praise the God of our sal - va - tion! Hosts on high, His pow'r pro - claim.
All the saints in heav'n a - dore Thee; We would bow be - fore Thy throne.

Laws which nev - er shall be bro - ken For their guid - ance hath He made.
Heav'n and earth, and all cre - a - tion, Laud and mag - ni - fy His name.
As Thine an - gels serve be - fore Thee, So on earth Thy will be done.

TEXT: *Foundling Hospital Collection, 1796;* Edward Osler, stanza 3;
based on Psalm 148
MUSIC: Franz Joseph Haydn

AUSTRIAN HYMN
8.7.8.7.D.

There's Something About That Name 83

There is no other name by which we must be saved. Acts 4:12

Je-sus, Je-sus, Je - sus! There's just some-thing a - bout that name! Mas-ter, Sav-ior, Je - sus! Like the fra-grance af-ter the rain. Je - sus, Je - sus, Je - sus! Let all heav-en and earth pro - claim: Kings and king-doms will all pass a - way, But there's some-thing a - bout that name!

TEXT: Gloria Gaither and William J. Gaither
MUSIC: William J. Gaither

THAT NAME
Irregular meter

84 Jesus, What a Wonder You Are

God made His light shine in our hearts to give us the light of God in the face of Christ. 2 Corinthians 4:6

Je - sus, what a won-der You are;

You are so gen - tle, so

pure, and so kind. You shine

like the morn - ing star; Je -

sus, what a won-der You are.

TEXT: Dave Bolton
MUSIC: Dave Bolton

BOLTON
Irregular meter

NAME ABOVE EVERY NAME
A Worship Sequence

85

Jesus, Name Above All Names
Fairest Lord Jesus; stanzas 1,3,4
More Precious than Silver
Suggested stanzas have been marked with an arrow: ➤

WORSHIP LEADER

Therefore God exalted Him to the highest place
and gave Him the name that is above every name,
that at the name of Jesus every knee should bow,
in heaven and on earth and under the earth,
and every tongue confess that Jesus Christ is Lord,
to the glory of God the Father.

from Philippians 2:9-11 (NIV)

Jesus, Name Above All Names 86
Your name will be great forever. 2 Samuel 7:26

*Optional segue to "Fairest Lord
Jesus." No transition is needed.*

TEXT: Naida Hearn
MUSIC: Naida Hearn

HEARN
Irregular meter

87 Fairest Lord Jesus

Your eyes will see the King in His beauty. Isaiah 33:17

1. Fair - est Lord Je - sus; Rul - er of all na - ture, O Thou of
2. Fair are the mead - ows; Fair - er still the wood - lands, Robed in the
3. Fair is the sun - shine; Fair - er still the moon - light And all the
4. Beau - ti - ful Sav - ior! Lord of the na - tions! Son of

God and man the Son. Thee will I cher - ish; Thee will I
bloom - ing garb of spring. Je - sus is fair - er; Je - sus is
twin - kling star - ry host. Je - sus shines bright - er; Je - sus shines
God and Son of man! Glo - ry and hon - or, Praise, ad - o -

hon - or, Thou my soul's glo - ry, joy, and crown. *Optional*
pur - er, Who makes the woe - ful heart to sing. *transition to*
pur - er, Than all the an - gels heav'n can boast. *"More Precious*
ra - tion, Now and for - ev - er - more be Thine! *than Silver"*

TEXT: Anonymous German hymn, *Münster Gesangbuch*, 1677;
translated, Source unknown, stanzas 1-3; Joseph A. Seiss, stanza 4
MUSIC: *Schlesische Volkslieder*, 1842; arranged by Richard S. Willis
A lower setting may be found at No. 452

CRUSADERS' HYMN
5.6.8.5.5.8.

88 More Precious than Silver

You are my Lord; apart from You I have no good thing. Psalm 16:2

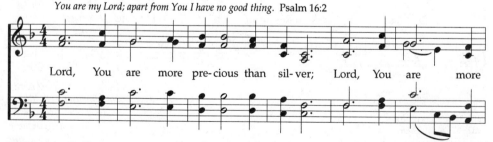

Lord, You are more pre - cious than sil - ver; Lord, You are more

TEXT: Lynn De Shazo
MUSIC: Lynn De Shazo

MORE PRECIOUS
Irregular meter

cost-ly than gold. Lord, You are more beau-ti-ful than

dia-monds, And noth-ing I de-sire com-pares with You.

Optional extended or choral ending

Noth-ing I de-sire, noth-ing I de-sire com-pares with You.

The end of NAME ABOVE EVERY NAME - A Worship Sequence

Jesus, the Very Thought of Thee 89

I have set the Lord always before me. Therefore my heart is glad. Psalm 16:8-9

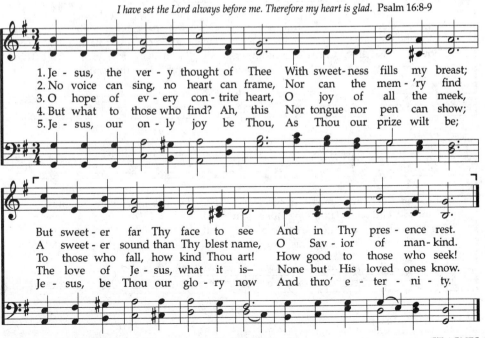

1. Je - sus, the ver - y thought of Thee With sweet-ness fills my breast;
2. No voice can sing, no heart can frame, Nor can the mem - 'ry find
3. O hope of ev - er - y con - trite heart, O joy of all the meek,
4. But what to those who find? Ah, this Nor tongue nor pen can show;
5. Je - sus, our on - ly joy be Thou, As Thou our prize wilt be;

But sweet - er far Thy face to see And in Thy pres - ence rest.
A sweet - er sound than Thy blest name, O Sav - ior of man - kind.
To those who fall, how kind Thou art! How good to those who seek!
The love of Je - sus, what it is— None but His loved ones know.
Je - sus, be Thou our glo - ry now And thro' e - ter - ni - ty.

TEXT: Attributed to Bernard of Clairvaux; translated by Edward Caswall
MUSIC: John B. Dykes

ST. AGNES
C.M.

90 Joyful, Joyful, We Adore Thee

My lips will shout for joy when I sing praise to You. Psalm 71:23

1. Joy - ful, joy - ful, we a - dore Thee, God of glo - ry, Lord of love;
2. All Thy works with joy sur - round Thee, Earth and heav'n re - flect Thy rays.
3. Thou art giv - ing and for - giv - ing, Ev - er bless - ing, ev - er blest,
4. Mor - tals, join the might - y cho - rus Which the morn - ing stars be - gan;

Hearts un - fold like flow'rs be - fore Thee, Open - ing to the sun a - bove.
Stars and an - gels sing a - round Thee, Cen - ter of un - bro - ken praise.
Well - spring of the joy of liv - ing, O - cean depth of hap - py rest!
Love di - vine is reign - ing o'er us, Lead - ing us with mer - cy's hand.

Melt the clouds of sin and sad - ness; Drive the dark of doubt a - way.
Field and for - est, vale and moun - tain, Flow - ery mead - ow, flash - ing sea,
Thou our Fa - ther, Christ our Broth - er— All who live in love are Thine.
Ev - er sing - ing, march we on - ward, Vic - tors in the midst of strife.

Giv - er of im - mor - tal glad - ness, Fill us with the light of day!
Chant - ing bird and flow - ing foun - tain Call us to re - joice in Thee!
Teach us how to love each oth - er; Lift us to the joy di - vine!
Joy - ful mu - sic leads us sun - ward In the tri - umph song of life!

TEXT: Henry van Dyke
MUSIC: Ludwig van Beethoven; melody from *Ninth Symphony*;
adapted by Edward Hodges; Last stanza setting and Choral ending by Dan Burgess

HYMN TO JOY
8.7.8.7.D.

Optional last stanza setting

Unison - (melody octave lower)

ff

4. Mor - tals, join the might-y cho-rus

Which the morn - ing stars be-gan;

melody as written

Love di - vine is reign-ing o'er us, Lead-ing us with mer - cy's hand. Ev - er sing-ing, march we on-ward, Vic - tors in the midst of strife.

melody octave lower

Joy - ful mu - sic leads us sun-ward In the tri - umph song of life!

Optional choral ending

f Sing harmony

Joy-ful mu-sic leads us sun-ward In the joy-ous tri-umph song of life!

91 In Moments like These

I love You, O Lord, my strength. Psalm 18:1

In mo-ments like these, I sing out a song, I sing out a love song to Je - sus. In mo-ments like these, I lift up my hands, I lift up my hands to the Lord. Sing-ing, "I love You, Lord." Sing-ing, "I love You, Lord." Sing-ing, "I love You, Lord. I love You."

Optional transition to "O How I Love Jesus"

TEXT: David Graham
MUSIC: David Graham

GRAHAM
Irregular meter

O How I Love Jesus 92

Though you have not seen Him, you love Him. 1 Peter 1:8

1. There is a name I love to hear, I love to sing its worth;
2. It tells me of a Sav-ior's love, Who died to set me free;
3. It tells me what my Fa-ther hath In store for ev-ery day
4. It tells of One whose lov-ing heart Can feel my deep-est woe,

It sounds like mu-sic in my ear, The sweet-est name on earth.
It tells me of His pre-cious blood, The sin-ner's per-fect plea.
And, tho' I tread a dark-some path, Yields sun-shine all the way.
Who in each sor-row bears a part That none can bear be-low.

Refrain

O how I love Je-sus! O how I love Je-sus!

O how I love Je-sus, Be-cause He first loved me!

TEXT: Frederick Whitfield
MUSIC: Traditional American melody

O HOW I LOVE JESUS
C.M. with Refrain

Optional extended or choral ending

Be-cause He first loved me! (He first loved me!)

93 God, Our Father, We Adore Thee

Our Father in heaven, hallowed be Your name. Matthew 6:9

1. God, our Fa - ther, we a - dore Thee! We, Thy chil - dren, bless Thy name!
2. Son E - ter - nal, we a - dore Thee! Lamb up - on the throne on high!
3. Ho - ly Spir - it, we a - dore Thee! Par - a - clete and heav'n - ly guest!
4. Fa - ther, Son, and Ho - ly Spir - it— Three in One! we give Thee praise!

Cho - sen in the Christ be - fore Thee, We are "ho - ly, with - out blame."
Lamb of God, we bow be - fore Thee, Thou hast bro't Thy peo - ple nigh!
Sent from God and from the Sav - ior, Thou hast led us in - to rest.
For the rich - es we in - her - it, Heart and voice to Thee we raise!

We a - dore Thee! we a - dore Thee! Ab - ba's prais - es we pro - claim!
We a - dore Thee! we a - dore Thee! Son of God, who came to die!
We a - dore Thee! we a - dore Thee! By Thy grace for - ev - er blest;
We a - dore Thee! we a - dore Thee! Thee we bless thro' end - less days!

We a - dore Thee! we a - dore Thee! Ab - ba's prais - es we pro - claim!
We a - dore Thee! we a - dore Thee! Son of God, who came to die!
We a - dore Thee! we a - dore Thee! By Thy grace for - ev - er blest;
We a - dore Thee! we a - dore Thee! Thee we bless thro' end - less days!

TEXT: George W. Frazier; Alfred S. Loizeaux, stanza 3
MUSIC: John Zundel
A lower setting may be found at No. 407

BEECHER
8.7.8.7.D.

I LOVE YOU, O LORD

from Psalms 62, 63 and 18 (NIV)

WORSHIP LEADER
O God, You are my God;
Earnestly I seek You.
I have seen You in the sanctuary
and beheld Your power and Your glory.

EVERYONE
Because Your love is better than life,
my lips will glorify You.
I will praise You as long as I live,
and in Your name I will lift up my hands.

WORSHIP LEADER
On my bed I remember You;
I think of You through the watches of the night.
Because You are my help,
I sing in the shadow of Your wings.

EVERYONE
I love You, O Lord, my strength.

WORSHIP LEADER
The Lord is my rock, my fortress and my deliverer.

EVERYONE
I love You, O Lord, my strength.

WORSHIP LEADER
My God is my rock, in whom I take refuge.

EVERYONE
I love You, O Lord, my strength.

WORSHIP LEADER
He is my shield and the horn of my salvation–
my stronghold.

EVERYONE
I love You, O Lord, my strength.

WORSHIP LEADER
One thing God has spoken,
two things have I heard;
That You, O God, are strong,
and that You, O God, are loving.

EVERYONE
O God, You are my God;
Earnestly I seek You.
I have seen You in the sanctuary
and beheld Your power and Your glory.

WORSHIP LEADER
The Lord lives! Praise be to my rock!
Exalted be God our Savior!

95

A NEW SONG

from Psalms 18, 40, 116 and 117 (NIV)

WORSHIP LEADER
I waited patiently for the Lord;
He turned to me and heard my cry.

SOLO 1
He lifted me out of the slimy pit;
out of the mud and mire.

SOLO 2
He set my feet on a rock
and gave me a firm place to stand.

SOLO 1 and SOLO 2
He put a new song in my mouth,
a hymn of praise to our God.

WORSHIP LEADER
I love the Lord, for He heard my voice;
He heard my cry for mercy.
The Lord is gracious and righteous;
Our God is full of compassion.
Because He turned His ear to me,
I will call on Him as long as I live.

SOLO 1
May all who seek You
rejoice and be glad in You;
May those who love Your salvation always say,
"The Lord be exalted."

SOLO 2
Many, O Lord my God,
are the wonders You have done.

SOLO 1
The things You planned for us
no one can recount to You;

SOLO 2
Were I to speak and tell of them,
they would be too many to declare.

WORSHIP LEADER
How can I repay the Lord
for all His goodness to me?

SOLO 1
I will lift up the cup of salvation
and call on the name of the Lord.

SOLO 2
I will sacrifice a thank offering to You
and call on the name of the Lord.
I call to the Lord, who is worthy of praise.

EVERYONE
Great is His love toward us,
and the faithfulness of the Lord endures forever.

To Thee We Ascribe Glory 96

Ascribe to the Lord glory and strength. Psalm 29:1

Optional repeat setting

Optional extended or choral ending

TEXT: Kirk Dearman; based on Psalm 29:1
MUSIC: Kirk Dearman

ASCRIBE GLORY
Irregular meter

97 Sing Praise to God Who Reigns Above

The Lord reigns, let the earth be glad. Psalm 97:1

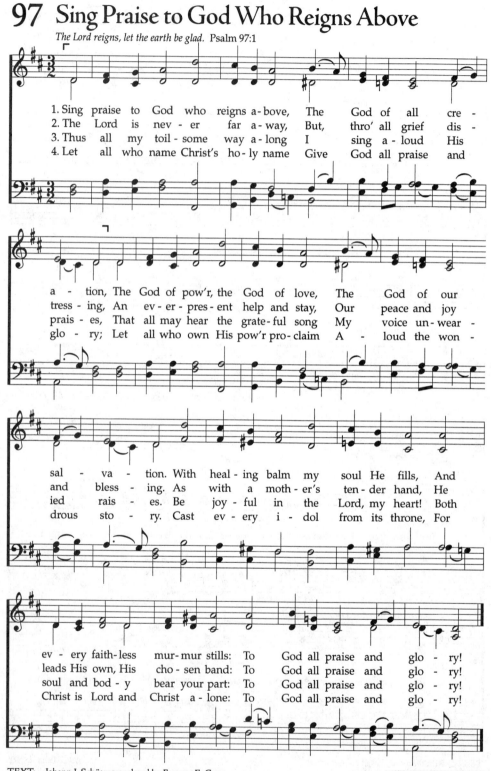

1. Sing praise to God who reigns a-bove, The God of all cre-
2. The Lord is nev-er far a-way, But, thro' all grief dis-
3. Thus all my toil-some way a-long I sing a-loud His
4. Let all who name Christ's ho-ly name Give God all praise and

a-tion, The God of pow'r, the God of love, The God of our
tress-ing, An ev-er-pres-ent help and stay, Our peace and joy
prais-es, That all may hear the grate-ful song My voice un-wear-
glo-ry; Let all who own His pow'r pro-claim A-loud the won-

sal-va-tion. With heal-ing balm my soul He fills, And
and bless-ing. As with a moth-er's ten-der hand, He
ied rais-es. Be joy-ful in the Lord, my heart! Both
drous sto-ry. Cast ev-ery i-dol from its throne, For

ev-ery faith-less mur-mur stills: To God all praise and glo-ry!
leads His own, His cho-sen band: To God all praise and glo-ry!
soul and bod-y bear your part: To God all praise and glo-ry!
Christ is Lord and Christ a-lone: To God all praise and glo-ry!

TEXT: Johann J. Schütz; translated by Frances E. Cox
MUSIC: Bohemian Brethren's *Kirchengesänge*, Berlin, 1566

MIT FREUDEN ZART
8.7.8.7.8.8.7.

HE IS WORTHY OF GLORY
A Worship Sequence

Thou Art Worthy, Great Jehovah
Thou Art Worthy

WORSHIP LEADER

"You are worthy, O Lord,
To receive glory and honor and power;
For You created all things,
And by Your will they exist and were created."

from Revelation 4:11 (NKJV)

Thou Art Worthy, Great Jehovah 99

Worthy is the Lamb to receive honor and glory and praise! Revelation 5:12

Thou art wor - thy, Great Je - ho - vah. Thou art
wor - thy, Might - y God. Thou art wor - thy, Ab - ba
Fa - ther. Thou art wor - thy, Lamb of God. Thou art God.

Optional segue to "Thou Art Worthy." No transition is needed.

TEXT: Karen Eagen
MUSIC: Karen Eagen

EAGAN
8.7.8.7.

100 Thou Art Worthy

You are worthy, our Lord and God, to receive glory and honor and power. Revelation 4:11

Thou art wor-thy, Thou art wor-thy, Thou art wor-thy, O Lord,

To re-ceive glo-ry, glo-ry and hon-or, Glo-ry and

hon-or and pow'r. For Thou hast cre-at-ed, hast all things cre-

at-ed; Thou hast cre-at-ed all things. And for Thy

plea-sure they are cre-at-ed; For Thou art wor-thy, O Lord.

TEXT: Pauline M. Mills; based on Revelations 4:11; 5:9
MUSIC: Pauline M. Mills

WORTHY
Irregular meter

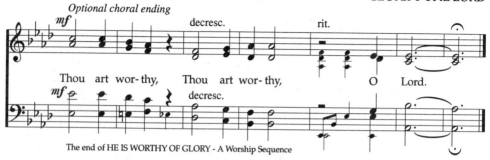

Optional choral ending

Thou art wor-thy, Thou art wor-thy, O Lord.

The end of HE IS WORTHY OF GLORY - A Worship Sequence

All People That on Earth Do Dwell 101

Shout for joy to the Lord, all the earth. Psalm 100:1

1. All peo - ple that on earth do dwell, Sing to the
2. The Lord, ye know, is God in - deed; With - out our
3. O en - ter then His gates with praise; Ap - proach with
4. For why? The Lord our God is good; His mer - cy
5. To Fa - ther, Son, and Ho - ly Ghost, The God whom

Lord with cheer - ful voice. Him serve with fear; His praise forth
aid He did us make. We are His flock; He doth us
joy His courts un - to. Praise, laud, and bless His name al -
is for - ev - er sure. His truth at all times firm - ly
heav'n and earth a - dore, From earth and from the an - gel

tell. Come ye be - fore Him and re - joice.
feed, And for His sheep He doth us take.
ways, For it is seem - ly so to do.
stood, And shall from age to age en - dure.
host Be praise and glo - ry ev - er - more. A - men.

TEXT: William Kethe and *Scottish Psalter*, 1565; based on Psalm 100   OLD HUNDREDTH
MUSIC: *Genevan Psalter*, 1551; attributed to Louis Bourgeois   L. M.

102 PRAISE TO THE KING
A Worship Sequence

All Hail King Jesus
O Worship the King; stanzas 1,2,5
Suggested stanzas have been marked with an arrow: ➤

WORSHIP LEADER
Hallelujah!
Salvation and glory and power belong to our God.
Hallelujah!
For our Lord God Almighty reigns.
Let us rejoice and be glad and give Him glory!
Hallelujah!
To Him who sits on the throne and to the Lamb
be praise and honor and glory and power,
for ever and ever!
Hallelujah!

from Revelation 19:16, 6-7; 5:13 (NIV)

Optional introduction to
"All Hail King Jesus"

103 All Hail King Jesus

He has this name written: KING OF KINGS AND LORD OF LORDS. Revelation 19:16

All hail King Je - sus! All hail Em - man - u - el:

King of kings, Lord of lords, Bright Morn - ing Star.

TEXT: Dave Moody
MUSIC: Dave Moody

KING JESUS
Irregular meter

Optional transition to
"O Worship the King"

104 O Worship the King

O Lord my God, You are very great; You are clothed with splendor and majesty. Psalm 104:1

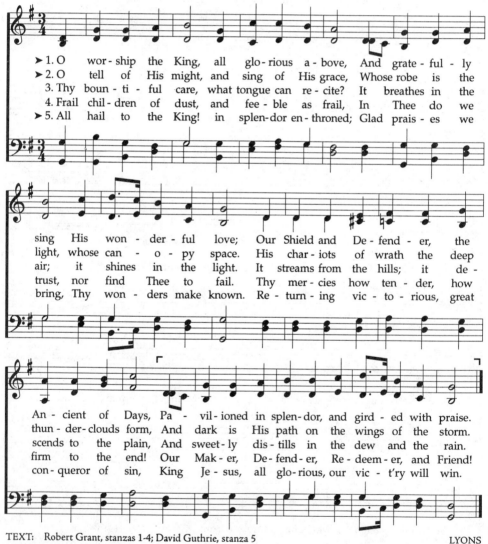

► 1. O wor - ship the King, all glo - rious a - bove, And grate - ful - ly
► 2. O tell of His might, and sing of His grace, Whose robe is the
3. Thy boun - ti - ful care, what tongue can re - cite? It breathes in the
4. Frail chil - dren of dust, and fee - ble as frail, In Thee do we
► 5. All hail to the King! in splen - dor en - throned; Glad prais - es we

sing His won - der - ful love; Our Shield and De - fend - er, the
light, whose can - o - py space. His char - iots of wrath the deep
air; it shines in the light. It streams from the hills; it de -
trust, nor find Thee to fail. Thy mer - cies how ten - der, how
bring, Thy won - ders make known. Re - turn - ing vic - to - rious, great

An - cient of Days, Pa - vil - ioned in splen-dor, and gird - ed with praise.
thun - der-clouds form, And dark is His path on the wings of the storm.
scends to the plain, And sweet-ly dis - tills in the dew and the rain.
firm to the end! Our Mak - er, De - fend - er, Re - deem - er, and Friend!
con - queror of sin, King Je - sus, all glo - rious, our vic - t'ry will win.

TEXT: Robert Grant, stanzas 1-4; David Guthrie, stanza 5
MUSIC: William Gardiner's *Sacred Melodies*, 1815; arranged from Johann M. Haydn;
Last stanza setting and Choral ending by Don Marsh

LYONS
10.10.11.11.

Optional last stanza setting

Unison

➤ 5. All hail to the King! in splen-dor en-throned; Glad prais-es we bring, Thy won-ders make known. Re-turn-ing vic-to-rious, great con-queror of sin, King Je-sus, all glo-rious, our vic-t'ry will win.

sub. *mf*

cresc.

Optional choral ending

All hail King Je-sus! Wor-ship the King!

The end of PRAISE TO THE KING - A Worship Sequence

105 We Will Glorify

To Him who sits on the throne and to the Lamb be praise and honor and glory. Revelation 5:13

1. We will glo - ri - fy the King of kings; We will glo - ri - fy the
2. Lord Je - ho - vah reigns in maj - es - ty; We will bow be - fore His
3. He is Lord of heav - en, Lord of earth; He is Lord of all who
4. Hal - le - lu - jah to the King of kings; Hal - le - lu - jah to the

Lamb. We will glo - ri - fy the Lord of lords, Who is the great I AM.
throne. We will wor - ship Him in righ - teous - ness, We will wor - ship Him a - lone.
live. He is Lord a - bove the u - ni - verse; All praise to Him we give.
Lamb. Hal - le - lu - jah to the Lord of lords, Who is the great I AM.

Optional last stanza setting   Broader

rit.

4. Hal - le - lu - jah to the King of kings;

Hal - le - lu - jah to the Lamb. Hal - le - lu - jah to the

1   2

Lord of lords, Who is the great I AM. Hal - le - AM.

TEXT: Twila Paris
MUSIC: Twila Paris; arranged by David Allen

WE WILL GLORIFY
9.7.9.6.

Worthy, You Are Worthy 106

Worthy is the Lamb to receive honor and glory and praise. Revelation 5:12

1. Wor - thy, You are wor - thy; King of kings, Lord of lords, You are wor - thy.
2. Ho - ly, You are ho - ly; King of kings, Lord of lords, You are ho - ly.
3. Je - sus, You are Je - sus; King of kings, Lord of lords, You are Je - sus.

Wor - thy, You are wor - thy; King of kings, Lord of lords, I wor-ship You.
Ho - ly, You are ho - ly; King of kings, Lord of lords, I wor-ship You.
Je - sus, You are Je - sus; King of kings, Lord of lords, I wor-ship You.

Optional last stanza setting

3. Je - sus, You are Je - sus; King of kings, Lord of lords, You are

Je - sus. Je - sus, You are Je - sus; King of kings, Lord of lords, I wor-ship You.

TEXT: Don Moen
MUSIC: Don Moen

WORTHY
6.6.4.6.6.4.

Optional extended or choral ending

King of kings, Lord of lords, I wor - ship You.

107 Lord, I Lift Your Name on High

My lips will shout for joy when I sing praise to You – I, whom You have redeemed. Psalm 71:23

Lord, I lift Your name on high; Lord, I love to sing Your prais-es. I'm so glad You're in my life; I'm so glad You came to save us. You came from heav-en to earth to show the way; From the earth to the cross, my debt to pay. From the cross to the grave, From the grave to the

sky;   Lord, I lift Your name   on   high.

GLORIFY THE LAMB OF GOD   108
A Worship Sequence

Lamb of Glory; complete
Hallelujah! Praise the Lamb
Glory to the Lamb
Suggested stanzas have been marked with an arrow: ➤

WORSHIP LEADER

He was oppressed and He was afflicted,
Yet He opened not His mouth;
He was led as a lamb to the slaughter,
And as a sheep before its shearers is silent,
So He opened not His mouth.
He was wounded for our transgressions,
He was bruised for our iniquities;
And by His stripes we are healed.
"Worthy is the Lamb who was slain,
to receive power and riches and wisdom,
and strength and honor and glory and blessing!"

EVERYONE

Hallelujah! Praise the Lamb!

from Isaiah 53: 7, 5; Revelation 5:12 (NKJV)

Optional introduction to
"Lamb of Glory"

mf

109 Lamb of Glory

Look, the Lamb of God, who takes away the sin of the world! John 1:29

1. Hear the sto - ry from God's Word That kings and priests and proph - ets heard: There would be a sac - ri - fice, And blood would flow to pay sin's price.

2. On the cross God loved the world While all the pow'rs of hell were hurled; No one there could un - der - stand The One they saw was Christ, the Lamb.

Refrain

Pre - cious Lamb of glo - ry, Love's most won - drous sto - ry, Heart of God's re - demp - tion of man— Wor - ship the Lamb of glo - ry.

TEXT: Greg Nelson and Phill McHugh
MUSIC: Greg Nelson and Phill McHugh

LAMB OF GLORY
7.8.7.8. with Refrain

Optional transition to
"Hallelujah! Praise the Lamb"

great rit.　　　　　　　　　　　　　　　slower

Hallelujah! Praise the Lamb 110

To Him who sits on the throne and to the Lamb be praise. Revelation 5:13

Hal - le - lu - jah! Praise the Lamb! Hal- le- lu - jah! Praise the Lamb! My heart

sings　this song a - gain:　Hal - le - lu - jah! Praise the Lamb! Hal- le- Lamb!

Optional repeat setting

Hal- le - lu - jah! Praise the Lamb! Hal- le- lu - jah! Praise the

Lamb!　My heart sings this song a - gain:　Hal - le - lu - jah! Praise the Lamb!

TEXT:　Pam Thum, Dawn Thomas and Gary McSpadden
MUSIC:　Pam Thum, Dawn Thomas and Gary McSpadden

PRAISE THE LAMB
L.M.

Optional transition to
"Glory to the Lamb"

111 Glory to the Lamb

Worthy is the Lamb to receive honor and glory and praise! Revelation 5:12

Glo - ry, glo - ry, glo - ry to the Lamb. Glo - ry,

glo - ry, glo - ry to the Lamb. For He is glo - ri - ous and

wor-thy to be praised, the Lamb up-on the throne; And un - to

Him we lift our voice in praise, the Lamb up-on the throne.

TEXT: Larry Dempsey
MUSIC: Larry Dempsey; Choral ending by Ken Barker

DEMPSEY
Irregular meter

The end of GLORIFY THE LAMB OF GOD - A Worship Sequence

112 Give to Our God Immortal Praise

Give thanks to the Lord, for He is good. His love endures forever. Psalm 136:1

1. Give to our God im-mor-tal praise; Mer - cy and truth are all His ways:
2. Give to the Lord of lords re - nown; The King of kings with glo - ry crown:
3. He built the earth, He spread the sky, And fixed the star-ry lights on high:

Hal-le-lu - jah, Hal-le-lu - jah! Won - ders of grace to God be-long,
Hal-le-lu - jah, Hal-le-lu - jah! His mer-cies ev - er shall en - dure,
Hal-le-lu - jah, Hal-le-lu - jah! Won - ders of grace to God be-long,

Re - peat His mer-cies in your song: Hal-le-lu - jah, Hal-le-lu - jah,
When lords and kings are known no more: Hal-le-lu - jah, Hal-le-lu - jah,
Re - peat His mer-cies in your song: Hal-le-lu - jah, Hal-le-lu - jah,

Hal-le - lu - jah, Hal-le - lu - jah, Hal-le - lu - jah!
Hal-le - lu - jah, Hal-le - lu - jah, Hal-le - lu - jah!
Hal-le - lu - jah, Hal-le - lu - jah, Hal-le - lu - jah!

TEXT: Isaac Watts; based on Psalm 136
MUSIC: *Geistliche Kirchengesänge*, Cologne, 1623; harmonized by Ralph Vaughan Williams
A lower setting may be found at No. 63

LASST UNS ERFREUEN
L.M. with Alleluias

THE KING OF GLORY 113

from Psalm 24 (NIV)

SOLO 1 *(Female)*
The earth is the Lord's, and everything in it; the world, and all who live in it.

SOLO 2 *(Male)*
For He founded it upon the seas and established it upon the waters.

CHILDREN and WOMEN
Who may ascend the hill of the Lord?
Who may stand in His holy place?

MEN
He who has clean hands and a pure heart,
who does not lift up his soul to an idol or swear by what is false.

SOLO I *(Female)*
He will receive blessings from the Lord,

SOLO 2 *(Male)*
and vindication from God, his Savior.

CHOIR
Such is the generation of those who seek Him–
who seek Your face, O God of Jacob.

EVERYONE
Lift up your heads, O you gates;
Be lifted up, you ancient doors, that the King of glory may come in.

CHILDREN and WOMEN
Who is this King of glory?

SOLO 1 *(Female)*
The Lord, strong and mighty;

SOLO 2 *(Male)*
The Lord, mighty in battle.

EVERYONE
Lift up your heads, O you gates;
Lift them up, you ancient doors, that the King of glory may come in.

CHILDREN and WOMEN
Who is He, this King of glory?

EVERYONE
The Lord Almighty - He is the King of glory.

THE HEAVENS DECLARE HIS GLORY 114

from Psalm 19:1-4 (NIV)

WORSHIP LEADER
The heavens declare the glory of God;
the skies proclaim the work of His hands.
Day after day they pour forth speech;
night after night they display knowledge.
There is no speech or language
where their voice is not heard.
Their voice goes out into all the earth,
their words to the ends of the world.

115   LET THE EARTH BE GLAD

from Psalm 96 (NIV)

WORSHIP LEADER
Sing to the Lord a new song; sing to the Lord, all the earth.

CHOIR
Sing to the Lord.

EVERYONE
Sing to the Lord, all the earth.

WORSHIP LEADER
Sing to the Lord, praise His name; proclaim His salvation day after day.

WOMEN
Declare His glory among the nations, His marvelous deeds among all peoples.

WORSHIP LEADER
For great is the Lord and most worthy of praise.

CHOIR
Great is the Lord.

EVERYONE
He is worthy of praise.

WORSHIP LEADER
Splendor and majesty are before Him; strength and glory are in His sanctuary.

MEN
Ascribe to the Lord, O families of nations; ascribe to the Lord glory and strength.

CHOIR
Ascribe to the Lord.

EVERYONE
Ascribe to the Lord glory and strength.

WORSHIP LEADER
Ascribe to the Lord the glory due His name; bring an offering and come into His courts.

EVERYONE
Worship the Lord in the splendor of His holiness; tremble before Him, all the earth.

WOMEN
Let the heavens rejoice.

MEN
Let the earth be glad.

WOMEN
Let the sea resound,

MEN
And all that is in it.

WOMEN
Let the fields be jubilant,

MEN
And everything in them.

WORSHIP LEADER
Sing to the Lord!

CHOIR
Sing to the Lord!

EVERYONE
Sing to the Lord, all the earth!

Name of All Majesty 116

Yours, O Lord, is the greatness and the power and the glory and the majesty. 1 Chronicles 29:11

1. Name of all maj - es - ty, fath - om - less mys - ter - y,
2. Child of our des - ti - ny, God from e - ter - ni - ty,
3. Sav - ior of Cal - va - ry, cost - li - est vic - to - ry,
4. Source of all sov - 'reign - ty, light, im - mor - tal - i - ty,

King of the a - ges by an - gels a - dored;
Love of the Fa - ther on sin - ners out - poured;
Dark - ness de - feat - ed and E - den re - stored;
Life ev - er - last - ing and heav - en as - sured;

Pow'r and au - thor - i - ty, splen - dor and dig - ni - ty,
See now what God has done send - ing His on - ly Son,
Born as a man to die, nailed to a cross on high,
So with the ran - somed, we praise Him e - ter - nal - ly,

Bow to His mas - ter - y— Je - sus is Lord!
Christ the be - lov - ed One— Je - sus is Lord!
Cold in the grave to lie— Je - sus is Lord!
Christ in His maj - es - ty— Je - sus is Lord!

TEXT: Timothy Dudley-Smith
MUSIC: Michael Baughen; arranged by Noel Tredinnick, altered

MAJESTAS
6.6.5.5.5.6.6.6.4.

117 His Name Is Life

I am the life. John 14:6

His name is Mas-ter, Sav-ior, Li-on of Ju-dah, Bless-ed Prince of Peace; Shep-herd, For-tress, Rock of Sal-va-tion– Lamb of God is He. Son of Da-vid, King of the Ag-es, E-ter-nal Life; Ho-ly Lord of Glo-ry– His name is Life.

TEXT: Carman, Gloria Gaither and William J. Gaither
MUSIC: Carman, Gloria Gaither and William J. Gaither

HIS NAME IS LIFE
Irregular meter

Optional extended ending

Optional transition to "His Name Is Wonderful"

Ho-ly Lord of Glo-ry– His name is Life. *rit.*

His Name Is Wonderful 118

No one can say, "Jesus is Lord," except by the Holy Spirit. 1 Corinthians 12:3

His name is Won-der-ful, His name is Won-der-ful, His name is Won-der-ful, Je-sus, my Lord; He is the might-y King, Mas-ter of ev-ery-thing, His name is Won-der-ful, Je-sus, my Lord. He's the great Shep-herd, the Rock of all ag-es, Al-might-y God is He; Bow down be-fore Him, Love and a-dore Him; His name is Won-der-ful, Je-sus, my Lord. Lord.

Slower on repeat

1 Repeat optional 2

TEXT: Audrey Mieir
MUSIC: Audrey Mieir

MIEIR
Irregular meter

119 Jesus, Your Name

I will do whatever you ask in My name, so that the Son may bring glory to the Father. John 14:13

Unison

1. Je - sus, Your name is pow - er; Je - sus, Your name is might.
2. Je - sus, Your name is heal - ing; Je - sus, Your name gives sight.
3. Je - sus, Your name is ho - ly; Je - sus, Your name brings light.
4. Je - sus, Your name is pow - er; Je - sus, Your name is might.

Je - sus, Your name will break ev - ery strong-hold; Je - sus, Your name is life.
Je - sus, Your name will free ev - ery cap - tive; Je - sus, Your name is life.
Je - sus, Your name a - bove ev - ery oth - er; Je - sus, Your name is life.
Je - sus, Your name will break ev - ery strong-hold; Je - sus, Your name is life.

TEXT: Claire Cloninger and Morris Chapman
MUSIC: Claire Cloninger and Morris Chapman

JESUS, YOUR NAME
6.6.10.6.

120 MAJESTIC AND GLORIOUS

A Worship Sequence

How Majestic Is Your Name
Glorious Is Thy Name; stanzas 1,2,4
Suggested stanzas have been marked with an arrow: ➤

WORSHIP LEADER

Yours, O Lord, is the greatness, the power and the glory,
the victory and the majesty; for all that is in heaven and in earth is Yours;
Yours is the kingdom, O Lord, and You are exalted as head over all.

EVERYONE

Now therefore, our God, we thank You and praise Your glorious name.

from 1 Chronicles 29:11, 13 (NKJV)

Optional introduction to "How Majestic Is Your Name"

MAJESTIC AND GLORIOUS - A Worship Sequence

How Majestic Is Your Name 121

O Lord, our Lord, how majestic is Your name in all the earth! Psalm 8:1

O Lord, our Lord, how ma- jes - tic is Your name in all the

earth. O earth. O Lord, we praise Your name. O

Lord, we mag- ni- fy Your name: Prince of Peace, Might- y

God; O Lord God Al- might - y. O y.

TEXT: Michael W. Smith
MUSIC: Michael W. Smith

HOW MAJESTIC
Irregular meter

Optional transition to "Glorious Is Thy Name"

♩ = ♩ A little slower

122 Glorious Is Thy Name

Our God, we give You thanks, and praise Your glorious name. 1 Chronicles 29:13

1. Bless - ed Sav - ior, we a - dore Thee; We Thy love and grace pro - claim.
2. Great Re - deem - er, Lord and Mas - ter, Light of all e - ter - nal days,
3. From the throne of heav - en's glo - ry To the cross of sin and shame,
4. Come, O come, im - mor - tal Sav - ior; Come and take Thy roy - al throne.

Thou art might - y; Thou art ho - ly. Glo - rious is Thy match - less name!
Let the saints of ev - ery na - tion Sing Thy just and end - less praise!
Thou didst come to die a ran - som, Guilt - y sin - ners to re - claim!
Come, and reign, and reign for - ev - er; Be the king - dom all Thine own!

Refrain

Glo - ri - ous, glo - ri - ous,
Glo - rious is Thy name, O Lord!   Glo - rious is Thy name, O Lord!

Glo - rious is Thy name, O Lord!   Glo - ri - ous,
Glo - rious is Thy name, O Lord!

TEXT: B. B. McKinney
MUSIC: B. B. McKinney

GLORIOUS NAME
8.7.8.7. with Refrain

glo - ri-ous, Glo-rious is Thy name, O Lord!

Glo - rious is Thy name, O Lord!

Optional choral ending

O how glo-rious, How ma-jes-tic is Your name, O Lord!

The end of MAJESTIC AND GLORIOUS - A Worship Sequence

How Sweet the Name of Jesus Sounds 123

To those who call on the name of our Lord Jesus Christ: Grace and peace to you. 1 Corinthians 1:2-3

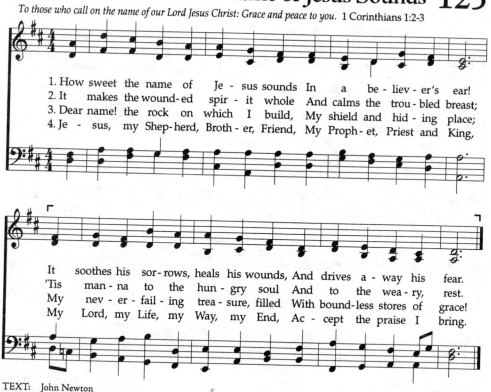

1. How sweet the name of Je - sus sounds In a be - liev - er's ear!
2. It makes the wound-ed spir - it whole And calms the trou - bled breast;
3. Dear name! the rock on which I build, My shield and hid - ing place;
4. Je - sus, my Shep-herd, Broth - er, Friend, My Proph - et, Priest and King,

It soothes his sor - rows, heals his wounds, And drives a - way his fear.
'Tis man - na to the hun - gry soul And to the wea - ry, rest.
My nev - er - fail - ing trea - sure, filled With bound-less stores of grace!
My Lord, my Life, my Way, my End, Ac - cept the praise I bring.

TEXT: John Newton
MUSIC: Alexander R. Reinagle

ST. PETER
C.M.

124 O Magnify the Lord

Glorify the Lord with me; let us exalt His name together. Psalm 34:3

1. O mag - ni - fy, O mag - ni - fy the Lord with me, And
(2. O) wor - ship Him; O wor - ship Christ the Lord with me, And

let us ex - alt His name to - geth - er! O mag - ni - fy the Lord;
let us ex - alt His name to - geth - er! O wor - ship Christ, the Lord;

O mag - ni - fy the Lord; And may His name be lift - ed high for -
O wor - ship Christ, the Lord; And may His name be lift - ed high for -

Last time to Coda

1
ev - er! 2. O
ev - er!
2
King of kings and Lord of

D.S. al Coda

lords; May His name be lift - ed high for - ev - er! 1. O

TEXT: Melodie and Dick Tunney
MUSIC: Melodie and Dick Tunney

TUNNEY
Irregular meter

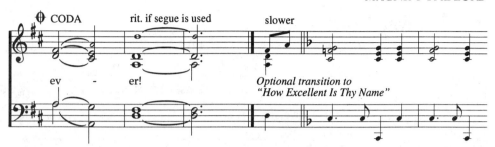

How Excellent Is Thy Name 125

O Lord, our Lord, how majestic is Your name in all the earth. Psalm 8:1, 9

TEXT: Paul Smith and Melodie Tunney
MUSIC: Dick Tunney

HOW EXCELLENT
Irregular meter

126 Holy Lord

The glory of the Lord fills the whole earth. Numbers 14:21

3-part canon

Ho - ly, ho - ly, Lord God Al-might-y; Your glo-ry fills the earth, Lord God of hosts.

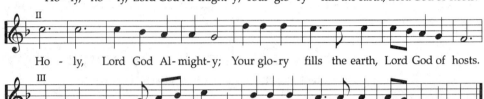

Ho - ly, Lord God Al-might-y; Your glo-ry fills the earth, Lord God of hosts.

Ho - ly, Lord God Al-might-y; Your glo-ry fills the earth, Lord God of hosts.

TEXT: Gerald S. Henderson; based on Isaiah 6:3
MUSIC: Source unknown; adapted by Gerald S. Henderson

DONA NOBIS PACEM
Irregular meter

127 THE LORD ON HIGH IS MIGHTY!

A Worship Sequence

I Sing the Mighty Power of God; complete
Great and Mighty
Suggested stanzas have been marked with an arrow: ➤

WORSHIP LEADER The Lord reigns, He is robed in majesty.

EVERYONE The Lord is robed in majesty and is armed with strength.

WORSHIP LEADER The world is firmly established.

MEN It cannot be moved.

EVERYONE Your throne was established long ago; You are from all eternity.

WORSHIP LEADER The seas have lifted up, O Lord,

WOMEN The seas have lifted up their voice;

EVERYONE The seas have lifted up their pounding waves.

WORSHIP LEADER Mightier than the thunder of the great waters,

MEN Mightier than the breakers of the sea –

EVERYONE The Lord on high is mighty!

WORSHIP LEADER Your statutes stand firm;

WOMEN Holiness adorns Your house for endless days, O Lord!

EVERYONE The Lord on high is mighty!

from Psalm 93 (NIV)

Optional introduction to "I Sing the Mighty Power of God"

I Sing the Mighty Power of God 128

The Lord made the heavens and the earth, the sea, and all that is in them. Exodus 20:11

1. I sing the might-y pow'r of God That made the moun-tains rise,
2. I sing the good-ness of the Lord That filled the earth with food;
3. There's not a plant or flow'r be-low But makes Thy glo-ries known;

That spread the flow-ing seas a-broad, And built the loft-y skies.
He formed the crea-tures with His word And then pro-nounced them good.
And clouds a-rise and tem-pests blow By or-der from Thy throne;

I sing the wis-dom that or-dained The sun to rule the day;
Lord, how Thy won-ders are dis-played Wher-e'er I turn my eye:
While all that bor-rows life from Thee Is ev-er in Thy care,

The moon shines full at His com-mand And all the stars o-bey.
If I sur-vey the ground I tread Or gaze up-on the sky!
And ev-ery-where that man can be, Thou, God, art pres-ent there.

TEXT: Isaac Watts, altered
MUSIC: From *Gesangbuch der Herzogl*, Würtemberg, 1784
A lower setting may be found at No. 297

ELLACOMBE
C.M.D.

Optional transition to "Great and Mighty"

129 Great and Mighty

Who is this King of glory? The Lord, strong and mighty. Psalm 24:8

Great and might-y is the Lord our God, Great and might-y is

He. Great and might-y is the Lord our God,

Great and might-y is He. Lift up your ban-ner, let the

an-thems ring prais-es to our King; Great and might-y is the

Lord our God, Great and might-y is He.

TEXT: Marlene Bigley
MUSIC: Marlene Bigley

GREAT AND MIGHTY
Irregular meter

Optional extended or choral ending
Unison

Great and might - y is, great and might - y is, great and might - y is He.

The end of THE LORD ON HIGH IS MIGHTY! - A Worship Sequence

His Glorious Name 130

He will be called Wonderful Counselor, Mighty God, Everlasting Father, Prince of Peace. Isaiah 9:6

His glo - rious name shall be called Won - der - ful. His match-less name shall

be called Coun - sel - or, The Might-y God, the Ev - er - last-ing Fa - ther,

The Prince of Peace thro' all e - ter - ni - ty. The Might-y God, the

Ev - er - last-ing Fa - ther, The Prince of Peace thro' all e - ter - ni - ty.

TEXT: Adapted from Isaiah 9:6
MUSIC: Jean Sibelius

FINLANDIA
10.10.11.10.11.10.

131 Almighty

Lord God, who is like You? You are mighty, and Your faithfulness surrounds You. Psalm 89:8

Al - might - y, most ho - ly God;
Faith - ful thro' the ag - es. Al - might - y, most ho - ly Lord;
Glo - ri - ous, Al - might - y God.
Al - might - y, most ho - ly God; Faith - ful thro' the
ag - es. Al - might - y, most ho - ly Lord;

TEXT: Wayne Watson
MUSIC: Wayne Watson

ALMIGHTY
Irregular meter

Glo-ri-ous, Al-might-y God. God.

Join All the Glorious Names 132

Praise be to His glorious name forever; may the whole earth be filled with His glory. Psalm 72:19

1. Join all the glo-rious names Of wis-dom, love, and pow'r, That
2. Great Proph-et of my God, My tongue would bless Thy name: By
3. Je - sus, my great High Priest, Of-fered His blood, and died; My
4. Thou art my Coun-sel - or, My Pat - tern, and my Guide, And
5. My Sav - ior and my Lord, My Con - qu'ror and my King, Thy

ev - er mor - tals knew, That an - gels ev - er bore: All are too
Thee the joy - ful news Of our sal - va - tion came, The joy - ful
guilt - y con-science seeks No sac - ri - fice be - side; His pow'r - ful
Thou my Shep-herd art; O keep me near Thy side: Nor let my
scep - ter and Thy sword, Thy reign-ing grace, I sing: Thine is the

poor to speak His worth, Too poor to set my Sav - ior forth.
news of sins for - giv'n, Of hell sub - dued and peace with heav'n.
blood did once a - tone And now it pleads be - fore the throne.
feet e'er turn a - stray To wan - der in the crook - ed way.
pow'r; be - hold I sit In will - ing bonds be - neath Thy feet.

TEXT: Isaac Watts
MUSIC: John Darwall

DARWALL
6.6.6.6.8.8.

133 We Declare Your Majesty

The Lord is robed in majesty and is armed with strength. Psalm 93:1

We de-clare Your maj-es-ty; We pro-claim that Your name is ex-alt-ed! For You reign mag-nif-i-cent, You rule vic-to-ri-ous, Your pow'r is shown thro'-out the earth. And we ex-claim: "Our God is might-y!" Lift up Your name, for You are ho-ly! Sing it a-gain, all hon-or and glo-ry! In ad-o-ra-tion we bow be-fore Your throne!

TEXT: Malcolm du Plessis
MUSIC: Malcolm du Plessis

WE DECLARE YOUR MAJESTY
Irregular meter

SEE HIS GLORY

134

from Psalm 97 (NIV)

WORSHIP LEADER
The Lord reigns!

EVERYONE
The Lord reigns!

WOMEN
Let the earth be glad;

MEN
Let the distant shores rejoice.

WORSHIP LEADER
Clouds and thick darkness surround Him;
Righteousness and justice are the foundation of His throne.

MEN
Fire goes before Him.

WOMEN
His lightning lights up the world;

MEN
The earth sees and trembles.

WOMEN
The mountains melt like wax before the Lord,

EVERYONE
Before the Lord of all the earth.

WORSHIP LEADER
The heavens proclaim His righteousness.

EVERYONE
And all the peoples see His glory.
Praise His holy name!

PRAISE AND MAGNIFY THE LORD

135

from Psalm 148 (NIV)

WORSHIP LEADER
Praise the Lord!

EVERYONE
Praise the Lord from the heavens,
Praise Him in the heights above.
Praise Him, all His angels; praise Him, all His heavenly hosts.
Praise Him, sun and moon; praise Him all you shining stars.
Praise Him, you highest heavens and you waters above the skies.
Let them praise the name of the Lord!
Praise the Lord from the earth,
You great sea creatures and all ocean depths,
Lightning and hail, snow and clouds, stormy winds that do His bidding;
You mountains and all hills, fruit trees and all cedars;
Wild animals and all cattle, small creatures and flying birds;
Kings of the earth and all nations, you princes and all rulers on earth;
Young men and maidens, old men and children.
Let them praise the name of the Lord!
For His name alone is exalted;
His splendor is above the earth and the heavens.
Praise the name of the Lord!

136

CRIES OF JOY

from Psalm 47 (NIV)

SOLO I
Clap your hands, all you nations;
Shout to God with cries of joy.

EVERYONE
How awesome is the Lord Most High,
The great King over all the earth!

SOLO 2
God has ascended amid shouts of joy,
The Lord amid the sounding of trumpets.

CHOIR and SOLO 1 and 2
Sing praises to God.

EVERYONE
Sing His praise!

CHOIR and SOLO 1 and 2
Sing praises to our King.

EVERYONE
Sing His praise!

SOLO 1
For God is the King of all the earth.

SOLO 2
God reigns over the nations.

SOLO 1
The kings of earth belong to God.
He is greatly exalted.

SOLO 2
Sing to Him a psalm of praise.

CHOIR and SOLO 1 and 2
Clap your hands, all you nations;
Shout to God with cries of joy.

EVERYONE
How awesome is the Lord Most High,
The great King over all the earth!

137

HE IS A HOLY GOD

from Psalm 99 (NIV)

WORSHIP LEADER
The Lord reigns; let the nations tremble.

EVERYONE
The Lord our God is holy.

WORSHIP LEADER
Great is the Lord. He is exalted over all nations.
Let them praise His great and awesome name.

EVERYONE
Our God is holy.

Holy Ground 138

The place where you are standing is holy ground. Exodus 3:5

We are stand-ing on ho-ly ground, And I know that there are an-gels all a-round. Let us praise Je-sus now; We are stand-ing in His pres-ence on ho-ly ground.

Optional extended or choral ending
Sing harmony

We are stand-ing in His pres-ence on ho-ly ground. (ho-ly ground.)

TEXT: Geron Davis
MUSIC: Geron Davis

HOLY GROUND
Irregular meter

139 Great Is Thy Faithfulness

The Lord's compassions are new every morning; great is Your faithfulness. Lamentations 3:22-23

1. Great is Thy faith - ful - ness, O God, my Fa - ther;
2. Sum - mer and win - ter, and spring - time and har - vest,
3. Par - don for sin and a peace that en - dur - eth,

There is no shad - ow of turn - ing with Thee.
Sun, moon and stars in their cours - es a - bove,
Thy own dear pres - ence to cheer and to guide.

Thou chang - est not; Thy com - pas - sions, they fail not.
Join with all na - ture in man - i - fold wit - ness
Strength for to - day and bright hope for to - mor - row—

As Thou hast been Thou for - ev - er wilt be.
To Thy great faith - ful - ness, mer - cy and love.
Bless - ings all mine with ten thou - sand be - side!

Refrain

Great is Thy faith - ful - ness! Great is Thy faith - ful - ness! Morn - ing by

TEXT: Thomas O. Chisholm
MUSIC: William M. Runyan

FAITHFULNESS
11.10.11.10. with Refrain

morn - ing new mer - cies I see; All I have need - ed Thy

hand hath pro - vid - ed. Great is Thy faith - ful - ness, Lord, un - to me!

Optional last refrain setting Broader

Great is Thy faith - ful - ness! Great is Thy faith - ful - ness!

Morn - ing by morn - ing new mer - cies I see; All I have

need - ed Thy hand hath pro - vid - ed. Great is Thy faith - ful - ness,

Soprano divisi Slowly
rit.

Great is Thy faith - ful - ness, Great is Thy faith - ful - ness, Lord, un - to me!

140 Great Is the Lord

Great is the Lord and most worthy of praise; His greatness no one can fathom. Psalm 145:3

Unison

Great is the Lord, He is ho-ly and just; By His pow-er we trust in His love. Great is the Lord, He is faith-ful and true; By His mer-cy He proves He is love.

Harmony optional

1.2. Great is the Lord and wor-thy of glo-ry!
(D.S.) Great are You, Lord, and wor-thy of glo-ry!

Great is the Lord and wor-thy of praise! Great is the Lord! Now
Great are You, Lord, and wor-thy of praise! Great are You, Lord! I

lift up your voice, now lift up your voice: Great is the
lift up my voice, I lift up my voice: Great are You,

TEXT: Michael W. Smith and Deborah D. Smith
MUSIC: Michael W. Smith and Deborah D. Smith

GREAT IS THE LORD
Irregular meter

Lord!   Great   is the Lord!   Lord!   Lord!
Lord!   Great   are You,   Lord!

Father God 141

Our Father in heaven, hallowed be Your name. Matthew 6:9

Fa - ther God, I give all thanks and praise to Thee;

Fa - ther God, my hands I hum - bly raise to Thee.

For Thy might - y pow'r and love a - maze me, a - maze me;

And I stand in awe and wor - ship, Fa - ther God.

TEXT: Jack W. Hayford
MUSIC: Jack W. Hayford

FATHER GOD
Irregular meter

142 Holy, Holy, Holy Is the Lord of Hosts

Holy, holy, holy is the Lord Almighty; the whole earth is full of His glory. Isaiah 6:3

TEXT: Nolene Prince; based on Isaiah 6:3
MUSIC: Nolene Prince

PRINCE
Irregular meter

This Is My Father's World 143

The earth is the Lord's, and everything in it, the world, and all who live in it. Psalm 24:1

1. This is my Fa-ther's world, And to my lis-t'ning ears
2. This is my Fa-ther's world, The birds their car-ols raise;
3. This is my Fa-ther's world, O let me ne'er for-get

All na-ture sings, and round me rings The mu-sic of the spheres.
The morn-ing light, the lil-y white De-clare their Mak-er's praise.
That though the wrong seems oft so strong, God is the Rul-er yet.

This is my Fa-ther's world, I rest me in the thought
This is my Fa-ther's world, He shines in all that's fair;
This is my Fa-ther's world, The bat-tle is not done;

Of rocks and trees, of skies and seas– His hand the won-ders wrought.
In the rus-tling grass I hear Him pass, He speaks to me ev-ery-where.
Je-sus, who died, shall be sat-is-fied, And earth and heav'n be one.

TEXT: Maltbie D. Babcock
MUSIC: Traditional English melody; adapted by Franklin L. Sheppard

TERRA BEATA
S.M.D.

144 Great Are You, O Lord

Great is our Lord and mighty in power. Psalm 147:5

3-part Canon

1. God, our Fa - ther, we a - dore You, mag - ni - fy You;
2. Heav'n and earth pro - claim Your pow - er, show Your glo - ry;

God, our Fa - ther, we a - dore You, mag - ni - fy You.
Heav'n and earth pro - claim Your pow - er, show Your glo - ry.

Great are You, O Lord!
Great are You, O Lord!

TEXT: Gerald S. Henderson
MUSIC: Traditional English melody; adapted by Gerald S. Henderson

ENGLAND
Irregular meter

145 SING OF HIS GREATNESS

A Worship Sequence

I Worship You, Almighty God
How Great Thou Art; stanzas 1,3,4
Suggested stanzas have been marked with an arrow: ➤

WORSHIP LEADER	Great is the Lord and most worthy of praise; His greatness no one can fathom.
EVERYONE	**There is no one like You, O Lord.**
WORSHIP LEADER	One generation will commend Your works to another; They will tell of Your mighty acts.
EVERYONE	**There is no one like You, O Lord.**
WORSHIP LEADER	They will speak of the glorious splendor of Your majesty; They will tell of the power of Your awesome works, and will celebrate Your abundant goodness.
EVERYONE	**There is no one like You, O Lord.**

from Psalm 145:3-7; 1 Chronicles 17:20 (NIV)

Optional introduction to "I Worship You, Almighty God"

mp

I Worship You, Almighty God **146**

I worship the Lord, the God of heaven, who made the sea and land. Jonah 1:9

I wor-ship You, Al-might-y God; There is none like You. I

wor-ship You, O Prince of Peace; That is what I want to do. I

give You praise for You are my righ-teous-ness. I

wor-ship You, Al-might-y God; There is none like You. I You.

TEXT: Sondra Corbett
MUSIC: Sondra Corbett

I WORSHIP YOU
Irregular meter

*Optional transition to
"How Great Thou Art"*

slowing gradually   more rit.

147 How Great Thou Art

You are great and do marvelous deeds: You alone are God. Psalm 86:10

➤ 1. O Lord, my God, when I in awe-some won-der Con-sid-er
2. When thro' the woods and for-est glades I wan-der And hear the
➤ 3. And when I think that God, His Son not spar-ing, Sent Him to
➤ 4. When Christ shall come with shout of ac-cla-ma-tion And take me

all the *worlds Thy hands have made, I see the stars, I hear the
birds sing sweet-ly in the trees, When I look down from loft-y
die, I scarce can take it in; That on the cross, my bur-den
home, what joy shall fill my heart! Then I shall bow in hum-ble

*roll-ing thun-der, Thy pow'r thro'-out the u-ni-verse dis-played.
moun-tain gran-deur, And hear the brook and feel the gen-tle breeze;
glad-ly bear-ing, He bled and died to take a-way my sin.
ad-o-ra-tion And there pro-claim: my God, how great Thou art!

Refrain

Then sings my soul, my Sav-ior God, to Thee; How great Thou

Author's original words are "works" and "mighty."

TEXT: Stuart K. Hine
MUSIC: Swedish Folk melody; adapted by Stuart K. Hine;
             Choral ending arranged by Eugene Thomas

O STORE GUD
11.10.11.10. with Refrain

art! How great Thou art! Then sings my soul, my Sav-ior

God, to Thee; How great Thou art! How great Thou art!

Optional choral ending

rit. ff

How great Thou art! How great Thou art! How great Thou art!

The end of SING OF HIS GREATNESS - A Worship Sequence

Isaiah 6:3 148

Holy, holy, holy is the Lord Almighty; the whole earth is full of His glory. Isaiah 6:3

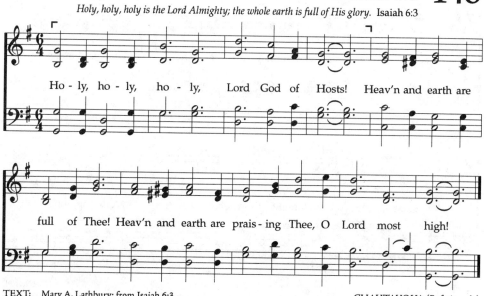

Ho-ly, ho-ly, ho-ly, Lord God of Hosts! Heav'n and earth are

full of Thee! Heav'n and earth are prais-ing Thee, O Lord most high!

TEXT: Mary A. Lathbury; from Isaiah 6:3
MUSIC: William F. Sherwin

CHAUTAUQUA (Refrain only)
Irregular meter

149 Ah, Lord God

Lord, You have made the heavens and the earth. Nothing is too hard for You. Jeremiah 32:17

Ah, Lord God, Thou hast made the heav-ens and the earth by Thy great

pow-er; Ah, Lord God, Thou hast made the heav-ens and the

earth by Thine out-stretched arm. Noth-ing is too dif-fi-cult for

Thee. Noth-ing is too dif-fi-cult for Thee. Great and might-y God,

great in coun-sel and might-y in deed. Noth-ing, noth-ing,

TEXT: Kay Chance
MUSIC: Kay Chance

AH, LORD GOD
Irregular meter

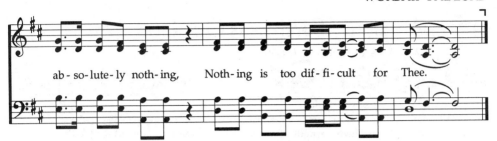

ab - so - lute - ly noth - ing, Noth - ing is too dif - fi - cult for Thee.

Awesome Power 150

The Lord your God is God of gods and Lord of lords, the great and mighty God. Deuteronomy 10:17

Awe - some pow - er, bound - less grace; None can fath - om all Your ways.

Truth and love are found in Your heart a - lone; Righ - teous - ness sur -

rounds Your throne. Ho - ly, ho - ly, ho - ly Lord Most

High; Ho - ly, ho - ly, ho - ly Lord Most High. High.

1 *Repeat optional* 2 *Final ending*

TEXT: John G. Elliott
MUSIC: John G. Elliott

AWESOME POWER
Irregular meter

151 A Mighty Fortress Is Our God

The Lord Almighty is with us; the God of Jacob is our fortress. Psalm 46:7

1. A might-y for-tress is our God, A bul-wark nev-er fail - ing;
2. Did we in our own strength con-fide, Our striv-ing would be los - ing,
3. And tho' this world, with dev-ils filled, Should threat-en to un-do us,
4. That word a-bove all earth-ly pow'rs, No thanks to them, a-bid - eth;

Our help-er He a-mid the flood Of mor-tal ills pre-vail - ing.
Were not the right man on our side, The man of God's own choos - ing.
We will not fear, for God hath willed His truth to tri-umph thro' us.
The Spir-it and the gifts are ours Thro' Him who with us sid - eth.

For still our an-cient foe Doth seek to work us woe— His craft and pow'r are
Dost ask who that may be? Christ Je-sus, it is He— Lord Sab-a-oth His
The prince of dark-ness grim, We trem-ble not for him— His rage we can en -
Let goods and kin-dred go, This mor-tal life al-so— The bod-y they may

great, And armed with cru-el hate, On earth is not his e - qual.
name, From age to age the same, And He must win the bat - tle.
dure, For lo, his doom is sure: One lit-tle word shall fell him.
kill; God's truth a-bid-eth still: His king-dom is for-ev - er.

TEXT: Martin Luther; translated by Frederick H. Hedge; based on Psalm 46
MUSIC: Martin Luther; Last stanza setting and Choral ending by Bruce Greer

EIN' FESTE BURG
8.7.8.7.6.6.6.6.7.

Optional last stanza setting
Unison   Broader

4. That word a - bove all earth - ly pow'rs, No thanks to them, a - bid - eth; The Spir - it and the gifts are ours Thro' Him who with us sid - eth. Let goods and kin - dred go, This mor - tal life al - so— The bod - y they may kill; God's truth a - bid - eth still: His king-dom is for - ev - er.

Optional choral ending
f Unison   *Divisi*   rit. *ff*

A might - y for - tress is our God!   A - men!

f Unison   *Divisi*   *ff*

152 The Majesty and Glory of Your Name

O Lord, our Lord, how majestic is Your name in all the earth! Psalm 8:9

TEXT: Linda Lee Johnson; based on Psalm 8
MUSIC: Tom Fettke

SOLI DEO GLORIA
Irregular meter

Worthy of Worship 153

You are worthy to receive glory and honor and power. Revelation 4:11

1. Wor-thy of wor-ship, wor-thy of praise, Wor-thy of hon-or and
2. Wor-thy of rev-'rence, wor-thy of fear, Wor-thy of love and de-
3. Al-might-y Fa-ther, Mas-ter and Lord, King of all kings and Re-

glo-ry; Wor-thy of all the glad songs we can sing, Wor-thy of
vo-tion; Wor-thy of bow-ing and bend-ing of knees, Wor-thy of
deem-er, Won-der-ful Coun-sel-or, Com-fort-er, Friend, Sav-ior and

Refrain

all of the off-'rings we bring.
all this and add-ed to these... You are wor-thy, Fa-ther, Cre-
Source of our life with-out end;

a-tor. You are wor-thy, Sav-ior, Sus-tain-er. You are wor-thy,

wor-thy and won-der-ful; Wor-thy of wor-ship and praise.

TEXT: Terry W. York
MUSIC: Mark Blankenship

JUDSON
Irregular meter

154 We Bow Down

Come, let us bow down and worship, let us kneel before the Lord our Maker. Psalm 95:6

1. You are Lord of cre-a - tion and Lord of my life,
2. You are King of cre-a - tion and King of my life,

Lord of the land and the sea. You were Lord of the heav-
King of the land and the sea. You were King of the heav-

-ens be-fore there was time, And Lord of all lords You will be!
-ens be-fore there was time, And King of all kings You will be!

Refrain

We bow down, (bow down,) and we wor-ship You,
We bow down, (bow down,) and we crown You the

Lord. We bow down, (bow down,) and we wor-ship You,
King. We bow down, (bow down,) and we crown You the

TEXT: Twila Paris
MUSIC: Twila Paris

WE BOW DOWN
Irregular meter

Lord. We bow down, (bow down,) and we wor-ship You,
King. We bow down, (bow down,) and we crown You the

Lord. Lord of all lords You will be!
King. King of all kings You will be!

Praise Ye the Triune God 155

I will praise Your name for Your love and Your faithfulness. Psalm 138:2

1. Praise ye the Fa-ther for His lov-ing-kind-ness; Ten-der-ly
2. Praise ye the Sav-ior— great is His com-pas-sion; Gra-cious-ly
3. Praise ye the Spir-it, Com-fort-er of Is-rael, Sent of the

cares He for His err-ing chil-dren. Praise Him, ye an-gels,
cares He for His cho-sen peo-ple. Young men and maid-ens,
Fa-ther and the Son to bless us. Praise ye the Fa-ther,

praise Him in the heav-ens. Praise ye Je-ho-vah!
ye old men and chil-dren, Praise ye the Sav-ior!
Son, and Ho-ly Spir-it— Praise ye the Tri-une God!

TEXT: Elizabeth R. Charles
MUSIC: Friedrich F. Flemming

FLEMMING
11.11.11.6.

156 OUR FATHER'S LOVE

A Worship Sequence

The Love of God; stanzas 1,3
Think About His Love
Suggested stanzas have been marked with an arrow: ➤

WORSHIP LEADER

The Lord is compassionate and gracious, slow to anger, abounding in love.
He will not always accuse, nor will He harbor His anger forever;
He does not treat us as our sins deserve
or repay us according to our iniquities.
For as high as the heavens are above the earth,
so great is His love for those who fear Him.

from Psalm 103:8-11 (NIV)

Optional introduction to "The Love of God"

157 The Love of God

I have loved you with an everlasting love. Jeremiah 31:3

➤ 1. The love of God is great-er far Than tongue or pen can ev - er
2. When years of time shall pass a - way And earth - ly thrones and king-doms
➤ 3. Could we with ink the o-cean fill And were the skies of parch-ment

tell; It goes be - yond the high-est star, And reach-es to the low - est
fall, When men who here re - fuse to pray, On rocks and hills and moun-tains
made, Were ev - ery stalk on earth a quill And ev - ery man a scribe by

TEXT: Frederick M. Lehman; Meir Ben Isaac Nehorai, stanza 3
MUSIC: Frederick M. Lehman

LOVE OF GOD
Irregular meter

hell; The guilt - y pair, bowed down with care, God gave His Son to
call, God's love so sure shall still en - dure, All mea - sure - less and
trade, To write the love of God a - bove Would drain the o - cean

win; His err - ing child He rec - on - ciled, And par - doned from his sin.
strong; Re - deem - ing grace to Ad - am's race— The saints' and an - gels' song.
dry; Nor could the scroll con - tain the whole, Tho' stretched from sky to sky.

Refrain

O love of God, how rich and pure! How mea - sure - less and strong!

It shall for - ev - er - more en - dure— The saints' and an - gels' song!

Optional transition to "Think About His Love"

158 Think About His Love

As high as the heavens are above the earth, so great is His love for those who fear Him. Psalm 103:11

Think a-bout His love, think a-bout His good-ness,

Think a-bout His grace that's bro't us through. For as

high as the heav-ens a-bove, so great is the mea-sure of our Fa-ther's

love. Great is the mea-sure of our Fa-ther's love.

TEXT: Walt Harrah
MUSIC: Walt Harrah

HARRAH
Irregular meter

Optional extended or choral ending **p**

Great is the mea-sure of our Fa-ther's love; God's love.

The end of OUR FATHER'S LOVE - A Worship Sequence

Great Are You, Lord 159

O Lord, You are great. Jeremiah 10:6

Ho - ly Lord, most ho - ly Lord, You a - lone are wor - thy of my praise. O ho - ly Lord, most ho - ly Lord, with all of my heart I sing. Great are You, Lord; wor - thy of praise, Ho - ly and true. Great are You, Lord, most ho - ly Lord.

TEXT: Steve and Vikki Cook
MUSIC: Steve and Vikki Cook

GREAT ARE YOU, LORD
Irregular meter

160 Antiphonal Praise

Worship the Lord in the splendor of His holiness. 1 Chronicles 16:29

ANTIPHONAL PRAISE
Irregular meter

I Will Sing of the Mercies 161

I will sing of the Lord's great love forever. Psalm 89:1

TEXT: Psalm 89:1
MUSIC: James H. Fillmore; arranged by Lee Herrington

FILLMORE
Irregular meter

162 BE STILL, AND KNOW

from Psalm 46 (NIV)

WORSHIP LEADER
Be still, and know that I am God.

EVERYONE
God is our refuge and strength,
an ever present help in trouble.
Therefore we will not fear,

WORSHIP LEADER
Though the earth give way and the mountains fall into the heart of the sea,
though its waters roar and foam
and the mountains quake with their surging.

EVERYONE
Be still, and know that I am God.

WORSHIP LEADER
There is a river whose streams make glad the city of God,
the holy place where the Most High dwells.
God is within her, she will not fall.

EVERYONE
Be still, and know that I am God.

WORSHIP LEADER
Nations are in uproar, kingdoms fall;
He lifts His voice, the earth melts.

EVERYONE
Be still, and know that I am God.

WORSHIP LEADER
The Lord Almighty is with us;
The God of Jacob is our fortress.
He makes wars cease to the ends of the earth.

EVERYONE
Be still, and know that I am God.
I will be exalted among the nations;
I will be exalted in the earth.

WORSHIP LEADER
The Lord Almighty is with us.

EVERYONE
Be still, and know that I am God.

163 I AM

from Revelation 22:13; John 14:6; 6:48; 8:12; 10:11; 11:25 (NKJV)

WORSHIP LEADER or SOLO
"I am the Alpha and the Omega,
the First and the Last.
I am the way, the truth and the life.
No one comes to the Father except through Me.
I am the bread of life.
I am the light of the world.
I am the good shepherd.
I am the resurrection and the life."

THE MAJESTY OF HIS NAME   **164**

from Psalm 8 (NIV)

WORSHIP LEADER
O Lord, our Lord–

EVERYONE
How majestic is Your name in all the earth!

WORSHIP LEADER
You have set Your glory above the heavens.

WOMEN
From the lips of children and infants You have ordained praise.

SOLO 1
When I consider Your heavens, the work of Your fingers,

SOLO 2
When I consider the moon and the stars, which You have set in place,

MEN
What is man that You are mindful of him?

EVERYONE
You made him a little lower than the heavenly beings
and crowned him with glory and honor.

WORSHIP LEADER
You made him ruler over the works of Your hands;
You put everything under his feet:

SOLO 1
All flocks and herds, and the beasts of the field,

SOLO 2
The birds of the air, and the fish of the sea;
All that swim the paths of the seas.

WORSHIP LEADER
O Lord, our Lord–

EVERYONE
How majestic is Your name in all the earth!

ROBED IN MAJESTY   **165**

from Psalm 93 (NIV)

WORSHIP LEADER
The Lord is robed in majesty and is armed with strength.
The seas have lifted up their voice;

EVERYONE
The seas have lifted up their pounding waves.

WORSHIP LEADER
Mightier than the thunder of the great waters,

EVERYONE
Mightier than the breakers of the sea–
The Lord on high is mighty!

WORSHIP LEADER
Holiness adorns Your house for endless days, O Lord!

EVERYONE
The Lord on high is mighty!

166 Praise God from Whom All Blessings Flow

Let everything that has breath praise the Lord. Psalm 150:6

Praise God from whom all bless-ings flow. Praise Him, all crea-tures here be-low. Al-le-lu-ia! Al-le-lu-ia! Praise Him a-bove, ye heav'n-ly host. Praise Fa-ther, Son, and Ho-ly Ghost. Al-le-lu-ia! Al-le-lu-ia! Al-le-lu-ia! Al-le-lu-ia! Al-le-lu-ia!

TEXT: Thomas Ken, adapted
MUSIC: *Geistliche Kirchengesänge*, Cologne, 1623, arranged by Ralph Vaughan Williams
A lower setting may be found at No. 63

LASST UNS ERFREUEN
L.M. with Alleluias

It Is a Good Thing to Give Thanks 167

It is good to praise the Lord and make music to Your name, O Most High. Psalm 92:1

It is a good thing to give thanks un-to the Lord; It is a good thing to give thanks un-to the Lord, And to sing prais-es un-to Thy name, O Most High.

TEXT: Judy Horner Montemayor; based on Psalm 92:1
MUSIC: Judy Horner Montemayor

IT IS A GOOD THING
Irregular meter

ENTER HIS GATES 168
A Worship Sequence

Rejoice, Ye Pure in Heart; stanzas 1,2,5
Give Thanks
Come into His Presence
Suggested stanzas have been marked with an arrow: ➤

WORSHIP LEADER
Shout for joy to the Lord, all the earth.
Worship the Lord with gladness; come before Him with joyful songs.

EVERYONE
Know that the Lord is God.
It is He who made us, and we are His;
We are His people, the sheep of His pasture.

WORSHIP LEADER
Enter His gates with thanksgiving and His courts with praise.
Give thanks to Him and praise His name.

from Psalm 100:1-4 (NIV)

Optional introduction to
"Rejoice, Ye Pure in Heart"

f

169 Rejoice, Ye Pure in Heart

Rejoice in the Lord and be glad, you who are upright in heart! Psalm 32:11

1. Re - joice, ye pure in heart; Re - joice, give thanks, and sing.
2. With all the an - gel choirs, With all the saints on earth,
3. Yes, on thro' life's long path, Still chant - ing as ye go;
4. Still lift your stand - ard high; Still march in firm ar - ray;
5. Praise God who reigns on high, The Lord whom we a - dore;

Your fes - tal ban - ner wave on high– The cross of Christ, your King.
Pour out the strains of joy and bliss, True rap - ture, no - blest mirth!
From youth to age, by night and day, In glad-ness and in woe,
As war - riors, thro' the dark - ness toil Till dawns the gold - en day.
The Fa - ther, Son, and Ho - ly Ghost– One God for - ev - er - more.

Refrain   Last refrain: great ritard

Re - joice, re - joice, Re - joice, give thanks, and sing!   *Optional transition to "Give Thanks"*
Re - joice, re - joice,

TEXT: Edward H. Plumptre
MUSIC: Arthur H. Messiter

MARION
S.M. with Refrain

170 Give Thanks

The Lord has done great things for us, and we are filled with joy. Psalm 126:3

Unison

Give thanks with a grate - ful heart; Give thanks to the Ho - ly One;

TEXT: Henry Smith
MUSIC: Henry Smith

GIVE THANKS
Irregular meter

Optional segue to "Come into His Presence." No transition is needed. Tempo is much faster.

171 Come into His Presence

Enter His gates with thanksgiving and His courts with praise; give thanks to Him. Psalm 100:4

Come in-to His pres-ence with thanks-giv-ing in your heart and give Him

praise, and give Him praise; Come in-to His pres-ence with thanks-

giv-ing in your heart, your voic-es raise, your voic-es raise.

Give glo-ry and hon-or and pow-er un-to

Him, Je - sus, the name a-bove all names.

TEXT: Lynn Baird
MUSIC: Lynn Baird

BAIRD
Irregular meter

Optional extended or choral ending

Give glo-ry and hon-or and pow-er un-to Him,

Je - sus, the name a-bove all names. Give Him thanks.

The end of ENTER HIS GATES - A Worship Sequence

All the Glory Belongs to Jesus 172

I glory in Christ Jesus in my service to God. Romans 15:17

All the glo-ry be-longs to Je - sus. All the praise

be-longs to Him. All that I am or ev-er

hope to be, All the glo - ry be-longs to Him.

TEXT: Gloria Gaither
MUSIC: William J. Gaither

ALL THE GLORY
Irregular meter

173 I'm Forever Grateful

The Son of Man came to seek and to save what was lost. Luke 19:10

Unison

You did not wait for me to draw near to You, But You

clothed Your-self with frail hu-man-i-ty. You

did not wait for me to cry out to You, But You let me hear Your

Refrain

voice call-ing me. And I'm for-ev-er grate-ful to You,

I'm for-ev-er grate-ful for the cross. I'm for-ev-er

TEXT: Mark Altrogge
MUSIC: Mark Altrogge

FOREVER GRATEFUL
Irregular meter

1 *Repeat refrain optional*

grate-ful to You that You came to seek and save the lost.

2

And I'm for - ev - er seek and save the lost.

I Will Bless Thee, O Lord 174

I will praise You as long as I live, and in Your name I will lift up my hands. Psalm 63:4

I will bless Thee, O Lord. I will bless Thee, O
hands lift - ed up, And my mouth filled with

Lord. With a heart of thanks- giv - ing, I will
praise, With a heart of thanks- giv - ing, I will

1

bless Thee, O Lord. With my
bless Thee, O

2

Lord.

TEXT: Esther Watanabe
MUSIC: Esther Watanabe

I WILL BLESS THEE
Irregular meter

175 O Lord, Our Lord

Your great mercy and love are from of old. Psalm 25:6

1. O Lord, our Lord, we praise You for Your mer-cy;   O Lord, our Lord, we
2. O Lord, our Lord, en-throned in high-est heav-en;   O Lord, our Lord, en-
3. O Lord, our Lord, we praise You for Your mer-cy;   O Lord, our Lord, we

praise You for Your love;   For ev-ery grace Your kind-ness has pro-vid-ed,
throned in grate-ful hearts;   Your love ex-tends to ev-ery gen-er-a-tion
praise You for Your love;   For ev-ery grace Your kind-ness has pro-vid-ed,

To ev-ery soul who calls up-on Your name.   For ev-ery grace Your
With joy-ful news of Your re-demp-tion plan.   Your love ex-tends to
To ev-ery soul who calls up-on Your name.   For ev-ery grace Your

kind-ness has pro-vid-ed,   To ev-ery soul who calls up-on Your name.
ev-ery gen-er-a-tion   With joy-ful news of Your re-demp-tion plan.
kind-ness has pro-vid-ed,   To ev-ery soul who calls up-on Your name.

TEXT: Phill McHugh and Tom Fettke
MUSIC: Jean Sibelius

FINLANDIA
11.10.11.10.11.10

HE HAS BLESSED US

from Ephesians 1:3-14; Romans 11:36 (NASB)

WORSHIP LEADER and EVERYONE
Blessed be the God and Father of our Lord Jesus Christ,
who has blessed us with every spiritual blessing
in the heavenly places in Christ.

WORSHIP LEADER
He chose us in Him before the foundation of the world,
that we should be holy and blameless before Him.

EVERYONE
For from Him, and through Him, and to Him are all things.

WORSHIP LEADER
In love He predestined us to adoption as sons through
Jesus Christ to Himself, according to the kind intention
of His will, to the praise of the glory of His grace,
which He freely bestowed on us in the Beloved.

EVERYONE
For from Him, and through Him, and to Him are all things.

WORSHIP LEADER
In Him we have redemption through His blood,
the forgiveness of our trespasses, according to the
riches of His grace which He lavished upon us.

EVERYONE
For from Him, and through Him, and to Him are all things.

WORSHIP LEADER
In all wisdom and insight He made known to us
the mystery of His will, according to His kind intention
which He purposed in Him with a view to an
administration suitable to the fullness of the times;
that is, the summing up of all things in Christ,
things in the heavens and things upon the earth.

EVERYONE
For from Him, and through Him, and to Him are all things.

WORSHIP LEADER
In Him also we have obtained an inheritance,
having been predestined according to His purpose,
who works all things after the counsel of His will,
to the end that we who were the first to hope in Christ
should be to the praise of His glory.

EVERYONE
For from Him, and through Him, and to Him are all things.

WORSHIP LEADER
In Him, you also, after listening to the message of truth,
the gospel of your salvation – having also believed,
you were sealed in Him with the Holy Spirit of promise,
who is given as a pledge of our inheritance,
with a view to the redemption of God's own possession,
to the praise of His glory.

EVERYONE
Blessed be the God and Father of our Lord Jesus Christ,
who has blessed us with every spiritual blessing
in the heavenly places in Christ.

177 GOD'S GOODNESS

from Psalm 107 (NKJV)

WORSHIP LEADER
Let the redeemed of the Lord say so.

EVERYONE
O give thanks to the Lord, for He is good!

WORSHIP LEADER
Let the redeemed of the Lord say so,
whom He has redeemed from the hand of the enemy;

EVERYONE
His mercy endures forever.

WORSHIP LEADER
O that men would give thanks to the Lord for His goodness,
and for His wonderful works to the children of men!

EVERYONE
For He satisfies the longing soul,
and fills the hungry soul with goodness.

WORSHIP LEADER
O that men would give thanks to the Lord for His goodness,
and for His wonderful works to the children of men!

EVERYONE
And let them sacrifice the sacrifices of thanksgiving,
and declare His works with rejoicing.

WORSHIP LEADER
O that men would give thanks to the Lord for His goodness,
and for His wonderful works to the children of men!

EVERYONE
Let them exalt Him also in the assembly of the people,
and praise Him in the company of the elders.
O give thanks to the Lord, for He is good;
For His mercy endures forever.

178 O GIVE THANKS

from Psalm 105 (NKJV)

WORSHIP LEADER
O give thanks to the Lord! Call upon His name;

SOLO
Make known His deeds among the peoples.

WORSHIP LEADER
Sing to Him;

SOLO
Sing psalms to Him.

WORSHIP LEADER
Talk of all His wondrous works.

SOLO
Glory in His holy name;
Remember His marvelous works which He has done.

WORSHIP LEADER and SOLO
O give thanks to the Lord!

Awesome God 179

The great and awesome God keeps His covenant of love. Nehemiah 1:5

Our God is an awe-some God; He reigns from heav-en a-bove With wis-dom, pow'r and love; Our God is an awe-some God! Our God! Our God is an awe-some God; He reigns from heav-en a-bove With wis-dom, pow'r and love; Our God is an awe-some God! Our God! Our God is an awe-some God! Our God is an awe-some God!

TEXT: Rich Mullins
MUSIC: Rich Mullins

AWESOME GOD
Irregular meter

Suggestions for effective usage
Youth choir or ensemble (or all youth) sing the chorus in E minor (including repeat).
Everyone (adults, children and remaining youth) sing the chorus in F minor with all repeats and tag.

180 GOOD AND PERFECT GIFTS
A Worship Sequence

Everything Was Made by God
For the Beauty of the Earth; complete
Everything Was Made by God - Reprise
Suggested stanzas have been marked with an arrow: ➤

WORSHIP LEADER
(A young person is preferable)
Every good gift and every perfect gift is from above,
and comes down from the Father of the heavenly lights.

James 1:17 (NKJV)

181 Everything Was Made by God
God made the world and everything in it. Acts 17:24

Ev-ery-thing was made by God, ev-ery-thing you see.

Ev-ery-thing was made by God for you and me. me.

Optional transition to "For the Beauty of the Earth"

TEXT: Tina English
MUSIC: Tina English

CANDICE CHRISTOPHER
Irregular meter

182 For the Beauty of the Earth - *Family Worship Setting*
Give thanks to the Lord for His unfailing love and His wonderful deeds. Psalm 107:8

➤ 1. For the beau-ty of the earth, For the glo-ry of the skies,
➤ 2. For the won-der of each hour Of the day and of the night,
➤ 3. For the joy of hu-man love, Broth-er, sis-ter, par-ent, child;

TEXT: Folliott S. Pierpoint, altered
MUSIC: Conrad Kocher; arranged by William H. Monk

DIX
7.7.7.7.7.7.

GOOD AND PERFECT GIFTS - A Worship Sequence

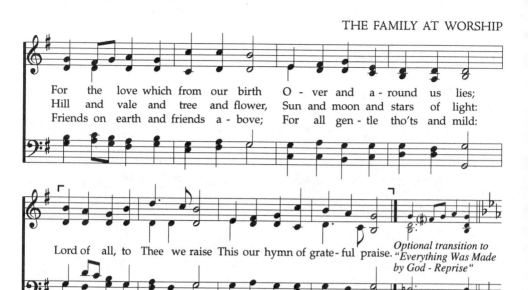

For the love which from our birth
O - ver and a - round us lies;

Hill and vale and tree and flower,
Sun and moon and stars of light:

Friends on earth and friends a - bove;
For all gen - tle tho'ts and mild:

Lord of all, to Thee we raise This our hymn of grate - ful praise.

Optional transition to "Everything Was Made by God - Reprise"

Everything Was Made by God - *Reprise* 183

God made the world and everything in it. Acts 17:24

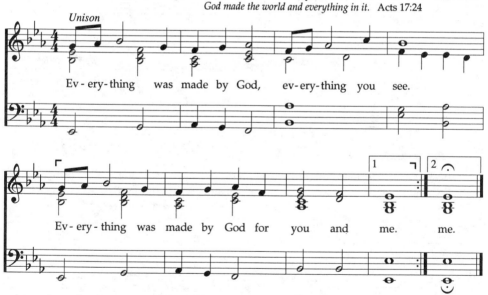

Unison

Ev - ery-thing was made by God, ev - ery-thing you see.

Ev - ery - thing was made by God for you and me. me.

TEXT: Tina English
MUSIC: Tina English

CANDICE CHRISTOPHER
Irregular meter

Suggestions for effective usage of GOOD AND PERFECT GIFTS
Everyone sing "Everything Was Made by God" once through; Children sing the repeat.
Children sing the 1st Stanza of "For the Beauty of the Earth;" Everyone sing the 2nd and 3rd Stanzas.
Children sing "Everything Was Made by God-Reprise" once through; Everyone sing the repeat.
You may wish to repeat the "Reprise" once or twice more.

The end of GOOD AND PERFECT GIFTS - A Worship Sequence

184 Thy Word

Your word is a lamp to my feet and a light for my path. Psalm 119:105

TEXT: Amy Grant; based on Psalm 119:105
MUSIC: Michael W. Smith

THY WORD
Irregular meter

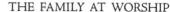

D.C. twice

Please be near me to the end.
I will love You to the end.

Suggestions for effective usage

Everyone sing the 1st Refrain. Both Stanzas may be sung by soloists, youth choir (or adult ensemble) or by everyone. Youth (including children) sing the 2nd Refrain. Everyone sing the last Refrain. The Stanzas are optional; you may wish to sing the Refrain only.

Jesus Loves Me 185

Christ loved us and gave Himself up for us. Ephesians 5:2

1. Je - sus loves me! This I know, For the Bi - ble tells me so. Lit - tle ones to Him be - long; They are weak, but He is strong.
2. Je - sus loves me! This I know, As He loved so long a - go, Tak - ing chil - dren on His knee, Say - ing, "Let them come to Me." Yes, Je - sus loves me!
3. Je - sus loves me! He will stay Close be - side me on my way. He's pre-pared a home for me, And some - day His face I'll see.

Refrain

Yes, Je - sus loves me! Yes, Je - sus loves me! The Bi - ble tells me so.

TEXT: Anna B. Warner, stanzas 1,3; David R. McGuire, stanza 2
MUSIC: William B. Bradbury

JESUS LOVES ME
7.7.7.7. with Refrain

Suggestions for effective usage

Children (or everyone) sing the 1st Stanza and Refrain. Senior adults and/or choir sing the 2nd Stanza, children join on the Refrain. All adults, choir (and children, if desired) sing the 3rd Stanza. Everyone sing the final Refrain (and repeat it, if you wish).

186 Lord, Be Glorified

Christ will be exalted in my body, whether by life or by death. Philippians 1:20

Optional Stanzas: "In my song", "In Your church".

TEXT: Bob Kilpatrick
MUSIC: Bob Kilpatrick

BE GLORIFIED
Irregular meter

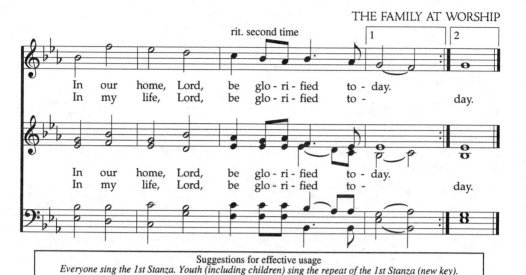

rit. second time

In our home, Lord, be glo-ri-fied to-day.
In my life, Lord, be glo-ri-fied to- day.

In our home, Lord, be glo-ri-fied to-day.
In my life, Lord, be glo-ri-fied to- day.

Suggestions for effective usage
Everyone sing the 1st Stanza. Youth (including children) sing the repeat of the 1st Stanza (new key).
Adults sing the 2nd Stanza (children and/or adult choirs may sing the descant).
Everyone sing the 3rd Stanza (children and/or adult choirs may sing the descant).

PRAISE, LOVE AND THANKS   187
A Worship Sequence

Praise Him, All Ye Little Children; stanza 1
Alleluia; stanzas 1,4
Praise Him, All Ye Little Children - Reprise I
Father, I Adore You; stanzas 1,2
Praise Him, All Ye Little Children - Reprise II
God Is So Good; stanzas 1,3,4
Suggested stanzas have been marked with an arrow: ➤

WORSHIP LEADER — CHILD 1

Give thanks to the Lord, for He is good;
His love endures forever.

CHILD 2   Praise and glory,

CHILD 3   Wisdom and honor,

CHILD 4   Power and strength be to our God

ALL CHILDREN   forever and ever. Amen!

from Psalm 118:29; Revelation 7:12 (NIV)

Optional introduction to "Praise Him, All Ye Little Children"

mf

PRAISE, LOVE AND THANKS - A Worship Sequence

Suggestions for effective usage of PRAISE, LOVE AND THANKS
Instructions appear at the beginning of each selection.
A children's choir or child soloist may be substituted for all the children in the congregation on any
or all of the selections designated for children.

188 Praise Him, All Ye Little Children

From the lips of children and infants You have ordained praise. Matthew 21:16

Stanza 1: Adults and youth

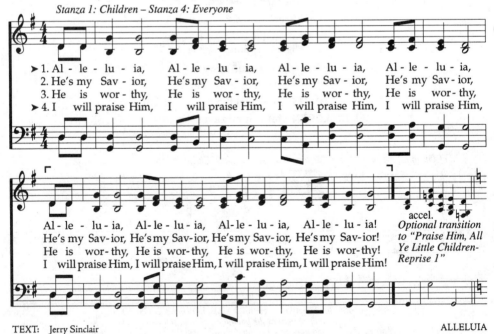

1. Praise Him, praise Him, all ye lit-tle chil-dren, God is love, God is love;
2. Love Him, love Him, all ye lit-tle chil-dren, God is love, God is love;
3. Thank Him, thank Him, all ye lit-tle chil-dren, God is love, God is love;

great rit.

Praise Him, praise Him, all ye lit-tle chil-dren, God is love, God is love.
Love Him, love Him, all ye lit-tle chil-dren, God is love, God is love.
Thank Him, thank Him, all ye lit-tle chil-dren, God is love, God is love.

Optional transition to "Alleluia"

TEXT: Anonymous
MUSIC: Carey Bonner

BONNER
10.6.10.6.

189 Alleluia

Hallelujah! Salvation and glory and power belong to our God. Revelation 19:1

Stanza 1: Children – Stanza 4: Everyone

1. Al - le - lu - ia, Al - le - lu - ia, Al - le - lu - ia, Al - le - lu - ia,
2. He's my Sav - ior, He's my Sav - ior, He's my Sav - ior, He's my Sav - ior,
3. He is wor - thy, He is wor - thy, He is wor - thy, He is wor - thy,
4. I will praise Him, I will praise Him, I will praise Him, I will praise Him,

Al - le - lu - ia, Al - le - lu - ia, Al - le - lu - ia, Al - le - lu - ia!
He's my Sav - ior, He's my Sav - ior, He's my Sav - ior, He's my Sav - ior!
He is wor - thy, He is wor - thy, He is wor - thy, He is wor - thy!
I will praise Him, I will praise Him, I will praise Him, I will praise Him!

accel.

Optional transition to "Praise Him, All Ye Little Children-Reprise 1"

TEXT: Jerry Sinclair
MUSIC: Jerry Sinclair

ALLELUIA
L.M.

Praise Him, All Ye Little Children - *Reprise I* 190

From the lips of children and infants You have ordained praise. Matthew 21:16

Adults and youth

Love Him, love Him, all ye lit-tle chil-dren, God is love, God is love;

Love Him, love Him, all ye lit-tle chil-dren, God is love, God is love.

great rit.

*Optional transition
to "Father, I Adore You"*

TEXT: Anonymous
MUSIC: Carey Bonner

BONNER
10.6.10.6.

Father, I Adore You 191

Our Father in heaven, hallowed be Your name. Matthew 6:9

Stanza 1: Children – Stanza 2: Everyone

*I Unison

1. Fa - ther, I a - dore You, Lay my life be -
2. Je - sus, I a - dore You, Lay my life be -
3. Spir - it, I a - dore You, Lay my life be -

fore You; How I love You.
fore You; How I love You.
fore You; How I love You.

accel.

*Optional 3-part round

*Optional transition to "Praise Him,
All Ye Little Children - Reprise II."*

TEXT: Terrye Coelho
MUSIC: Terrye Coelho

MARANATHA
6.6.4.

192 Praise Him, All Ye Little Children - *Reprise II*

From the lips of children and infants You have ordained praise. Matthew 21:16

Adults and youth

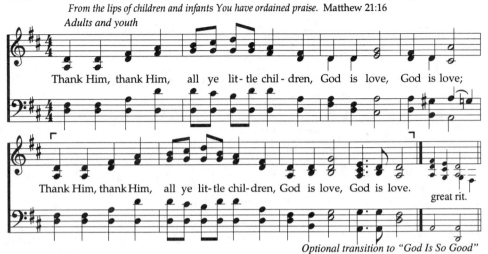

Thank Him, thank Him, all ye lit-tle chil-dren, God is love, God is love;

Thank Him, thank Him, all ye lit-tle chil-dren, God is love, God is love.

great rit.

Optional transition to "God Is So Good"

TEXT: Anonymous
MUSIC: Carey Bonner

BONNER
10.6.10.6.

193 God Is So Good

Give thanks to the Lord, for He is good; His love endures forever. 1 Chronicles 16:34

Stanza 1: Children – Stanza 3: Children and youth – Stanza 4: Everyone

➤ 1. God is so good, God is so good, God is so good, He's so
2. He cares for me, He cares for me, He cares for me, He's so
➤ 3. He loves me so, He loves me so, He loves me so, He's so
➤ 4. God is so good, God is so good, God is so good, He's so

Optional last stanza setting

good to me. ➤ 4. God is so good, God is so good,

God is so good, He's so good to me. me.

TEXT: Traditional
MUSIC: Traditional

GOD IS SO GOOD
Irregular meter

The end of PRAISE, LOVE AND THANKS - A Worship Sequence

We Worship and Adore You 194

They sang praises with gladness and bowed their heads and worshipped. 2 Chronicles 29:30

1. We wor - ship and a - dore You, Bow - ing down be - fore You,
2. We wor - ship and a - dore You, Bow - ing down be - fore You,

Songs of prais - es sing - ing, Hal - le - lu - jahs ring - ing. Hal - le -
Songs of prais - es sing - ing, Hal - le - lu - jahs ring - ing. Hal - le -

lu - jah, hal - le - lu - jah, hal - le - lu - jah! A - men. 2. We
lu - jah, hal - le - lu - jah, hal - le - lu - jah! A - men.

Optional half chorus setting

3. Hal - le - lu - jah, hal - le -

lu - jah, hal - le - lu - jah! A - men. men.

TEXT: Anonymous
MUSIC: Anonymous

WORSHIP AND ADORE
7.6.6.6.8.6.

Suggestions for effective usage
Adults or everyone sing the 1st chorus. Youth and children sing the 2nd chorus.
Everyone sing the half chorus setting twice (chorus 3).

195 Bless the Name of Jesus

I glory in Christ Jesus in my service to God. Romans 15:17

TEXT: Carman
MUSIC: Carman

BLESS THE NAME
Irregular meter

Suggestions for effective usage

Youth choir or ensemble (or all youth) sing the Stanza. Everyone (adults, children and remaining youth) join in on repeat of Refrain. More than one repeat of Refrain is desirable.

O Come, Let Us Adore Him 196

We have come to worship Him. Matthew 2:2

1. O come, let us a - dore Him, O come, let us a - dore
2. We'll praise His name for - ev - er, We'll praise His name for - ev -
3. We'll give Him all the glo - ry, We'll give Him all the glo -
4. For He a - lone is wor - thy, For He a - lone is wor -

Him, O come, let us a - dore Him, Christ the Lord.
er, We'll praise His name for - ev - er, Christ the Lord.
ry, We'll give Him all the glo - ry, Christ the Lord.
thy, For He a - lone is wor - thy, Christ the Lord.

Optional last stanza setting   Broader

rit.

5. O come, let us a - dore Him, O come, let us a - dore

last time

Him, O come, let us a - dore Him, Christ the Lord. O Lord.

TEXT: Traditional
MUSIC: Wade's *Cantus Diversi*, 1751

ADESTE FIDELES (Refrain only)
7.7.10.

Suggestions for effective usage
Everyone sing the 1st Stanza. All females (including youth) sing the 2nd Stanza. All males (including youth) sing the 3rd Stanza. Everyone sing the 4th Stanza and last Stanza setting, which is a repeat of the 1st stanza.

197 HALLELUJAH TO THE LORD!

A Worship Sequence

Sing Hallelujah (to the Lord)
King of Kings

WORSHIP LEADER — CHILD 1
Hallelujah! For our Lord God Almighty reigns.

CHILD 2
Let us rejoice and be glad and give Him glory!

from Revelation 19:6-7 (NKJV)

198 Sing Hallelujah (to the Lord)

The elders and the living creatures worshiped God. They cried: "Amen, Hallelujah!" Revelation 19:4

TEXT: Linda Stassen-Benjamin
MUSIC: Linda Stassen-Benjamin

SING HALLELUJAH
Irregular meter

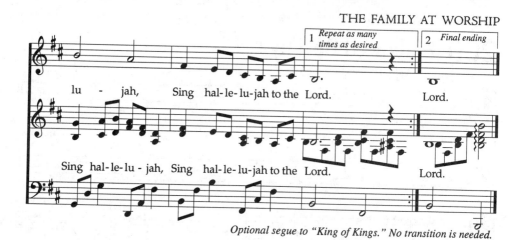

Repeat as many times as desired

Final ending

lu - jah, Sing hal-le-lu-jah to the Lord.

Lord.

Sing hal-le-lu - jah, Sing hal-le-lu-jah to the Lord.

Lord.

Optional segue to "King of Kings." No transition is needed.

King of Kings 199

The Lamb will overcome them because He is Lord of lords and King of kings. Revelation 17:14

2-part round (optional)   1 Unison

Introduction

King of kings and Lord of   lords,   glo-ry,   hal - le - lu - jah!

King of kings and Lord of   lords,   glo-ry,   hal - le - lu - jah!   Je - sus, Prince of Peace,

Repeat as many times as desired

glo-ry,   hal-le-lu-jah!   Je-sus, Prince of Peace,   glo-ry,   hal-le-lu-jah!   Play after final repeat

TEXT: Sophie Conty and Naomi Batya
MUSIC: Ancient Hebrew Folk song

KING OF KINGS
Irregular meter

The end of HALLELUJAH TO THE LORD! - A Worship Sequence

Suggestions for effective usage of HALLELUJAH TO THE LORD!
"Sing Hallelujah (to the Lord)": Everyone sing unison melody the 1st time through. The 2nd time (and subsequent repeats) all children (or the children's choir) sing the descant while the adults and youth sing the unison melody. More than one repeat is desirable. You may also reverse this procedure-adults and youth sing the descant on the repetition while the children sing the unison melody.
"King of Kings": Everyone sing the 1st time through. The 2nd time, adults and youth sing Part I of the 2-part round, and the children (and/or children's choir) sing Part II. Repeat as many times as desired. Another option would be to divide the congregation equally into two parts (mixing adults, children and youth). Give clear instructions to the instrumentalists as to the number of repeats of each of the two songs in this sequence.

200 Hallowed Be Thy Name

Our Father in heaven, hallowed be Your name. Matthew 6:9

Unison

Introduction

You are love,
You are life, You are Lord o - ver ev-ery-thing, Al-pha, O-me - ga, Je-ho-
-vah, the King of kings, Won-der-ful Way Mak-er, wor - thy of my of-fer-ing;

1,2 Hal-low-ed be Thy name. You are love,

3

Hal-low-ed be Thy name. Hal-low-ed be Thy name!

TEXT: Babbie Mason and Robert Lawson
MUSIC: Babbie Mason and Robert Lawson

HALLOWED BE THY NAME
Irregular meter

Suggestions for effective usage

Children's choir (or all children) sing the 1st chorus. Everyone (adults, youth and children) sing the repeat choruses and tag. This segues effectively into "He Is the King of Kings."

He Is the King of Kings 201

He has this name written: KING OF KINGS AND LORD OF LORDS. Revelation 19:16

TEXT: Virgil Meares
MUSIC: Virgil Meares; arranged by Joseph Linn

HE IS THE KING
Irregular meter

Suggestions for effective usage
*Children's choir (or all children) sing the 1st chorus. Everyone (adults, youth and remaining children)
sing the repeat choruses and tag.*

202   HIS LOVE ENDURES FOREVER

from Psalm 136:1-9, 26 (NIV)

WORSHIP LEADER *(preferably a child or teenager)*
Give thanks to the Lord, for He is good.

EVERYONE
His love endures forever.

YOUTH and CHILDREN
Give thanks to the God of gods.

ADULTS
His love endures forever.

YOUTH and CHILDREN
Give thanks to the Lord of lords.

ADULTS
His love endures forever.

WORSHIP LEADER
To Him who alone does great wonders.

EVERYONE
His love endures forever.

YOUTH and CHILDREN
Who by His understanding made the heavens.

ADULTS
His love endures forever.

WORSHIP LEADER
Who spread out the earth upon the waters.

EVERYONE
His love endures forever.

YOUTH and CHILDREN
Who made the great lights.

ADULTS
His love endures forever.

YOUTH and CHILDREN
The sun to govern the day.

ADULTS
His love endures forever.

WORSHIP LEADER
The moon and stars to govern the night.

EVERYONE
His love endures forever.

YOUTH and CHILDREN
Give thanks to the God of heaven.

ADULTS
His love endures forever.

WORSHIP LEADER
Give thanks to the Lord, for He is good.

EVERYONE
His love endures forever.

WORSHIP WITH GLADNESS 203

from Psalm 100 (NIV)

WORSHIP LEADER *(preferably a child)*
Shout for joy to the Lord!

EVERYONE
Shout for joy to the Lord, all the earth.

CHILDREN and YOUTH
Worship the Lord with gladness.

WORSHIP LEADER
Come before Him with joyful songs.

EVERYONE
The Lord is God.

CHILDREN and YOUTH
He made us, and we are His.

PARENTS
We are His people, the sheep of His pasture.

WORSHIP LEADER
Shout for joy to the Lord!

EVERYONE
Shout for joy to the Lord, all the earth.

PARENTS
Enter His gates with thanksgiving and His courts with praise.

CHILDREN and YOUTH
Give thanks to Him and praise His name.

WORSHIP LEADER
For the Lord is good and His love endures forever.

PARENTS
His faithfulness continues through all generations.

CHILDREN and YOUTH
Shout for joy to the Lord!

EVERYONE
Shout to the Lord, all the earth.
Worship the Lord with gladness.

MAKER OF HEAVEN AND EARTH 204

from Psalm 121 (NIV)

WORSHIP LEADER *(preferably a teenager)*
I lift my eyes to the hills– where does my help come from?

YOUTH and CHILDREN
My help comes from the Lord, the Maker of heaven and earth.

WORSHIP LEADER
He will not let your foot slip–
He who watches over you will not slumber.

YOUTH and CHILDREN
My help comes from the Lord, the Maker of heaven and earth.

WORSHIP LEADER
The Lord will keep you from all harm– He will watch over your life.

EVERYONE
My help comes from the Lord, the Maker of heaven and earth.

205 THE LORD IS MY SHEPHERD

from Psalm 23 (NKJV)

WORSHIP LEADER *(preferably a child)*
The Lord is my shepherd, I shall not want.

WORSHIP LEADER and CHILDREN
The Lord is my shepherd, I shall not want.

PARENTS and YOUTH
He makes me to lie down in green pastures;
He leads me beside the still waters.

WORSHIP LEADER and CHILDREN
The Lord is my shepherd, I shall not want.

PARENTS and YOUTH
He restores my soul; He leads me in the paths
of righteousness for His name's sake.

WORSHIP LEADER and CHILDREN
The Lord is my shepherd, I shall not want.

PARENTS and YOUTH
Even though I walk through the valley of
the shadow of death, I will fear no evil;

WORSHIP LEADER
For You are with me;
Your rod and Your staff, they comfort me.

WORSHIP LEADER and CHILDREN
The Lord is my shepherd, I shall not want.

PARENTS and YOUTH
You prepare a table before me in the presence of my enemies;
You anoint my head with oil;
My cup runs over.

WORSHIP LEADER
Surely goodness and mercy shall follow me
All the days of my life;

EVERYONE
And I will dwell in the house of the Lord forever.
The Lord is my shepherd, I shall not want.

206 THE ROCK OF OUR SALVATION

from Psalm 95:1-5 (NIV)

WORSHIP LEADER *(preferably a teenager)*
Come! Let us sing for joy to the Lord. Let us shout aloud to the rock of our salvation.

PARENTS
Let us come before Him with thanksgiving and extol Him with music and song.

YOUTH and CHILDREN
The Lord is the great God. He is the greatest king.

WORSHIP LEADER
In His hand are the depths of the earth, and the mountain peaks belong to Him.

YOUTH and CHILDREN
The sea is His, for He made it.

EVERYONE
Come! Let us sing for joy to the Lord. Let us shout aloud to the rock of our salvation!

We Have Come to Join in Worship 207

Worship the Lord in the splendor of His holiness. 1 Chronicles 16:29

1. We have come to join in wor-ship And a-dore the Lord our God.
2. See them gath-er all a-round you, Those He bought at such a cost;
3. Let us love our God su-preme-ly; Let us love each oth-er, too.

Let us come in prayer, ex-pect-ing God to speak His might-y Word.
See the wea-ry, see the hurt-ing, See the lone-ly, see the lost.
Let us care for all His peo-ple Till our God makes all things new.

All is vain un-less the Spir-it Of the Ho-ly One comes down.
Be His hand, and touch the need-y; Be His gos-pel, let it sound!
Christ will call us home to heav-en; At His ban-quet we'll sit down;

Chris-tians, pray, and ho-ly man-na Will be show-ered all a-round.
Be His bod-y, and sweet man-na Will be show-ered all a-round.
Christ Him-self will rise and serve us Liv-ing man-na all a-round.

TEXT: Ken Bible and George Atkins
MUSIC: William Moore

HOLY MANNA
8.7.8.7.D.

208 Let the Redeemed

The Lord is good; His love endures forever. Let the redeemed of the Lord say this. Psalm 107:1-2

TEXT: Ward L. Ellis; based on Psalm 107:2
MUSIC: Ward L. Ellis

LET THE REDEEMED
Irregular meter

Optional extended or choral ending

Let the re-deemed of the Lord say so; I'm re-deemed!

This Is the Day 209

This is the day the Lord has made; let us rejoice and be glad in it. Psalm 118:24

Unison

This is the day, this is the day that the Lord has made, that the Lord has made;

We will re-joice, we will re-joice and be glad in it, and be glad in it.

This is the day that the Lord has made; We will re-joice and be glad in it.

This is the day, this is the day that the Lord has made.

TEXT: Les Garrett; based on Psalm 118:24
MUSIC: Les Garrett

THIS IS THE DAY
Irregular meter

210 Praise to the Lord, the Almighty

Praise and exalt and glorify the King of heaven. Daniel 4:37

1. Praise to the Lord, the Al - might - y, the King of cre - a - tion! O my soul, praise Him, for He is thy health and sal - va - tion! All ye who hear, Now to His tem - ple draw near; Join me in glad ad - o - ra - tion!

2. Praise to the Lord, who o'er all things so won - drous - ly reign - eth, Shel - ters thee un - der His wings, yea, so gent - ly sus - tain - eth! Hast thou not seen How thy de - sires all have been Grant - ed in what He or - dain - eth?

3. Praise to the Lord, who doth pros - per thy work and de - fend thee; Sure - ly His good - ness and mer - cy here dai - ly at - tend thee. Pon - der a - new What the Al - might - y can do If with His love He be - friend thee.

4. Praise to the Lord! O let all that is in me a - dore Him! All that hath life and breath, come now with prais - es be - fore Him! Let the "a - men" Sound from His peo - ple a - gain; Glad - ly for - ev - er a - dore Him!

TEXT: Joachim Neander; translated by Catherine Winkworth
MUSIC: *Stralsund Gesangbuch*, 1665; Last stanza setting and Choral ending by Susan Caudill

LOBE DEN HERREN
14.14.4.7.8.

211 Let There Be Praise

Let them praise the name of the Lord, for His name alone is exalted. Psalm 148:13

Let there be praise, let there be joy in our hearts.
Let there be praise, let there be joy in our hearts.

Sing to the Lord, give Him the glo - ry; (glo - ry;)
For - ev - er - more let His love

1

2

fill the air, and let there be praise.

Optional choral ending

Let there be praise.

TEXT: Dick and Melodie Tunney
MUSIC: Dick and Melodie Tunney

LET THERE BE PRAISE
Irregular meter

212 OFFERING OF THANKS

A Worship Sequence

We Bring the Sacrifice of Praise
He Has Made Me Glad (I Will Enter His Gates)

WORSHIP LEADER

Shout for joy to the Lord, all the earth.
Serve the Lord with gladness;
Come before Him with joyful songs.
Give thanks to Him and praise His name.

from Psalm 100:1-2,4 (NIV)

Optional introduction to
"We Bring the Sacrifice of Praise"

f

OFFERING OF THANKS - A Worship Sequence

We Bring the Sacrifice of Praise 213

Let us continually offer to God a sacrifice of praise. Hebrews 13:15

We bring the sac-ri-fice of praise in-to the house of the Lord; We bring the sac-ri-fice of praise in-to the house of the Lord. And we of-fer up to You the sac-ri-fic-es of thanks-giv-ing; And we of-fer up to You the sac-ri-fic-es of joy. joy.

Optional transition to "He Has Made Me Glad"

TEXT: Kirk Dearman
MUSIC: Kirk Dearman

WE BRING THE SACRIFICE
Irregular meter

214 He Has Made Me Glad (I Will Enter His Gates)

Enter His gates with thanksgiving and His courts with praise. Psalm 100:4

I will en-ter His gates with thanks-giv-ing in my heart; I will en-ter His courts with praise. I will say, "This is the day that the Lord has made!" I will re-joice for He has made me glad. He has made me glad, He has made me glad, I will re-joice for He has made me glad. will re-joice for He has made me glad. I will

TEXT: Leona Von Brethorst
MUSIC: Leona Von Brethorst

HE HAS MADE ME GLAD
Irregular meter

Optional choral ending

The end of OFFERING OF THANKS - A Worship Sequence

215 When Morning Gilds the Skies

Worthy is the Lamb, who was slain, to receive honor and glory and praise! Revelation 5:12

1. When morn-ing gilds the skies, My heart a-wak-ing cries;
2. The night be-comes as day When from the heart we say,
3. Ye na-tions of man-kind, In this your con-cord find:
4. Be this, while life is mine, My can-ti-cle di-vine:

May Je-sus Christ be praised! A-like at work and prayer,
May Je-sus Christ be praised! The pow'rs of dark-ness fear,
May Je-sus Christ be praised! Let all the earth a-round
May Je-sus Christ be praised! Be this th'e-ter-nal song

To Je-sus I re-pair; May Je-sus Christ be praised!
When this sweet song they hear: May Je-sus Christ be praised!
Ring joy-ous with the sound: May Je-sus Christ be praised!
Thro' all the a-ges long: May Je-sus Christ be praised!

TEXT: *Katholisches Gesangbuch*, Würzburg, 1828; translated by Edward Caswall
MUSIC: Joseph Barnby

LAUDES DOMINI
6.6.6.6.6.6.

Optional last stanza setting

4. Be this, while life is mine, My can-ti-cle di-

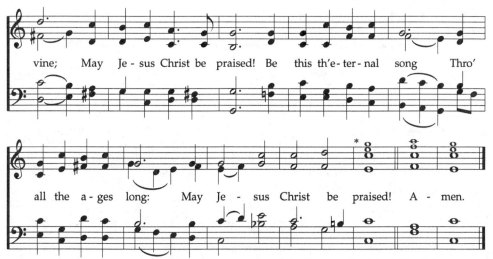

vine; May Je - sus Christ be praised! Be this th'e - ter - nal song Thro'

all the a - ges long: May Je - sus Christ be praised! A - men.

Cued notes optional for a few choir sopranos.

The Lord Is in His Holy Temple 216

The Lord is in His holy temple; let all the earth be silent before Him. Habakkuk 2:20

The Lord is in His ho - ly tem - ple, The Lord is in His ho - ly

tem - ple; Let all the earth keep si - lence, Let all the earth keep

si - lence be - fore Him, Keep si - lence, keep si - lence be - fore Him.

TEXT: Habakkuk 2:20
MUSIC: George F. Root

QUAM DILECTA
Irregular meter

217 Holy Ground

Take off your sandals, for the place where you are standing is holy ground. Exodus 3:5

1. This is ho - ly ground; We're stand-ing on ho - ly ground,
2. These are ho - ly hands; He's giv - en us ho - ly hands.

For the Lord is pre-sent and where He is is ho - ly.
He works through these hands and so these hands are ho - ly.

This is ho - ly ground; We're stand-ing on ho - ly ground,
These are ho - ly hands; He's giv - en us ho - ly hands.

For the Lord is pre-sent and where He is is ho - ly.
He works through these hands and so these hands are ho - ly.

TEXT: Christopher Beatty
MUSIC: Christopher Beatty

BEATTY
Irregular meter

Optional extended or choral ending
Softly (a cappella preferred)

This is ho - ly ground; We're stand-ing on ho - ly ground, ho - ly ground.

Come into the Holy of Holies 218

We have confidence to enter the Most Holy Place by the blood of Jesus. Hebrews 10:19

Come in-to the Ho-ly of Ho - lies, En-ter by the

blood of the Lamb; Come in-to His pres-ence with sing - ing,

1 Wor-ship at the throne of God. **2** Wor-ship at the throne of God.

Lift-ing ho-ly hands To the King of

kings; Wor - ship Je - sus.

TEXT: John Sellers
MUSIC: John Sellers

SELLERS
Irregular meter

219 Surely the Presence (of the Lord Is in This Place)

Surely the Lord is in this place. Genesis 28:16

Sure-ly the pres-ence of the Lord is in this place; I can feel His might-y pow-er and His grace. I can hear the brush of an-gels' wings, I see glo-ry on each face; Sure-ly the pres-ence of the Lord is in this place.

Optional transition to "He Is Here"

TEXT: Lanny Wolfe
MUSIC: Lanny Wolfe

SURELY THE PRESENCE
Irregular meter

220 He Is Here

Where two or three come together in My name, there am I with them. Matthew 18:20

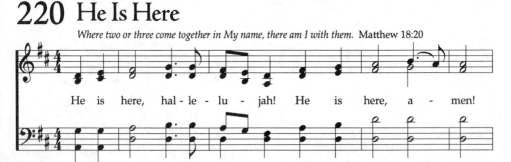

He is here, hal-le-lu-jah! He is here, a-men!

TEXT: Kirk Talley
MUSIC: Kirk Talley

HE IS HERE
Irregular meter

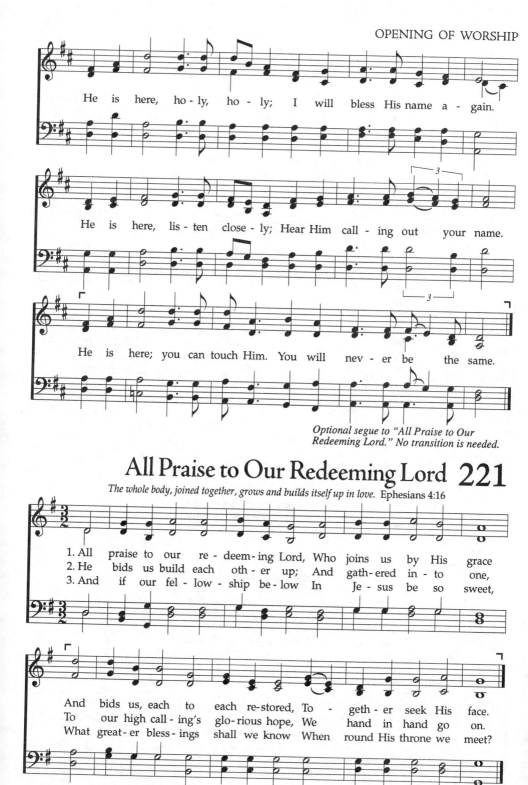

He is here, ho-ly, ho-ly; I will bless His name a-gain.

He is here, lis-ten close-ly; Hear Him call-ing out your name.

He is here; you can touch Him. You will nev-er be the same.

Optional segue to "All Praise to Our Redeeming Lord." No transition is needed.

All Praise to Our Redeeming Lord 221

The whole body, joined together, grows and builds itself up in love. Ephesians 4:16

1. All praise to our re-deem-ing Lord, Who joins us by His grace,
2. He bids us build each oth-er up; And gath-ered in-to one,
3. And if our fel-low-ship be-low In Je-sus be so sweet,

And bids us, each to each re-stored, To-geth-er seek His face.
To our high call-ing's glo-rious hope, We hand in hand go on.
What great-er bless-ings shall we know When round His throne we meet?

TEXT: Charles Wesley; altered
MUSIC: Carl G. Gläser; arranged by Lowell Mason
A higher setting may be found at No. 21

AZMON
C.M.

222 Lord, We Praise You

Praise be to the God and Father of our Lord Jesus Christ. 2 Corinthians 1:3

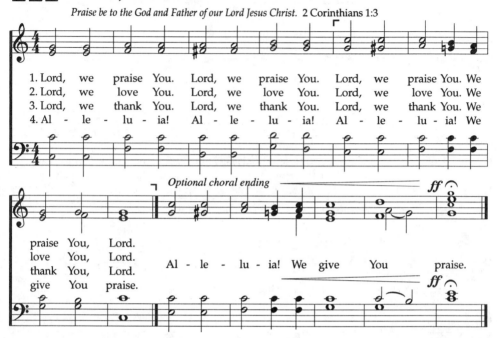

1. Lord, we praise You. Lord, we praise You. Lord, we praise You. We
2. Lord, we love You. Lord, we love You. Lord, we love You. We
3. Lord, we thank You. Lord, we thank You. Lord, we thank You. We
4. Al - le - lu - ia! Al - le - lu - ia! Al - le - lu - ia! We

Optional choral ending

praise You, Lord.
love You, Lord.
thank You, Lord.   Al - le - lu - ia! We give You praise.
give You praise.

TEXT: Otis Skillings
MUSIC: Otis Skillings

LORD, WE PRAISE YOU
4.4.4.4.

223 THE HOUSE OF THE LORD
A Worship Sequence

We Have Come into His House; stanza 1
Come, Christians, Join to Sing; complete
Suggested stanzas have been marked with an arrow: ➤

WORSHIP LEADER

I rejoiced with those who said to me,
"Let us go to the house of the Lord."
Splendor and majesty are before Him;
Strength and glory are in His sanctuary.
Ascribe to the Lord the glory due His name;
Worship the Lord in the splendor of His holiness.

from Psalm 122:1; 96:6, 8-9 (NIV)

Optional introduction to
"We Have Come into His House"

mf

THE HOUSE OF THE LORD - *A Worship Sequence*

We Have Come into His House **224**

Let us go to the house of the Lord. Psalm 122:1

1. We have come in-to His house and gath-ered in His name to wor-ship Him. We have come in-to His house and gath-ered in His name to wor-ship Him. We have come in-to His house and gath-ered in His name to wor-ship Christ the Lord. Wor-ship Him, Christ the Lord.

2. Let's for-get a-bout our-selves and mag-ni-fy His name and wor-ship Him. Let's for-get a-bout our-selves and mag-ni-fy His name and wor-ship Him. Let's for-get a-bout our-selves and mag-ni-fy His name and wor-ship Christ the Lord. Wor-ship Him, Christ the Lord.

TEXT: Bruce Ballinger
MUSIC: Bruce Ballinger

WORSHIP HIM
Irregular meter

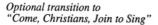

Optional transition to
"Come, Christians, Join to Sing"

225 Come, Christians, Join to Sing

Sing and make music in your heart to the Lord, always giving thanks. Ephesians 5:19-20

➤ 1. Come, Chris-tians, join to sing Al - le - lu - ia! A - men!
➤ 2. Come, lift your hearts on high: Al - le - lu - ia! A - men!
➤ 3. Praise yet our Christ a - gain, Al - le - lu - ia! A - men!

Loud praise to Christ, our King; Al - le - lu - ia! A - men!
Let prais - es fill the sky; Al - le - lu - ia! A - men!
Life shall not end the strain; Al - le - lu - ia! A - men!

Let all, with heart and voice, Be - fore His throne re - joice;
He is our Guide and Friend; To us He'll con - de-scend;
On heav - en's bliss - ful shore His good - ness we'll a - dore,

Praise is His gra - cious choice: Al - le - lu - ia! A - men!
His love shall nev - er end: Al - le - lu - ia! A - men!
Sing - ing for - ev - er-more, "Al - le - lu - ia! A - men!"

TEXT: Christian H. Bateman
MUSIC: Traditional Spanish melody; arranged by David Evans;
Choral ending arranged by Lee Herrington

MADRID
6.6.6.6.D.

Optional choral ending

A - men, a - men! Al - le - lu - ia! A - men!

The end of THE HOUSE OF THE LORD - A Worship Sequence

Oh, the Glory of Your Presence 226

The glory of the Lord filled the temple of God. 2 Chronicles 5:14

Oh, the glo - ry of Your pres - ence, We, Your

tem - ple, give You rev - 'rence. *Come and rise to Your

rest and be blest by our praise as we glo - ry in Your em -

brace; As Your pres - ence now fills this place.

*2 Chronicles 6:41

TEXT: Steve Fry
MUSIC: Steve Fry

HIS PRESENCE
Irregular meter

227 Come, Let Us Worship and Bow Down

Come, let us bow down in worship. Psalm 95:6

Come, let us wor-ship and bow down, Let us kneel be-fore the Lord, our God, our

Mak - er. Mak - er. For He is our

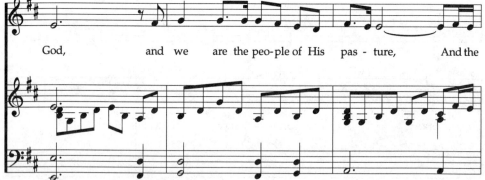

God, and we are the peo-ple of His pas - ture, And the

TEXT: Dave Doherty; adapted from Psalm 95:6
MUSIC: Dave Doherty

WORSHIP AND BOW DOWN
Irregular meter

sheep of His hand, just the sheep of His hand.

Optional segue to "I Will Come and Bow Down." No transition is needed. Tempo is a little faster.

I Will Come and Bow Down 228

You will fill me with joy in Your presence, with eternal pleasures at Your right hand. Psalm 16:11

I will come and bow down at Your feet, Lord Je-sus. In Your pres-ence is full-ness of joy. There is noth-ing, there is no one who com-pares with You. I take plea-sure in wor-ship-ing You, Lord.

TEXT: Martin Nystrom
MUSIC: Martin Nystrom

NYSTROM
Irregular meter

229 Cast Thy Burden upon the Lord

Cast your cares on the Lord and He will sustain you. Psalm 55:22

Cast thy bur-den up-on the Lord, And He shall sustain thee. He nev-er will suf-fer the righ-teous to fall;
He is at thy right hand. Thy mer-cy, Lord, is great and
far a-bove the heav'ns; Let none be made a-
sham-ed that wait up-on Thee. A-men.

TEXT: Based on Psalms 55:22; 16:8
MUSIC: Felix Mendelssohn, from *Elijah*

CAST THY BURDEN
Irregular meter

Christ, We Do All Adore Thee 230

Worthy is the Lamb, who was slain, to receive honor and glory and praise! Revelation 5:12

Christ, we do all a - dore Thee, and we do praise Thee for - ev - er.

Christ, we do all a - dore Thee, and we do praise Thee for - ev - er,

For on the ho - ly cross hast Thou the world from sin re - deem - ed.

Christ, we do all a - dore Thee, and we do praise Thee for - ev - er.

Instruments   Christ, we do all a - dore Thee!

These 2 measures may be omitted.

TEXT: *Adoramus Te*, English version by Theodore Baker
MUSIC: Theodore Dubois; from *The Seven Last Words of Christ*

ADORE THEE
Irregular meter

231 Let the Peace of Christ Rule in Your Heart

Let the peace of Christ rule in your hearts. And be thankful. Colossians 3:15

Let the peace of Christ rule in your heart; Let the peace of Christ rule in your heart,

And what-ev-er you do, in word or deed, Do it all in the name of the Lord.

Giv-ing thanks, giv-ing thanks to God, thro' Christ, the Lord;

Giv-ing thanks, giv-ing thanks to God, thro' Christ, the Lord.

TEXT: Denny Cagle; based on Colossians 3:15
MUSIC: Denny Cagle

PEACE OF CHRIST
Irregular meter

232 God Be with You

The grace of our Lord Jesus Christ be with you. 1 Thessalonians 5:28

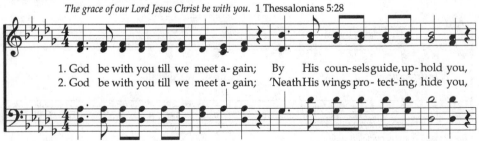

1. God be with you till we meet a-gain; By His coun-sels guide, up-hold you,
2. God be with you till we meet a-gain; 'Neath His wings pro-tect-ing, hide you,

TEXT: Jeremiah E. Rankin
MUSIC: William G. Tomer

GOD BE WITH YOU
Irregular meter

With His sheep se-cure-ly fold you; God be with you till we meet a-gain.
Dai - ly man-na still pro-vide you; God be with you till we meet a-gain.

Grace, Love and Fellowship 233

May grace, love and fellowship of the Holy Spirit be with you all. 2 Corinthians 13:14

Unison

May the grace of Christ, our Sav-ior, and the love of God, our

Fa-ther, and the fel-low-ship of the Spir-it be with us.

May the us for-ev-er and

rit.

ev - er, for - ev - er-more. A - men.

TEXT: Tom Fettke; based on 2 Corinthians 13:14
MUSIC: Tom Fettke

CANE PEAK
Irregular meter

234 Now unto Him

To Him who is able to keep you be glory, majesty, power and authority. Jude 24-25

Introduction Now un-to Him who is a - ble to keep you from fall - ing And to make you stand in His pres - ence blame- less and with great joy. To the on - ly God, our Sav - ior, thro' Je - sus Christ, our Lord, Be the glo - ry and the maj-es-ty, do - min - ion and au-thor-i-ty, Both now and for -

TEXT: David Morris
MUSIC: David Morris; arranged by Tom Fettke

NOW UNTO HIM
Irregular meter

ev - er. A - men!   Give Him the   men!

Take the Name of Jesus with You 235

Whatever you do, do it all in the name of the Lord Jesus. Colossians 3:17

1. Take the name of Je - sus with you, Child of sor - row and of woe;
2. Take the name of Je - sus ev - er, As a shield from ev - ery snare;
3. O the pre - cious name of Je - sus! How it thrills our souls with joy,
4. At the name of Je - sus bow - ing, Fall - ing pros - trate at His feet;

It will joy and com - fort give you— Take it, then, wher - e'er you go.
If temp - ta - tions round you gath - er, Breathe that ho - ly name in prayer.
When His lov - ing arms re - ceive us And His songs our tongues em - ploy!
King of kings in heav'n we'll crown Him When our jour - ney is com - plete.

Refrain

Pre - cious name, O how sweet! Hope of earth and joy of heav'n;

Pre - cious name, O how sweet! Hope of earth and joy of heav'n.

TEXT: Lydia Baxter
MUSIC: William H. Doane

PRECIOUS NAME
8.7.8.7. with Refrain

236 The Lord Bless You and Keep You

The Lord bless you and keep you and give you peace. Numbers 6:24, 26

*The "Amens" may be used separately. Bass begins with the first "Amen" on the downbeat of the measure (cued half note).

TEXT: Numbers 6:24-26
MUSIC: Peter C. Lutkin

BENEDICTION
Irregular meter

men,   A - men,   A - men,   A - men.

Lord, Dismiss Us with Thy Blessing 237

May Your blessing be on Your people. Psalm 3:8

1. Lord, dis - miss us with Thy bless - ing; Fill our hearts with joy and peace.
2. Thanks we give and ad - o - ra - tion For Thy gos - pel's joy - ful sound;

Let us each, Thy love pos - sess - ing, Tri - umph in re - deem - ing grace.
May the fruits of Thy sal - va - tion In our hearts and lives a - bound.

O re - fresh us, O re - fresh us, Trav - el - ing thro' this wil - der - ness.
Ev - er faith - ful, ev - er faith - ful To Thy truth may we be found.

TEXT: John Fawcett, altered
MUSIC: Tattersall's *Psalmody,* 1794

SICILIAN MARINERS
8.7.8.7.8.7.

238 CALLS TO WORSHIP

1 Come, let us sing for joy to the Lord; let us shout aloud to the Rock of our salvation. Let us come before Him with thanksgiving and extol Him with music and song. *Psalm 95:1-2*

2 Come, let us bow down in worship, let us kneel before the Lord our Maker; for He is our God and we are the people of His pasture, the flock under His care. *Psalm 95:6-7*

3 Shout for joy to the Lord, all the earth. Worship the Lord with gladness; come before Him with joyful songs. Know that the Lord is God. It is He who made us, and we are His; we are His people, the sheep of His pasture. *Psalm 100:1-3*

4 Enter His gates with thanksgiving and His courts wth praise; give thanks to Him and praise His name. For the Lord is good and His love endures forever; His faithfulness continues through all generations. *Psalm 100:4-5*

5 Be still, and know that I am God. I will be exalted among the nations; I will be exalted in the earth. *Psalm 46:10*

6 A time is coming and has now come when the true worshipers will worship the Father in spirit and truth, for they are the kind of worshipers the Father seeks. God is spirit, and His worshipers must worship in spirit and in truth. *John 4:23-24*

239 BENEDICTIONS

1 The Lord bless you and keep you; the Lord make His face shine upon you and be gracious to you; the Lord turn His face toward you and give you peace. *Numbers 6:24-26*

2 May the grace of the Lord Jesus Christ, and the love of God, and the fellowship of the Holy Spirit be with you all. *2 Corinthians 13:14*

3 To Him who is able to keep you from falling and to present you before His glorious presence without fault and with great joy—to the only God, our Savior– be glory, majesty, power and authority, through Jesus Christ our Lord, before all ages, now and forevermore! Amen. *Jude 24-25*

4 May our Lord Jesus Christ Himself and God our Father, who loved us and by His grace gave us eternal encouragement and good hope, encourage your hearts and strengthen you in every good deed and word. *2 Thessalonians 2:16-17*

5 Now to Him who is able to do immeasurably more than all we ask or imagine, according to His power that is at work within us, to Him be glory in the church and in Christ Jesus throughout all generations, for ever and ever! Amen. *Ephesians 3:20-21*

6 Now to the King eternal, immortal, invisible, the only God, be honor and glory for ever and ever. Amen. *1 Timothy 1:17*

All spoken Calls to Worship and Benedictions are from the NIV.

Of the Father's Love Begotten 240

I am the Alpha and the Omega, the Beginning and the End. Revelation 22:13

Unison

1. Of the Fa-ther's love be-got - ten, Ere the worlds be-gan to be,
2. O ye heights of heav'n, a-dore Him; An-gel hosts, His prais - es sing;
3. Christ, to Thee with God the Fa - ther, And, O Ho-ly Ghost, to Thee,

He is Al-pha and O-me - ga, He the Source, the End - ing He
Pow'rs, do-min-ions, bow be-fore Him And ex-tol our God and King;
Hymn and chant and high thanks-giv - ing, And un-wear-ied prais - es be:

Of the things that are, that have been, And that fu - ture
Let no tongue on earth be si - lent; Ev - ery voice in
Hon-or, glo-ry, and do-min - ion And e - ter - nal

years shall see, Ev-er-more and ev-er-more.
con - cert ring, Ev-er-more and ev-er-more.
vic - to - ry, Ev-er-more and ev-er-more. A - men.

TEXT: Aurelius C. Prudentius, 4th century;
      translated by John M. Neale and Henry W. Baker
MUSIC: Plainsong, 13th century; arranged by C. Winfred Douglas

DIVINUM MYSTERIUM
8.7.8.7.8.7.7.

241 Arise, Shine

Arise, shine, for your light has come, and the glory of the Lord rises upon you. Isaiah 60:1

A - rise, shine, for thy Light is come. A -
rise, shine, for thy Light is come: And the
glo-ry of the Lord is ris-en, The glo-ry of the Lord is
come, The glo-ry of the Lord is ris-en up-on thee.

TEXT: Steven Urspringer and Jay Robinson
MUSIC: Steven Urspringer and Jay Robinson

ARISE, SHINE
Irregular meter

242   GOD WITH US
A Worship Sequence
Emmanuel
Come, Thou Long-Expected Jesus; complete
Suggested stanzas have been marked with an arrow: ➤

WORSHIP LEADER

"Behold, a virgin shall be with child, and bear a Son,
and they shall call His name Immanuel," which is translated,

EVERYONE
"God with us."

from Matthew 1:23 (NKJV)

Optional introduction to "Emmanuel"

Emmanuel 243

They will call Him Immanuel—which means, "God with us." Matthew 1:23

Em - man - u - el, Em - man - u - el,

His name is called Em - man - u - el;

God with us, re - vealed in us;

His name is called Em - man - u - el.

Optional segue to "Come, Thou Long-Expected Jesus." No transition is needed.

TEXT: Bob McGee
MUSIC: Bob McGee

EMMANUEL
Irregular meter

244 Come, Thou Long-Expected Jesus

The Lord has sent Me to bind up the brokenhearted, to proclaim freedom for the captives. Isaiah 61:1

1. Come, Thou long - ex - pect - ed Je - sus, Born to set Thy peo - ple free.
2. Born Thy peo - ple to de - liv - er, Born a Child and yet a King,

From our fears and sins re - lease us; Let us find our rest in Thee.
Born to reign in us for - ev - er, Now Thy gra - cious king - dom bring.

Is - rael's Strength and Con - so - la - tion, Hope of all the earth Thou art;
By Thine own e - ter - nal Spir - it, Rule in all our hearts a - lone;

Dear De - sire of ev - ery na - tion, Joy of ev - ery long - ing heart.
By Thine all - suf - fi - cient mer - it, Raise us to Thy glo - rious throne.

TEXT: Charles Wesley
MUSIC: Rowland H. Prichard; arranged by Robert Harkness
A lower setting may be found at No. 309

HYFRYDOL
8.7.8.7.D.

Optional choral ending

Em - man - u - el, Em - man - u - el.

The end of GOD WITH US - A Worship Sequence

O Come, O Come, Emmanuel 245

The virgin will give birth to a Son, and will call Him Immanuel. Isaiah 7:14

1. O come, O come, Em - man - u - el And ran-som cap-tive
2. O come, Thou Day-spring, come and cheer Our spir-its by Thine
3. O come, Thou Wis-dom from on high And or-der all things,
4. O come, De-sire of na - tions, bind All peo-ples in one

Is - ra - el, That mourns in lone-ly ex - ile here,
ad - vent here; Dis-perse the gloom-y clouds of night,
far and nigh; To us the path of knowl-edge show
heart and mind. Bid en-vy, strife, and quar - rels cease;

Refrain

Un - til the Son of God ap - pear.
And death's dark shad-ows put to flight.
And cause us in her ways to go. Re - joice! Re - joice!
Fill the whole world with heav - en's peace.

Em - man - u - el Shall come to thee, O Is - ra - el!

TEXT: Latin Hymn, *Psalteriolum Cantionum Catholicarum,* 1710;
translated by John M. Neale, stanzas 1,2, altered;
Henry S. Coffin, stanzas 3,4 altered
MUSIC: Adapted from Plainsong by Thomas Helmore, altered

VENI EMMANUEL
L. M. with Refrain

246 PRINCE OF PEACE
A Worship Sequence
Let's Worship and Adore Him
I Extol You
O Come, All Ye Faithful; complete
Suggested stanzas have been marked with an arrow: ➤

WORSHIP LEADER
For unto us a Child is born, unto us a Son is given;
And the government will be upon His shoulder. And His name will be called:

EVERYONE
Wonderful, Counselor, Mighty God, Everlasting Father, Prince of Peace.
from Isaiah 9:6 (NKJV)

247 Let's Worship and Adore Him
All nations will come and worship before You. Revelation 15:4

Let's wor-ship and a-dore Him, Let's wor-ship and a-dore Him, Let's wor-ship and a-dore Him, Christ the Lord.

Optional additional stanza setting
Unison

For ' He a-lone is wor-thy, For He a-lone is wor-thy,

For He a-lone is wor-thy, Christ the Lord.

Optional transition to "I Extol You"

TEXT: Traditional
MUSIC: Wade's *Cantus Diversi*, 1751; arranged by Tom Fettke

ADESTE FIDELES (Refrain only)
7.7.10.

I Extol You 248

I will extol the Lord with all my heart in the council of the upright. Psalm 111:1

Unison

Prince of Peace, Coun-se-lor, mer-ci-ful Son of God, Lord of Hosts, Con-quer-or, Com-ing King and Ev-er liv-ing God, I ex-tol You; Lord, I ex-tol You. You are high a-bove the earth; All cre-a-tion shouts Your worth! I ex-tol You; Lord, I ex-tol You. My Je-ho-vah, I ex-tol You.

In the context of the Worship Sequence, "I Extol You" may be sung by choir, ensemble or soloist, if desired.

TEXT: Jennifer Randolph
MUSIC: Jennifer Randolph

I EXTOL YOU
Irregular meter

Optional transition to
"O Come, All Ye Faithful"

mf a little faster

249 O Come, All Ye Faithful

Let's go to Bethlehem and see this thing that has happened. Luke 2:15

➤ 1. O come, all ye faith - ful, joy - ful and tri - um - phant; O come
➤ 2. Sing, choirs of an - gels; sing in ex - ul - ta - tion; O sing,
➤ 3. Yea, Lord, we greet Thee, born this hap - py morn - ing; Je -

ye, O come ye to Beth - le - hem! Come and be - hold Him—
all ye bright hosts of heav'n a - bove! Glo - ry to God, all
sus, to Thee be all glo - ry giv'n: Word of the Fa - ther,

Refrain

born the King of an - gels! O come, let us a - dore Him! O
glo - ry in the high - est!
now in flesh ap - pear - ing!

TEXT: Latin Hymn; ascribed to John Francis Wade;
translated by Frederick Oakeley
MUSIC: John Francis Wade;
Last refrain setting, Descant and Choral ending by Tom Fettke

ADESTE FIDELES
Irregular meter

The end of PRINCE OF PEACE - A Worship Sequence

250 O Little Town of Bethlehem

Bethlehem, out of you will come for Me One who will be ruler over Israel. Micah 5:2

1. O lit - tle town of Beth - le - hem, How still we see thee lie!
2. For Christ is born of Mar - y, And gath - ered all a - bove,
3. How si - lent - ly, how si - lent - ly The won - drous Gift is giv'n!
4. O ho - ly Child of Beth - le - hem, De - scend on us, we pray.

A - bove thy deep and dream - less sleep The si - lent stars go by.
While mor - tals sleep, the an - gels keep Their watch of won - d'ring love.
So God im - parts to hu - man hearts The bless - ings of His heav'n.
Cast out our sin, and en - ter in; Be born in us to - day.

Yet in thy dark streets shin - eth The ev - er - last - ing Light;
O morn - ing stars, to - geth - er Pro - claim the ho - ly birth;
No ear may hear His com - ing, But in this world of sin,
We hear the Christ - mas an - gels The great glad tid - ings tell.

The hopes and fears of all the years Are met in thee to - night.
And prais - es sing to God, the King, And peace to men on earth.
Where meek souls will re - ceive Him still, The dear Christ en - ters in.
O come to us, a - bide with us, Our Lord, Em - man - u - el.

TEXT: Phillips Brooks
MUSIC: Lewis H. Redner

ST. LOUIS
8.6.8.6.7.6.8.6.

It Came upon the Midnight Clear 251

An angel of the Lord appeared to them, and the glory of the Lord shone around them. Luke 2:9

1. It came up-on the mid-night clear, That glo-rious song of old,
2. Still thro' the clo-ven skies they come With peace-ful wings un-furled,
3. And ye, be-neath life's crush-ing load, Whose forms are bend-ing low,
4. For lo, the days are has-t'ning on, By proph-ets seen of old,

From an-gels bend-ing near the earth To touch their harps of gold:
And still their heav'n-ly mu-sic floats O'er all the wea-ry world;
Who toil a-long the climb-ing way With pain-ful steps and slow,
When with the ev-er-cir-cling years Shall come the time fore-told,

"Peace on the earth, good-will to men, From heav'n's all-gra-cious King!"
A-bove its sad and low-ly plains They bend on hov-'ring wing,
Look now! for glad and gold-en hours Come swift-ly on the wing:
When peace shall o-ver all the earth Its an-cient splen-dors fling,

The world in sol-emn still-ness lay To hear the an-gels sing.
And ev-er o'er its Ba-bel sounds The bless-ed an-gels sing.
O rest be-side the wea-ry road And hear the an-gels sing.
And the whole world send back the song Which now the an-gels sing.

TEXT: Edmund H. Sears
MUSIC: Richard S. Willis

CAROL
C.M.D.

252

TINY KING
A Worship Sequence
Silent Night! Holy Night!; stanzas 1,2,4
Isn't He?
Suggested stanzas have been marked with an arrow: ➤

WORSHIP LEADER
And Mary brought forth her firstborn Son,
and wrapped Him in swaddling clothes,
and laid Him in a manger.

from Luke 2:7 (NKJV)

253 Silent Night! Holy Night!

There were shepherds living out in the fields nearby, keeping watch over their flocks at night. Luke 2:8

➤ 1. Si - lent night, ho - ly night, All is calm, all is bright
➤ 2. Si - lent night, ho - ly night, Shep-herds quake at the sight.
3. Si - lent night, ho - ly night, Won-drous star, lend thy light.
➤ 4. Si - lent night, ho - ly night, Son of God, love's pure light

Round yon vir - gin moth-er and Child. Ho - ly In - fant so ten-der and mild,
Glo - ries stream from heav-en a - far; Heaven-ly hosts sing al - le-lu - ia.
With the an - gels let us sing Al - le-lu - ia to our King.
Ra - diant beams from Thy ho-ly face, With the dawn of re - deem-ing grace,

Sleep in heav - en - ly peace, Sleep in heav - en - ly peace.
Christ the Sav - ior is born! Christ the Sav - ior is born!
Christ the Sav - ior is born! Christ the Sav - ior is born!
Je - sus, Lord, at Thy birth, Je - sus, Lord, at Thy birth.

TEXT: Joseph Mohr; translated by John F. Young, stanzas 1,2,4; Anonymous, stanza 3
MUSIC: Franz Grüber

STILLE NACHT
Irregular meter

Optional transition to "Isn't He?"

Isn't He? 254

For to us a Child is born, to us a Son is given. Isaiah 9:6

* Unison

Is-n't He beau- ti- ful? Beau- ti- ful, is- n't He?
Is-n't He won- der- ful? Won- der- ful, is- n't He?

Prince of Peace, Son of God, is- n't He?
Coun- sel- or, Al- might- y God,

is- n't He, is- n't He, is- n't

He, is- n't He?

*In the context of the Worship Sequence, "Isn't He?" may be sung by choir, ensemble or soloist, if desired.

TEXT: John Wimber
MUSIC: John Wimber

WIMBER
Irregular meter

The end of TINY KING - A Worship Sequence

255 Lo! How a Rose E'er Blooming

A shoot will come up from the stump of Jesse. Isaiah 11:1

1. Lo, how a Rose e'er bloom-ing From ten-der stem hath sprung! Of Jes-se's lin-eage com-ing As men of old have sung. It came, a Flow-'ret bright, A-mid the cold of win-ter When half-spent was the night.

2. I - sa-iah 'twas fore-told it, The Rose I have in mind; With Mar-y we be-hold it, The vir-gin moth - er kind. To show God's love a - right She bore to men a Sav - ior When half-spent was the night.

3. This Flow'r, whose fra-grance ten-der With sweet-ness fills the air, Dis - pels with glo-rious splen-dor The dark-ness ev - ery-where. True man, yet ver - y God, From sin and death He saves us And light-ens ev - ery load.

TEXT: German carol, 16th century; translated by Theodore
Baker, stanzas 1,2 and Harriet Krauth Spaeth, stanza 3
MUSIC: *Geistliche Kirchengesäng*, Cologne, 1599;
harmonized by Michael Praetorius

ES IST EIN' ROS'
7.6.7.6.6.7.6.

Love Has Come! 256

God so loved the world that He gave His one and only Son. John 3:16

1. Love has come— a light in the dark-ness! Love ex-plodes in the
2. Love is born! Come share in the won-der; Love is God now a-
3. Love has come— He nev-er will leave us! Love is life ev-er-

Beth-le-hem skies. See, all heav-en has come to pro-claim it;
sleep in the hay. See the glow in the eyes of His moth-er;
last-ing and free. Love is Je-sus with-in and a-mong us;

Hear how their song of joy a-ris-es: Love! Love! Born un-to
What is the name her heart is say-ing? Love! Love! Love is the
Love is the peace our hearts are seek-ing. Love! Love! Love is the

you, a Sav-ior! Love! Love! Glo-ry to God on high.
name she whis-pers; Love! Love! Je-sus, Im-man-u-el.
gift of Christ-mas; Love! Love! Praise to You, God on high!

TEXT: Ken Bible
MUSIC: French carol melody; attributed to Saboly, 17th c.; arranged by Tom Fettke

BRING A TORCH
Irregular meter

257 JESUS CHRIST IS BORN!

A Worship Sequence

Go, Tell It on the Mountain; stanzas 1,3
Angels, from the Realms of Glory; stanzas 1,2,5
Worthy, You Are Worthy; complete
Suggested stanzas have been marked with an arrow: ➤

WORSHIP LEADER

And the shepherds came with haste and found Mary and Joseph, and the Babe lying in a manger. Now when they had seen Him, they made widely known the saying which was told them concerning this Child. And all those who heard it marveled at those things which were told them by the shepherds. But Mary kept all these things and pondered them in her heart. Then the shepherds returned, glorifying and praising God for all the things that they had heard and seen.

from Luke 2:16-20 (NKJV)

*Optional introduction to
"Go, Tell It on the Mountain"*

258 Go, Tell It on the Mountain

When they had seen Him, they spread the word about this Child. Luke 2:17

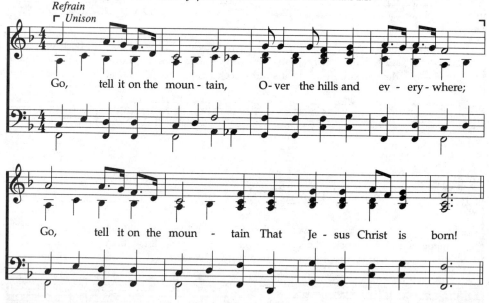

Go, tell it on the moun - tain, O - ver the hills and ev - ery - where;

Go, tell it on the moun - tain That Je - sus Christ is born!

TEXT: John W. Work, Jr.
MUSIC: Traditional Spiritual; Refrain harmonized by Eugene Thomas

GO TELL IT
7.6.7.6. with Refrain

Harmony optional

1. While shep-herds kept their watch-ing O'er si-lent flocks by night,
(2. The) shep-herds feared and trem-bled When lo! a-bove the earth
(3. Down) in a low-ly man-ger The hum-ble Christ was born,

Be-hold! thro'-out the heav-ens There shone a ho-ly light.
Rang out the an-gel cho-rus That hailed our Sav-ior's birth.
And brought us God's sal-va-tion That bless-ed Christ-mas morn.

Refrain
Unison

Go, tell it on the moun-tain, O-ver the hills and ev-ery-where;

1, 2   ‖ 3

Go, tell it on the moun-tain That Je-sus Christ is born!

2. The
3. Down   born!

Optional extended ending or transition to
"Angels, from the Realms of Glory"

That Je-sus Christ is born, That Je-sus Christ is born!

8ᵛᵇ

Segue to "Angels, from the Realms of Glory."
No further transition is needed.

259 Angels, from the Realms of Glory

Bethlehem, out of you will come a Ruler who will be the Shepherd of My people. Matthew 2:6

➤ 1. An - gels, from the realms of glo - ry, Wing your flight o'er all the earth;
➤ 2. Shep - herds, in the field a - bid - ing, Watch - ing o'er your flocks by night,
3. Sag - es, leave your con - tem - pla - tions, Bright - er vi - sions beam a - far;
4. Saints be - fore the al - tar bend - ing, Watch - ing long in hope and fear,
➤ 5. Tho' an in - fant now we view Him, He will share His Fa - ther's throne;

Ye who sang cre - a - tion's sto - ry Now pro - claim Mes - si - ah's birth:
God with man is now re - sid - ing; Yon - der shines the In - fant Light:
Seek the great De - sire of na - tions; Ye have seen His na - tal star:
Sud - den - ly the Lord, de - scend - ing In His tem - ple shall ap - pear:
Gath - er all the na - tions to Him; Ev - ery knee shall then bow down:

Refrain

Come and wor - ship, come and wor - ship; Wor - ship Christ, the new - born King.

TEXT: James Montgomery
MUSIC: Henry T. Smart

REGENT SQUARE
8.7.8.7.8.7.

*Optional extended ending

Come and wor - ship, come and wor - ship;

rit.   *more rit. and decresc.*

Wor - ship Christ, the new - born King.

*Optional transition to
"Worthy, You Are Worthy"*

*Choir or ensemble may sing the extended ending, if desired.

Worthy, You Are Worthy - *Christmas Setting* 260

He has this name written: KING OF KINGS AND LORD OF LORDS. Revelation 19:16

1. Wor - thy, You are wor - thy; King of kings, Lord of lords, You are wor - thy.
2. Ho - ly, You are ho - ly; King of kings, Lord of lords, You are ho - ly.
3. Je - sus, You are Je - sus; King of kings, Lord of lords, You are Je - sus.

Wor - thy, You are wor - thy; King of kings, Lord of lords, I wor-ship You.
Ho - ly, You are ho - ly; King of kings, Lord of lords, I wor-ship You.
Je - sus, You are Je - sus; King of kings, Lord of lords, I wor-ship You.

Optional last stanza setting

3. Je - sus, You are Je - sus; King of kings, Lord of lords, You are

Je - sus. Je - sus, You are Je - sus; King of kings, Lord of lords, I wor-ship You.

TEXT: Don Moen
MUSIC: Don Moen

WORTHY
6.6.4.6.6.4.

© *Copyright 1986 by Integrity's Hosanna! Music. All rights reserved. Used by permission.*

Optional extended or choral ending

King of   kings,   Lord of   lords,   I wor-ship You.

The end of JESUS CHRIST IS BORN! - A Worship Sequence

261 Away in a Manger

She gave birth to her firstborn, a Son, and placed Him in a manger. Luke 2:7

1. A-way in a man-ger, no crib for a bed, The lit-tle Lord Je-sus laid down His sweet head. The stars in the bright sky looked down where He lay; The lit-tle Lord Je-sus a-sleep on the hay.
2. The cat-tle are low-ing; the Ba-by a-wakes, But lit-tle Lord Je-sus— no cry-ing He makes. I love Thee, Lord Je-sus; look down from the sky, And stay by my side un-til morn-ing is nigh.
3. Be near me, Lord Je-sus; I ask Thee to stay Close by me for-ev-er, and love me, I pray. Bless all the dear chil-dren in Thy ten-der care, And fit us for heav-en, to live with Thee there.

TEXT: Source unknown, stanzas 1, 2; John Thomas McFarland, stanza 3
MUSIC: William J. Kirkpatrick

CRADLE SONG
11.11.11.11.

262 Away in a Manger

She gave birth to her firstborn, a Son, and placed Him in a manger. Luke 2:7

1. A - way in a man-ger, no crib for a bed, The lit - tle Lord
2. The cat - tle are low-ing; the Ba - by a - wakes, But lit - tle Lord
3. Be near me, Lord Je - sus; I ask Thee to stay Close by me for-

TEXT: Source unknown, stanzas 1, 2; John Thomas McFarland, stanza 3
MUSIC: James R. Murray

AWAY IN A MANGER
11.11.11.11.

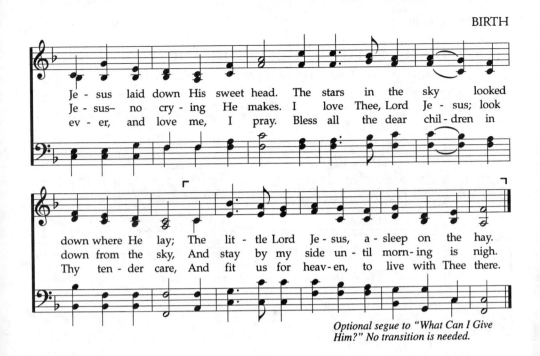

Je - sus laid down His sweet head. The stars in the sky looked
Je - sus— no cry - ing He makes. I love Thee, Lord Je - sus; look
ev - er, and love me, I pray. Bless all the dear chil - dren in

down where He lay; The lit - tle Lord Je - sus, a - sleep on the hay.
down from the sky, And stay by my side un - til morn - ing is nigh.
Thy ten - der care, And fit us for heav - en, to live with Thee there.

Optional segue to "What Can I Give Him?" No transition is needed.

What Can I Give Him? 263

They gave themselves first to the Lord. 2 Corinthians 8:5

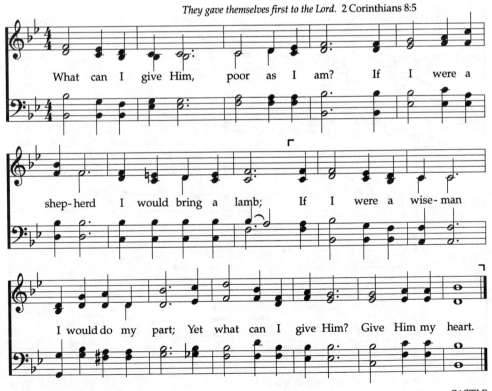

What can I give Him, poor as I am? If I were a

shep - herd I would bring a lamb; If I were a wise - man

I would do my part; Yet what can I give Him? Give Him my heart.

TEXT: Christina Rossetti
MUSIC: Don Cason

CASTLE
9.11.11.10.

264 Break Forth, O Beauteous Heavenly Light

...a light for revelation to the Gentiles and for glory to Your people Israel. Luke 2:32

1. Break forth, O beau-teous heav'n-ly light, And ush-er in the morn - ing; Ye shep-herds, shrink not with af-fright But hear the an-gel's warn - ing. This Child, now weak in in-fan-cy, Our con-fi-dence and joy shall be. The pow'r of Sa-tan break - ing, Our peace e-ter-nal mak - ing.

2. He comes, a Child from realms on high; He comes the heav'ns a-dor - ing. He comes to earth to live and die, A bro-ken race re-stor - ing. Al-though the King of kings is He, He comes in deep hu-mil-i-ty; His peo-ple to de-liv - er And reign in us for-ev - er.

TEXT: Johann Rist, stanza 1; translated by John Troutbeck;
        Joseph Barlowe, stanza 2
MUSIC: Johann Schop; harmonized by J. S. Bach

ERMUNTRE DICH
8.7.8.7.8.8.7.7.

The First Noel 265

Today in the town of David a Savior has been born to you; He is Christ the Lord. Luke 2:11

1. The first No - el, the an-gel did say, Was to cer-tain poor shep-herds in fields as they lay; In fields where they lay keep-ing their sheep, On a cold win-ter's night that was so deep.
2. They look - ed up and saw a star Shin-ing in the east, be - yond them far, And to the earth it gave great light, And so it con - tin - ued both day and night.
3. And by the light of that same star Three Wise Men came from coun - try far; To seek for a King was their in - tent, And to fol - low the star wher - ev - er it went.
4. This star drew nigh to the north-west, O'er Beth - le - hem it took its rest, And there it did both stop and stay, Right o - ver the place where Je - sus lay.
5. Then en - tered in those Wise Men three, Full rev - 'rent-ly up - on their knee, And of - fered there in His pres - ence Their gold, and myrrh, and frank - in - cense.
6. Then let us all with one ac - cord Sing prais - es to our heav'n - ly Lord, That hath made heav'n and earth of naught, And with His blood man - kind hath bought.

Refrain

No - el, No - el, No - el, No - el, Born is the King of Is - ra - el.

TEXT: Traditional English carol
MUSIC: W. Sandys' *Christmas Carols*, 1833; arranged by John Stainer

THE FIRST NOEL
Irregular meter

266 That Beautiful Name

God gave Him the name that is above every name. Philippians 2:9

1. I know of a name, A beau-ti-ful name, That an-gels bro't
2. I know of a name, A beau-ti-ful name, That un-to a
3. The One of that name My Sav-ior be-came, My Sav-ior of
4. I love that blest name, That won-der-ful name, Made high-er than

down to earth; They whis-pered it low, One night long a-go,
Babe was giv-en; The stars glit-tered bright Thro'-out that glad night,
Cal-va-ry; My sins nailed Him there, My bur-dens to bear,
all in heav-en; 'Twas whis-pered, I know, In my heart long a-go,

To a maid-en of low-ly birth.
And an-gels praised God in heav'n.
He suf-fered all this for me.
To Je-sus my life I've given.

Refrain

That beau-ti-ful name, That beau-ti-ful name From sin has power to free us! That beau-ti-ful name, That won-der-ful name, That match-less name is Je-sus!

TEXT: Jean Perry
MUSIC: Mabel Johnston Camp

BEAUTIFUL NAME
Irregular meter

I Heard the Bells on Christmas Day 267

He will be their peace. Micah 5:5

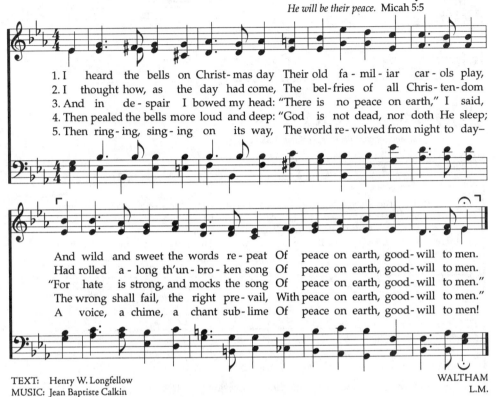

1. I heard the bells on Christ-mas day Their old fa - mil - iar car - ols play,
2. I thought how, as the day had come, The bel-fries of all Chris-ten-dom
3. And in de - spair I bowed my head: "There is no peace on earth," I said,
4. Then pealed the bells more loud and deep: "God is not dead, nor doth He sleep;
5. Then ring-ing, sing-ing on its way, The world re-volved from night to day—

And wild and sweet the words re - peat Of peace on earth, good-will to men.
Had rolled a - long th'un-bro-ken song Of peace on earth, good-will to men.
"For hate is strong, and mocks the song Of peace on earth, good-will to men."
The wrong shall fail, the right pre-vail, With peace on earth, good-will to men."
A voice, a chime, a chant sub-lime Of peace on earth, good-will to men!

TEXT: Henry W. Longfellow
MUSIC: Jean Baptiste Calkin

WALTHAM
L.M.

REJOICE WITH EXCEEDING GREAT JOY! 268

A Worship Sequence

How Great Our Joy!; stanzas 1,2,4
Joy to the World!; stanzas 1,2,4
Joyful, Joyful, We Adore You; complete
Suggested stanzas have been marked with an arrow: ➤

WORSHIP LEADER

Now there were in the same country shepherds living out in the fields, keeping watch over their flock by night. And behold, an angel of the Lord stood before them, and the glory of the Lord shone around them, and they were greatly afraid. Then the angel said to them, "Do not be afraid, for behold, I bring you good tidings of great joy which will be to all people. For there is born to you this day in the city of David a Savior, who is Christ the Lord. And this will be the sign to you: You will find a Babe wrapped in swaddling clothes, lying in a manger." And suddenly there was with the angel a multitude of the heavenly host praising God and saying:

EVERYONE

"Glory to God in the highest, and on earth peace, goodwill toward men!"

from Luke 2:8-14 (NKJV)

Optional introduction to "How Great Our Joy!"

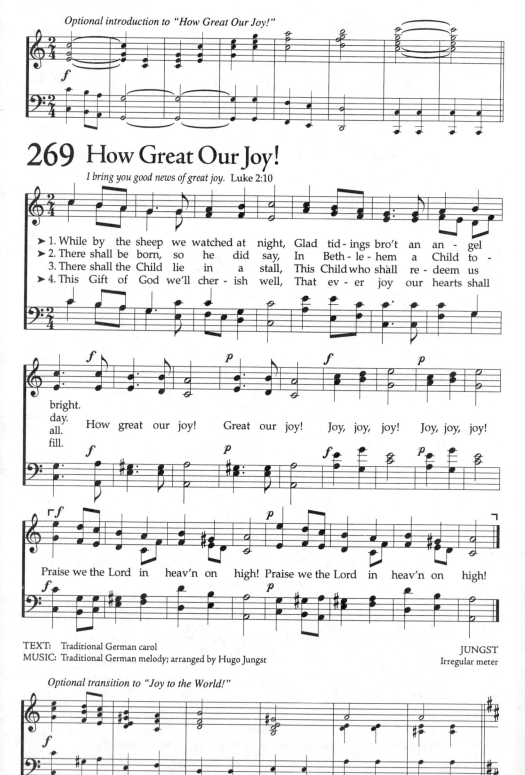

269 How Great Our Joy!

I bring you good news of great joy. Luke 2:10

1. While by the sheep we watched at night, Glad tid-ings bro't an an - gel
2. There shall be born, so he did say, In Beth - le - hem a Child to -
3. There shall the Child lie in a stall, This Child who shall re - deem us
4. This Gift of God we'll cher - ish well, That ev - er joy our hearts shall

bright.
day.
all.
fill.

How great our joy! Great our joy! Joy, joy, joy! Joy, joy, joy!

Praise we the Lord in heav'n on high! Praise we the Lord in heav'n on high!

TEXT: Traditional German carol
MUSIC: Traditional German melody; arranged by Hugo Jungst

JUNGST
Irregular meter

Optional transition to "Joy to the World!"

Joy to the World! 270

Shout for joy to the Lord, all the earth, for He comes. Psalm 98:4, 9

1. Joy to the world! the Lord is come; Let earth re - ceive her King. Let ev - ery heart pre - pare Him room, And heav'n and na - ture sing, And heav'n and na - ture sing, And heav'n, and heav'n and na - ture sing.

2. Joy to the world! the Sav - ior reigns; Let men their songs em - ploy, While fields and floods, rocks, hills and plains Re - peat the sound - ing joy, Re - peat the sound - ing joy, Re - peat, re - peat the sound - ing joy.

3. No more let sin and sor - row grow, Nor thorns in - fest the ground. He comes to make His bless - ings flow Far as the curse is found, Far as the curse is found, Far as, far as the curse is found.

4. He rules the world with truth and grace And makes the na - tions prove The glo - ries of His righ - teous - ness And won - ders of His love, And won - ders of His love, And won - ders, won - ders of His love.

1. And heav'n and na - ture sing,

1. And heav'n and na - ture sing, And heav'n and na - ture sing,

TEXT: Isaac Watts
MUSIC: George Frederick Handel; arranged by Lowell Mason

ANTIOCH
C.M.

Optional transition to "Joyful, Joyful, We Adore You"

271 Joyful, Joyful, We Adore You

Shout for joy, O heavens; rejoice, O earth! For the Lord comforts His people. Isaiah 49:13

1. Joy - ful, joy - ful, we a - dore You, God of glo - ry, Lord of light;
2. All Your works de - clare Your glo - ry; All cre - a - tion joins to sing.

An - gels lift - ing praise be - fore You Sing thro' - out this ho - ly night.
Praise re - sounds as earth re - joic - es In the birth of Christ, the King.

In a man - ger lies a Ba - by— Child of Mar - y, Son of God.
Shep - herds kneel be - fore the In - fant. Trum - pets sound and an - thems raise

Voic - es joined in joy - ful cho - rus Praise You for Your gift of love.
As with joy our hearts are lift - ed, Joined in won - der, love, and praise.

TEXT: Linda Lee Johnson
MUSIC: Ludwig van Beethoven; adapted by Edward Hodges; Choral ending by Eugene Thomas

HYMN TO JOY
8.7.8.7.D.

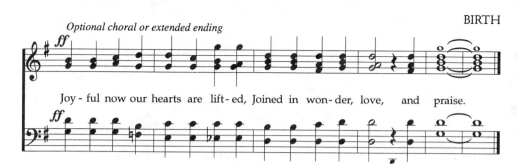

Optional choral or extended ending

ff

Joy-ful now our hearts are lift-ed, Joined in won-der, love, and praise.

ff

The end of REJOICE WITH EXCEEDING GREAT JOY! - A Worship Sequence

While Shepherds Watched Their Flocks 272

There were shepherds living out in the fields nearby, keeping watch over their flocks at night. Luke 2:8

1. While shep - herds watched their flocks by night, All seat - ed
2. "Fear not," said he, for might - y dread Had seized their
3. "To you, in Da - vid's town this day Is born, of
4. "The heav'n - ly Babe you there shall find To hu - man
5. "All glo - ry be to God on high And to the

on the ground, The an - gel of the Lord came down,
trou - bled mind, "Glad tid - ings of great joy I bring
Da - vid's line, The Sav - ior, who is Christ the Lord;
view dis - played, All mean-ly wrapped in swath - ing bands,
earth be peace. Good - will hence- forth from heav'n to men

And glo - ry shone a - round, And glo - ry shone a - round.
To you and all man - kind, To you and all man - kind.
And this shall be the sign, And this shall be the sign:
And in a man - ger laid, And in a man - ger laid.
Be - gin and nev - er cease, Be - gin and nev - er cease!"

TEXT: Nahum Tate
MUSIC: George Frederick Handel; from Weyman's, *Melodia Sacra*, 1815

CHRISTMAS
C.M with Repeats

273 Good Christian Men, Rejoice

My spirit rejoices in God my Savior. Luke 1:47

1. Good Chris-tian men, re-joice With heart and soul and voice! Give ye heed to what we say: News! News! Je-sus Christ is born to-day! Ox and ass be-fore Him bow, And He is in the man-ger now. Christ is born to-day! Christ is born to-day!

2. Good Chris-tian men, re-joice With heart and soul and voice! Now ye hear of end-less bliss: Joy! Joy! Je-sus Christ was born for this! He hath o-pened heav-en's door And man is blessed for-ev-er-more. Christ was born for this! Christ was born for this!

3. Good Chris-tian men, re-joice With heart and soul and voice! Now ye need not fear the grave: Peace! Peace! Je-sus Christ was born to save! Calls you one and calls you all To gain His ev-er-last-ing hall. Christ was born to save! Christ was born to save!

TEXT: Latin carol, 14th century; translated by John M. Neale
MUSIC: German melody, 14th century; harmonized by John Stainer

IN DULCI JUBILO
Irregular meter

O Hearken Ye 274

Glory to God in the highest, and on earth peace. Luke 2:14

1. O heark-en ye who would be-lieve, The gra-cious tid-ings now re-ceive: Glo-ri-a, glo-ri-a, In ex-cel-sis De - o. The might-y Lord of heav'n and earth To - day is come to hu-man birth. Glo - ri-a, glo - ri-a, In ex-cel-sis De - o.

2. O heark-en ye who long for peace, Your trou-bled search-ing now may cease. Glo-ri-a, glo-ri-a, In ex-cel-sis De - o. For at this cra-dle you shall find God's heal-ing grace for all man-kind. Glo - ri-a, glo - ri-a, In ex-cel-sis De - o.

3. O heark-en ye who long for love And turn your hearts to God a-bove. Glo-ri-a, glo-ri-a, In ex-cel-sis De - o. The an-gel's song the won-der tells: Now Love In-car-nate with us dwells! Glo - ri-a, glo - ri-a, In ex-cel-sis De - o.

TEXT: Wihla Hutson
MUSIC: Alfred Burt

O HEARKEN YE
8.8.6.6.D.

275 Sing We Now of Christmas

The heavenly host appeared, saying, "Glory to God in the highest." Luke 2:13-14

1. Sing we now of Christ-mas, No - el sing we here! Lis - ten to our
2. Shep-herds on the hill - side heard the an-gels sing: Glo - ry, hon-or,
3. In the town they found Him; Son of Ma - ry mild. Sleep-ing in a
4. Wise Men sought and found Him, trea-sures did they bring; Bow-ing down they

prais - es to the Babe so dear.
prais - es to the in - fant King.
man - ger was the Ho - ly Child. Sing we No - el, the
wor - shiped Christ, the King of kings.

No- el, the

King is born, No - el! Sing we now of Christ-mas, sing we all No - el!

TEXT: Traditional French carol; Tom Fettke, stanzas 2, 3, 4   FRENCH CAROL
MUSIC: Traditional French melody; arranged by Tom Fettke   11.11.10.11.

Text for stanzas 2, 3, 4, and Arr. © Copyright 1997 by Integrity's Hosanna! Music and Word Music (a div. of WORD MUSIC). All rights reserved. Used by permission.

276 THE WORD BECAME FLESH

A Worship Sequence

Hark! the Herald Angels Sing; complete
Angels We Have Heard on High; stanzas 1,3,4
Suggested stanzas have been marked with an arrow: ➤

WORSHIP LEADER

The Word became flesh and lived for a while among us.
We have seen His glory, the glory of the One and Only,
who came from the Father, full of grace and truth.

from John 1:14 (NIV)

THE WORD BECAME FLESH - A Worship Sequence
Compilation © Copyright 1997 by Integrity's Hosanna! Music and Word Music (a div. of WORD MUSIC). All rights reserved. Used by permission.

Hark! the Herald Angels Sing 277

Glory to God in the highest, and on earth peace. Luke 2:14

1. Hark! the her - ald an - gels sing, "Glo - ry to the new - born King;
2. Christ, by high - est heav'n a - dored; Christ, the ev - er - last - ing Lord!
3. Hail, the heav'n - born Prince of Peace! Hail, the Sun of Righ - teous - ness!

Peace on earth, and mer - cy mild, God and sin - ners rec - on - ciled!"
Late in time be - hold Him come, Off - spring of the Vir - gin's womb:
Light and life to all He brings, Ris'n with heal - ing in His wings.

Joy - ful, all ye na - tions, rise, Join the tri - umph of the skies;
Veiled in flesh the God - head see; Hail th'in - car - nate De - i - ty,
Mild He lays His glo - ry by, Born that men no more may die,

With th'an - gel - ic host pro - claim, "Christ is born in Beth - le - hem!"
Pleased as man with men to dwell, Je - sus, our Em - man - u - el.
Born to raise the sons of earth, Born to give them sec - ond birth.

Refrain

Hark! the her - ald an - gels sing, "Glo - ry to the new - born King."

Optional segue to "Angels We Have Heard on High." No transition is needed.

TEXT: Charles Wesley, altered
MUSIC: Felix Mendelssohn; arranged by William H. Cummings

MENDELSSOHN
7.7.7.7.D. with Refrain

278 Angels We Have Heard on High

The heavenly host appeared with the angel, praising God. Luke 2:13

► 1. An - gels we have heard on high, Sweet - ly sing - ing o'er the plains
2. Shep - herds, why this ju - bi - lee? Why your joy - ous strains pro - long?
► 3. Come to Beth - le - hem, and see Him whose birth the an - gels sing;
► 4. See with - in a man - ger laid Je - sus, Lord of heav'n and earth!

And the moun - tains in re - ply, Ech - o back their joy - ous strains.
Say what may the tid - ings be Which in - spire your heav'n - ly song?
Come, a - dore on bend - ed knee Christ the Lord, the new - born King.
Mar - y, Jo - seph, lend your aid, With us sing our Sav - ior's birth.

Refrain

Glo - - - - ri - a in ex - cel - sis De - o,

Glo - - - - ri - a in ex - cel - sis De - o.

TEXT: Traditional French carol

MUSIC: Traditional French melody; Choral ending by Ken Barker

GLORIA

7.7.7.7. with Refrain

Optional choral ending

Glo-ry to God! Glo-ry to God! Glo-ry to God!

The end of THE WORD BECAME FLESH - A Worship Sequence

8vb - - - ┐

Infant Holy, Infant Lowly 279

He has this name written: KING OF KINGS AND LORD OF LORDS. Revelation 19:16

1. In - fant ho - ly, In - fant low - ly, For His bed– a cat - tle stall;
2. Flocks were sleep-ing; shep-herds keep-ing Vig - il till the morn-ing new

Ox - en low - ing, lit - tle know - ing Christ, the Babe, is Lord of all.
Saw the glo - ry, heard the sto - ry– Tid - ings of a gos - pel true.

Swift are wing-ing an - gels sing-ing, No - els ring - ing, tid-ings bring-ing:
Thus re - joic-ing, free from sor - row, Prais-es voic-ing greet the mor - row:

Christ, the Babe, is Lord of all! Christ, the Babe, is Lord of all!
Christ, the Babe, was born for you! Christ, the Babe, was born for you!

TEXT: Polish carol; paraphrase by Edith E. M. Reed
MUSIC: Traditional Polish melody

W ZLOBIE LEZY
8.7.8.7.8.8.7.

280 One Small Child

She gave birth to a male Child, who will rule all the nations. Revelation 12:5

1. One small Child in a land of a thou-sand, One small dream of a
2. One king bring-ing his gold and rich-es, One King rul-ing an
3. One small light from the flame of a can-dle, One small light from a
4. One small Child in a land of a thou-sand, One small dream in a

Sav-ior to-night, One small hand reach-ing out to the star-light,
ar-my of might, One king kneel-ing with in-cense and can-dle light,
cit-y of might, One small light from the stars in the end-less night,
peo-ple of might, One small hand reach-ing out to the star-light,

1, 4   Fine   2, 3

One small cit-y of life. O!
One King bring-ing us life. O!
One small light from a face. O!
One small Sav-ior of life. O!

After Fine - Optional segue to "What Child Is This?" No transition is needed.

2. See Him ly-ing, a cra-dle be-neath Him; See Him smil-ing in the stall.
3. See the shep-herds kneel-ing be-fore Him; See the kings on bend-ed knee.

TEXT: David Meece
MUSIC: David Meece

ONE SMALL CHILD
Irregular meter

D.S. al Fine

See His moth-er prais-ing His Fa-ther; See His ti-ny   eye-lids fall.
See His moth-er prais-ing His Fa-ther; See the Bless-ed   In-fant sleep.

What Child Is This? 281

They spread the word concerning what had been told them about this Child. Luke 2:17

1. What Child is this, who, laid to rest, On Mar-y's lap is sleep-ing?
2. Why lies He in such mean es-tate Where ox and ass are feed-ing?
3. So bring Him in-cense, gold, and myrrh; Come, peas-ant, king to own Him.

Whom an-gels greet with an-thems sweet, While shep-herds watch are keep-ing?
Good Chris-tian, fear, for sin-ners here The si-lent Word is plead-ing.
The King of kings sal-va-tion brings; Let lov-ing hearts en-throne Him.

Refrain

This, this is Christ, the King, Whom shep-herds guard and an-gels sing.

Haste, haste to bring Him laud, The Babe, the Son of Ma-ry.

TEXT: William C. Dix
MUSIC: Traditional English melody, 16th century

GREENSLEEVES
8.7.8.7. with Refrain

282 O Thou Joyful, O Thou Wonderful

Our Lord Jesus Christ, though He was rich, yet for your sakes He became poor. 2 Corinthians 8:9

1. O thou joy - ful, O thou won- der- ful Grace - re - veal - ing Christ- mas - tide! Je - sus came to win us From all sin with- in us; Glo - ri - fy the Ho - ly Child!
2. O thou joy - ful, O thou won- der- ful Love - re - veal - ing Christ- mas - tide! Loud ho- san- nas sing - ing And all prais - es bring - ing: May Thy love with us a - bide!
3. O thou joy - ful, O thou won- der- ful Peace - re - veal - ing Christ- mas - tide! Dark - ness dis - ap- pear - eth, God's own light now near - eth: Peace and joy to all be - tide!

TEXT: Johannes D. Falk, stanzas 1, 2; Source unknown, stanza 3; translated by Henry Katterjohn
MUSIC: Tattersall's *Psalmody*, 1794

O SANCTISSIMA
4.5.7.6.6.7.

283 NIGHT OF MIRACLES

A Worship Sequence

The Birthday of a King; complete
O Holy Night!; stanzas 1,3
Suggested stanzas have been marked with an arrow: ➤

WORSHIP LEADER

But you, Bethlehem, out of you will come for Me One who will be ruler over Israel. He will stand and shepherd His flock in the strength of the Lord, in the majesty of the name of the Lord His God. And they will live securely, for then His greatness will reach to the ends of the earth. And He will be their peace.

from Micah 5:2, 4-5 (NIV)

Optional introduction to "The Birthday of a King"

mp

The Birthday of a King 284

I will raise up to David a righteous Branch, a King who will reign wisely. Jeremiah 23:5

* Unison

1. In the lit-tle vil-lage of Beth-le-hem, there lay a Child one day, And the sky was bright with a ho-ly light o'er the place where Je-sus lay.

2. 'Twas a hum-ble birth-place, but O how much God gave to us that day; From the man-ger bed what a path has led, what a per-fect, ho-ly way.

Refrain *Harmony optional*

Al-le-lu-ia! O how the an-gels sang. Al-le-lu-ia! How it rang! And the sky was bright with a ho-ly light, 'Twas the birth-day of a King.

*Verses may be sung by a soloist.

Optional segue to "O Holy Night!"
No transition is needed.

TEXT: William Harold Neidlinger
MUSIC: William Harold Neidlinger; arranged by Robert F. Douglas

NEIDLINGER
10.6.10.7. with Refrain

285 O Holy Night!

The Holy One to be born will be called the Son of God. Luke 1:35

Introduction

1. O ho-ly night! the stars are bright-ly
2. Led by the light of faith se-rene-ly
3. Tru-ly He taught us to love one an-

shin - ing; It is the night of the dear Sav-ior's birth.
beam - ing, With glow-ing hearts by His cra - dle we stand.
oth - er; His law is love and His gos-pel is peace.

Long lay the world in sin and er-ror pin - ing, Till He ap-
So led by light of a star sweet-ly gleam - ing, Here came the
Chains shall He break, for the slave is our broth - er, And in His

peared and the soul felt its worth. A thrill of hope— the
Wise Men from O - ri - ent land. The King of kings lay
name all op-pres-sion shall cease. Sweet hymns of joy in

TEXT: John S. Dwight
MUSIC: Adolphe Adam

CANTIQUE DE NOEL
Irregular meter

wea - ry world re - joic - es, For yon - der breaks a new and glo - rious morn!
thus in low - ly man - ger, In all our tri - als born to be our Friend.
grate - ful cho - rus raise we; Let all with - in us praise His ho - ly name.

Fall on your knees! O hear the an - gel voic - es! O night
He knows our need— to our weak - ness is no strang - er. Be - hold
Christ is the Lord! O praise His name for - ev - er! His pow'r

di - vine, O night when Christ was born! O night, O
your King, be - fore Him low - ly bend! Be - hold your
and glo - ry ev - er - more pro - claim! His pow'r and

ho - ly night, O night di - vine!
King, be - fore Him low - ly bend!
glo - ry ev - er - more pro - claim!

Optional extended or choral ending

His pow'r and glo - ry ev - er - more pro - claim!

The end of NIGHT OF MIRACLES - A Worship Sequence

286 Once in Royal David's City

He will reign on David's throne and over his kingdom. Isaiah 9:7

1. Once in roy - al Da - vid's cit - y Stood a low - ly
2. He came down to earth from heav - en Who is God and
3. Je - sus is our child - hood's pat - tern; Day by day like
4. And our eyes at last shall see Him Thro' His own re -

cat - tle shed, Where a moth - er laid her Ba - by In a
Lord of all, And His shel - ter was a sta - ble, And His
us He grew. He was lit - tle, weak, and help - less; Tears and
deem - ing love; For that Child so dear and gen - tle Is our

man - ger for His bed. Ma - ry was that moth - er
cra - dle was a stall. With the poor, and mean, and
smiles like us He knew. And He feel - eth for our
Lord in heav'n a - bove. And He leads His chil - dren

mild, Je - sus Christ, her lit - tle Child.
low - ly Lived on earth, our Sav - ior ho - ly.
sad - ness, And He shar - eth in our glad - ness.
on To the place where He is gone.

TEXT: Cecil F. Alexander
MUSIC: Henry J. Gauntlett

IRBY
8.7.8.7.7.7.

A Communion Hymn for Christmas 287

Proclaim the Lord's death until He comes. 1 Corinthians 11:26

Unison

1. Gath - ered 'round Your ta - ble on this ho - ly eve,
2. Prince of Glo - ry, grac - ing Heav'n ere time be - gan,
3. Beth - l'hem's In - car - na - tion, Cal - v'ry's bit - ter cross,
4. With pro - found - est won - der we Your bod - y take-
5. Christ- mas Babe so ten - der, Lamb who bore our blame,

View - ing Beth - l'hem's sta - ble we re - joice and grieve.
Now for us em - brac - ing death as Son of Man.
Wrought for us sal - va - tion by Your pain and loss.
Laid in man - ger yon - der, bro - ken for our sake.
How shall sin - ners ren - der prais - es due Your name?

Joy to see You ly - ing in Your man - ger bed;
By Your birth so low - ly, by Your love so true,
Now we fall be - fore You in this ho - ly place;
Hushed in ad - o - ra - tion we ap - proach the cup;
Do Your own good plea - sure in the lives we bring;

Weep to see You dy - ing in our sin - ful stead.
By Your cross most ho - ly, Lord, we wor - ship You!
Pros - trate we a - dore You for Your gift of grace.
Beth - l'hem's pure ob - la - tion free - ly of - fered up.
In Your ran - somed trea - sure reign for - ev - er King!

TEXT: Margaret Clarkson
MUSIC: Tom Fettke

GREENRIDGE
11.11.11.11.

288 We Three Kings

After Jesus was born in Bethlehem, Magi from the east came. Matthew 2:1

1. We three kings of O - ri - ent are; Bear - ing gifts we tra - verse a - far—
2. Born a King on Beth - le - hem's plain; Gold I bring to crown Him a - gain,
3. Frank - in - cense to of - fer have I; In - cense owns a De - i - ty nigh.
4. Myrrh is mine: its bit - ter per - fume Breathes a life of gath - er - ing gloom—
5. Glo - rious now be - hold Him a - rise, King and God and Sac - ri - fice;

Field and foun - tain, moor and moun - tain— Fol - low - ing yon - der star.
King for - ev - er, ceas - ing nev - er O - ver us all to reign.
Prayer and prais - ing, all men rais - ing, Wor - ship Him, God on high.
Sor - r'wing, sigh - ing, bleed - ing, dy - ing, Sealed in the stone - cold tomb.
Al - le - lu - ia, al - le - lu - ia! Earth to heav'n re - plies.

Refrain

O star of won - der, star of night, Star with roy - al beau - ty bright,

West - ward lead - ing, still pro - ceed - ing, Guide us to thy per - fect light.

TEXT: John H. Hopkins, Jr.
MUSIC: John H. Hopkins, Jr.

KINGS OF ORIENT
8.8.4.4.6. with Refrain

Optional extended ending and transition to "Adoration"

Guide us to thy per - fect light.

rit.

Segue to "Adoration" ♪ = ♩

Adoration 289

Worship the Lord in the splendor of His holiness. Psalm 96:9

1. Wor - ship the Lord in the beau - ty of ho - li - ness!
2. Fear not to en - ter His pres - ence in pov - er - ty,

Bow down be - fore Him, His glo - ry pro - claim.
Bear - ing no gifts to pre - sent as your own.

With gold of o - be - dience and in - cense of low - li - ness,
Bring truth in its beau - ty and love in its pu - ri - ty–

Kneel and a - dore Him– the Lord is His name!
These are the of - f'rings to lay at His throne.

TEXT: John S. B. Monsell, stanza 1; Ken Bible, stanza 2
MUSIC: Tom Fettke

JANICE
12.10.13.10.

290 As with Gladness Men of Old

When they saw the star, they were overjoyed. Matthew 2:10

1. As with glad - ness men of old Did the guid - ing star be - hold; As with joy they hailed its light, Lead - ing on - ward, beam - ing bright; So, most gra - cious Lord, may we Ev - er - more be led to Thee.

2. As with joy - ful steps they sped To that low - ly man - ger bed; There to bend the knee be - fore Him whom heav'n and earth a - dore; So, may we with will - ing feet Ev - er seek the mer - cy seat.

3. As they of - fered gifts most rare At that man - ger rude and bare, So may we with ho - ly joy, Pure and free from sin's al - loy, All our cost - liest trea - sures bring, Christ, to Thee our heav'n - ly King.

4. Ho - ly Je - sus, ev - ery day Keep us in the nar - row way; And, when earth - ly things are past, Bring our ran - somed souls at last Where they need no star to guide, Where no clouds Thy glo - ry hide.

TEXT: William C. Dix
MUSIC: Conrad Kocher

DIX
7.7.7.7.7.7.

O Sing a Song of Bethlehem 291

He appeared in a body, was believed on in the world, was taken up in glory. 1 Timothy 3:16

1. O sing a song of Beth - le - hem, Of shep-herds watch-ing there,
2. O sing of song of Naz - a - reth, Of sun - ny days of joy.
3. O sing a song of Gal - i - lee, Of lake and woods and hill,
4. O sing a song of Cal - va - ry, Its glo - ry and dis - may;

And of the news that came to them From an - gels in the air:
O sing of fra - grant flow-ers' breath And of the sin - less Boy:
Of Him who walked up - on the sea And bade the waves be still:
Of Him who hung up - on the tree, And took our sins a - way:

The light that shone on Beth - le - hem Fills all the world to - day;
For now the flow-ers on Naz - a - reth In ev - ery heart may grow;
For tho' like waves on Gal - i - lee, Dark seas of trou - ble roll,
For He who died on Cal - va - ry Is ris - en from the grave,

Of Je - sus' birth and peace on earth The an - gels sing al - way.
Now spreads the fame of His dear name On all the winds that blow.
When faith has heard the Mas - ter's word, Falls peace up - on the soul.
And Christ, our Lord, by heav'n a - dored, Is might - y now to save.

TEXT: Louis F. Benson
MUSIC: English melody; arranged by Ralph Vaughan Williams

KINGSFOLD
C.M.D.

292 Thou Didst Leave Thy Throne

He came to that which was His own, but His own did not receive Him. John 1:11

1. Thou didst leave Thy throne and Thy king - ly crown When Thou cam - est to earth for me; But in Beth - le - hem's home was there found no room For Thy ho - ly na - tiv - i - ty.

2. Heav-en's arch - es rang when the an - gels sang, Pro - claim - ing Thy roy - al de - gree; But of low - ly birth didst Thou come to earth, And in great hu - mil - i - ty.

3. The fox - es found rest and the birds their nest In the shade of the for - est tree; But Thy couch was the sod, O Thou Son of God, In the des - erts of Gal - i - lee.

4. Thou cam - est, O Lord, with the liv - ing word That should set Thy peo - ple free; But with mock - ing scorn and with crown of thorn They bore Thee to Cal - va - ry.

5. When the heav'ns shall ring and the an - gels sing At Thy com - ing to vic - to - ry, Let Thy voice call me home, say - ing, "Yet there is room— There is room at My side for thee." My

Refrain

O come to my heart, Lord Je - sus— There is room in my heart for Thee!
O come to my heart, Lord Je - sus— There is room in my heart for Thee!
O come to my heart, Lord Je - sus— There is room in my heart for Thee!
O come to my heart, Lord Je - sus— There is room in my heart for Thee!
My heart shall re - joice, Lord Je - sus, When Thou com - est and call - est for me!

TEXT: Emily E. S. Elliott
MUSIC: Timothy R. Matthews

MARGARET
Irregular meter

Praise the One Who Breaks the Darkness 293

The people living in darkness have seen a great light. Matthew 4:16

1. Praise the One who breaks the dark - ness With a lib - er - at - ing light;
2. Praise the One who blessed the chil - dren With a strong yet gen - tle word;
3. Praise the one true love in - car - nate: Christ, who suf - fered in our place;

Praise the One who frees the pris - 'ners, Turn - ing blind-ness in - to sight.
Praise the One who drove out de - mons With a pierc - ing two-edged sword.
Je - sus died and rose for man - y That we may know God by grace.

Praise the One who preached the gos - pel, Heal - ing ev - ery dread dis - ease,
Praise the One who brings cool wa - ter To the des - ert's burn - ing sand;
Let us sing for joy and glad - ness, See - ing what our God has done.

Calm - ing storms and feed - ing thou-sands With the ver - y bread of peace.
From this well comes liv - ing wa - ter Quench-ing thirst in ev - ery land.
Praise the one re - deem - ing glo - ry; Praise the One who makes us one.

TEXT: Rusty Edwards
MUSIC: Traditional American melody; John Wyeth's *Repository of Sacred Music*, 1813

NETTLETON
8.7.8.7.D

294 One Day

At just the right time, when we were still powerless, Christ died for the ungodly. Romans 5:6

1. One day when heav - en was filled with His prais - es, One day when
2. One day they led Him up Cal - va - ry's moun - tain, One day they
3. One day they left Him a - lone in the gar - den, One day He
4. One day the grave could con - ceal Him no long - er, One day the
5. One day the trum - pet will sound for His com - ing, One day the

sin was as black as can be, Je - sus came forth to be born of a
nailed Him to die on the tree; Suf - fer - ing an - guish, de - spised and re -
rest - ed, from suf - fer - ing free; An - gels came down o'er His tomb to keep
stone rolled a - way from the door; Then He a - rose— o - ver death He had
skies with His glo - ries will shine; Won - der - ful day, my be - lov - ed ones

vir - gin, Dwelt a - mong men— my ex - am - ple is He!
ject - ed, Bear - ing our sins— my Re - deem - er is He!
vig - il; Hope of the hope - less— my Sav - ior is He!
con - quered, Now is as - cend - ed, my Lord ev - er - more!
bring - ing; Glo - ri - ous Sav - ior— this Je - sus is mine!

Refrain

Liv - ing, He loved me; Dy - ing, He saved me; Bur - ied, He

TEXT: J. Wilbur Chapman
MUSIC: Charles H. Marsh

ONE DAY
11.10.11.10 with Refrain

car - ried my sins far a - way; Ris - ing, He jus - ti - fied free - ly for -

ev - er; One day He's com - ing— O glo - ri - ous day!

Optional repeat refrain setting

Liv - ing, He loved me; Dy - ing, He saved me;

Bur - ied, He car - ried my sins far a - way; Ris - ing, He jus - ti - fied

free - ly for - ev - er; One day He's com - ing— O glo - ri - ous day!

Optional choral ending

rit. *ff*

One day He's com - ing— O glo - ri - ous day! Glo - ri - ous day!

ff

*Congregation may sing up to this point.

295 Tell Me the Story of Jesus

Philip began with that very passage of Scripture and told him the good news about Jesus. Acts 8:35

1. Tell me the sto - ry of Je - sus; Write on my heart ev - ery word.
2. Fast - ing a - lone in the des - ert, Tell of the days that are past,
3. Tell of the cross where they nailed Him, Writh-ing in an - guish and pain;

Refrain: Tell me the sto - ry of Je - sus; Write on my heart ev - ery word.

Fine

Tell me the sto - ry most pre - cious, Sweet - est that ev - er was heard.
How for our sins He was tempt - ed, Yet was tri - um - phant at last.
Tell of the grave where they laid Him. Tell how He liv - eth a - gain.
Tell me the sto - ry most pre - cious, Sweet - est that ev - er was heard.

Tell how the an - gels in cho - rus Sang as they wel - comed His birth:
Tell of the years of His la - bor; Tell of the sor - row He bore.
Love in that sto - ry so ten - der, Clear - er than ev - er I see.

D.C. for Refrain

"Glo - ry to God in the high - est! Peace and good tid - ings to earth."
He was de - spised and af - flict - ed, Home - less, re - ject - ed and poor.
Stay, let me weep while you whis - per, Love paid the ran - som for me.

TEXT: Fanny J. Crosby
MUSIC: John R. Sweney

STORY OF JESUS
8.7.8.7.D. with Refrain

Hosanna 296

Hosanna to the Son of David! Hosanna in the highest! Matthew 21:9

1. Ho - san - na, Ho - san - na, Ho - san - na in the high - est! Ho - san - na, Ho - san - na, Ho - san - na in the high - est! Lord, we lift up Your name, With hearts full of praise; Be ex - alt - ed, O Lord my God! Ho - san - na in the high - est!

2. Glo - ry, glo - ry, glo - ry to the King of kings! Glo - ry, glo - ry, glo - ry to the King of kings! Glo - ry to the King of kings!

TEXT: Carl Tuttle
MUSIC: Carl Tuttle

HOSANNA
Irregular meter

297 Hosanna, Loud Hosanna

Hosanna to the Son of David! Hosanna in the highest! Matthew 21:9

1. "Ho - san - na, loud ho - san - na," The lit - tle chil - dren sang;
2. From Ol - i - vet they fol - lowed 'Mid an ex - ul - tant crowd,
3. "Ho - san - na in the high - est!" That an - cient song we sing,

Thro' pil - lared court and tem - ple The love - ly an - them rang;
The vic - tor palm branch wav - ing And chant - ing clear and loud;
For Christ is our Re - deem - er, The Lord of heav'n, our King;

To Je - sus, who had blessed them Close fold - ed to His breast,
The Lord of earth and heav - en Rode on in low - ly state,
O may we ev - er praise Him With heart and life and voice,

The chil - dren sang their prais - es, The sim - plest and the best.
Nor scorned that lit - tle chil - dren Should on His bid - ding wait.
And in His bliss - ful pres - ence E - ter - nal - ly re - joice!

TEXT: Jenette Threlfall; based on Matthew 21:15,16
MUSIC: From *Gesangbuch der Herzogl, Würtemburg*, 1784
A higher setting may be found at No. 128

ELLACOMBE
7.6.7.6.D.

HOSANNA TO THE SON OF DAVID 298

A Worship Sequence

In the Name of the Lord
All Glory, Laud and Honor, complete
We Will Glorify
Suggested stanzas have been marked with an arrow: ➤

WORSHIP LEADER
As the time approached for Him to be taken up to heaven, Jesus resolutely set out for Jerusalem.
As He went along, people spread their cloaks on the road,
while others cut branches from the trees and spread them on the road.
When He came near the place where the road goes down the Mount of Olives, the whole crowd
of disciples began joyfully to praise God in loud voices for all the miracles they had seen:

EVERYONE
"Blessed is the King who comes in the name of the Lord!"

WORSHIP LEADER
The crowds that went ahead of Him and those that followed shouted:

EVERYONE
"Hosanna to the Son of David!"
"Blessed is He who comes in the name of the Lord!"
"Hosanna in the highest!"
from Luke 9:51; 19:36; Matthew 21:8; Luke 19:37-38; Matthew 21:9 (NIV)

In the Name of the Lord 299

The name of the Lord is a strong tower. Proverbs 18:10

There is strength in the name of the Lord. There is pow'r in the
name of the Lord. There is hope in the name of the Lord.
Bless-ed is He who comes in the name of the Lord! Lord!

If song follows reading, use the first two beats of measure 1 as the introduction.

TEXT: Sandi Patty, Phill McHugh, Gloria Gaither
MUSIC: Sandi Patty, Phill McHugh, Gloria Gaither

NAME OF THE LORD
Irregular meter

Optional transition to "All Glory, Laud and Honor"

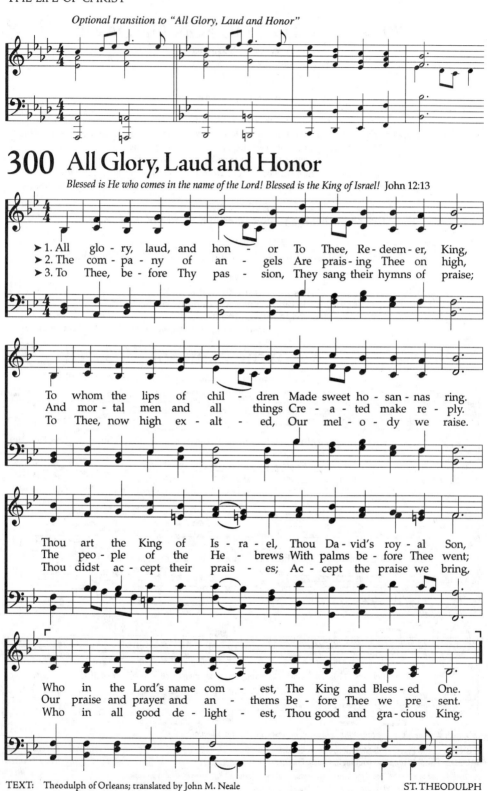

300 All Glory, Laud and Honor

Blessed is He who comes in the name of the Lord! Blessed is the King of Israel! John 12:13

1. All glo-ry, laud, and hon-or To Thee, Re-deem-er, King,
2. The com-pa-ny of an-gels Are prais-ing Thee on high,
3. To Thee, be-fore Thy pas-sion, They sang their hymns of praise:

To whom the lips of chil-dren Made sweet ho-san-nas ring.
And mor-tal men and all things Cre-a-ted make re-ply.
To Thee, now high ex-alt-ed, Our mel-o-dy we raise.

Thou art the King of Is-ra-el, Thou Da-vid's roy-al Son,
The peo-ple of the He-brews With palms be-fore Thee went;
Thou didst ac-cept their prais-es; Ac-cept the praise we bring,

Who in the Lord's name com-est, The King and Bless-ed One.
Our praise and prayer and an-thems Be-fore Thee we pre-sent.
Who in all good de-light-est, Thou good and gra-cious King.

TEXT: Theodulph of Orleans; translated by John M. Neale
MUSIC: Melchior Teschner

ST. THEODULPH
7.6.7.6.D.

Optional transition to "We Will Glorify"

f slower

We Will Glorify - *Palm Sunday Setting* **301**

To Him who sits on the throne and to the Lamb be praise and honor and glory. Revelation 5:13

We will glo-ri-fy the King of kings; We will glo-ri-fy the Lamb. We will

rit.

glo-ri-fy the Lord of lords, Who is the great I Am. Hal-le-

Broader

lu-jah to the King of kings; Hal-le-lu-jah to the Lamb. Hal-le-lu-jah to the

| 1 | 2 | *Optional choral ending* |

Lord of lords, Who is the great I Am. Hal-le- Am. Ho-san-na to the King.

TEXT: Twila Paris
MUSIC: Twila Paris; arranged by David Allen

WE WILL GLORIFY
9.7.9.6.

The end of HOSANNA TO THE SON OF DAVID - A Worship Sequence

302 Lamb of God

Look, the Lamb of God, who takes away the sin of the world! John 1:29

Unison

1. Your on-ly Son, no sin to hide, But You have sent Him from Your
2. Your gift of love they cru-ci-fied, They laughed and scorned Him as He
3. I was so lost I should have died, But You have brought me to Your

side To walk up-on this guilt-y sod, And to be-come the Lamb of God.
died; The hum-ble King they named a fraud, And sac-ri-ficed the Lamb of God.
side To be led by Your staff and rod, And to be called a lamb of God.

Refrain

O Lamb of God, sweet Lamb of God; I love the

ho-ly Lamb of God. O wash me in His pre-cious

last time rit.

blood.
1,2. My Je-sus Christ, the Lamb of God.
3. Till I am just a lamb of God.

TEXT: Twila Paris
MUSIC: Twila Paris

LAMB OF GOD
L.M.D.

Worthy Is the Lamb 303

Worthy is the Lamb, who was slain, to receive honor and glory and praise! Revelation 5:12

Wor-thy is the Lamb that was slain; Wor-thy is the Lamb that was slain. Wor-thy is the Lamb that was slain, to re-ceive Pow-er and rich-es and wis-dom and strength, Hon-or and glo-ry and bless-ing! Wor-thy is the Lamb, Wor-thy is the Lamb, Wor-thy is the Lamb that was slain. Wor-thy is the Lamb!

TEXT: Revelation 5:12; adapted by Don Wyrtzen
MUSIC: Don Wyrtzen

WORTHY IS THE LAMB
Irregular meter

304 Behold the Lamb

The Lamb was slain from the creation of the world. Revelation 13:8

mf Introduction

Be - hold the Lamb, be - hold the Lamb, Slain from the foun-

da - tion of the world. For sin - ners cru - ci - fied, O ho - ly

sac - ri - fice, Be - hold the Lamb of God, be - hold the Lamb.

play cued notes first time only

More movement

Crown Him, crown Him, Wor - thy is the Lamb.

TEXT: Dottie Rambo
MUSIC: Dottie Rambo

BEHOLD THE LAMB
Irregular meter

D.S. al Fine

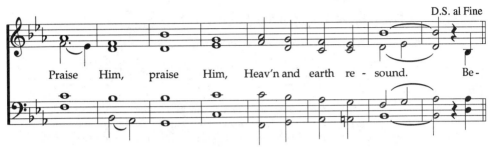

Praise Him, praise Him, Heav'n and earth re - sound. Be-

Jesus Paid It All 305

You are not your own; you were bought at a price. Therefore honor God. 1 Corinthians 6:19-20

1. I hear the Sav - ior say: "Thy strength in - deed is small.
2. Lord, now in - deed I find Thy pow'r, and Thine a - lone
3. For noth - ing good have I Where - by Thy grace to claim;
4. And when be - fore the throne I stand in Him com - plete,

Child of weak - ness, watch and pray; Find in Me thine all in all."
Can change the lep - er's spots And melt the heart of stone.
I'll wash my gar - ments white In the blood of Cal - v'ry's Lamb.
"Je - sus died my soul to save," My lips shall still re - peat.

Refrain

Je - sus paid it all; All to Him I owe.

Sin had left a crim - son stain; He washed it white as snow.

TEXT: Elvina M. Hall
MUSIC: John T. Grape

ALL TO CHRIST
6.6.7.7. with Refrain

306 Alas! and Did My Savior Bleed?

The message of the cross is the power of God. 1 Corinthians 1:18

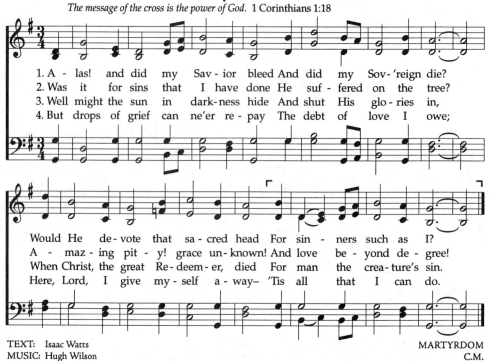

1. A - las! and did my Sav - ior bleed And did my Sov - 'reign die?
2. Was it for sins that I have done He suf - fered on the tree?
3. Well might the sun in dark - ness hide And shut His glo - ries in,
4. But drops of grief can ne'er re - pay The debt of love I owe;

Would He de - vote that sa - cred head For sin - ners such as I?
A - maz - ing pit - y! grace un - known! And love be - yond de - gree!
When Christ, the great Re - deem - er, died For man the crea - ture's sin.
Here, Lord, I give my - self a - way– 'Tis all that I can do.

TEXT: Isaac Watts
MUSIC: Hugh Wilson

MARTYRDOM
C.M.

307 MY REDEEMER

A Worship Sequence

There Is a Redeemer; stanzas 1,2
I Will Sing of My Redeemer; stanzas 1,3,4
Suggested stanzas have been marked with an arrow: ➤

WORSHIP LEADER

You were not redeemed with perishable things like silver or gold,
but with precious blood, as of a lamb unblemished and spotless,
the blood of Christ.
He took up our infirmities and carried our sorrows.
He was pierced for our transgressions, He was crushed for our iniquities;
The punishment that brought us peace was upon Him,
and by His wounds we are healed.

from 1 Peter 1:18-19 (NASB); Isaiah 53:4-5 (NIV)

Optional introduction to "There Is a Redeemer"

mp

MY REDEEMER - A Worship Sequence

There Is a Redeemer 308

Christ Jesus has become our righteousness, holiness and redemption. 1 Corinthians 1:30

1. There is a Re-deem-er— Je-sus, God's own Son;
2. Je-sus, my Re-deem-er, name a-bove all names;
3. When I stand in Glo-ry, I will see His face;

Pre-cious Lamb of God, Mes-si-ah, Ho-ly One.
Pre-cious Lamb of God, Mes-si-ah, Hope for sin-ners slain.
There I'll serve my King for-ev-er in that ho-ly place.

Refrain

Thank You, O my Fa-ther, for giv-ing us Your Son, And

leav-ing Your Spir-it till the work on earth is done.

TEXT: Melody Green
MUSIC: Melody Green

GREEN
Irregular meter

Optional transition to "I Will Sing of My Redeemer"

faster *mf*

309 I Will Sing of My Redeemer

In Him we have redemption through His blood, the forgiveness of sins. Ephesians 1:7

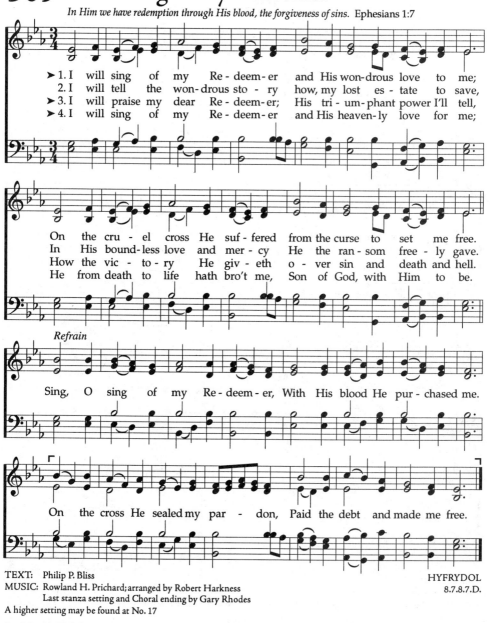

1. I will sing of my Re-deem-er and His won-drous love to me;
2. I will tell the won-drous sto-ry how, my lost es-tate to save,
3. I will praise my dear Re-deem-er; His tri-um-phant power I'll tell,
4. I will sing of my Re-deem-er and His heaven-ly love for me;

On the cru-el cross He suf-fered from the curse to set me free.
In His bound-less love and mer-cy He the ran-som free-ly gave.
How the vic-to-ry He giv-eth o-ver sin and death and hell.
He from death to life hath bro't me, Son of God, with Him to be.

Refrain

Sing, O sing of my Re-deem-er, With His blood He pur-chased me.

On the cross He sealed my par - don, Paid the debt and made me free.

TEXT: Philip P. Bliss
MUSIC: Rowland H. Prichard; arranged by Robert Harkness
    Last stanza setting and Choral ending by Gary Rhodes
A higher setting may be found at No. 17

HYFRYDOL
8.7.8.7.D.

Optional last stanza setting   ***ff*** *Unison (melody octave lower)*

4. I will sing of my Re-deem-er

Melody as written

Optional choral ending　　　Broadening

The end of MY REDEEMER - A Worship Sequence

310 Lead Me to Calvary

I resolved to know nothing except Jesus Christ and Him crucified. 1 Corinthians 2:2

1. King of my life I crown Thee now, Thine shall the glo - ry be;
2. Show me the tomb where Thou wast laid, Ten - der - ly mourned and wept;
3. Let me, like Mar - y, through the gloom, Come with a gift to Thee;
4. May I be will - ing, Lord, to bear Dai - ly my cross for Thee;

Lest I for - get Thy thorn - crowned brow, Lead me to Cal - va - ry.
An - gels in robes of light ar - rayed Guard - ed Thee whilst Thou slept.
Show to me now the emp - ty tomb, Lead me to Cal - va - ry.
E - ven Thy cup of grief to share, Thou hast borne all for me.

Refrain

Lest I for - get Geth - sem - a - ne; Lest I for - get Thine ag - o - ny;

Lest I for - get Thy love for me, Lead me to Cal - va - ry.

TEXT: Jennie Evelyn Hussey
MUSIC: William J. Kirkpatrick; Choral ending by Tom Fettke

DUNCANNON
C.M. with Refrain

Optional choral ending

King of my life I crown Thee now; Thine shall the glo - ry be.

Hallelujah, What a Savior! 311

We know that this Man really is the Savior of the world. John 4:42

1. "Man of Sor-rows!" what a name   For the Son of God, who came
2. Bear-ing shame and scoff-ing rude,   In my place con-demned He stood–
3. Guilt-y, vile and help-less we,   Spot-less Lamb of God was He;
4. Lift-ed up was He to die,   "It is fin-ished," was His cry;
5. When He comes, our glo-rious King,   All His ran-somed home to bring,

Ru-ined sin-ners to re-claim! Hal-le-lu-jah, what a Sav-ior!
Sealed my par-don with His blood: Hal-le-lu-jah, what a Sav-ior!
Full a-tone-ment! can it be? Hal-le-lu-jah, what a Sav-ior!
Now in heav'n ex-alt-ed high: Hal-le-lu-jah, what a Sav-ior!
Then a-new this song we'll sing: Hal-le-lu-jah, what a Sav-ior!

TEXT: Philip P. Bliss
MUSIC: Philip P. Bliss

MAN OF SORROWS
7.7.7.8.

Optional last stanza setting

Broader

rit.

5. When He comes, our glo-rious King,   All His ran-somed

home to bring, Then a-new this song we'll sing: Hal-le-lu-jah, what a Sav-ior!

rit.

312 Calvary Covers It All

He forgave us all our sins. Colossians 2:13

1. Far dear-er than all that the world can im-part Was the mes-sage that
2. The stripes that He bore and the thorns that He wore Told His mer-cy and
3. How match-less the grace, when I looked on the face Of this Je-sus, my
4. How bless-ed the tho't, that my soul, by Him bo't, Shall be His in the

came to my heart; How that Je-sus a-lone for my sin did a-tone,
love ev-er-more; And my heart bowed in shame as I called on His name,
cru-ci-fied Lord; My re-demp-tion com-plete I then found at His feet,
glo-ry on high; Where with glad-ness and song I'll be one of the throng,

Refrain

And Cal-va-ry cov-ers it all. Cal-va-ry cov-ers it all,

My past with its sin and stain; My guilt and de-spair Je-sus

took on Him there, And Cal-va-ry cov-ers it all.

TEXT: Mrs. Walter G. Taylor
MUSIC: Mrs. Walter G. Taylor

CALVARY COVERS IT
Irregular meter

Optional last refrain setting

Cal - va - ry cov - ers it all, My past with its sin and stain; My

guilt and de - spair Je - sus took on Him there, And Cal - va - ry cov - ers it all.

*Optional segue to "Worthy
the Lamb That Was Slain."
No transition is needed.*

Worthy the Lamb That Was Slain 313

Worthy is the Lamb, who was slain, to receive power, wisdom, honor and glory. Revelation 5:12

Unison

Wor - thy the Lamb that was slain. Wor - thy the

Lamb that was slain To re - ceive glo - ry and hon - or,

Wis - dom and pow - er. Wor - thy the Lamb that was slain.

TEXT: Don Moen
MUSIC: Don Moen

WORTHY THE LAMB
Irregular meter

314 What Wondrous Love Is This

Praise be to the Lord, for He showed His wonderful love to me. Psalm 31:21

Unison

1. What won-drous love is this, O my soul, O my soul! What
2. When I was sink-ing down, sink-ing down, sink-ing down, When
3. To God and to the Lamb I will sing, I will sing; To
4. And when from death I'm free, I'll sing on, I'll sing on; And

won-drous love is this, O my soul! What won-drous love is
I was sink-ing down, sink-ing down, When I was sink-ing
God and to the Lamb I will sing. To God and to the
when from death I'm free, I'll sing on. And when from death I'm

this That caused the Lord of bliss To bear the dread-ful curse for my
down Be - neath God's righ-teous frown, Christ laid a - side His crown for my
Lamb Who is the great "I AM," While mil-lions join the theme, I will
free, I'll sing and joy - ful be, And thro' e - ter - ni - ty, I'll sing

soul, for my soul, To bear the dread-ful curse for my soul.
soul, for my soul, Christ laid a - side His crown for my soul.
sing, I will sing, While mil-lions join the theme, I will sing.
on, I'll sing on, And thro' e - ter - ni - ty, I'll sing on.

TEXT: American Folk Hymn
MUSIC: William Walker's *Southern Harmony*, 1835

WONDROUS LOVE
12.9.6.6.12.9.

Were You There? 315

It was the third hour when they crucified Him. Mark 15:25

1. Were you there when they cru-ci-fied my Lord? Were you
2. Were you there when they nailed Him to the tree? Were you
3. Were you there when they laid Him in the tomb? Were you
* 4. Were you there when He rose up from the dead? Were you

there when they cru-ci-fied my Lord? O!
there when they nailed Him to the tree? O!
there when they laid Him in the tomb? O!
there when He rose up from the dead? O!

Some-times it caus-es me to trem-ble, trem-ble, trem-ble!
Some-times it caus-es me to trem-ble, trem-ble, trem-ble!
Some-times it caus-es me to trem-ble, trem-ble, trem-ble!
Some-times I feel like shout-ing glo-ry, glo-ry, glo-ry!

Were you there when they cru-ci-fied my Lord?
Were you there when they nailed Him to the tree?
Were you there when they laid Him in the tomb?
Were you there when He rose up from the dead?

*May be omitted; especially for Holy Week services.

TEXT: Traditional Spiritual
MUSIC: Traditional Spiritual

WERE YOU THERE?
Irregular meter

316 O Sacred Head, Now Wounded

They twisted together a crown of thorns and set it on Him. Mark 15:17

1. O sa-cred Head, now wound-ed With grief and shame weighed down;
2. What Thou, my Lord, hast suf-fered Was all for sin-ners' gain;
3. What lan-guage shall I bor-row To thank Thee, dear-est Friend,

Now scorn-ful-ly sur-round-ed With thorns, Thine on-ly crown.
Mine, mine was the trans-gres-sion, But Thine the dead-ly pain.
For this, Thy dy-ing sor-row, Thy pit-y with-out end?

How pale Thou art with an-guish, With sore a-buse and scorn;
Lo, here I fall, my Sav-ior; 'Tis I de-serve Thy place.
O make me Thine for-ev-er; And, should I faint-ing be,

How does that vis-age lan-quish, Which once was bright as morn!
Look on me with Thy fa-vor; As-sist me with Thy grace.
Lord, let me nev-er, nev-er Out-live my love to Thee.

TEXT: Paul Gerhardt; based on Medieval Latin poem ascribed to Bernard
of Clairvaux; translated from the German by James W. Alexander
MUSIC: Hans Leo Hassler; harmonized by J. S. Bach

PASSION CHORALE
7.6.7.6.D.

O Mighty Cross 317

The message of the cross is the power of God. 1 Corinthians 1:18

1. O might-y cross, Love lift-ed high,
2. O might-y cross, what throne of grace,
3. O might-y cross, O Christ, so pure,
4. O might-y cross, my soul's re-lease;

The Lord of life raised there to die;
He knew no sin, yet took my place;
Love held Him there, such shame en-dured;
The stripes He bore have brought me peace;

His sac-ri-fice on Cal-va-ry

Has made the might-y cross a tree of life to me.

TEXT: David Baroni and John Chisum
MUSIC: David Baroni and John Chisum; arranged by Tom Fettke

O MIGHTY CROSS
8.8.8.12.

Optional extended or choral ending   rit.

Has made the might-y cross a tree of life to me.

318 I Believe in a Hill Called Mount Calvary

Those who would come after Me must take up their cross daily and follow Me. Luke 9:23

1. There are things as we trav-el this earth's shift-ing sands That tran-
2. I be-lieve that the Christ who was slain on that cross Has the
3. I be-lieve that this life with its great mys-ter-ies Sure-ly

scend all the rea-son of man; But the things that mat-ter the
pow-er to change lives to-day; For He changed me com-plete-ly, a
some-day will come to an end; But faith will con-quer the

most in this world, They can nev-er be held in our hand.
new life is mine, That is why by the cross I will stay.
dark-ness and death And will lead me at last to my friend.

Refrain

I be-lieve in a hill called Mount Cal-v'ry— I'll be-lieve what-

ev-er the cost; And when time has sur-ren-dered and

TEXT: Dale Oldham, Gloria Gaither and William J. Gaither
MUSIC: William J. Gaither

MOUNT CALVARY
Irregular meter

earth is no more, I'll still cling to that old rug-ged cross.

Near the Cross 319

May I never boast except in the cross of our Lord Jesus Christ. Galatians 6:14

1. Je - sus, keep me near the cross— There a pre - cious foun - tain,
2. Near the cross, a trem - bling soul, Love and mer - cy found me;
3. Near the cross! O Lamb of God, Bring its scenes be - fore me;
4. Near the cross I'll watch and wait, Hop - ing, trust - ing ev - er,

Free to all, a heal - ing stream, Flows from Cal - v'ry's moun - tain.
There the Bright and Morn - ing Star Sheds its beams a - round me.
Help me walk from day to day With its shad - ows o'er me.
Till I reach the gold - en strand, Just be - yond the riv - er.

Refrain

In the cross, in the cross Be my glo - ry ev - er,

Till my rap - tured soul shall find Rest be - yond the riv - er.

TEXT: Fanny J. Crosby
MUSIC: William H. Doane

NEAR THE CROSS
7.6.7.6. with Refrain

320 Beneath the Cross of Jesus

Near the cross of Jesus stood His mother. John 19:25

1. Be - neath the cross of Je - sus I fain would take my stand;
2. There lies be - neath its shad - ow, But on the far - ther side,
3. Up - on the cross of Je - sus Mine eyes at times can see
4. I take, O cross, thy shad - ow For my a - bid - ing place;

The sha - dow of a might - y rock With - in a wea - ry land,
The dark - ness of an aw - ful grave That gapes both deep and wide,
The ver - y dy - ing form of One Who suf - fered there for me.
I ask no oth - er sun - shine than The sun - shine of His face;

A home with - in the wil - der - ness, A rest up - on the way
And there be - tween us stands the cross, Two arms out - stretched to save,
And from my smit - ten heart, with tears, These won - ders I con - fess:
Con - tent to let the world go by, To know no gain nor loss,

From the burn - ing of the noon - tide heat And the bur - den of the day.
Like a watch - man set to guard the way From that e - ter - nal grave.
The won - der of His glo - rious love, And my un - wor - thi - ness.
My sin - ful self— my on - ly shame, My glo - ry— all the cross.

TEXT: Elizabeth C. Clephane
MUSIC: Frederick C. Maker

ST. CHRISTOPHER
7.6.8.6.8.6.8.6.

When I Survey the Wondrous Cross 321

May I never boast except in the cross of our Lord Jesus Christ. Galatians 6:14

Unison

1. When I sur - vey the won - drous cross
2. For - bid it, Lord, that I should boast,
3. See, from His head, His hands, His feet,
4. Were the whole realm of na - ture mine,

On which the Prince of Glo - ry died,
Save in the death of Christ, my God;
Sor - row and love flow min - gled down;
That were a pres - ent far too small:

My rich - est gain I count but loss,
All the vain things that charm me most—
Did e'er such love and sor - row meet,
Love so a - maz - ing, so di - vine,

rit. last stanza

And pour con - tempt on all my pride.
I sac - ri - fice them to His blood.
Or thorns com - pose so rich a crown?
De - mands my soul, my life, my all.

TEXT: Isaac Watts
MUSIC: Appalachian Folk melody; arranged by Michael James

O WALY WALY
8.8.9.8.

322 THE CROSS - TREE OF LIFE

A Worship Sequence

At the Cross; stanzas 1,2
When I Survey the Wondrous Cross; complete
Suggested stanzas have been marked with an arrow: ➤

WORSHIP LEADER

God forbid that I should boast except in the cross of our Lord Jesus Christ,
by whom the world has been crucified to me, and I to the world.
It is no longer I who live, but Christ lives in me; and the life which I now live
in the flesh I live by faith in the Son of God,
who loved me and gave Himself for me.

from Galatians 6:14; 2:20 (NKJV)

Optional introduction to
"At the Cross"

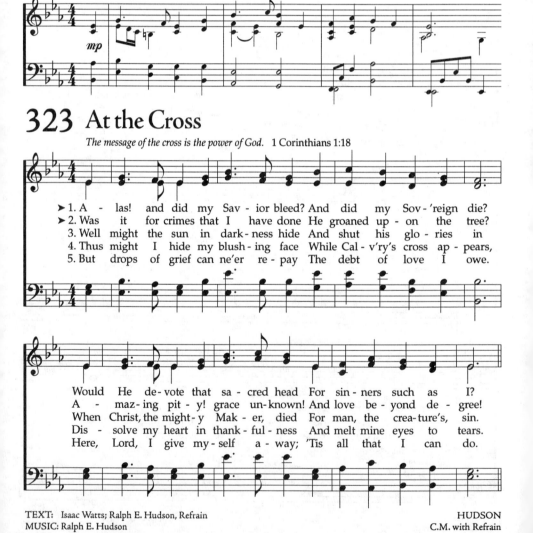

323 At the Cross

The message of the cross is the power of God. 1 Corinthians 1:18

➤ 1. A - las! and did my Sav - ior bleed? And did my Sov - 'reign die?
➤ 2. Was it for crimes that I have done He groaned up - on the tree?
3. Well might the sun in dark - ness hide And shut his glo - ries in
4. Thus might I hide my blush - ing face While Cal - v'ry's cross ap - pears,
5. But drops of grief can ne'er re - pay The debt of love I owe.

Would He de - vote that sa - cred head For sin - ners such as I?
A - maz - ing pit - y! grace un - known! And love be - yond de - gree!
When Christ, the might - y Mak - er, died For man, the crea - ture's, sin.
Dis - solve my heart in thank - ful - ness And melt mine eyes to tears.
Here, Lord, I give my - self a - way; 'Tis all that I can do.

TEXT: Isaac Watts; Ralph E. Hudson, Refrain
MUSIC: Ralph E. Hudson

HUDSON
C.M. with Refrain

Refrain

At the cross, at the cross, where I first saw the light, And the

bur-den of my heart rolled a-way. rolled a-way. It was there by

faith I re-ceived my sight, And now I am hap-py all the day!

Optional repeat refrain setting

At the cross, at the cross, where I first saw the light, And the

bur-den of my heart rolled a-way. It was there by faith I re-ceived my

sight, And now I am hap-py all the day!

rit.

Optional transition to "When I Survey the Wondrous Cross"

324 When I Survey the Wondrous Cross

They will look on the One they have pierced. John 19:37

1. When I sur-vey the won-drous cross On which the Prince of Glo-ry died, My rich-est gain I count but loss, And pour con-tempt on all my pride.

2. For-bid it, Lord, that I should boast, Save in the death of Christ, my God. All the vain things that charm me most, I sac-ri-fice them to His blood.

3. See, from His head, His hands, His feet, Sor-row and love flow min-gled down. Did e'er such love and sor-row meet, Or thorns com-pose so rich a crown?

4. Were the whole realm of na-ture mine, That were a pres-ent far too small. Love so a-maz-ing, so di-vine, De-mands my soul, my life, my all!

Optional third and fourth stanzas setting

Unison

mp 3. See, from His head, His hands, His feet, Sor-row and love flow min-gled down.

TEXT: Isaac Watts

MUSIC: Lowell Mason; based on plainsong; arranged by Tom Fettke

HAMBURG
L.M.

Did e'er such love and sor - row meet, Or thorns com -

pose so rich a crown? rit.

Broader

➤ 4. Were the whole realm of na - ture mine,

That were a pres - ent far too small. Love so a -

maz - ing, so di - vine, De - mands my soul, my

1

2 Choir harmonize

life, my all! life, my all!

The end of THE CROSS - TREE OF LIFE - A Worship Sequence

325 Why Should He Love Me So?

Christ loved the church and gave Himself up for her. Ephesians 5:25

1. Love sent my Savior to die in my stead; Why should He
2. Nails pierced His hands and His feet for my sin; Why should He
3. O how He ag-o-nized there in my place; Why should He

love me so? Meek-ly to Cal-va-ry's cross He was led;
love me so? He suf-fered sore my sal-va-tion to win;
love me so? Noth-ing with-hold-ing my sin to ef-face;

Refrain

Why should He love me so?
Why should He love me so? Why should He love me so?
Why should He love me so?

Why should He love me so? Why should my Sav-ior to

Cal-va-ry go? Why should He love me so?

TEXT: Robert Harkness
MUSIC: Robert Harkness

LOVE ME
10.6.10.6. with Refrain

Blessed Redeemer 326

Christ redeemed us from the curse of the law by becoming a curse for us. Galatians 3:13

1. Up Cal-v'ry's moun-tain one dread-ful morn Walked Christ, my Sav - ior,
2. "Fa-ther, for - give them," thus did He pray, E'en while His life - blood
3. O how I love Him, Sav - ior and Friend! How can my prais - es

wea - ry and worn; Fac - ing for sin - ners death on the cross,
flowed fast a - way. Pray - ing for sin - ners while in such woe,
ev - er find end? Thro' years un - num - bered on heav-en's shore,

Refrain

That He might save them from end-less loss.
No one but Je - sus ev - er loved so! Bless-ed Re - deem-er! Pre - cious Re-
My tongue shall praise Him for - ev - er - more.

deem - er! Seems now I see Him on Cal-va-ry's tree; Wound-ed and

bleed - ing, for sin-ners plead - ing, Blind and un - heed - ing, dy-ing for me!

TEXT: Avis B. Christiansen
MUSIC: Harry Dixon Loes

REDEEMER
9.9.9.9. with Refrain

327 The Old Rugged Cross

He humbled Himself and became obedient to death—even death on a cross. Philippians 2:8

1. On a hill far a-way stood an old rug-ged cross, The em-blem of
2. O the old rug-ged cross, so de-spised by the world, Has a won-drous at-
3. In the old rug-ged cross, stained with blood so di-vine, A won-drous
4. To the old rug-ged cross I will ev-er be true; Its shame and re-

suf-f'ring and shame; And I love that old cross, where the dear-est and best
trac-tion for me; For the dear Lamb of God left His glo-ry a-bove
beau-ty I see; For 'twas on that old cross Je-sus suf-fered and died
proach glad-ly bear. Then He'll call me some-day to my home far a-way,

Refrain

For a world of lost sin-ners was slain.
To bear it to dark Cal-va-ry.
To par-don and sanc-ti-fy me.
Where His glo-ry for-ev-er I'll share.

So I'll cher-ish the old rug-ged cross, the

cross, Till my tro-phies at last I lay down. I will cling to the
old rug-ged cross,

TEXT: George Bennard
MUSIC: George Bennard

OLD RUGGED CROSS
Irregular meter

old rug-ged cross, And ex-change it some-day for a crown.
cross, the old rug-ged cross,

In the Cross of Christ I Glory 328

May I never boast except in the cross of our Lord Jesus Christ. Galatians 6:14

1. In the cross of Christ I glo - ry, Tow'r - ing
2. When the woes of life o'er - take me, Hopes de -
3. When the sun of bliss is beam - ing Light and
4. Bane and bless - ing, pain and plea - sure By the

o'er the wrecks of time. All the light of
ceive, and fears an - noy, Nev - er shall the
love up - on my way, From the cross, the
cross are sanc - ti - fied. Peace is there that

sa - cred sto - ry Gath - ers round its head sub - lime.
cross for - sake me. Lo! it glows with peace and joy.
ra - diance stream-ing Adds more lus - ter to the day.
knows no mea - sure, Joys that through all time a - bide.

TEXT: John Bowring
MUSIC: Ithamar Conkey

RATHBUN
8.7.8.7.

329 There Is Power in the Blood

They overcame him by the blood of the Lamb. Revelation 12:11

1. Would you be free from your bur-den of sin? There's pow'r in the blood,
2. Would you be free from your pas-sion and pride? There's pow'r in the blood,
3. Would you be whit-er, much whit-er than snow? There's pow'r in the blood,
4. Would you do ser-vice for Je-sus, your King? There's pow'r in the blood,

pow'r in the blood; Would you o'er e-vil a vic-to-ry win? There's
pow'r in the blood; Come for a cleans-ing to Cal-va-ry's tide. There's
pow'r in the blood; Sin-stains are lost in its life-giv-ing flow. There's
pow'r in the blood; Would you live dai-ly His prais-es to sing? There's

Refrain

won-der-ful pow'r in the blood. There is pow'r, pow'r, won-der-work-ing
There is pow'r, there is pow'r, won-der-work-ing

pow'r In the blood of the Lamb. There is pow'r, pow'r,
pow'r In the blood of the Lamb. There is pow'r, there is pow'r,

won-der-work-ing pow'r In the pre-cious blood of the Lamb.

Optional segue to "Are You Washed in the Blood?" No transition is needed.

TEXT: Lewis E. Jones
MUSIC: Lewis E. Jones

POWER IN THE BLOOD
10.9.10.8. with Refrain

Are You Washed in the Blood? 330

They have washed their robes and made them white in the blood of the Lamb. Revelation 7:14

1. Have you been to Je - sus for the cleans - ing pow'r? Are you washed in the
2. Are you walk - ing dai - ly by the Sav - ior's side? Are you washed in the
3. When the Bride - groom com - eth, will your robes be white? Are you washed in the
4. Lay a - side the gar - ments that are stained with sin, And be washed in the

blood of the Lamb? Are you ful - ly trust - ing in His grace this hour? Are you
blood of the Lamb? Do you rest each mo - ment in the Cru - ci - fied? Are you
blood of the Lamb? Will your soul be read - y for the man - sions bright, And be
blood of the Lamb. There's a foun - tain flow - ing for the soul un - clean; O be

Refrain

washed in the blood of the Lamb? Are you washed in the blood,
washed in the blood of the Lamb? Are you washed in the blood,
washed in the blood of the Lamb?
washed in the blood of the Lamb!

In the soul - cleans - ing blood of the Lamb? Are your gar - ments
of the Lamb?

spot - less? Are they white as snow? Are you washed in the blood of the Lamb?

TEXT: Elisha A. Hoffman
MUSIC: Elisha A. Hoffman

WASHED IN THE BLOOD
11.9.11.9. with Refrain

331 HIS CLEANSING BLOOD

A Worship Sequence

I Know a Fount
O the Blood of Jesus; stanzas 1,2,4
The Blood Will Never Lose Its Power, complete
Suggested stanzas have been marked with an arrow: ➤

WORSHIP LEADER

If we walk in the light as He is in the light,
we have fellowship with one another,
and the blood of Jesus Christ His Son
cleanses us from all sin.

from 1 John 1:7 (NKJV)

Optional introduction to "I Know a Fount"

332 I Know a Fount

A fountain will be opened to cleanse them from sin and impurity. Zechariah 13:1

I know a fount where sins are washed a-way; I know a
place where night is turned to day. Bur-dens are lift-ed; blind eyes made to
see. There's a won-der-work-ing pow'r in the blood of Cal-va-ry. rit.

Optional transition to
"O the Blood of Jesus"

TEXT: Oliver Cook
MUSIC: Oliver Cook

I KNOW A FOUNT
Irregular meter

O the Blood of Jesus 333

They have washed their robes and made them white in the blood of the Lamb. Revelation 7:14

➤1. O the blood of Je - sus, O the blood of Je - sus,
➤2. O the cross of Je - sus, O the cross of Je - sus,
3. O the love of Je - sus, O the love of Je - sus,
➤4. O the blood of Je - sus, O the blood of Je - sus,

O the blood of Je - sus, It wash - es white as snow.
O the cross of Je - sus, His death brings life to me.
O the love of Je - sus, He free - ly gives to me.
O the blood of Je - sus, It wash - es white as snow.

Optional last stanza setting

➤4. O the blood of Je - sus, O the blood of Je - sus, O the blood of Je - sus, It wash - es white as snow.

Optional transition to "The Blood Will Never Lose Its Power"

TEXT: Traditional, stanzas 1, 4; Brenda Barker, stanzas 2, 3
MUSIC: Traditional; arranged by Ken Barker

O THE BLOOD OF JESUS
6.6.6.6.

334 The Blood Will Never Lose Its Power

This is My blood of the covenant, which is poured out for the forgiveness of sins. Matthew 26:28

1. The blood that Je - sus shed for me
2. It soothes my doubt and calms my fears,

'Way back on Cal - va - ry, The blood that gives me strength from
And it dries all my tears; The blood that gives me strength from

day to day— It will nev - er lose its pow'r.
day to day— It will nev - er lose its pow'r.

Refrain

It reach - es to the high - est moun - tain; It flows to the

low - est val - ley. The blood that gives me strength from

TEXT: Andraé Crouch
MUSIC: Andraé Crouch

THE BLOOD
Irregular meter

day to day– It will nev - er lose its pow'r.

Optional extended or choral ending

It will nev - er lose, it will nev - er lose its pow'r!

The end of HIS CLEANSING BLOOD - A Worship Sequence

Cross of Jesus, Cross of Sorrow 335

He humbled Himself and become obedient to death–even death on a cross! Philippians 2:8

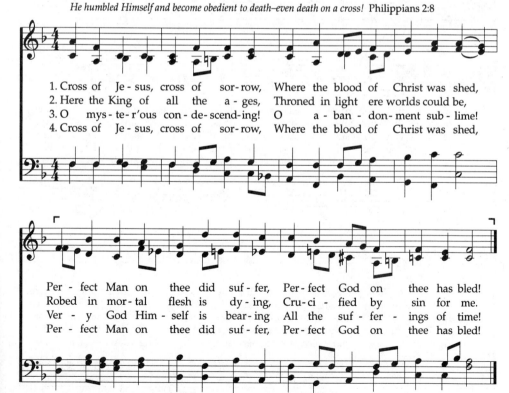

1. Cross of Je - sus, cross of sor - row, Where the blood of Christ was shed,
2. Here the King of all the a - ges, Throned in light ere worlds could be,
3. O mys - te - r'ous con - de - scend-ing! O a - ban - don - ment sub - lime!
4. Cross of Je - sus, cross of sor - row, Where the blood of Christ was shed,

Per - fect Man on thee did suf - fer, Per - fect God on thee has bled!
Robed in mor - tal flesh is dy - ing, Cru - ci - fied by sin for me.
Ver - y God Him - self is bear-ing All the suf - fer - ings of time!
Per - fect Man on thee did suf - fer, Per - fect God on thee has bled!

TEXT: William J. Sparrow-Simpson
MUSIC: John Stainer

CROSS OF JESUS
8.7.8.7.

336 There Is a Fountain

A fountain will be opened to cleanse them from sin. Zechariah 13:1

1. There is a foun-tain filled with blood Drawn from Im-man-uel's veins,
2. The dy-ing thief re-joiced to see That foun-tain in his day,
3. Dear dy-ing Lamb, Thy pre-cious blood Shall nev-er lose its pow'r,
4. E'er since, by faith, I saw the stream Thy flow-ing wounds sup-ply,
5. When this poor lisp-ing, stam-m'ring tongue Lies si-lent in the grave,

And sin-ners plunged be-neath that flood Lose all their guilt-y stains:
And there may I, though vile as he, Wash all my sins a-way:
Till all the ran-somed Church of God Be saved to sin no more:
Re-deem-ing love has been my theme And shall be till I die:
Then in a no-bler, sweet-er song I'll sing Thy pow'r to save:

Lose all their guilt-y stains, Lose all their guilt-y stains;
Wash all my sins a-way, Wash all my sins a-way;
Be saved to sin no more, Be saved to sin no more;
And shall be till I die, And shall be till I die;
I'll sing Thy pow'r to save, I'll sing Thy pow'r to save;

And sin-ners plunged be-neath that flood Lose all their guilt-y stains.
And there may I, though vile as he, Wash all my sins a-way.
Till all the ran-somed Church of God Be saved to sin no more.
Re-deem-ing love has been my theme And shall be till I die.
Then in a no-bler, sweet-er song I'll sing Thy pow'r to save.

TEXT: William Cowper
MUSIC: Traditional American melody; arranged by Lowell Mason

CLEANSING FOUNTAIN
C.M.D.

Nothing but the Blood 337

The blood of Jesus, His Son, purifies us from all sin. 1 John 1:7

1. What can wash a - way my sin? Noth-ing but the blood of Je - sus;
2. For my par - don this I see, Noth-ing but the blood of Je - sus;
3. Noth-ing can for sin a - tone, Noth-ing but the blood of Je - sus;
4. This is all my hope and peace, Noth-ing but the blood of Je - sus;

What can make me whole a - gain? Noth-ing but the blood of Je - sus.
For my cleans-ing, this my plea, Noth-ing but the blood of Je - sus.
Naught of good that I have done, Noth-ing but the blood of Je - sus.
This is all my righ-teous-ness, Noth-ing but the blood of Je - sus.

Refrain

O pre - cious is the flow That makes me white as snow;

No oth - er fount I know, Noth-ing but the blood of Je - sus.

TEXT: Robert Lowry
MUSIC: Robert Lowry; Choral ending by Ken Barker

PLAINFIELD
7.8.7.8. with Refrain

Optional choral ending

cresc.

Noth-ing but the blood, Noth-ing but the blood of Je - sus.
cresc.

338 Wonderful Grace of Jesus

You know the grace of our Lord Jesus Christ. 2 Corinthians 8:9

1. Won - der - ful grace of Je - sus, Great - er than all my sin.
2. Won - der - ful grace of Je - sus, Reach - ing to all the lost.
3. Won - der - ful grace of Je - sus, Reach - ing the most de - filed.

How shall my tongue de - scribe it? Where shall its praise be - gin?
By it I have been par - doned, Saved to the ut - ter - most.
By its trans - form - ing pow - er Mak - ing him God's dear child.

Tak - ing a - way my bur - den, Set - ting my spir - it free;
Chains have been torn a - sun - der, Giv - ing me lib - er - ty;
Pur - chas - ing peace and heav - en For all e - ter - ni - ty;

For the won - der - ful grace of Je - sus reach - es me.
For the won - der - ful grace of Je - sus reach - es me.
For the won - der - ful grace of Je - sus reach - es me.

Refrain

Won - der - ful the match - less grace, the match - less grace of Je - sus;

Won - der - ful the match - less grace of Je - sus;

Men unison

TEXT: Haldor Lillenas
MUSIC: Haldor Lillenas

WONDERFUL GRACE
Irregular meter

339 By His Grace

By grace you have been saved, through faith–it is the gift of God. Ephesians 2:8

1. By His grace I am re - deemed, By His blood I am made clean;
2. By Your grace I am re - deemed, By Your blood I am made clean;

And I now can know Him face to face.
And I now can know You face to face.

By His pow'r I have been raised, Hid-den now in Christ by faith;
By Your pow'r I have been raised, Hid-den now in You by faith;

I will praise the glo - ry of His grace.
I will praise the glo - ry of Your grace.

TEXT: Steve Fry
MUSIC: Steve Fry

BY HIS GRACE
Irregular meter

340 Turn Your Eyes upon Jesus

We reflect the Lord's glory, being transformed into His likeness. 2 Corinthians 3:18

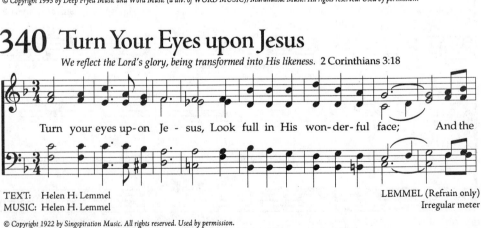

Turn your eyes up-on Je - sus, Look full in His won-der-ful face; And the

TEXT: Helen H. Lemmel
MUSIC: Helen H. Lemmel

LEMMEL (Refrain only)
Irregular meter

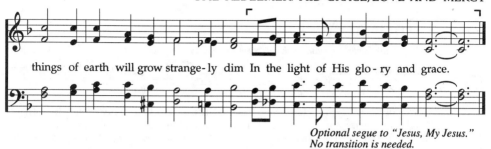

things of earth will grow strange-ly dim In the light of His glo-ry and grace.

Optional segue to "Jesus, My Jesus."
No transition is needed.

Jesus, My Jesus 341

Live a life of love, just as Christ loved us and gave Himself up for us. Ephesians 5:2

Unison

Je - sus, my Je - sus,

Your love means so much to me.

Je - sus, my Je - sus,

Your love is all that I need.

TEXT: Carol Cymbala
MUSIC: Carol Cymbala

MY JESUS
7.5.7.5.

342 Rock of Ages

They drank from the spiritual rock that accompanied them; that rock was Christ. 1 Corinthians 10:4

1. Rock of A - ges, cleft for me, Let me hide my - self in Thee;
2. Could my tears for - ev - er flow, Could my zeal no lan - guor know,
3. While I draw this fleet - ing breath, When my eyes shall close in death,

Let the wa - ter and the blood, From Thy wound - ed side which flowed,
These for sin could not a - tone; Thou must save, and Thou a - lone.
When I rise to worlds un - known And be - hold Thee on Thy throne,

Be of sin the dou - ble cure, Save from wrath and make me pure.
In my hand no price I bring; Sim - ply to Thy cross I cling.
Rock of A - ges, cleft for me, Let me hide my - self in Thee.

TEXT: Augustus M. Toplady
MUSIC: Thomas Hastings

TOPLADY
7.7.7.7.7.7.

343 Amazing Grace

One thing I do know, I was blind but now I see! John 9:25

1. A - maz - ing grace! how sweet the sound That saved a wretch like me!
2. 'Twas grace that taught my heart to fear, And grace my fears re - lieved.
3. The Lord has prom - ised good to me; His word my hope se - cures.
4. Thro' man - y dan - gers, toils, and snares I have al - read - y come.
5. When we've been there ten thou - sand years, Bright shin - ing as the sun,

TEXT: John Newton; John P. Rees, stanza 5
MUSIC: Traditional American melody from Carrell and Clayton's
Virginia Harmony, 1831; arranged by Edwin O. Excell;
Last stanza setting and Choral ending by O. D. Hall, Jr.

AMAZING GRACE
C.M.

344 Grace Greater than Our Sin

Where sin increased, grace increased all the more. Romans 5:20

1. Mar - vel - ous grace of our lov - ing Lord, Grace that ex - ceeds our
2. Sin and de - spair, like the sea waves cold, Threat - en the soul with
3. Dark is the stain that we can - not hide— What can a - vail to
4. Mar - vel - ous, in - fi - nite, match - less grace, Free - ly be - stowed on

sin and our guilt, Yon - der on Cal - va - ry's mount out - poured,
in - fi - nite loss; Grace that is great - er, yes, grace un - told,
wash it a - way? Look! there is flow - ing a crim - son tide;
all who be - lieve! You that are long - ing to see His face,

Refrain

There where the blood of the Lamb was spilt.
Points to the ref - uge, the might - y cross. Grace, grace,
Whit - er than snow you may be to - day. Mar - vel - ous grace,
Will you this mo - ment His grace re - ceive?

God's grace, Grace that will par - don and cleanse with - in! Grace,
in - fi - nite grace, Mar - vel - ous

TEXT: Julia H. Johnston
MUSIC: Daniel B. Towner

MOODY
9.9.9.9. with Refrain

grace, God's grace,
grace, in-fi-nite grace, Grace that is great-er than all our sin!

What a Wonderful Savior! 345

We know that this Man really is the Savior of the world. John 4:42

1. Christ has for sin a-tone-ment made– What a won-der-ful Sav-ior!
2. I praise Him for the cleans-ing blood– What a won-der-ful Sav-ior!
3. He cleansed my heart from all its sin– What a won-der-ful Sav-ior!
4. He gives me o-ver-com-ing pow'r– What a won-der-ful Sav-ior!

We are re-deemed, the price is paid– What a won-der-ful Sav-ior!
That rec-on-ciled my soul to God– What a won-der-ful Sav-ior!
And now He reigns and rules there-in– What a won-der-ful Sav-ior!
And tri-umph in each try-ing hour– What a won-der-ful Sav-ior!

Refrain

What a won-der-ful Sav-ior is Je-sus, my Je-sus!

What a won-der-ful Sav-ior is Je-sus, my Lord!

TEXT: Elisha A. Hoffman
MUSIC: Elisha A. Hoffman

BENTON HARBOR
8.7.8.7. with Refrain

346

THIS IS LOVE
A Worship Sequence

And Can It Be?; stanzas 1, 2, 4
My Savior's Love; stanzas 1, 4
O How He Loves You and Me; complete
Suggested stanzas have been marked with an arrow: ➤

WORSHIP LEADER

Because of His great love for us, God, who is rich in mercy,
made us alive with Christ even when we were dead in transgressions–
it is by grace you have been saved.

EVERYONE

Thank You, Father, for Your amazing love.

WORSHIP LEADER

This is how God showed His love among us:
He sent His one and only Son into the world that we might live through Him.
This is love: not that we loved God, but that He loved us and sent His Son
as an atoning sacrifice for our sins.

EVERYONE

Thank You, Father, for Your amazing love.

from Ephesians 2:4-5; 1 John 4:9-10 (NIV)

Optional introduction to
"And Can It Be?"

347 And Can It Be?

While we were still sinners, Christ died for us. Romans 5:8

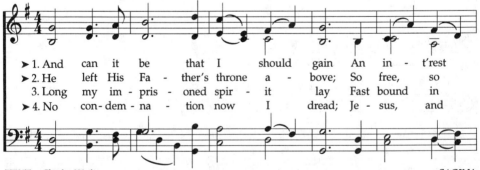

➤ 1. And can it be that I should gain An in - t'rest
➤ 2. He left His Fa - ther's throne a - bove; So free, so
3. Long my im - pris - oned spir - it lay Fast bound in
➤ 4. No con - dem - na - tion now I dread; Je - sus, and

TEXT: Charles Wesley
MUSIC: Thomas Campbell

SAGINA
8.8.8.8.8.8. with Refrain

in the Sav-ior's blood? Died He for me, who caused His pain?
in-fi - nite His grace. Emp-tied Him-self of all but love,
sin and na-ture's night; Thine eye dif-fused a quick-'ning ray,
all in Him is mine! A - live in Him, my liv-ing Head,

For me, who Him to death pur-sued? A - maz-ing love! how
And bled for Ad - am's help-less race. 'Tis mer-cy all, im -
I woke, the dun-geon flamed with light. My chains fell off; my
And clothed in righ-teous-ness di - vine; Bold I ap-proach th'e -

can it be That Thou, my God, shouldst die for me?
mense and free, For, O my God, it found out me.
heart was free. I rose, went forth and fol - lowed Thee.
ter - nal throne And claim the crown, thro' Christ, my own.

Refrain

A - maz - ing love! how can it be That
A - maz-ing love! how can it be

Thou, my God, shouldst die for me?
That Thou, my God,

*Optional transition to
"My Savior's Love"*

348 My Savior's Love

The Son of God loved me and gave Himself for me. Galatians 2:20

➤ 1. I stand a-mazed in the pres-ence Of Je - sus, the Naz - a - rene,
2. For me it was in the gar - den He prayed, "Not My will, but Thine."
3. In pit - y an - gels be - held Him And came from the world of light
➤ 4. He took my sins and my sor - rows; He made them His ver - y own.
5. When with the ran-somed in glo - ry His face I at last shall see,

And won- der how He could love me, A sin - ner, con-demned, un - clean.
He had no tears for His own griefs, But sweat drops of blood for mine.
To com-fort Him in the sor - rows He bore for my soul that night.
He bore the bur - den to Cal - v'ry And suf - fered and died a - lone.
'Twill be my joy thro' the a - ges To sing of His love for me.

Refrain

How mar-vel- ous, How won-der-ful!
O how mar-vel- ous, O how won-der-ful! And my song shall ev-er be:

How mar-vel- ous, How won-der-ful
O how mar-vel- ous, O how won-der-ful Is my Sav-ior's love for me!

TEXT: Charles H. Gabriel
MUSIC: Charles H. Gabriel

MY SAVIOR'S LOVE
8.7.8.7. with Refrain

Optional transition to "O How He Loves You and Me"

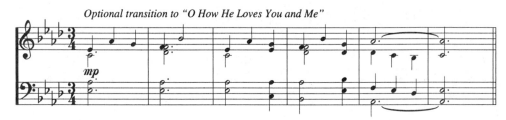

O How He Loves You and Me 349

As the Father has loved Me, so have I loved you. John 15:9

1. O how He loves you and me! O how He loves you and me! He gave His life; what more could He give? O how He loves you; O how He loves me; O how He loves you and me!

2. Je - sus to Cal - v'ry did go; His love for sin - ners to show. What He did there bro't hope from de - spair. O how He loves you; O how He loves me; O how He loves you and me!

TEXT: Kurt Kaiser
MUSIC: Kurt Kaiser

PATRICIA
Irregular meter

Optional choral ending - a cappella preferred

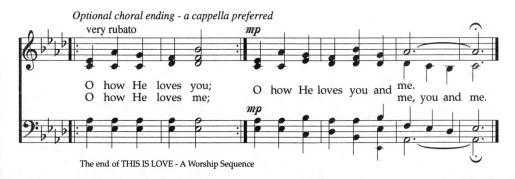

very rubato   *mp*

O how He loves you; O how He loves you and me.
O how He loves me; O how He loves me, you and me.

mp

The end of THIS IS LOVE - A Worship Sequence

350 God So Loved the World

God so loved the world that He gave His one and only Son. John 3:16

God so loved the world. God so loved the world, that He gave His on-ly be-got-ten Son, that who-so be-liev-eth, be-liev-eth in Him should not per-ish, should not per-ish but have ev-er-last-ing life. For God sent not His Son in-to the world to con-

TEXT: John 3:16, 17
MUSIC: John Stainer

STAINER
Irregular meter

351 Amazing Love

Greater love has no one than this, that he lay down his life for his friends. John 15:13

Unison

1. My Lord, what love is this that pays so dear-ly; That I, the guilt-y one, may go free?
2. And so they watched Him die, de-spised, re-ject-ed; But, O the blood He shed flowed for me.
3. And now this love of Christ shall flow like riv-ers; Come wash your guilt a-way, live a-gain.

Refrain

A-maz-ing love, O what sac-ri-fice, The Son of God giv'n for me; My debt He pays and my death He dies, That I might live, that I might live.

TEXT: Graham Kendrick
MUSIC: Graham Kendrick

AMAZING LOVE
Irregular meter

O the Deep, Deep Love of Jesus 352

How wide and long and high and deep is the love of Christ. Ephesians 3:18

1. O the deep, deep love of Je - sus, Vast, un - mea - sured, bound - less, free,
2. O the deep, deep love of Je - sus— Spread His praise from shore to shore!
3. O the deep, deep love of Je - sus, Love of ev - ery love the best;

Roll - ing as a might - y o - cean In its full - ness o - ver me.
How He lov - eth, ev - er lov - eth, Chang - eth nev - er, nev - er - more;
'Tis an o - cean vast of bless - ing, 'Tis a ha - ven sweet of rest.

Un - der - neath me, all a - round me, Is the cur - rent of Thy love;
How He watch - es o'er His loved ones, Died to call them all His own;
O the deep, deep love of Je - sus, 'Tis a heav'n of heav'ns to me;

Lead - ing on - ward, lead - ing home - ward To my glo - rious rest a - bove.
How for them He in - ter - ced - eth, Watch - eth o'er them from the throne.
And it lifts me up to glo - ry, For it lifts me up to Thee.

TEXT: Samuel Trevor Francis
MUSIC: Thomas J. Williams
A higher setting may be found at No. 733

EBENEZER
8.7.8.7.D.

353 Victory in Jesus

He gives us the victory through our Lord Jesus Christ. 1 Corinthians 15:57

1. I heard an old, old story, how a Sav-ior came from glo-ry,
2. I heard a-bout His heal-ing, of His cleans-ing pow'r re-veal-ing,
3. I heard a-bout a man-sion He has built for me in glo-ry,

How He gave His life on Cal-va-ry to save a wretch like me.
How He made the lame to walk a-gain and caused the blind to see.
And I heard a-bout the streets of gold be-yond the crys-tal sea;

I heard a-bout His groan-ing, of His pre-cious blood's a-ton-ing,
And then I cried, "Dear Je-sus, come and heal my bro-ken spir-it,"
A-bout the an-gels sing-ing, and the old re-demp-tion sto-ry;

Then I re-pent-ed of my sins and won the vic-to-ry.
And some-how Je-sus came and bro't to me the vic-to-ry.
And some sweet day I'll sing up there the song of vic-to-ry.

Refrain

O vic-to-ry in Je-sus, my Sav-ior for-ev-er! He sought me and

TEXT: Eugene M. Bartlett
MUSIC: Eugene M. Bartlett

HARTFORD
Irregular meter

bo't me with His re-deem-ing blood. He loved me ere I knew Him, and all my

love is due Him. He plunged me to vic-to-ry be-neath the cleans-ing flood.

Optional last refrain setting

O vic-to-ry in Je-sus, my Sav-ior for-ev-er! He sought me and

bo't me with His re-deem-ing blood. He loved me ere I knew Him, and all my love

is due Him. He plunged me to vic-to-ry be-neath the cleans-ing flood. O flood.

Optional choral ending

Vic-to-ry! Vic-to-ry! Vic-to-ry in Christ, our Lord. Vic-to-ry!

354 I Cannot Tell

Christ loved us and gave Himself up for us. Ephesians 5:2

1. I cannot tell why He, the King of Heav-en, Should leave the peace of all e-ter-ni-ty, Why God Him-self should lay a-side His splen-dor To leave the Fa-ther's side and come to me. But this I know: our si-lence filled with sing-ing, And all our

2. I cannot tell why He, the Joy of Heav-en, Should give Him-self to suf-fer for my sin, Why Ho-ly God should love me in my shame-ful-ness, Why He should die to draw my soul to Him. But this I know: that Christ the Lord is ris-en, And praise His

3. I cannot tell when He will rule the na-tions, How He will claim His loved ones as His own; And who can tell the ho-ly ju-bi-la-tion When all His chil-dren gath-er 'round His throne. But this I know: all flesh will see His glo-ry, And skies will

TEXT: Ken Bible; inspired by William Y. Fullerton
MUSIC: Traditional Irish melody

LONDONDERRY AIR
11.10.11.10.11.10.11.12.

dark - ness fled from heav - en's light   When Christ the Lord,   so hu - man, yet so
name, He's ris - en now in   me!   Be - cause He lives,   I'll rise to life e -
burst   as   all   cre - a - tion sings.   The   Son will   rise   on   one   e - ter - nal

ho - ly,   In   love was born   a   child   for   me   that   ho - ly   night.
ter - nal!   He   took my   guilt - y   heart, and I'm   for - ev - er   free!
morn - ing   When Christ, the   Sav - ior   of   the world, is   Lord and King!

There's a Wideness in God's Mercy 355

Let me fall into the hands of the Lord, for His mercy is very great. 1 Chronicles 21:13

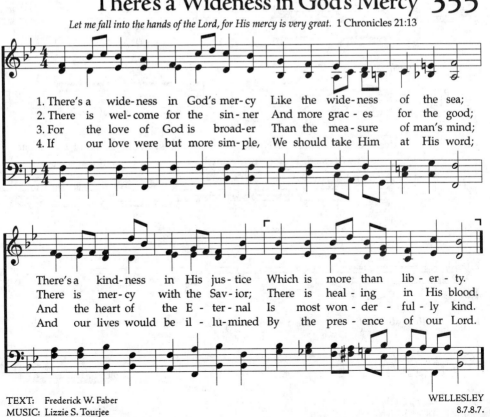

1. There's a   wide - ness   in   God's mer - cy   Like   the   wide - ness   of   the   sea;
2. There   is   wel - come for the   sin - ner   And more   grac - es   for   the   good;
3. For   the   love of   God is   broad - er   Than the   mea - sure   of man's mind;
4. If   our love were but more sim - ple,   We should take Him   at   His word;

There's a   kind - ness   in   His   jus - tice   Which   is   more   than   lib - er - ty.
There   is   mer - cy   with the   Sav - ior;   There   is   heal - ing   in   His blood.
And   the heart of   the   E - ter - nal   Is   most won - der - ful - ly   kind.
And   our lives would be   il - lu - mined   By   the   pres - ence   of   our Lord.

TEXT: Frederick W. Faber
MUSIC: Lizzie S. Tourjee

WELLESLEY
8.7.8.7.

356 Redeemed

You were redeemed with the precious blood of Christ, a lamb. 1 Peter 1:18-19

1. Re-deemed, how I love to pro-claim it! Re-deemed by the blood of the Lamb;
2. Re-deemed and so hap-py in Je-sus, No lan-guage my rap-ture can tell;
3. I think of my bless-ed Re-deem-er, I think of Him all the day long;
4. I know I shall see in His beau-ty The King in whose law I de-light;

Re-deemed thro' His in-fi-nite mer-cy, His child, and for-ev-er, I am.
I know that the light of His pres-ence With me doth con-tin-ual-ly dwell.
I sing, for I can-not be si-lent; His love is the theme of my song.
Who lov-ing-ly guard-eth my foot-steps, And giv-eth me songs in the night.

Refrain

Re-deemed, re-deemed, Re-deemed by the blood of the Lamb;
re-deemed, re-deemed,

Re-deemed, re-deemed, His child, and for-ev-er, I am.
re-deemed, re-deemed,

TEXT: Fanny J. Crosby
MUSIC: William J. Kirkpatrick

REDEEMED
9.8.9.8. with Refrain

Christ Arose 357

It was impossible for death to keep its hold on Him. Acts 2:24

1. Low in the grave He lay— Je-sus, my Sav-ior! Wait-ing the
2. Vain-ly they watch His bed— Je-sus, my Sav-ior! Vain-ly they
3. Death can-not keep his prey— Je-sus, my Sav-ior! He tore the

Refrain faster

com-ing day— Je-sus, my Lord! Up from the grave He a-rose,   With a
seal the dead— Je-sus, my Lord! He a-rose,
bars a-way— Je-sus, my Lord!

might-y tri-umph o'er His foes.   He a-rose a vic-tor from the
He a-rose!

dark do-main, And He lives for-ev-er with His saints to reign. He a-

rose!   He a-rose!   Hal-le-lu-jah! Christ a-rose!
He a-rose!   He a-rose!

TEXT: Robert Lowry
MUSIC: Robert Lowry

CHRIST AROSE
6.5.6.4. with Refrain

358 Because He Lives

Because I live, you also will live. John 14:19

1. God sent His Son— they called Him Je - sus; He came to
2. How sweet to hold a new - born ba - by, And feel the
3. And then one day I'll cross the riv - er; I'll fight life's

love, heal and for - give. He lived and died to buy my
pride and joy he gives; But great - er still the calm as -
fi - nal war with pain. And then, as death gives way to

par - don; An emp - ty grave is there to prove my Sav - ior lives.
sur - ance: This child can face un - cer - tain days be - cause He lives.
vic - t'ry, I'll see the lights of glo - ry and I'll know He reigns.

Refrain

Be - cause He lives I can face to - mor - row; Be - cause He

lives, all fear is gone. Be - cause I know He holds the

TEXT: Gloria Gaither and William J. Gaither
MUSIC: William J. Gaither

RESURRECTION
Irregular meter

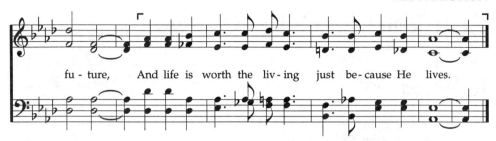

fu - ture, And life is worth the liv - ing just be - cause He lives.

Alleluia, Alleluia! Give Thanks 359

Thanks be to God! He gives us the victory through our Lord Jesus Christ. 1 Corinthians 15:57

Al - le - lu - ia, al - le - lu - ia! Give thanks to the ris - en Lord;

Al - le - lu - ia, al - le - lu - ia! Give praise to His name.

Fine

1. Je - sus is Lord of all the earth;
2. Spread the good news o'er all the earth;
3. We have been cru - ci - fied with Christ;
4. Come, let us praise the liv - ing God;

D.S. al Fine

He is the King of cre - a - tion.
Je - sus has died and has ris - en.
Now we shall live for - ev - er.
Joy - ful - ly sing to our Sav - ior.

Al - le -

TEXT: Donald Fishel
MUSIC: Donald Fishel

ALLELUIA No. 1
Irregular meter

360 Jesus Christ Is Risen Today

He has risen! He is not here. **Mark 16:6**

1. Je - sus Christ is risen to - day, Al - le - lu - ia!
2. Hymns of praise, then, let us sing, Al - le - lu - ia!
3. Sing we to our God a - bove, Al - le - lu - ia!

Our tri - um - phant ho - ly day, Al - le - lu - ia!
Un - to Christ, our heaven - ly King, Al - le - lu - ia!
Praise e - ter - nal as His love: Al - le - lu - ia!

Who did once, up - on the cross, Al - le - lu - ia!
Who en - dured the cross and grave, Al - le - lu - ia!
Praise Him, all you heaven - ly host, Al - le - lu - ia!

Suf - fer to re - deem our loss, Al - le - lu - ia!
Sin - ners to re - deem and save, Al - le - lu - ia!
Fa - ther, Son and Ho - ly Ghost, Al - le - lu - ia!

TEXT: Latin hymn, 14th century; translated in *Lyra Davidica*, 1708, altered;
Charles Wesley, stanza 3
MUSIC: Robert Williams

LLANFAIR
7.7.7.7. with Alleluias

Worship Christ, the Risen King 361

He has risen! He is not here. Mark 16:6

1. Rise, O Church, and lift your voic - es; Christ has con - quered
2. See the tomb where death had laid Him; Emp - ty now, its
3. Hear the earth pro - test and trem - ble; See the stone re -
4. Doubt may lift its head to mur - mur, Scoff - ers mock and
5. We ac - claim Your life, O Je - sus; Now we sing Your

death and hell. Sing as all the earth re - joic - es;
mouth de - clares: "Death and I could not con - tain Him,
moved with pow'r. All hell's min - ions may as - sem - ble,
sin - ners jeer; But the truth pro - claims a won - der
vic - to - ry. Sin and hell may seek to seize us,

Res - ur - rec - tion an - thems swell. Come and wor - ship,
For the throne of life He shares." Come and wor - ship,
But can - not with - stand His hour. He has con - quered,
Tho't - ful hearts re - ceive with cheer. He is ris - en,
But Your con - quest keeps us free. Stand in tri - umph,

come and wor - ship; Wor - ship Christ, the ris - en King!
come and wor - ship; Wor - ship Christ, the ris - en King!
He has con - quered; Christ the Lord, the ris - en King!
He is ris - en; Now re - ceive the ris - en King!
stand in tri - umph; Wor - ship Christ, the ris - en King!

TEXT: Jack W. Hayford
MUSIC: Henry T. Smart
A lower setting may be found at No. 754

REGENT SQUARE
8.7.8.7.8.7.

362 Celebrate Jesus

I am the Living One; I was dead, and behold I am alive for ever and ever! Revelation 1:18

TEXT: Gary Oliver
MUSIC: Gary Oliver

CELEBRATE JESUS
Irregular meter

363 Be Joyful

They worshiped Him and returned to Jerusalem with great joy. Luke 24:52

2-part Canon

Be joy - ful, joy - ful, the Lord is a - live.

Come on be joy - ful, joy - ful, the Lord is a - live!

TEXT: Kurt Kaiser
MUSIC: Kurt Kaiser

BE JOYFUL
Irregular meter

364 THE LORD HAS RISEN!

A Worship Sequence

Alleluia! Alleluia!; complete
I Live
Christ the Lord Is Risen Today; complete
Suggested stanzas have been marked with an arrow: ➤

WORSHIP LEADER	Why do you look for the living among the dead? He is not here; the Lord has risen!
CHOIR	**He has risen indeed!**
WORSHIP LEADER	The Lord has risen!
EVERYONE	**He has risen indeed!**
WORSHIP LEADER	The Lord has risen!
EVERYONE	**He has risen indeed!**
WORSHIP LEADER	Where, O death, is your victory? Where, O death, is your sting? Death has been swallowed up in victory!
CHOIR	**Christ has risen indeed!**
WORSHIP LEADER	Jesus said, "I am the resurrection and the life. He who believes in Me will live, even though he dies; and whoever lives and believes in Me will never die."
EVERYONE	**Thanks be to God! He gives us the victory through our Lord Jesus Christ.**
WORSHIP LEADER	The Lord has risen!
EVERYONE	**He has risen indeed! Alleluia!**

from Luke 24:5-6; 1 Corinthians 15:54-55, 57; John 11:25-26 (NIV)

Optional introduction to "Alleluia! Alleluia!"

Alleluia! Alleluia! 365

After His suffering, He gave many convincing proofs that He was alive. Acts 1:3

➤ 1. Al - le - lu - ia! Al - le - lu - ia! Hearts to heav'n and voic - es raise;
➤ 2. Now the i - ron bars are bro - ken, Christ from death to life is born;

Sing to God a hymn of glad - ness, Sing to God a hymn of praise.
Glo - rious life, and life im - mor - tal, On this res - ur - rec - tion morn.

He who on the cross as Sav - ior For the world's sal - va - tion bled,
Christ has tri - umphed, and we con - quer By His might - y en - ter - prise;

Je - sus Christ, the King of Glo - ry, Now is ris - en from the dead.
We with Him to life e - ter - nal By His res - ur - rec - tion rise.

TEXT: Christopher Wordsworth, altered
MUSIC: Ludwig van Beethoven; adapted by Edward Hodges

HYMN TO JOY
8.7.8.7.D.

Optional transition to "I Live"

decresc.   *mf*

366 I Live

Because I live, you also will live. John 14:19

I live, I live be-cause He is ris-en; I live, I live with pow'r o-ver sin. I live, I live be-cause He is ris-en; I live, I live to wor-ship Him. Thank You, Je-sus, thank You, Je-sus; Be-cause You're a-live, be-cause You're a-live, Be-cause You're a-live, I live!

TEXT: Rich Cook
MUSIC: Rich Cook

I LIVE
Irregular meter

Optional repeat setting

cresc.

I live, I live be-cause He is ris-en; I live, I live with pow'r o - ver sin. I live, I live be-cause He is ris-en; I live, I live to wor-ship Him. Thank You, Je - sus, thank You, Je - sus; Be-cause You're a - live, be-cause You're a - live, Be-cause You're a - live, I live!

Optional transition to "Christ the Lord Is Risen Today"

367 Christ the Lord Is Risen Today

He is not here; He has risen, just as He said. Matthew 28:6

1. Christ the Lord is ris'n to-day. Al - le - lu - ia!
2. Lives a - gain our glo-rious King. Al - le - lu - ia!
3. Love's re - deem-ing work is done. Al - le - lu - ia!
4. Soar we now where Christ has led. Al - le - lu - ia!

Sons of men and an - gels say: Al - le - lu - ia!
Where, O death, is now thy sting? Al - le - lu - ia!
Fought the fight, the bat - tle won. Al - le - lu - ia!
Fol - l'wing our ex - alt - ed Head. Al - le - lu - ia!

Raise your joys and tri - umphs high. Al - le - lu - ia!
Dy - ing once, He all doth save. Al - le - lu - ia!
Death in vain for - bids Him rise. Al - le - lu - ia!
Made like Him, like Him we rise. Al - le - lu - ia!

Sing, ye heav'ns, and earth, re - ply: Al - le - lu - ia!
Where thy vic - to - ry, O grave? Al - le - lu - ia!
Christ has o - pened par - a - dise. Al - le - lu - ia!
Ours the cross, the grave, the skies. Al - le - lu - ia!

TEXT: Charles Wesley
MUSIC: *Lyra Davidica*, 1708; Last stanza setting and Choral ending by Don Hart

EASTER HYMN
7.7.7.7. with Alleluias

The end of THE LORD HAS RISEN! - A Worship Sequence

368 He Lives

I am the Living One; I was dead, and behold I am alive for ever and ever! Revelation 1:18

1. I serve a ris - en Sav - ior, He's in the world to - day; I
2. In all the world a - round me I see His lov - ing care; And
3. Re - joice, re - joice, O Chris - tian, lift up your voice and sing E -

know that He is liv - ing, what - ev - er men may say. I see His
tho' my heart grows wea - ry, I nev - er will de - spair. I know that
ter - nal hal - le - lu - jahs to Je - sus Christ, the King! The Hope of

hand of mer - cy, I hear His voice of cheer, And just the time I
He is lead - ing thro' all the storm - y blast; The day of His ap -
all who seek Him, the Help of all who find, None oth - er is so

Refrain

need Him, He's al - ways near. He lives, He lives! Christ
pear - ing will come at last. He lives, He lives!
lov - ing, so good and kind.

Je - sus lives to - day! He walks with me and talks with me a - long life's

TEXT: Alfred H. Ackley
MUSIC: Alfred H. Ackley

ACKLEY
13.13.13.11. with Refrain

nar - row way. He lives, He lives, sal - va - tion to im - part!
He lives, He lives,

rit.

You ask me how I know He lives? He lives with - in my heart!

He Rose Triumphantly 369

We believe that Jesus died and rose again. 1 Thessalonians 4:14

He rose tri - um - phant-ly, In pow'r and maj - es - ty, The Sav - ior

rose no more to die; O let us now pro - claim The glo - ry of His name,

1 And tell to all He lives to - day. **2** He rose tri - day. He lives!

TEXT: Oswald J. Smith
MUSIC: Bentley D. Ackley

HE ROSE TRIUMPHANTLY
Irregular meter

370 Rejoice, the Lord Is King

Rejoice in the Lord always. I will say it again: Rejoice! Philippians 4:4

1. Re - joice, the Lord is King; Your Lord and King a - dore!
2. Je - sus, the Sav - ior, reigns, The God of truth and love.
3. His king - dom can - not fail; He rules o'er earth and heav'n.
4. Re - joice in glo - rious hope! Our Lord, the Judge, shall come

Re - joice, give thanks and sing And tri - umph ev - er - more. Lift
When He had purged our stains, He took His seat a - bove. Lift
The keys of death and hell Are to our Je - sus giv'n. Lift
And take His ser - vants up To their e - ter - nal home. Lift

up your heart; Lift up your voice! Re - joice, a - gain I say, re - joice!
up your heart; Lift up your voice! Re - joice, a - gain I say, re - joice!
up your heart; Lift up your voice! Re - joice, a - gain I say, re - joice!
up your heart; Lift up your voice! Re - joice, a - gain I say, re - joice!

TEXT: Charles Wesley
MUSIC: John Darwall

DARWALL
6.6.6.6.8.8.

371 Oh for a Thousand Tongues

My tongue will sing of Your righteousness. Psalm 51:14

Unison

Glo - ry to the Lamb Whose throne for -

TEXT: David Binion
MUSIC: David Binion

BINION
Irregular meter

ev - er reigns; God in the

high - est, Wor - thy to mer - it our praise.

Refrain

Oh for a thou - sand tongues to sing

prais - es un - to Thee; Oh for a

thou - sand hands to raise in hon - or to the

1 *Repeat of refrain optional*   *Introduction take D.C.*   2

King. King.

8vb

372 Our God Reigns

How beautiful are the feet of those who bring good news, "Your God reigns!" Isaiah 52:7

1. How love - ly on the moun - tains are the feet of him
2. He had no state - ly form; He had no maj - es - ty,
3. Out of the tomb He came with grace and maj - es - ty;

Who brings good news, good news An - nounc - ing
That we should be drawn to Him. He was de -
He is a - live, He is a - live. God loves us

peace, pro - claim - ing news of hap - pi - ness. Our God
spised, and we took no ac - count of Him, Yet now He
so— see here His hands, His feet, His side. Yes, we

Refrain

reigns; our God reigns! Our God reigns!
reigns with the Most High.
know He is a - live.

TEXT: Leonard E. Smith, Jr.
MUSIC: Leonard E. Smith, Jr.

OUR GOD REIGNS
Irregular meter

Our God reigns! Our God reigns! Our God reigns!

Optional segue to "To Him Who Sits on the Throne." No transition is needed.

To Him Who Sits on the Throne 373

To Him who sits on the throne and to the Lamb be praise and honor and glory. Revelation 5:13

To Him who sits on the throne and un-to the Lamb,

To Him who sits on the throne and un-to the Lamb Be

bless-ing and hon-or and glo-ry and pow-er for-ev-er, Be

Cued notes for a few choir sopranos

bless-ing and hon-or and glo-ry and pow-er for-ev-er, -ev-er, for-ev-er!

TEXT: Debbye Graafsma
MUSIC: Debbye Graafsma

GRAAFSMA
Irregular meter

374 Victory Chant

God gives us the victory through our Lord Jesus Christ. 1 Corinthians 15:57

1. Hail, Je - sus, You're my King. Hail, Je - sus, You're my King.
2. Hail, Je - sus, You're my Lord. Hail, Je - sus, You're my Lord.
3. Glo - ry, glo - ry to the Lamb. Glo - ry, glo - ry to the Lamb.

Your life frees me to sing. Your life frees me to sing.
I will o - bey Your Word. I will o - bey Your Word. I
You take me in - to the land. You take me in - to the land.

I will praise You all my days. I will praise You all my days.
want to see Your King - dom come. I want to see Your King - dom come.
We will con - quer in Your name, We will con - quer in Your name,

Per - fect in all Your ways. Per - fect in all Your ways.
Not my will, but Yours be done. Not my will, but Yours be done.
And pro - claim that Je - sus reigns, And pro - claim that Je - sus reigns.

TEXT: Joseph Vogels
MUSIC: Joseph Vogels

VICTORY CHANT
Irregular meter

Optional extended ending

And pro-claim that Je-sus reigns, And pro-claim that Je-sus reigns.

Optional segue to "Jesus Shall Reign." No transition is needed, but use bracketed introduction.

Jesus Shall Reign 375

He will rule from sea to sea and from the River to the ends of the earth. Psalm 72:8

1. Je - sus shall reign wher - e'er the sun Does its suc -
2. To Him shall end - less prayer be made, And end - less
3. Peo - ple and realms of ev - ery tongue Dwell on His
4. Let ev - ery crea - ture rise and bring His grate - ful

ces - sive jour - neys run; His king-dom spread from
prais - es crown His head. His name like sweet per -
love with sweet - est song, And in - fant voic - es
hon - ors to our King; An - gels de - scend with

shore to shore, Till moons shall wax and wane no more.
fume shall rise With ev - ery morn - ing sac - ri - fice.
shall pro - claim Their ear - ly bless - ings on His name.
songs a - gain, And earth re - peat the loud "A - men!"

TEXT: Isaac Watts; based on Psalm 72
MUSIC: John Hatton

DUKE STREET
L.M.

376 Great Is the Lord Almighty!

Great is our Lord and mighty in power. Psalm 147:5

The Lord reigns! He is a might-y God, the Lord God reigns! The

Lord reigns! He is a might-y God, the Lord God reigns!

Harmony optional

Great is the Lord Al-might-y, He is Lord, He is God in-deed! Great is the Lord Al-

might-y, He is God su-preme! Great is the Lord Al-might-y, He is

Lord, He is God in-deed! Great is the Lord, Great is the Lord!

TEXT: Dennis L. Jernigan
MUSIC: Dennis L. Jernigan

ALMIGHTY
Irregular meter

Alleluia! Sing to Jesus 377

There was a great multitude from every nation standing in front of the Lamb. Revelation 7:9

1. Al - le - lu - ia! sing to Je - sus! His the scep - ter, His the throne.
2. Al - le - lu - ia! not as or - phans Are we left in sor - row now.
3. Al - le - lu - ia! Bread of Heav - en, You on earth our food and stay!

Al - le - lu - ia! His the tri - umph, His the vic - to - ry a - lone.
Al - le - lu - ia! He is near us; Faith be - lieves, nor ques - tions how.
Al - le - lu - ia! here the sin - ful Flee to You from day to day.

Hark! the songs of peace - ful Zi - on Thun - der like a might - y flood:
Tho' the clouds from sight re - ceived Him When the for - ty days were o'er,
In - ter - ces - sor, Friend of sin - ners, Earth's Re - deem - er, plead for me,

"Je - sus out of ev - ery na - tion Has re - deemed us by His blood."
Shall our hearts for - get His prom - ise: "I am with you ev - er - more"?
Where the songs of all the sin - less Sweep a - cross the crys - tal sea.

TEXT: William C. Dix
MUSIC: Rowland H. Prichard; arranged by Robert Harkness
A lower setting may be found at No. 309

HYFRYDOL
8.7.8.7.D.

378

THE LIGHT

from John 1:1-14 (NKJV)

SOLO 1
In the beginning was the Word,

SOLO 2
And the Word was with God,

SOLO 1
And the Word was God.

EVERYONE
He was in the beginning with God.

SOLO 1
All things were made through Him,
and without Him nothing was made that was made.

EVERYONE
In Him was life,
and the life was the light of men.

SOLO 2
And the light shines in the darkness,
and the darkness did not comprehend it.

SOLO 1
There was a man sent from God, whose name was John.
This man came for a witness, to bear witness of the light,
that all through Him might believe.

SOLO 2
He was not that light,
but was sent to bear witness of that light.

SOLO 1
That was the true light which gives light
to every man who comes into the world.

WOMEN
He was in the world,
and the world was made through Him,
and the world did not know Him.

MEN
He came to His own,
and His own did not receive Him.

EVERYONE
But as many as received Him,
to them He gave the right to become children of God,
even to those who believe in His name.

SOLO 2
These were born not of blood,
not of the will of the flesh,
not of the will of man, but of God.

EVERYONE
And the Word became flesh and dwelt among us,
and we beheld His glory—
the glory as of the only begotten of the Father,
full of grace and truth.

CHRIST, THE REDEEMER

from Mark 10:45; Romans 3:21-26; Ephesians 1:7-8;
Hebrews 9:15; 1 Peter 1:18-19, 21 (NIV)

WORSHIP LEADER
The Son of Man did not come to be served, but to serve,
and to give His life as a ransom for many.

MEN
But now a righteousness from God, apart from law,
has been made known, to which
the Law and the Prophets testify.

EVERYONE
The righteousness from God
comes through faith in Jesus Christ to all who believe.

WORSHIP LEADER
There is no difference;

EVERYONE
For all have sinned and fall short of the glory of God,
and are justified freely by His grace
through the redemption that came by Christ Jesus.

WORSHIP LEADER
God presented Him as a sacrifice of atonement,
through faith in His blood.
He did this to demonstrate His justice,
because in His forbearance He had left the sins
committed beforehand unpunished.

WOMEN
He did it to demonstrate His justice at the present time,
so as to be just and the one who justifies those
who have faith in Jesus.

EVERYONE
In Him we have redemption through His blood,
the forgiveness of sins,
in accordance with the riches of God's grace
that He lavished on us with all wisdom and understanding.

WORSHIP LEADER
For this reason Christ is the mediator of a New Covenant,
that those who are called may receive the promised eternal inheritance,
now that He has died as a ransom to set them free
from the sins committed under the First Covenant.

MEN
For you know that it was not with perishable things
such as silver or gold that you were redeemed from
the empty way of life handed down to you from your forefathers,

EVERYONE
But with the precious blood of Christ,
a lamb without blemish or defect.

WORSHIP LEADER
Through Him you believe in God,
who raised Him from the dead and glorified Him,
and so your faith and hope are in God.

EVERYONE
My faith and hope are in God.

380

THE LOVE OF CHRIST

from John 13:1, 34; 14:21; 15:12-13; Romans 8:35, 39;
2 Corinthians 5:14; Ephesians 3:17-19 (NKJV)

WORSHIP LEADER
Now before the feast of the Passover,
when Jesus knew that His hour had come
that He should depart from this world to the Father,
having loved His own who were in the world,
He loved them to the end.
And Jesus said;

EVERYONE
"A new commandment I give to you,
that you love one another; as I have loved you,
that you also love one another."

WORSHIP LEADER
"He who has My commandments and keeps them,
it is he who loves Me.
And he who loves Me will be loved by My Father,
and I will love him and manifest Myself to him."

WOMEN
"This is My commandment, that you love one another
as I have loved you."

EVERYONE
"Greater love has no one than this,
than to lay down one's life for his friends."

WORSHIP LEADER
Who shall separate us from the love of Christ?
Shall tribulation, or distress,
or persecution, or famine,
or nakedness, or peril, or sword?

EVERYONE
Neither height nor depth,
nor any other created thing
shall be able to separate us from the love of God
which is in Christ Jesus, our Lord.

WORSHIP LEADER
For the love of Christ compels us.

MEN
May you be rooted and established
in the love of Christ.

WOMEN
May you be able to comprehend with all the saints
what is the width and length and depth and height of the love of Christ.

MEN
May you know the love of Christ which passes knowledge.

WORSHIP LEADER
May you be filled with all the fullness of God.

EVERYONE
This is My commandment, that you love one another
as I have loved you.

CHRIST'S PRIESTHOOD

from Hebrews 3:1; 4:15-16; 7:24-27; 10:11-14, 19-22 (NKJV)

WORSHIP LEADER
Therefore, holy brethren, partakers of the heavenly calling,
consider the apostle and high priest of our confession,
Christ Jesus.

SOLO
For we do not have a high priest
who cannot sympathize with our weaknesses,
but was in all points tempted as we are,
yet without sin.

EVERYONE
**Let us therefore come boldly to the throne of grace,
that we may obtain mercy
and find grace to help in time of need.**

WORSHIP LEADER
Because He continues forever,
He has an unchangeable priesthood.

SOLO
Therefore He is also able to save to the uttermost
those who come to God through Him,
since He always lives to make intercession for them.

EVERYONE
**For such a high priest was fitting for us,
who is holy, harmless, undefiled, separate from sinners,
and has become higher than the heavens;**

WORSHIP LEADER
He does not need daily, as those high priests, to offer up sacrifices,
first for His own sins and then for the people's,
for this He did once for all when He offered up Himself.

SOLO
And every priest stands ministering daily
and offering repeatedly the same sacrifices,
which can never take away sins.

EVERYONE
**But this man,
after He had offered one sacrifice for sins forever,
sat down at the right hand of God.**

WORSHIP LEADER
For by one offering He has perfected forever
those who are being sanctified.

SOLO
Therefore, brethren, having boldness to enter
the holiest place by the blood of Jesus,
by a new and living way which He consecrated for us,
through the veil, that is, His flesh,
and having a high priest over the house of God,

EVERYONE
**Let us draw near with a true heart in full assurance of faith,
having our hearts sprinkled from an evil conscience
and our bodies washed with pure water.**

382 Come, Holy Spirit

The law of the Spirit of life set me free from the law of sin and death. Romans 8:2

1. Come as a wis-dom to chil-dren; Come as new
2. Come as a rest to the wea-ry; Come as a
3. Come like a spring in the des-ert; Come to the

sight to the blind. Come, Lord, as strength to my weak-ness;
balm for the sore. Come as a dew to my dry-ness;
with-ered of soul. O let Your sweet heal-ing pow-er

Refrain

Take me: soul, bod-y and mind.
Fill me with joy ev-er-more. Come, Ho-ly Spir-it, I
Touch me and make me whole.

need You; Come, sweet Spir-it, I pray. Come in Your

strength and Your pow-er; Come in Your own gen-tle way.

Optional segue to "Fill Me Now."
No transition is needed.

TEXT: Gloria Gaither and William J. Gaither
MUSIC: William J. Gaither

COME, HOLY SPIRIT
8.7.8.7.D.

Fill Me Now 383

Be filled with the Spirit. Ephesians 5:18

1. Hov - er o'er me, Ho - ly Spir - it; Bathe my trem - bling heart and brow.
2. Thou canst fill me, gra - cious Spir - it, Tho' I can - not tell Thee how.
3. I am weak - ness, full of weak - ness; At Thy sa - cred feet I bow.
4. Cleanse and com - fort, bless and save me; Bathe, O bathe my heart and brow.

Fill me with Thy hal - lowed pres - ence; Come, O come and fill me now.
But I need Thee, great - ly need Thee; Come, O come and fill me now.
Blest, di - vine, e - ter - nal Spir - it, Fill with pow'r and fill me now.
Thou art com - fort - ing and sav - ing; Thou art sweet - ly fill - ing now.

Refrain

Fill me now, fill me now, Je - sus, come and fill me now;

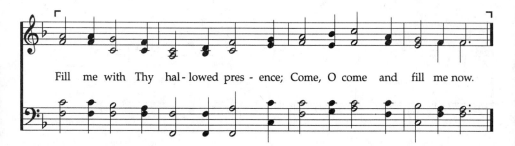

Fill me with Thy hal - lowed pres - ence; Come, O come and fill me now.

TEXT: Elwood H. Stokes
MUSIC: John R. Sweney

FILL ME NOW
8.7.8.7. with Refrain

384 Spirit Song

Whoever believes in Me will have streams of living water flowing from within. John 7:38

1. O let the Son of God en-fold you with His Spir-it
2. O come and sing this song with glad-ness as your hearts are

and His love; Let Him fill your heart and sat-is-fy your soul.
filled with joy; Lift your hands in sweet sur-ren-der to His name.

O let Him have the things that hold you, and His Spir-it, like a
O give Him all your tears and sad-ness; give Him all your years of

dove, Will de-scend up-on your life and make you whole.
pain, And you'll en-ter in-to life in Je-sus' name.

Refrain

Je-sus, O Je-sus, come and fill Your lambs.

TEXT: John Wimber
MUSIC: John Wimber

SPIRIT SONG
Irregular meter

Je - sus, O Je - sus, come and fill Your lambs.

Optional transition to
"Where the Spirit of the Lord Is"

Where the Spirit of the Lord Is 385

Where the Spirit of the Lord is, there is freedom. 2 Corinthians 3:17

Where the Spir - it of the Lord is, there is peace; Where the

Spir - it of the Lord is, there is love. There is com - fort in life's

dark - est hour; There is light and life, there is help and

pow - er In the Spir - it, in the Spir - it of the Lord.

TEXT: Stephen R. Adams
MUSIC: Stephen R. Adams

ADAMS
Irregular meter

386 The Comforter Has Come

I will ask the Father, and He will give you another Counselor to be with you forever. John 14:16

1. O spread the tid-ings 'round, wher-ev-er man is found, Wher-
2. The long, long night is past; the morn-ing breaks at last; And
3. Lo, the great King of kings, with heal-ing in His wings, To
4. O bound-less love di-vine! How shall this tongue of mine To

ev-er hu-man hearts and hu-man woes a-bound. Let ev-ery Chris-tian
hushed the dread-ful wail and fu-ry of the blast, As o'er the gold-en
ev-ery cap-tive soul a full de-liv-'rance brings; And thro' the va-cant
won-d'ring mor-tals tell the match-less grace di-vine— That I, a child of

tongue pro-claim the joy-ful sound: The Com-fort-er has come!
hills the day ad-vanc-es fast! The Com-fort-er has come!
cells the song of tri-umph rings: The Com-fort-er has come!
hell, should in His im-age shine? The Com-fort-er has come!

Refrain

The Com-fort-er has come! The Com-fort-er has come! The Ho-ly

TEXT: Frank Bottome
MUSIC: William J. Kirkpatrick

COMFORTER
12.12.12.6. with Refrain

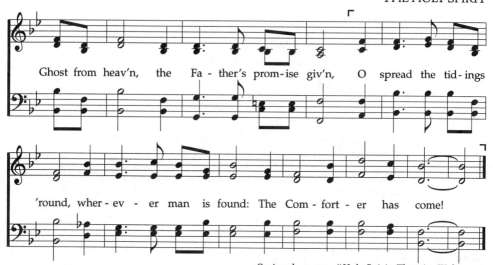

Ghost from heav'n, the Fa - ther's prom-ise giv'n, O spread the tid-ings 'round, wher - ev - er man is found: The Com - fort - er has come!

Optional segue to "Holy Spirit, Thou Art Welcome."
No transition is needed. Ritard the last phrase of
"The Comforter Has Come."

Holy Spirit, Thou Art Welcome 387

We have not received the spirit of the world but the Spirit who is from God. 1 Corinthians 2:12

Ho - ly Spir - it, Thou art wel - come in this place. Ho - ly

Spir - it, Thou art wel - come in this place. Om - nip - o - tent

Fa - ther of mer - cy and grace, Thou art wel - come in this place.

TEXT: Dottie Rambo and David Huntsinger
MUSIC: Dottie Rambo and David Huntsinger

THOU ART WELCOME
11.11.11.7.

388

BY HIS SPIRIT
A Worship Sequence
Spirit of the Living God; stanzas 1,3
Spirit of God, Descend upon My Heart; stanzas 1,2,4
Suggested stanzas have been marked with an arrow: ➤

WORSHIP LEADER

If Christ is in you, your spirit is alive because of righteousness.
If the Spirit of Him who raised Jesus from the dead is living in you,
He will also give life to your mortal bodies through His Spirit, who lives in you.
If by the Spirit you put to death the misdeeds of the body, you will live,
Because those who are led by the Spirit of God are sons of God.

from Romans 8:10-11, 13-14 (NIV)

389 Spirit of the Living God

Live by the Spirit, and you will not gratify the desires of the sinful nature. Galatians 5:16

➤ 1. Spir - it of the liv - ing God, fall fresh on me. Spir - it of the liv - ing God, fall fresh on me. Melt me, mold me, fill me, use me. Spir - it of the liv - ing God, fall fresh on me.

2. Soul of heav - en, heart of God, wash o - ver me. Soul of heav - en, heart of God, wash o - ver me. Cleanse me, teach me, hold me, reach me. Soul of heav - en, heart of God, wash o - ver me.

➤ 3. Ho - ly pres - ence, love di - vine, cast out my fear. Ho - ly pres - ence, love di - vine, cast out my fear. Shield me, free me, call me, lead me. Ho - ly pres - ence, love di - vine, cast out my fear.

Optional segue to "Spirit of God, Descend upon My Heart." No transition is necessary.

TEXT: Daniel Iverson, stanza 1; Lowell Alexander, stanzas 2, 3
MUSIC: Daniel Iverson

IVERSON
Irregular meter

Spirit of God, Descend upon My Heart 390

Since we live by the Spirit, let us keep in step with the Spirit. Galatians 5:25

1. Spir - it of God, de - scend up - on my heart; Wean it from
earth, thro' all its puls - es move; Stoop to my weak - ness, might - y
as Thou art, And make me love Thee as I ought to love.

2. Hast Thou not bid us love Thee, God and King? All, all Thine
own– soul, heart, and strength, and mind! I see Thy cross– there teach my
heart to cling; O let me seek Thee, and O let me find!

3. Teach me to feel that Thou art al - ways nigh; Teach me the
strug - gles of the soul to bear, To check the ris - ing doubt, the
reb - el sigh; Teach me the pa - tience of un - an - swered prayer.

4. Teach me to love Thee as Thine an - gels love, One ho - ly
pas - sion fill - ing all my frame; The bap - tism of the heav'n - de-
scend-ed Dove– My heart an al - tar, and Thy love the flame.

TEXT: George Croly
MUSIC: Frederick C. Atkinson;
Fourfold Amen by William David Young

MORECAMBE
10.10.10.10.

Optional choral ending

A - men, a - men, a - men, a - men.

The end of BY HIS SPIRIT - A Worship Sequence

391 Sweet, Sweet Spirit

The fruit of the Spirit is love, joy, peace. Galatians 5:22

There's a sweet, sweet Spir-it in this place, And I know that it's the Spir-it of the Lord. There are sweet ex-pres-sions on each face, And I know they feel the pres-ence of the Lord.

Refrain

Sweet Ho-ly Spir-it, sweet heav-en-ly Dove, Stay right here with us, fill-ing us with Your

TEXT: Doris Akers
MUSIC: Doris Akers

SWEET, SWEET SPIRIT
Irregular meter

love. And for these bless-ings we lift our hearts in praise.

With-out a doubt we'll know that we have been re-vived When

we shall leave this place.

Optional transition to
"Holy Spirit, Light Divine"

rit.

Holy Spirit, Light Divine 392

"Not by might nor by power, but by My Spirit," says the Lord Almighty. Zechariah 4:6

1. Ho - ly Spir - it, Light di - vine, Shine up - on this heart of mine.
2. Ho - ly Spir - it, Pow'r di - vine, Cleanse this guilt - y heart of mine.
3. Ho - ly Spir - it, Joy di - vine, Cheer this sad - dened heart of mine.
4. Ho - ly Spir - it, all di - vine, Dwell with - in this heart of mine.

Chase the shades of night a - way; Turn my dark - ness in - to day.
Long hath sin with - out con - trol Held do - min - ion o'er my soul.
Bid my man - y woes de - part; Heal my wound - ed, bleed - ing heart.
Cast down ev - ery i - dol throne; Reign su - preme, and reign a - lone.

TEXT: Andrew Reed
MUSIC: Louis M. Gottschalk; arranged by Edwin P. Parker

MERCY
7.7.7.7.

393 Breathe on Me, Breath of God

He breathed on them and said, "Receive the Holy Spirit." John 20:22

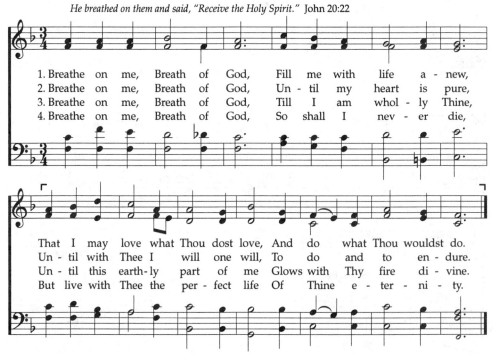

1. Breathe on me, Breath of God, Fill me with life a - new,
2. Breathe on me, Breath of God, Un - til my heart is pure,
3. Breathe on me, Breath of God, Till I am whol - ly Thine,
4. Breathe on me, Breath of God, So shall I nev - er die,

That I may love what Thou dost love, And do what Thou wouldst do.
Un - til with Thee I will one will, To do and to en - dure.
Un - til this earth - ly part of me Glows with Thy fire di - vine.
But live with Thee the per - fect life Of Thine e - ter - ni - ty.

TEXT: Edwin Hatch
MUSIC: Robert Jackson
A lower setting may be found at No. 466

TRENTHAM
S.M.

394 Greater Is He That Is in Me

The One who is in you is greater than the one who is in the world. 1 John 4:4

Great-er is He that is in me, Great-er is He that is in me;

Great-er is He that is in me Than he that is in the world.

TEXT: Lanny Wolfe; based on 1 John 4:4
MUSIC: Lanny Wolfe

GREATER IS HE
8.8.8.7.

Descend, O Holy Spirit 395

We do not know what we ought to pray for, but the Spirit Himself intercedes for us. Romans 8:26

1. De - scend, O Ho - ly Spir - it, de - scend on us we pray;
2. De - scend, O Ho - ly Spir - it, let heal - ing wa - ter flow
3. De - scend, O Ho - ly Spir - it, de - scend in tongues of fire,
4. De - scend, O Ho - ly Spir - it, as rush - ing, might - y wind;

And bless us with Your pres - ence, re - newed in us to - day.
To com - fort those in mourn - ing, a so - lace to the soul;
And fill us with great pow - er; Your will is our de - sire.
We stand in ad - o - ra - tion; O Spir - it, now de - scend.

A fer - vent in - ter - ces - sor be - fore the Fa - ther's throne;
A foun - tain in the des - ert, the wa - ter of Your Word,
O make our hearts an al - tar, con - sumed by ho - ly flame,
O cleanse us by Your pow - er, our weak - ened faith re - new;

Your gen - tle sup - pli - ca - tions make our pe - ti - tions known.
A - noint - ed with Your pow - er, the sweet - est mes - sage heard.
To draw the soul held cap - tive to faith in Je - sus' name.
Com - mis - sion us for ser - vice to lead the lost to You.

TEXT: Michaele Murphy
MUSIC: Alexander Ewing

EWING
7.6.7.6.D.

396 Breathe on Me

He breathed on them and said, "Receive the Holy Spirit." John 20:22

1. Ho - ly Spir - it, breathe on me Un - til my heart is clean;
2. Ho - ly Spir - it, breathe on me; My stub-born will sub - due.
3. Ho - ly Spir - it, breathe on me; Fill me with pow'r di - vine.
4. Ho - ly Spir - it, breathe on me Till I am all Thine own,

Let sun-shine fill its in - most part, With not a cloud be - tween.
Teach me in words of liv - ing flame What Christ would have me do.
Kin - dle a flame of love and zeal With - in this heart of mine.
Un - til my will is lost in Thine, To live for Thee a - lone.

Refrain

Breathe on me, breathe on me; Ho - ly Spir - it, breathe on me.

Take Thou my heart, cleanse ev - ery part; Ho - ly Spir - it, breathe on me.

TEXT: Edwin Hatch; adapted by B. B. McKinney; based on John 20:22
MUSIC: B. B. McKinney

TRUETT
7.6.8.6. with Refrain

THE SPIRIT OF TRUTH 397

from John 14:16-21, 23-24, 26 (NIV)

WORSHIP LEADER or DRAMATIC SOLO

Jesus said,
"I will ask the Father, and He will give you another Counselor
to be with you forever—the Spirit of truth.
The world cannot accept Him,
because it neither sees Him nor knows Him.
But you know Him, for He lives with you and will be in you.
I will not leave you as orphans; I will come to you.
Before long, the world will not see Me anymore, but you will see Me.
Because I live, you also will live.
On that day you will realize that I am in My Father,
and you are in Me, and I am in you.
Whoever has My commands and obeys them,
he is the one who loves Me.
He who loves Me will be loved by My Father,
and I too will love him and show Myself to him.
If anyone loves Me, he will obey My teaching.
My Father will love him, and We will come to him
and make Our home with him.
He who does not love Me will not obey My teaching.
These words you hear are not My own;
they belong to the Father who sent Me.
The Counselor, the Holy Spirit, will teach you all things."

LIFE IN THE SPIRIT 398

from Galatians 5:16-25 (NIV)

WORSHIP LEADER or DRAMATIC SOLO

I, Paul, say,
"Live by the Spirit, and you will not gratify the desires
of the sinful nature.
The sinful nature desires what is contrary to the Spirit,
and the Spirit what is contrary to the sinful nature.
They are in conflict with each other,
so that you do not do what you want.
If you are led by the Spirit, you are not under law.
The acts of the sinful nature are obvious:
Sexual immorality, impurity and debauchery;
Idolatry and witchcraft; hatred, discord, jealousy;
Fits of rage, selfish ambition; dissensions, factions and envy;
Drunkenness, orgies and the like.
I warn you…
Those who live like this will not inherit the kingdom of God.
But the fruit of the Spirit is love, joy, peace, patience, kindness,
goodness, faithfulness, gentleness and self-control.
Against such things there is no law.
Those who belong to Christ Jesus have crucified the sinful nature
with its passions and desires.
Since we live by the Spirit, let us keep in step with the Spirit."

399 We Are God's People

You are a chosen people, a royal priesthood, a holy nation, a people belonging to God. 1 Peter 2:9

Unison

1. We are God's peo - ple, the cho - sen of the Lord,
2. We are God's loved ones, the Bride of Christ, our Lord,
3. We are the Bod - y of which the Lord is Head,
4. We are a Tem - ple, the Spir - it's dwell - ing place,

Born of His Spir - it, es - tab - lished by His Word. Our
For we have known it, the love of God out - poured. Now
Called to o - bey Him, now ris - en from the dead. He
Formed in great weak - ness, a cup to hold God's grace. We

cor - ner - stone is Christ a - lone, And strong in Him we stand; O let us
let us learn how to re - turn The gift of love once given; O let us
wills us be a fam - i - ly Di - verse, yet tru - ly one; O let us
die a - lone, for on its own Each em - ber los - es fire; Yet joined in

live trans - par - ent - ly And walk heart to heart and hand in hand.
share each joy and care And live with a zeal that pleas - es Heav'n.
give our gifts to God And so shall His work on earth be done.
one the flame burns on To give warmth and light and to in - spire.

TEXT: Bryan Jeffery Leech
MUSIC: Johannes Brahms; adapted by Fred Bock

SYMPHONY
11.11.13.8.9.

Glorious Things of Thee Are Spoken 400

Glorious things are said of you, O city of God. Psalm 87:3

1. Glo - rious things of thee are spo - ken, Zi - on, cit - y of our God;
2. See, the streams of liv - ing wa - ters, Spring-ing from e - ter - nal Love,
3. Round each hab - i - ta - tion hov - 'ring, See the cloud and fire ap - pear
4. Sav - ior, since of Zi - on's cit - y I thro' grace a mem - ber am,

He whose word can - not be bro - ken Formed thee for His own a - bode.
Well sup - ply thy sons and daugh-ters, And all fear of want re - move.
For a glo - ry and a cov - 'ring, Show-ing that the Lord is near!
Let the world de - ride or pit - y; I will glo - ry in Thy name.

On the Rock of A - ges found - ed, What can shake thy sure re - pose?
Who can faint while such a riv - er Ev - er flows their thirst to as - suage?
Thus they march, the pil - lar lead - ing, Light by night and shade by day,
Fad - ing is the world's best plea - sure, All its boast - ed pomp and show;

With sal - va - tion's walls sur-round-ed, Thou may'st smile at all thy foes.
Grace which like the Lord, the Giv - er, Nev - er fails from age to age!
Dai - ly on the man - na feed - ing Which He gives them when they pray.
Sol - id joys and last - ing trea - sures None but Zi - on's chil-dren know.

TEXT: John Newton, altered
MUSIC: Franz Joseph Haydn

AUSTRIAN HYMN
8.7.8.7.D.

401 The Church's One Foundation

No one can lay any foundation other than the one already laid; Jesus Christ. 1 Corinthians 3:11

1. The Church's one foundation Is Jesus Christ, her Lord;
2. Elect from every nation, Yet one o'er all the earth,
3. 'Mid toil and tribulation And tumult of her war,
4. Yet she on earth hath union With God, the Three in One,

She is His new creation By water and the Word:
Her charter of salvation: One Lord, one faith, one birth;
She waits the consummation Of peace forevermore;
And mystic, sweet communion With those whose rest is won:

From heav'n He came and sought her To be His holy bride;
One holy name she blesses, Partakes one holy food;
Till with the vision glorious Her longing eyes are blest,
O happy ones and holy! Lord, give us grace that we

With His own blood He bought her, And for her life He died.
And to one hope she presses, With every grace endued.
And the great Church victorious Shall be the Church at rest.
Like them, the meek and lowly, On high may dwell with Thee.

TEXT: Samuel J. Stone
MUSIC: Samuel S. Wesley; Last stanza setting and Choral ending by David T. Clydesdale

AURELIA
7.6.7.6.D.

Optional last stanza setting

Unison (melody octave lower)

4. Yet she on earth hath un - ion With God, the Three in One,

melody as written

And mys- tic, sweet com - mun - ion With those whose rest is won:

O hap-py ones and ho - ly! Lord, give us grace that we

melody octave lower

Like them, the meek and low - ly, On high may dwell with Thee.

Optional choral ending

A - men.

402 Cornerstone

I lay a stone in Zion, a tested stone, a precious cornerstone for a sure foundation. Isaiah 28:16

I lay in Zi-on, for a foun-da-tion, a Stone. I lay in Zi-on, for a foun-da-tion, a Stone— A tried Stone, a pre-cious Cor-ner-stone, A sure foun-da-tion, a sure foun-da-tion; A tried Stone, a pre-cious Cor-ner-stone. He that be-liev-eth shall not make haste.

TEXT: Leon Patillo; based on Isaiah 28:16
MUSIC: Leon Patillo

CORNERSTONE
Irregular meter

Christ Is Made the Sure Foundation 403

No one can lay any foundation other than Jesus Christ. 1 Corinthians 3:11

1. Christ is made the sure foun-da-tion. Christ the head and cor-ner-stone, Cho-sen of the Lord and pre-cious, Bind-ing all the Church in one, Ho-ly Zi-on's help for-ev-er, And her con-fi-dence a-lone.

2. To this tem-ple, where we call Thee, Come, O Lord of hosts, to-day. With ac-cus-tomed lov-ing-kind-ness Hear Thy peo-ple as they pray, And Thy full-est ben-e-dic-tion Shed with-in its walls al-way.

3. Here vouch-safe to all Thy ser-vants What they ask of Thee to gain, What they gain from Thee for-ev-er With the bless-ed to re-tain, And here-af-ter in Thy glo-ry Ev-er-more with Thee to reign.

4. Laud and hon-or to the Fa-ther; Laud and hon-or to the Son. Laud and hon-or to the Spir-it; Ev-er Three and ev-er One. One in might and One in glo-ry While un-end-ing a-ges run.

TEXT: Latin Hymn, 7th century; translated by John M. Neale
MUSIC: Henry T. Smart
A lower setting may be found at No. 754

REGENT SQUARE
8.7.8.7.8.7.

404 Faith of Our Fathers

Contend for the faith that was once for all entrusted to the saints. Jude 3

1. Faith of our fa - thers, liv - ing still In spite of dun - geon,
2. Faith of our fa - thers! we will strive To win all na - tions
3. Faith of our fa - thers! we will love Both friend and foe in

fire, and sword; O how our hearts beat high with joy
un - to thee, And through the truth that comes from God,
all our strife, And preach thee, too, as love knows how,

When - e'er we hear that glo - rious word! Faith of our fa - thers,
Man - kind shall then be tru - ly free. Faith of our fa - thers,
By kind - ly words and vir - tuous life. Faith of our fa - thers,

ho - ly faith! We will be true to thee till death!
ho - ly faith! We will be true to thee till death!
ho - ly faith! We will be true to thee till death!

TEXT: Frederick W. Faber
MUSIC: Henri F. Hemy; arranged by James G. Walton

ST. CATHERINE
8.8.8.8.8.8.

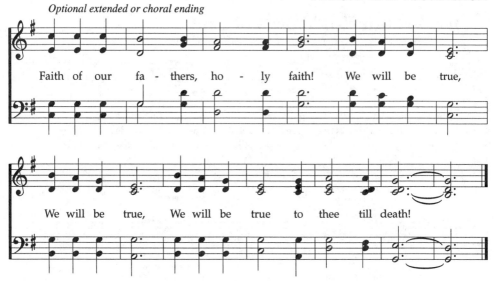

Optional extended or choral ending

Faith of our fa - thers, ho - ly faith! We will be true,

We will be true, We will be true to thee till death!

I Love Thy Kingdom, Lord 405

I love the house where You live, O Lord. Psalm 26:8

1. I love Thy king - dom, Lord, The house of Thine a - bode,
2. I love Thy Church, O God! Her walls be - fore Thee stand,
3. For her my tears shall fall; For her my prayers as - cend;
4. Be - yond my high - est joy I prize her heav'n - ly ways,
5. Sure as Thy truth shall last, To Zi - on shall be giv'n

The Church our blest Re - deem - er saved With His own pre - cious blood.
Dear as the ap - ple of Thine eye, And grav - en on Thy hand.
To her my cares and toils be giv'n, Till toils and cares shall end.
Her sweet com - mu - nion, sol - emn vows, Her hymns of love and praise.
The bright - est glo - ries earth can yield, And bright - er bliss of heav'n.

TEXT: Timothy Dwight
MUSIC: Aaron Williams
A higher setting may be found at No. 65

ST. THOMAS
S.M.

406 Wonderful Words of Life

The words I have spoken to you are spirit and they are life. John 6:63

1. Sing them o-ver a-gain to me, Won-der-ful words of Life;
2. Christ, the bless-ed One, gives to all Won-der-ful words of Life;
3. Sweet-ly ech-o the gos-pel call, Won-der-ful words of Life;

Let me more of their beau-ty see, Won-der-ful words of Life.
Sin-ner, list to the lov-ing call, Won-der-ful words of Life.
Of-fer par-don and peace to all, Won-der-ful words of Life.

Words of life and beau-ty, Teach me faith and du-ty.
All so free-ly giv-en, Woo-ing us to heav-en—
Je-sus, on-ly Sav-ior, Sanc-ti-fy for-ev-er.

Refrain

Beau-ti-ful words, won-der-ful words, Won-der-ful words of Life.

Beau-ti-ful words, won-der-ful words, Won-der-ful words of Life.

TEXT: Philip P. Bliss
MUSIC: Philip P. Bliss

WORDS OF LIFE
8.6.8.6.6.6. with Refrain

God Has Spoken by His Prophets 407

God spoke through the prophets; in these days He has spoken to us by His Son. Hebrews 1:1-2

1. God has spo-ken by His proph-ets, Spo-ken His un-chang-ing Word,
2. God has spo-ken by Christ Je - sus, Christ the ev - er - last - ing Son,
3. God is speak-ing by His Spir - it, Speak-ing to our hearts a - gain;

Each from age to age pro-claim-ing God, the one, the righ-teous Lord.
Bright-ness of the Fa-ther's glo-ry, With the Fa-ther ev - er one;
In the age-less Word ex-pound-ing God's own mes-sage, now as then.

In the world's de-spair and tur-moil One firm an-chor holds us fast:
Spo-ken by the Word in-car-nate, God of God, ere time was born;
Thro' the rise and fall of na-tions One sure faith yet stand-ing fast:

God is King, His throne e - ter-nal, God the First and God the Last.
Light of Light, to earth de-scend-ing, Christ as God in hu-man form.
God a-bides, His Word un-chang-ing, God the First and God the Last.

TEXT: George W. Briggs, altered
MUSIC: John Zundel

BEECHER
8.7.8.7.D.

A higher setting may be found at No. 93

408 How Firm a Foundation

God's solid foundation stands firm; The Lord knows those who are His. 2 Timothy 2:19

1. How firm a foun-da-tion, ye saints of the Lord,
2. "Fear not! I am with thee; O be not dis-mayed,
3. "When through fi-ery tri-als thy path-way shall lie,
4. "The soul that on Je-sus hath leaned for re-pose;

Is laid for your faith in His ex-cel-lent Word!
For I am thy God and will still give thee aid.
My grace, all suf-fi-cient, shall be thy sup-ply.
I will not, I will not de-sert to his foes.

What more can He say than to you He hath said,
I'll strength-en thee, help thee, and cause thee to stand,
The flame shall not hurt thee; I on-ly de-sign
That soul, though all hell should en-deav-or to shake,

To you who for ref-uge to Je-sus have fled?
Up-held by My righ-teous, om-nip-o-tent hand.
Thy dross to con-sume and thy gold to re-fine.
I'll nev-er, no nev-er, no nev-er for-sake!"

TEXT: Rippon's *Selection of Hymns*, 1787
MUSIC: Traditional American melody; Caldwell's *Union Harmony*, 1837

FOUNDATION
11.11.11.11.

Thanks to God Whose Word Was Spoken 409

I the Lord have spoken, and I will do it. Ezekiel 36:36

1. Thanks to God whose Word was spoken In the deed that made the earth. His the voice that called a nation; His the fires that tried her worth. God has spoken, God has spoken; Praise Him for His open Word.

2. Thanks to God whose Word incarnate Glorified the flesh of man. Deeds and words and death and rising Tell the grace in heaven's plan. God has spoken, God has spoken; Praise Him for His open Word.

3. Thanks to God whose Word was written In the Bible's sacred page, Record of the revelation Showing God to every age. God has spoken, God has spoken; Praise Him for His open Word.

4. Thanks to God whose Word is answered By the Spirit's voice within. Here we drink of joy unmeasured, Life redeemed from death and sin. God is speaking, God is speaking; Praise Him for His open Word.

TEXT: R. T. Brooks
MUSIC: Henry T. Smart

REGENT SQUARE
8.7.8.7.8.7.

A lower setting may be found at No. 754

410 Standing on the Promises

He has given us His very great and precious promises. 2 Peter 1:4

1. Stand-ing on the prom-is-es of Christ, my King! Thro' e-ter-nal
2. Stand-ing on the prom-is-es that can-not fail, When the howl-ing
3. Stand-ing on the prom-is-es, I now can see Per-fect, pres-ent
4. Stand-ing on the prom-is-es of Christ, the Lord, Bound to Him e-
5. Stand-ing on the prom-is-es, I can-not fall, Lis-t'ning ev-ery

a-ges let His prais-es ring; "Glo-ry in the high-est!" I will
storms of doubt and fear as-sail, By the liv-ing Word of God I
cleans-ing in the blood for me; Stand-ing in the lib-er-ty where
ter-nal-ly by love's strong cord, O-ver-com-ing dai-ly with the
mo-ment to the Spir-it's call, Rest-ing in my Sav-ior as my

shout and sing, Stand-ing on the prom-is-es of God.
shall pre-vail, Stand-ing on the prom-is-es of God.
Christ makes free, Stand-ing on the prom-is-es of God.
Spir-it's Sword, Stand-ing on the prom-is-es of God.
All in All, Stand-ing on the prom-is-es of God.

Refrain

Stand - ing, stand - ing, Stand-ing on the
Stand-ing on the prom-is-es, stand-ing on the prom-is-es, Stand-ing on the

TEXT: R. Kelso Carter
MUSIC: R. Kelso Carter; Choral ending by Tom Fettke

PROMISES
11.11.11.9. with Refrain

prom - is - es of God, my Sav - ior; Stand - - ing,
prom - is - es of God, my Sav - ior; Stand - ing on the prom - is - es,

stand - - ing, I'm stand - ing on the prom - is - es of God.
stand - ing on the prom - is - es, I'm stand - ing on the prom - is - es of God.

Optional last refrain setting

Stand - - ing, stand - - ing,
Stand - ing on the prom - is - es, stand - ing on the prom - is - es,

Stand - ing on the prom - is - es of God, my Sav - ior; Stand - - ing,
Stand - ing on the prom - is - es of God, my Sav - ior; Stand - ing on the prom - is - es,

stand - - ing, I'm stand - ing on the prom - is - es of God.
stand - ing on the prom - is - es, I'm stand - ing on the prom - is - es of God.

Optional choral ending cresc.

Stand - ing, stand - ing on the prom - is - es, Stand - ing on the prom - is - es of God.
cresc.

411 I Hide Your Word Within My Heart

I have hidden Your word in my heart that I might not sin against You. Psalm 119:11

1. I hide Your Word with-in my heart To keep me safe from sin;
2. I shine Your Word up-on my path And walk with-in its light;
3. I trust Your Word with all my heart And give You thanks and praise;

For where Your truth is in con-trol No lie can en-ter in.
For where Your wis-dom shines, O Lord, It drives a-way the night.
For all the beau-ty of Your truth That stands from age to age.

TEXT: Claire Cloninger
MUSIC: Alexander R. Reinagle

ST. PETER
C.M.

412 Holy Bible, Book Divine

All Scripture is God-breathed and is useful. 2 Timothy 3:16

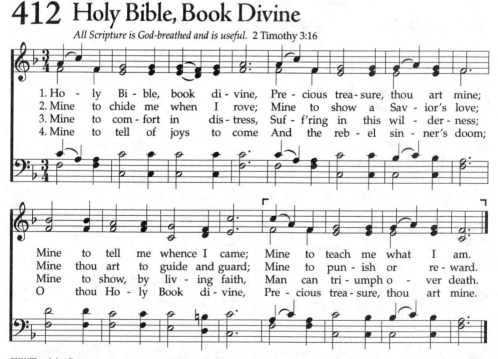

1. Ho-ly Bi-ble, book di-vine, Pre-cious trea-sure, thou art mine;
2. Mine to chide me when I rove; Mine to show a Sav-ior's love;
3. Mine to com-fort in dis-tress, Suf-f'ring in this wil-der-ness;
4. Mine to tell of joys to come And the reb-el sin-ner's doom;

Mine to tell me whence I came; Mine to teach me what I am.
Mine thou art to guide and guard; Mine to pun-ish or re-ward.
Mine to show, by liv-ing faith, Man can tri-umph o-ver death.
O thou Ho-ly Book di-vine, Pre-cious trea-sure, thou art mine.

TEXT: John Burton
MUSIC: William B. Bradbury

ALETTA
7.7.7.7.

Break Thou the Bread of Life 413

Looking up to heaven, He gave thanks and broke the loaves. Matthew 14:19

1. Break Thou the bread of life, Dear Lord, to me,
2. Break Thou the bread of life, O Lord, to me,
3. O - pen Thy Word of Truth That I may see
4. Bless Thou the truth, dear Lord, To me, to me,
5. O send Thy Spir - it, Lord, Now un - to me,

As Thou didst break the loaves Be - side the sea;
That hid with - in my heart Thy Word may be;
Thy mes - sage writ - ten clear And plain for me;
As Thou didst bless the bread By Gal - i - lee;
That He may touch my eyes And make me see;

Be - yond the sa - cred page I seek Thee, Lord;
Mold Thou each in - ward thought, From self set free,
Then in sweet fel - low - ship, Walk - ing with Thee,
Then shall all bond - age cease, All fet - ters fall,
Show me the truth con - cealed With - in Thy Word,

My spir - it pants for Thee, O Liv - ing Word.
And let my steps be all Con - trolled by Thee.
Thine im - age on my life En - graved will be.
And I shall find my peace, My All in All.
And in Thy Book re - vealed I see the Lord.

TEXT: Mary A. Lathbury; Alexander Groves, stanza 5
MUSIC: William F. Sherwin

BREAD OF LIFE
6.4.6.4.D.

414 O Word of God Incarnate

The unfolding of Your words gives light. Psalm 119:130

1. O Word of God in-car-nate, O Wis-dom from on high,
2. The Church from You, dear Mas-ter, Re-ceived the gift di-vine,
3. O make Your Church, dear Sav-ior, A lamp of bur-nished gold

O Truth un-changed, un-chang-ing, O Light of our dark sky:
And still that light is lift-ed O'er all the earth to shine.
To bear be-fore the na-tions Your true light, as of old;

We praise You for the ra-diance That from the hal-lowed page,
It is the chart and com-pass That o'er life's surg-ing sea,
O teach Your wan-d'ring pil-grims By this their path to trace,

A lan-tern to our foot-steps, Shines on from age to age.
A-mid the rocks and quick-sands, Still guides, O Christ, to Thee.
Till, clouds and dark-ness end-ed, They see You face to face.

TEXT: William W. How
MUSIC: *Neuvermehrtes Gesangbuch,* Meiningen, 1693; arranged by Felix Mendelssohn

MUNICH
7.6.7.6.D.

We Are Called to Be God's People 415

You are a chosen people, a people belonging to God. 1 Peter 2:9

1. We are called to be God's peo - ple, Show - ing by our lives His grace,
2. We are called to be God's ser - vants, Work - ing in His world to - day;
3. We are called to be God's proph - ets, Speak - ing for the truth and right;

One in heart and one in spir - it, Sign of hope for all the race.
Tak - ing His own task up - on us, All His sa - cred words o - bey.
Stand - ing firm for god - ly jus - tice, Bring - ing e - vil in - to light.

Let us show how He has changed us And re - made us as His own;
Let us rise, then, to His sum - mons, Ded - i - cate to Him our all,
Let us seek the cour - age need - ed, Our high call - ing to ful - fill,

Let us share our life to - geth - er As we shall a - round His throne.
That we may be faith - ful ser - vants, Quick to an - swer now His call.
That we all may know the bless - ing Of the do - ing of God's will.

TEXT: Thomas A. Jackson
MUSIC: Franz Joseph Haydn

AUSTRIAN HYMN
8.7.8.7.D.

416 We're Marching to Zion

The ransomed of the Lord will enter Zion with singing and joy. Isaiah 35:10

1. Come, we that love the Lord, And let our joys be known. Join in a song with sweet ac-cord, Join in a song with sweet ac-cord, And thus sur-round the throne, And thus sur-round the throne.
2. Let those re-fuse to sing Who nev-er knew our God; But chil-dren of the heav'n-ly King, But chil-dren of the heav'n-ly King May speak their joys a-broad, May speak their joys a-broad.
3. The hill of Zi-on yields A thou-sand sa-cred sweets Be-fore we reach the heav'n-ly fields, Be-fore we reach the heav'n-ly fields Or walk the gold-en streets, Or walk the gold-en streets.
4. Then let our songs a-bound, And ev-ery tear be dry. We're march-ing thro' Im-man-uel's ground, We're march-ing thro' Im-man-uel's ground To fair-er worlds on high, To fair-er worlds on high.

Refrain

We're march-ing to *Zi-on, Beau-ti-ful, beau-ti-ful Zi-on. We're
We're march-ing on to Zi-on, Beau-ti-ful, beau-ti-ful Zi-on. We're

*Psalm 2:6. By extension this refers to the New Jerusalem.

TEXT: Isaac Watts; Robert Lowry, Refrain
MUSIC: Robert Lowry

MARCHING TO ZION
6.6.8.8.6.6. with Refrain

march-ing up-ward to Zi - on, The beau-ti-ful cit-y of God.
march-ing up-ward to Zi - on, Zi-on, The beau-ti-ful cit-y of God.

We Will Stand 417

Stand firm then. Ephesians 6:14

Unison

You're my broth-er, you're my sis - ter, so take me by the hand.

To - geth-er we will work un-til He comes.

There's no foe that can de-feat us when we're walk-ing side by side;

As long as there is love, we will stand.

TEXT: Russ Taff and Tori Taff
MUSIC: James Hollihan

WE WILL STAND
Irregular meter

418 Make Us One

Brought to complete unity to let the world know that You have loved them. John 17:23

TEXT: Carol Cymbala
MUSIC: Carol Cymbala

MAKE US ONE
Irregular meter

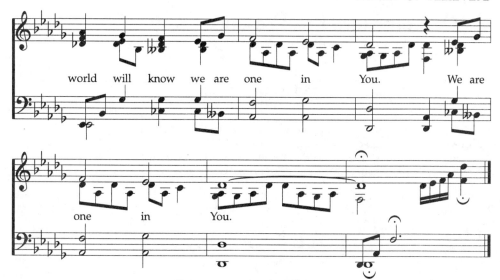

world will know we are one in You. We are

one in You.

The Family of God 419

We are God's children; heirs of God and co-heirs with Christ. Romans 8:16-17

I'm so glad I'm a part of the fam - 'ly of God— I've been washed in the

foun - tain, cleansed by His blood! Joint heirs with Je-sus as we trav-el this

sod; For I'm part of the fam - 'ly, the fam - 'ly of God.

TEXT: William J. Gaither
MUSIC: William J. Gaither

FAMILY OF GOD
Irregular meter

420 Come into His Presence

Come before Him with joyful songs. Psalm 100:2

4-Part Canon

1. Come in-to His pres-ence sing-ing Al - le - lu - ia, al - le - lu - ia, al - le - lu - ia.
2. Come in-to His pres-ence sing-ing Je - sus is Lord, Je - sus is Lord, Je - sus is Lord.
3. Praise the Lord to-geth-er sing-ing Wor-thy the Lamb, wor-thy the Lamb, wor-thy the Lamb.
4. Praise the Lord to-geth-er sing-ing Glo-ry to God, glo-ry to God, glo-ry to God.

TEXT: Source unknown
MUSIC: Source unknown

HIS PRESENCE
8.4.4.4.

421   LOVE THAT BINDS

A Worship Sequence

I Love You with the Love of the Lord
The Bond of Love; stanza 1
The Servant Song; stanzas 1,2,4,5,6
Suggested stanzas have been marked with an arrow: ➤

WORSHIP LEADER

As God's chosen people, holy and dearly loved,
clothe yourselves with compassion, kindness,
humility, gentleness and patience.
And over all these virtues put on love,
which binds them all together in perfect unity.

from Colossians 3:12, 14 (NIV)

Optional introduction to
"I Love You with the Love of the Lord"

mp

422 I Love You with the Love of the Lord

Love one another deeply, from the heart. 1 Peter 1:22

I love you with the love of the Lord. Yes, I love you with the

TEXT: Jim Gilbert
MUSIC: Jim Gilbert

GILBERT
Irregular meter

love of the Lord. I can see in you the glo-ry of my King,

And I love you with the love of the Lord.

Optional transition to "The Bond of Love"

The Bond of Love 423

We know that we have passed from death to life, because we love each other. 1 John 3:14

1. We are one in the bond of love, We are one in the bond of
2. Let us sing now, ev-ery one, Let us feel His love be-

love; We have joined our spir-it with the Spir-it of God,
gun; Let us join our hands that the world will know

We are one in the bond of love.
We are one in the bond of love.

Optional transition to "The Servant Song"

TEXT: Otis Skillings
MUSIC: Otis Skillings

BOND OF LOVE
Irregular meter

424 The Servant Song

Serve one another in love. Galatians 5:13

1. Broth - er, sis - ter, let me serve you, Let me be as Christ to you;
2. We are pil - grims on a jour - ney; We're to - geth - er on this road.
3. I will hold the Christ-light for you In the night-time of your fear;
4. I will weep when you are weep-ing; When you laugh, I'll laugh with you.
5. When we sing to God in heav - en, We shall find such har - mo - ny,
6. Broth - er, sis - ter, let me serve you, Let me be as Christ to you;

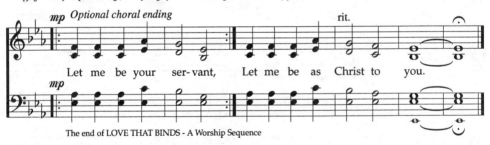

Pray that I may have the grace to Let you be my ser - vant too.
We are here to help each oth - er Walk the mile and bear the load.
I will hold my hand out to you, Speak the peace you long to hear.
I will share your joy and sor - row Till we've seen this jour - ney thro'.
Born of all we've known to - geth - er Of Christ's love and ag - o - ny.
Pray that I may have the grace to Let you be my ser - vant too.

TEXT: Richard Gillard
MUSIC: Richard Gillard
THE SERVANT SONG
8.7.8.7.

mp **Optional choral ending**   rit.

Let me be your ser - vant, Let me be as Christ to you.

mp

The end of LOVE THAT BINDS - A Worship Sequence

425 Bind Us Together

Over all these virtues put on love, which binds them all together in perfect unity. Colossians 3:14

Bind us to - geth - er, Lord; Bind us to - geth - er with cords that can - not be

TEXT: Bob Gillman
MUSIC: Bob Gillman
BIND US TOGETHER
Irregular meter

bro - ken. Bind us to - geth-er, Lord; Bind us to - geth-er, Lord; Bind us to -

Fine

geth-er with love. There is on-ly one God, There is on-ly one

D.C. al Fine

King, There is on-ly one bod-y; That is why we can sing:

Blest Be the Tie That Binds 426

You are all one in Christ Jesus. Galatians 3:28

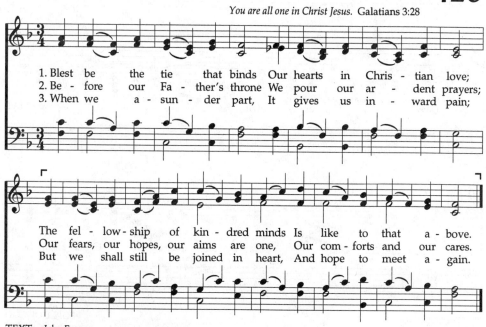

1. Blest be the tie that binds Our hearts in Chris - tian love;
2. Be - fore our Fa - ther's throne We pour our ar - dent prayers;
3. When we a - sun - der part, It gives us in - ward pain;

The fel - low-ship of kin - dred minds Is like to that a - bove.
Our fears, our hopes, our aims are one, Our com - forts and our cares.
But we shall still be joined in heart, And hope to meet a - gain.

TEXT: John Fawcett
MUSIC: Johann G. Naegeli; arranged by Lowell Mason

DENNIS
S.M.

427 People of God

You are a chosen people, a royal priesthood, a holy nation, a people belonging to God. 1 Peter 2:9

With our lips let us sing one con - fes - sion, With our hearts hold to one truth a - lone; For He has e - rased our trans - gres - sions, Claimed us and called us His own, His ver - y own. We're the peo - ple of God, called by His name, Called from the

TEXT: Wayne Watson
MUSIC: Wayne Watson

PEOPLE OF GOD
Irregular meter

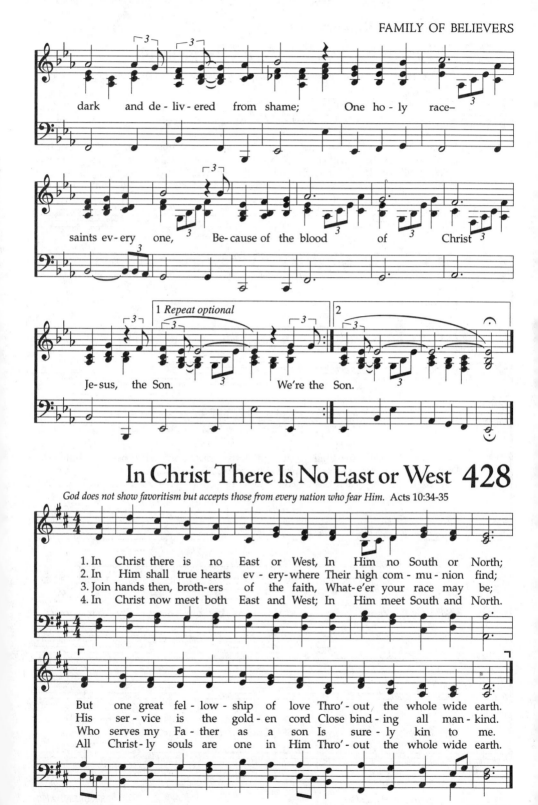

dark   and de - liv - ered   from shame;   One ho - ly   race–

saints ev - ery   one,   Be - cause of the blood   of   Christ

1 *Repeat optional*   2

Je - sus,   the Son.   We're the Son.

In Christ There Is No East or West 428

God does not show favoritism but accepts those from every nation who fear Him. Acts 10:34-35

1. In Christ there is no   East or West, In Him no South or North;
2. In Him shall true hearts ev - ery-where Their high com - mu - nion find;
3. Join hands then, broth-ers of the faith, What-e'er your race may be;
4. In Christ now meet both East and West; In Him meet South and North.

But   one great fel - low - ship of love Thro'- out the whole wide earth.
His   ser - vice is the gold - en cord Close bind - ing all man - kind.
Who   serves my Fa - ther as a son Is sure - ly kin to me.
All   Christ - ly souls are one in Him Thro'- out the whole wide earth.

TEXT: John Oxenham   ST. PETER
MUSIC: Alexander R. Reinagle   C.M.

429 They'll Know We Are Christians

By this everyone will know that you are My disciples, if you love one another. John 13:35

Unison

1. We are one in the Spir-it; we are one in the Lord.
2. We will walk with each oth-er; we will walk hand in hand.
3. We will work with each oth-er; we will work side by side.
4. All praise to the Fa-ther, from whom all things come.

We are one in the Spir-it; we are one in the Lord.
We will walk with each oth-er; we will walk hand in hand.
We will work with each oth-er; we will work side by side.
And all praise to Christ Je-sus, His on-ly Son.

And we pray that all u-ni-ty may one day be re-stored.
And to-geth-er we'll spread the news that God is in our land.
And we'll guard each one's dig-ni-ty and save each one's pride.
And all praise to the Spir-it, who makes us one.

Refrain

And they'll know we are Chris-tians by our love, by our love.

Yes, they'll know we are Chris-tians by our love.

TEXT: Peter Scholtes; based on John 13:35
MUSIC: Peter Scholtes

ST. BRENDAN'S
Irregular meter

There Shall Be Showers of Blessing 430

I will send down showers in season; there will be showers of blessing. Ezekiel 34:26

1. There shall be show-ers of bless-ing: This is the prom-ise of love.
2. There shall be show-ers of bless-ing— Pre-cious re-viv-ing a-gain;
3. There shall be show-ers of bless-ing; Send them up-on us, O Lord.
4. There shall be show-ers of bless-ing; O that to-day they might fall,

There shall be sea-sons re-fresh-ing, Sent from the Sav-ior a-bove.
O-ver the hills and the val-leys, Sound of a-bun-dance of rain.
Grant to us now a re-fresh-ing; Come and now hon-or Your Word.
Now as to God we're con-fess-ing, Now as on Je-sus we call!

Refrain

Show - ers of bless-ing, Show-ers of bless-ing we need.
Show - ers, show-ers of bless-ing,

Mer-cy-drops round us are fall-ing, But for the show-ers we plead.

TEXT: Daniel W. Whittle; based on Ezekiel 34:26
MUSIC: James McGranahan

SHOWERS OF BLESSING
8.7.8.7. with Refrain

431 Shine, Jesus, Shine

I am the Light of the world. John 8:12

1. Lord, the light of Your love is shin - ing, In the midst of the
2. Lord, I come to Your awe - some pres - ence, From the shad - ows in -
3. As we gaze on Your king - ly bright - ness So our fac - es dis -

dark - ness shin - ing; Je - sus, Light of the world, shine up - on us,
to Your ra - diance; By the blood I may en - ter Your bright-ness;
play Your like - ness, Ev - er chang-ing from glo - ry to glo - ry;

Set us free by the truth You now bring us; Shine on me,
Search me, try me, con - sume all my dark - ness; Shine on me,
Mir - rored here, may our lives tell Your sto - ry; Shine on me,

Harmony optional

Shine on me. Shine, Je - sus, shine, fill this
Shine on me. Flow, riv - er, flow, flood the
Shine on me.

TEXT: Graham Kendrick
MUSIC: Graham Kendrick

SHINE, JESUS, SHINE
Irregular meter

land with the Fa-ther's glo-ry. Blaze, Spir-it, blaze; set our
na-tions with grace and mer-cy. Send forth Your Word, Lord, and

1
hearts on fire.

2
let there be light.

rit.

Optional transition to
"Revive Us, O Lord"

Revive Us, O Lord 432

Revive us again, that Your people may rejoice in You. Psalm 85:6

Re-vive us, O Lord; re-vive us, O Lord; And
cleanse us from our im-pu-ri-ties, And make us ho-ly.

1   *2*

Hear our cry, and re-vive us, O Lord. Lord.

Optional segue to "Rise Up, O Church
of God." No transition is needed.

TEXT: Steve Camp and Carman
MUSIC: Steve Camp and Carman

REVIVE
Irregular meter

433 Rise Up, O Church of God

Wake up! Strengthen what remains and is about to die. Revelation 3:2

1. Rise up, O Church of God! Have done with less-er things;
2. Rise up, O Church of God! His king-dom tar-ries long;
3. Rise up, O sons of God! The Church for you doth wait,
4. Lift high the cross of Christ! Tread where His feet have trod;

Give heart and mind and soul and strength To serve the King of kings.
Bring in the day of broth-er-hood And end the night of wrong.
Her strength un-e-qual to her task, Rise up, and make her great!
As fol-l'wers of the Son of Man, Rise up, O Church of God!

Optional last stanza setting

4. Lift high the cross of Christ! Tread where His feet have

trod; As fol-l'wers of the Son of Man, Rise up, O Church of God!

TEXT: William P. Merrill, altered
MUSIC: Aaron Williams; arranged by Joseph Barlowe

ST. THOMAS
S.M.

f **Optional choral ending** *ff*

Rise up, rise up, rise up!

Revive Us Again 434

Revive us, and we will call on Your name. Psalm 80:18

1. We praise Thee, O God, for the Son of Thy love— For Jesus, who
2. We praise Thee, O God, for Thy Spirit of Light, Who has shown us our
3. All glory and praise to the Lamb that was slain, Who has borne all our
4. Revive us again; fill each heart with Thy love. May each soul be re-

died and is now gone above.
Savior and scattered our night.
sins and has cleansed every stain.
kindled with fire from above.

Refrain

Hallelujah! Thine the glory! Hallelujah! Amen! Hallelujah! Thine the glory! Revive us again.

Optional last refrain setting

Hallelujah! Thine the glory! Hallelujah! Amen! Hallelujah! Thine the glory! Revive us again.

f Optional choral ending

Revive us again.

TEXT: William P. Mackay
MUSIC: John J. Husband

REVIVE US AGAIN
11.11. with Refrain

435 God of Grace and God of Glory

Be strong and courageous; do not be discouraged, for the Lord your God will be with you. Joshua 1:9

1. God of grace and God of glo-ry, On Thy peo-ple pour Thy
2. Lo! the hosts of e-vil round us Scorn Thy Christ, as-sail His
3. Cure Thy chil-dren's war-ring mad-ness; Bend our pride to Thy con-
4. Set our feet on loft-y plac-es; Gird our lives that they may

pow'r. Crown Thine an-cient Church-'s sto-ry; Bring her bud to
ways! From the fears that long have bound us, Free our hearts to
trol. Shame our wan-ton, self-ish glad-ness, Rich in things and
be Ar-mored with all Christ-like grac-es In the fight to

glo-rious flow'r. Grant us wis-dom; Grant us cour-age
faith and praise. Grant us wis-dom; Grant us cour-age
poor in soul. Grant us wis-dom; Grant us cour-age
set men free. Grant us wis-dom; Grant us cour-age

For the fac-ing of this hour, For the fac-ing of this hour.
For the liv-ing of these days, For the liv-ing of these days.
Lest we miss Thy king-dom's goal, Lest we miss Thy king-dom's goal.
That we fail not man nor Thee, That we fail not man nor Thee.

TEXT: Harry Emerson Fosdick
MUSIC: John Hughes

CWM RHONDDA
8.7.8.7.8.7.7.

Freely, Freely 436

Freely you have received, freely give. Matthew 10:8

1. God for- gave my sin in Je - sus' name; I've been born a - gain in
2. All pow'r is giv'n in Je - sus' name, In earth and heav'n in

Je - sus' name; And in Je - sus' name I come to you To share
Je - sus' name; And in Je - sus' name I come to you To share

His love as He told me to. He said, "Free - ly, free - ly
His pow'r as He told me to.

Refrain

you have re- ceived; Free - ly, free - ly give. Go in My

name and be- cause you be - lieve, Oth - ers will know that I live."

TEXT: Carol Owens; based on Matthew 10:8, 28:18
MUSIC: Carol Owens

FREELY, FREELY
9.9.9.9. with Refrain

437 Send the Light

Let light shine out of darkness. 2 Corinthians 4:6

1. There's a call comes ring-ing o'er the rest-less wave, "Send the light!
2. We have heard the Mac-e-do-nian call to-day, "Send the light!
3. Let us pray that grace may ev-ery-where a-bound; "Send the light!
4. Let us not grow wea-ry in the work of love; "Send the light!

Send the light!" There are souls to res-cue; there are souls to save.
Send the light!" And a gold-en of-f'ring at the cross we lay;
Send the light!" And a Christ-like spir-it ev-ery-where be found;
Send the light!" Let us gath-er jew-els for a crown a-bove;

Send the light! Send the light!

Refrain

Send the light, the bless-ed gos-pel light; Let it shine from shore to shore! Send the light, the bless-ed gos-pel light; Let it shine for-ev-er-more!

Optional segue to "Jesus Saves!"
No transition is needed.

TEXT: Charles H. Gabriel
MUSIC: Charles H. Gabriel

McCABE
11.6.11.6. with Refrain

Jesus Saves! 438

Christ Jesus came into the world to save sinners. 1 Timothy 1:15

1. We have heard the joy - ful sound: Je - sus saves! Je - sus saves!
2. Waft it on the roll - ing tide: Je - sus saves! Je - sus saves!
3. Sing a - bove the bat - tle strife: Je - sus saves! Je - sus saves!
4. Give the winds a might - y voice: Je - sus saves! Je - sus saves!

Spread the tid - ings all a - round: Je - sus saves! Je - sus saves!
Tell to sin - ners far and wide: Je - sus saves! Je - sus saves!
By His death and end - less life, Je - sus saves! Je - sus saves!
Let the na - tions now re - joice: Je - sus saves! Je - sus saves!

Bear the news to ev - ery land; Climb the steeps and cross the waves.
Sing, ye is - lands of the sea! Ech - o back, ye o - cean caves!
Sing it soft - ly thro' the gloom When the heart for mer - cy craves;
Shout sal - va - tion full and free, High - est hills and deep - est caves;

On - ward! 'tis our Lord's com - mand. Je - sus saves! Je - sus saves!
Earth shall keep her ju - bi - lee. Je - sus saves! Je - sus saves!
Sing in tri - umph o'er the tomb: Je - sus saves! Je - sus saves!
This our song of vic - to - ry: Je - sus saves! Je - sus saves!

TEXT: Priscilla J. Owens
MUSIC: William J. Kirkpatrick

JESUS SAVES
7.6.7.6.7.7.7.6.

439 Song for the Nations

Go and make disciples of all nations. Matthew 28:19

1. May we be a shin-ing light to the na-tions, A shin-ing light to the peo-ples of the earth, Till the whole world sees the glo-ry of Your name. May Your pure light shine thro' us.
2. May we bring a word of hope to the na-tions, A word of life to the peo-ples of the earth, Till the whole world knows there's sal-va-tion thro' Your name. May Your mer-cy flow thro' us.
3. May we be a heal-ing balm to the na-tions, A heal-ing balm to the peo-ples of the earth, Till the whole world knows the pow-er of Your name. May Your heal-ing flow thro' us.
4. May we sing a song of joy to the na-tions, A song of praise to the peo-ples of the earth, Till the whole world rings with the prais-es of Your name. May Your song be sung thro' us.
5. May Your king-dom come to the na-tions, Your will be done in the peo-ples of the earth, Till the whole world knows that Je-sus Christ is Lord. May Your king-dom come on earth.

TEXT: Chris Christensen
MUSIC: Chris Christensen; Arrangement and Descant by Tom Fettke

SONG FOR THE NATIONS
11.11.11.7.

Optional last stanza setting

5. May Your

Optional descant

king - dom come to the na - tions, Your will be done in the

king - dom come to the na - tions, Your will be done in the

peo-ples of the earth, Till the whole world knows that Je - sus Christ is Lord.

peo-ples of the earth, Till the whole world knows that Je - sus Christ is Lord.

May Your king - dom come, May Your king - dom come,

Cued notes optional for a few choir sopranos

May Your king - dom come on earth.

440 So Send I You–by Grace Made Strong

As the Father has sent Me, I am sending you. John 20:21

1. So send I you— by grace made strong to tri - umph O'er hosts of hell, o'er dark - ness, death and sin, My name to bear and in that name to con - quer— So send I you, My vic - to - ry to win.

2. So send I you— to take to souls in bond - age The Word of truth that sets the cap - tive free, To break the bonds of sin, to loose death's fet - ters— So send I you, to bring the lost to Me.

3. So send I you— My strength to know in weak - ness, My joy in grief, My per - fect peace in pain, To prove My pow'r, My grace, My prom - ised pres - ence— So send I you, e - ter - nal fruit to gain.

4. So send I you— to bear My cross with pa - tience, And then one day with joy to lay it down, To hear My voice, "Well done, My faith - ful ser - vant— Come, share My throne, My king - dom, and My crown!" As the Fa - ther has sent Me, so send I you.

Optional segue to "Rescue the Perishing."
No transition is needed.

TEXT: Margaret Clarkson
MUSIC: John W. Peterson

TORONTO
11.10.11.10. with Coda

Rescue the Perishing 441

Snatch others from the fire and save them. Jude 23

1. Res - cue the per - ish - ing; care for the dy - ing. Snatch them in
2. Tho' they are slight - ing Him, still He is wait - ing— Wait - ing the
3. Down in the hu - man heart, crushed by the tempt - er, Feel - ings lie
4. Res - cue the per - ish - ing; du - ty de - mands it. Strength for your

pit - y from sin and the grave. Weep o'er the err - ing one; lift up the
pen - i - tent child to re - ceive. Plead with them ear - nest - ly; plead with them
bur - ied that grace can re - store. Touched by a lov - ing heart, wak - ened by
la - bor the Lord will pro - vide. Back to the nar - row way pa - tient - ly

Refrain

fall - en. Tell them of Je - sus, the might - y to save.
gent - ly. He will for - give if they on - ly be - lieve.
kind - ness, Cords that are bro - ken will vi - brate once more.
win them, Tell the poor wan - d'rer a Sav - ior has died.

Res - cue the

per - ish - ing; Care for the dy - ing. Je - sus is mer - ci - ful; Je - sus will save!

TEXT: Fanny J. Crosby
MUSIC: William H. Doane

RESCUE
11.10.11.10. with Refrain

442 Each One, Reach One

The first thing Andrew did was to find his brother Simon. And he brought him to Jesus. John 1:41-42

Unison

Each one can reach one; As we fol-low af-ter Christ we all can lead one; We can lead one to the Sav-ior; Then to-geth-er we can tell the world that Je-sus is the way— If we each one reach one.

Optional repeat setting

Each one can reach one; As we fol-low af-ter Christ we all can lead one; We can lead one to the Sav-ior; Then to-geth-er we can

TEXT: Babbie Mason
MUSIC: Babbie Mason

EACH ONE, REACH ONE
Irregular meter

tell the world that Je-sus is the way— If we each one reach one.

O Zion, Haste 443

O Zion, bringer of good tidings, lift up your voice. Isaiah 40:9

1. O *Zi - on, haste, thy mis-sion high ful-fill-ing, To tell to all the
2. Pro-claim to ev - ery peo-ple, tongue and na - tion That God, in whom they
3. Give of thy sons to bear the mes-sage glo - rious; Give of thy wealth to

world that God is Light; That He who made all na-tions is not will-ing
live and move, is love: Tell how He stooped to save His lost cre - a - tion
speed them on their way. Pour out thy soul for them in prayer vic-to-rious;

Refrain

One soul should per - ish, lost in shades of night.
And died on earth that man might live a - bove. Pub - lish glad tid-ings,
And all thy spend-ing Je - sus will re - pay.

tid - ings of peace; Tid-ings of Je - sus, re-demp-tion, and re - lease.

*Isaiah 40:9. By extension the word refers to the people of God.

TEXT: Mary A. Thomson
MUSIC: James Walch

TIDINGS
11.10.11.10. with Refrain

444 I Love to Tell the Story

Those who had been scattered preached the Word wherever they went. Acts 8:4

1. I love to tell the sto - ry Of un - seen things a - bove,
2. I love to tell the sto - ry; More won - der - ful it seems
3. I love to tell the sto - ry; 'Tis pleas - ant to re - peat
4. I love to tell the sto - ry, For those who know it best

Of Je - sus and His glo - ry, Of Je - sus and His love.
Than all the gold - en fan - cies Of all our gold - en dreams.
What seems each time I tell it More won - der - ful - ly sweet.
Seem hun - ger - ing and thirst - ing To hear it like the rest.

I love to tell the sto - ry Be - cause I know 'tis true.
I love to tell the sto - ry; It did so much for me,
I love to tell the sto - ry, For some have nev - er heard
And when in scenes of glo - ry I sing the new, new song,

It sat - is - fies my long - ings As noth - ing else can do.
And that is just the rea - son I tell it now to thee.
The mes - sage of sal - va - tion From God's own ho - ly Word.
'Twill be the old, old sto - ry That I have loved so long.

TEXT: A. Catherine Hankey
MUSIC: William G. Fischer

HANKEY
7.6.7.6.D. with Refrain

I love to tell the sto-ry! 'Twill be my theme in glo-ry

To tell the old, old sto-ry Of Je-sus and His love.

People Need the Lord 445

"Open your eyes and look at the fields! They are ripe for harvest." John 4:35

1. Peo-ple need the Lord, peo-ple need the
2. Peo-ple need the Lord, peo-ple need the

Lord; At the end of bro-ken dreams,
Lord; When will we re-al-ize

1. He's the o-pen door.

2. peo-ple need the Lord.

TEXT: Greg Nelson and Phill McHugh
MUSIC: Greg Nelson and Phill McHugh; arranged by David Allen

PEOPLE NEED THE LORD
Irregular meter

446 We've a Story to Tell to the Nations

This gospel of the kingdom will be preached in the whole world. Matthew 24:14

1. We've a sto-ry to tell to the na-tions That shall turn their hearts
2. We've a song to be sung to the na-tions That shall lift their hearts
3. We've a mes-sage to give to the na-tions– That the Lord who reign-
4. We've a Sav-ior to show to the na-tions Who the path of sor-

to the right, A sto-ry of truth and mer — cy, A sto-ry of
to the Lord, A song that shall con-quer e — vil And shat-ter the
eth a-bove Hath sent us His Son to save us And show us that
row hath trod, That all of the world's great peo — ples Might come to the

peace and light, A sto-ry of peace and light.
spear and sword, And shat-ter the spear and sword. **For the**
God is love, And show us that God is love.
truth of God, Might come to the truth of God.

Refrain

dark-ness shall turn to dawn-ing, And the dawn-ing to noon-day bright, And

TEXT: H. Ernest Nichol
MUSIC: H. Ernest Nichol

MESSAGE
Irregular meter

Christ's great king-dom shall come on earth– The king-dom of love and light.

Jesus Loves the Little Children 447

Let the little children come to Me, and do not hinder them. Matthew 19:14

1. Je - sus loves the lit - tle chil - dren, All the chil-dren of the
2. Je - sus died for all the chil - dren, All the chil-dren of the
3. We must pray for all the chil - dren, All the chil-dren of the
4. We must help the lit - tle chil - dren, All the chil-dren of the

world. Red and yel-low, black and white, They are pre-cious in His sight–
world. Red and yel-low, black and white, They are pre-cious in His sight–
world. Red and yel-low, black and white, They are pre-cious in His sight–
world. Red and yel-low, black and white, They are pre-cious in His sight–

Je - sus loves the lit - tle chil - dren of the world.
Je - sus died for all the chil - dren of the world.
We must pray for all the chil - dren of the world.
We must help the lit - tle chil - dren of the world.

TEXT: C. H. Woolston and Joseph Barlowe
MUSIC: George F. Root

CHILDREN
8.7.7.7.11.

448 I'll Tell the World That I'm a Christian

I am not ashamed of the gospel. Romans 1:16

1. I'll tell the world that I'm a Chris-tian; I'm not a-shamed His name to bear. I'll tell the world that I'm a Chris-tian; I'll take Him with me an-y-where. I'll tell the world how Je-sus saved me, And how He gave me a life brand new; And I know that if you trust Him That all He gave me He'll give to you. I'll tell the world

2. I'll tell the world that He is com-ing; It may be near or far a-way. But we must live as if His com-ing Would be to-mor-row or to-day. For when He comes and life is o-ver, For those who love Him there's more to be; Eyes have nev-er seen the won-ders That He's pre-par-ing for you and me. O tell the world

TEXT: Baynard L. Fox
MUSIC: Baynard L. Fox

TUCKER
Irregular meter

that He's my Sav - ior;   No oth - er one   could love me so.   My life, my
that you're a Chris - tian;   Be not a - shamed   His name to bear.   O tell the

all   is His for - ev - er,   And where He leads me   I will go.
world   that you're a Chris - tian,   And take Him with you   ev - ery - where.

Lord, Lay Some Soul upon My Heart 449

I make myself a slave to everyone, to win as many as possible.   1 Corinthians 9:19

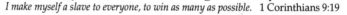

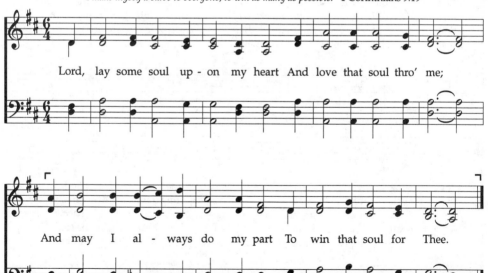

Lord, lay some soul up - on my heart And love that soul thro' me;

And may I al - ways do my part To win that soul for Thee.

TEXT: Leon Tucker
MUSIC: Ira D. Sankey

IRA
C.M.

450 Lift High the Cross

I, when I am lifted up from the earth, will draw all people to Myself. John 12:32

Refrain in unison

Lift high the cross; the love of Christ pro-claim, Till all the world a - dore His sa - cred name.

Harmony optional

1. Come, Chris - tians, fol - low where our Sav - ior trod,
2. Led on their way by this tri - um - phant sign,
3. O Lord, once lift - ed on this glo - rious tree,
4. Set up Thy throne, that earth's de-spair may cease
5. For Thy blest cross which doth for all a - tone,

D. C. al Fine

Our King vic - to - rious, Christ, the Son of God.
The hosts of God in con - qu'ring ranks com - bine.
As Thou hast prom - ised, draw men un - to Thee.
Be - neath the shad - ow of its heal - ing peace.
Cre - a - tion's prais - es rise be - fore Thy throne.

TEXT: George W. Kitchin and Michael R. Newbolt
MUSIC: Sydney H. Nicholson

CRUCIFER
10.10.10.10.

A Christian Home 451

From infancy you have known the holy Scriptures. 2 Timothy 3:15

1. O give us homes built firm up-on the Sav-ior, Where Christ is Head and Coun-sel-or and Guide; Where ev-ery child is taught His love and fa-vor And gives his heart to Christ, the Cru-ci-fied: How sweet to know that, tho' his foot-steps wa-ver, His faith-ful Lord is walk-ing by his side!

2. O give us homes with god-ly fa-thers, moth-ers, Who al-ways place their hope and trust in Him; Whose ten-der pa-tience tur-moil nev-er both-ers, Whose calm and cour-age trou-ble can-not dim; A home where each finds joy in serv-ing oth-ers, And love still shines, tho' days be dark and grim.

3. O give us homes where Christ is Lord and Mas-ter, The Bi-ble read, the pre-cious hymns still sung; Where pray'r comes first in peace or in di-sas-ter, And praise is nat-ural speech to ev-ery tongue; Where moun-tains move be-fore a faith that's vast-er, And Christ suf-fi-cient is for old and young.

4. O Lord, our God, our homes are Thine for-ev-er! We trust to Thee their prob-lems, toil, and care; Their bonds of love no en-e-my can sev-er If Thou art al-ways Lord and Mas-ter there: Be Thou the cen-ter of our least en-deav-or— Be Thou our guest, our hearts and homes to share.

TEXT: Barbara B. Hart
MUSIC: Jean Sibelius

FINLANDIA
11.10.11.10.11.10.

A higher setting may be found at No. 712

452 I Am a Woman

A woman who fears the Lord is to be praised. Proverbs 31:30

Women unison

1. I am a wom-an Called to be a ser-vant;
2. I am a wom-an Called to speak with wis-dom;
3. I am a wom-an Pur-chased by Your mer-cy;

Bound by the grace that Your love im-parts. Lord, make me hum-ble,
Shin-ing a light that will lead to You. Lord, give me cour-age
Bought by the love that would spare no cost. Lord, make me ho-ly,

Teach me to fol-low; Make me a wom-an of Your heart.
To be Your wit-ness; Make me a wom-an of Your truth.
Lov-ing You on-ly; Make me a wom-an of Your cross.

TEXT: Claire Cloninger
MUSIC: *Schlesische Volkslieder*, 1842; arranged by Richard S. Willis
A higher setting may be found at No. 87

CRUSADERS' HYMN
5.6.8.5.5.8.

453 Happy Our Home When God Is There

Those who love Me will obey My teaching and My Father will love them. John 14:23

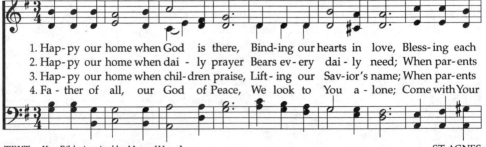

1. Hap-py our home when God is there, Bind-ing our hearts in love, Bless-ing each
2. Hap-py our home when dai-ly prayer Bears ev-ery dai-ly need; When par-ents
3. Hap-py our home when chil-dren praise, Lift-ing our Sav-ior's name; When par-ents
4. Fa-ther of all, our God of Peace, We look to You a-lone; Come with Your

TEXT: Ken Bible, inspired by Henry Ware, Jr.
MUSIC: John B. Dykes

ST. AGNES
C.M.

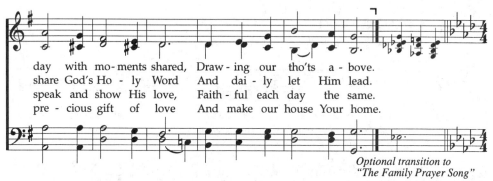

day with mo-ments shared, Draw-ing our tho'ts a-bove.
share God's Ho-ly Word And dai-ly let Him lead.
speak and show His love, Faith-ful each day the same.
pre-cious gift of love And make our house Your home.

*Optional transition to
"The Family Prayer Song"*

The Family Prayer Song 454

As for me and my household, we will serve the Lord. Joshua 24:15

Unison

Come and fill our homes with Your pres-ence; You a-lone are wor-thy of our

rev-'rence. As for me and my house, we will serve the Lord. As for

me and my house, we will serve the Lord. As for me and my house,

we will serve the Lord; We will serve the Lord.

TEXT: Morris Chapman
MUSIC: Morris Chapman

CHAPMAN
Irregular meter

455 I Am a Man

You have put on the new self, in the image of its Creator. Colossians 3:10

Men in unison

1. I am a man cre-at-ed in God's im-age, Of Ad-am's race, now
2. I am a man ap-point-ed by my Sav-ior To show His love in
3. I'll be a man who walks with God in wor-ship; I'll be a man who

marred by pride and sin. But thro' God's Son, Lord Je-sus Christ, my Sav-ior,
all I do and say. His Ho-ly Spir-it is my source of pow-er,
walks with men as friend. I'll be a man who loves and serves his fam-'ly;

I am a man who's now re-stored to Him. The Might-y God who
To live in light and point to Christ the Way. Lord, fill me now, and
I'll be a man on whom God can de-pend. Lord Je-sus Christ, my

made me has re-deemed me; Now I'm His man, for Je-sus reigns with-in.
help me seize this mo-ment, And as Your man, I'll serve Your cause to-day.
King and my Com-mand-er, I'll be Your man un-til my life shall end.

TEXT: Jack W. Hayford
MUSIC: Jean Sibelius

FINLANDIA
11.10.11.10.11.10.

A higher setting may be found at No. 712

Find Us Faithful 456

Those who have been given a trust must prove faithful. 1 Corinthians 4:2

O may all who come be-hind us find us faith - ful;

May the fire of our de-vo - tion light their way.

May the foot-prints that we leave Lead them to be - lieve,

And the lives we live in - spire them to o - bey.

O may all who come be-hind us find us faith - ful.

TEXT: Jon Mohr
MUSIC: Jon Mohr

FIND US FAITHFUL
Irregular meter

457 God, Give Us Christian Homes

Children of God—shine like stars. Philippians 2:15

1. God, give us Chris - tian homes! Homes where the Bi - ble is
2. God, give us Chris - tian homes! Homes where the fa - ther is
3. God, give us Chris - tian homes! Homes where the moth - er, in
4. God, give us Chris - tian homes! Homes where the chil - dren are

loved and taught, Homes where the Mas - ter's will is sought,
true and strong, Homes that are free from the blight of wrong,
car - ing quest, Strives to show oth - ers Your way is best,
led to know Christ in His beau - ty who loves them so,

Homes crowned with beau - ty Your love has wrought; God, give us
Homes that are joy - ous with love and song; God, give us
Homes where the Lord is an hon - ored guest; God, give us
Homes where the al - tar fires burn and glow; God, give us

Chris - tian homes; God, give us Chris - tian homes!
Chris - tian homes; God, give us Chris - tian homes!
Chris - tian homes; God, give us Chris - tian homes!
Chris - tian homes; God, give us Chris - tian homes!

TEXT: B. B. McKinney
MUSIC: B. B. McKinney

CHRISTIAN HOME
Irregular meter

O Perfect Love 458

Husbands, love your wives. Colossians 3:19 Women, love their husbands. Titus 2:4

1. O per - fect Love, all hu - man tho't tran - scend - ing,
2. O per - fect Life, be Thou their full as - sur - ance
3. Grant them the joy which bright - ens earth - ly sor - row;

Low - ly we kneel in prayer be - fore Thy throne,
Of ten - der char - i - ty and stead - fast faith,
Grant them the peace which calms all earth - ly strife,

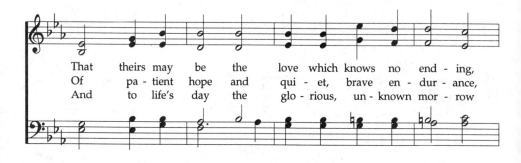

That theirs may be the love which knows no end - ing,
Of pa - tient hope and qui - et, brave en - dur - ance,
And to life's day the glo - rious, un - known mor - row

Whom Thou for - ev - er - more dost join in one.
With child - like trust that fears not pain nor death.
That dawns up - on e - ter - nal love and life.

TEXT: Dorothy F. Gurney
MUSIC: Joseph Barnby

O PERFECT LOVE
11.10.11.10.

459 We Remember You

This is My body given for you; do this in remembrance of Me. Luke 22:19

TEXT: Kirk Dearman
MUSIC: Kirk Dearman

WE REMEMBER YOU
Irregular meter

Optional extended or choral ending

We re-mem - ber and wor-ship You, O Lord.

Let Us Break Bread Together 460

They devoted themselves to the breaking of bread. Acts 2:42

1. Let us break bread to-geth-er on our knees; (on our knees;)
2. Let us drink the cup to-geth-er on our knees; (on our knees;)
3. Let us praise God to-geth-er on our knees; (on our knees;)

Let us break bread to-geth-er on our knees; (on our knees;)
Let us drink the cup to-geth-er on our knees; (on our knees;)
Let us praise God to-geth-er on our knees; (on our knees;)

Refrain

When I fall on my knees with my face to the ris-ing sun,

O Lord, have mer-cy on me. (on me.)

TEXT: Traditional Spiritual
MUSIC: Traditional Spiritual; arranged by Keith Phillips

LET US BREAK BREAD
Irregular meter

461 In Remembrance

This is My body given for you; do this in remembrance of Me. Luke 22:19

Introduction

1. In re - mem - brance of Me,
(2. In re -) mem - brance of Me,

eat this bread.   In re-mem-brance of Me, drink this wine.   In re-
heal the sick.   In re-mem-brance of Me, feed the poor.   In re-

mem - brance of Me,   pray for the time when God's own will   is
mem - brance of Me,   o - pen the door and let your broth - er

done.   2. In re - in,   let   him in.   Take,   eat, and be

com - fort - ed;   Drink   and re - mem - ber,   too,   that

TEXT: Ragan Courtney
MUSIC: Buryl Red

RED
Irregular meter

462 Come, Share the Lord

Is not the bread that we break a participation in the body of Christ? 1 Corinthians 10:16

1. We gath-er here in Je-sus' name; His love is burn-ing in our
2. He joins us here; He breaks the bread. The Lord who pours the cup is
3. We'll gath-er soon where an-gels sing; We'll see the glo-ry of our

hearts like liv-ing flame, For thro' the lov-ing Son, The Fa-ther
ris-en from the dead. The one we love the most Is now our
Lord and com-ing King. Now we an-tic-i-pate The feast for

makes us one: Come, take the bread; come, drink the cup; come, share the Lord.
gra-cious host: Come, take the bread; come, drink the cup; come, share the Lord.
which we wait: Come, take the bread; come, drink the cup; come, share the Lord.

TEXT: Bryan Jeffery Leech
MUSIC: Bryan Jeffery Leech

DIVERNON (Abridged)
Irregular meter

463 I Will Remember Thee

This is My body given for you; do this in remembrance of Me. Luke 22:19

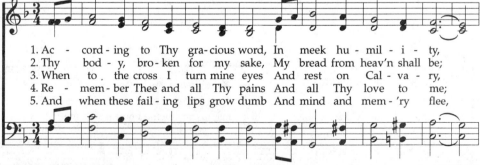

1. Ac - cord-ing to Thy gra-cious word, In meek hu-mil-i-ty,
2. Thy bod-y, bro-ken for my sake, My bread from heav'n shall be;
3. When to the cross I turn mine eyes And rest on Cal-va-ry,
4. Re-mem-ber Thee and all Thy pains And all Thy love to me;
5. And when these fail-ing lips grow dumb And mind and mem-'ry flee,

TEXT: James Montgomery
MUSIC: From Henry W. Greatorex's Collection of Church Music, 1851

MANOAH
C.M.

This will I do, my dy - ing Lord: I will re - mem - ber Thee.
Thy tes - ta - men - tal cup I take And thus re - mem - ber Thee.
O Lamb of God, my sac - ri - fice, I must re - mem - ber Thee.
Yea, while a breath, a pulse re - mains, Will I re - mem - ber Thee.
When Thou shalt in Thy king - dom come, Je - sus, re - mem - ber me!

Come to the Table 464

Proclaim the Lord's death until He comes. 1 Corinthians 11:26

Come to the ta - ble of mer - cy, Pre - pared with the wine and the bread;

All who are hun - gry and thirst - y, Come and your souls will be fed.

Come at the Lord's in - vi - ta - tion; Re - ceive from His nail - scarred hand.

Eat of the bread of sal - va - tion; Drink of the blood of the Lamb.

TEXT: Claire Cloninger
MUSIC: Martin J. Nystrom

COME TO THE TABLE
8.8.8.7.D.

465 Baptized in Water

We were buried with Him through baptism that we may live a new life. Romans 6:4

1. Bap-tized in wa - ter, Sealed by the Spir - it,
2. Bap-tized in wa - ter, Sealed by the Spir - it,
3. Bap-tized in wa - ter, Sealed by the Spir - it,

Cleansed by the blood of Christ, our King;
Dead in the tomb with Christ, our King;
Marked with the sign of Christ, our King;

Heirs of sal - va - tion, Trust-ing His prom - ise,
One with His ris - ing, Freed and for - giv - en,
Born of one Fa - ther, We are His chil - dren,

Faith - ful - ly now God's praise we sing.
Thank - ful - ly now God's praise we sing.
Joy - ful - ly now God's praise we sing.

TEXT: Michael Saward
MUSIC: Traditional Gaelic melody; arranged by Tom Fettke

BUNESSAN
5.5.5.4.D.

Jesus, Our Lord and King 466

Offer your bodies as living sacrifices. Romans 12:1

1. Je - sus, our Lord and King, To You our prais - es rise;
2. Now jus - ti - fied by grace And made a - live to God,
3. As dead in - deed to sin, We rise to walk a - new,
4. Bap - tized in - to Your death, With You a - gain we rise,

To You our bod - ies we pre - sent, A liv - ing sac - ri - fice.
Formed for Your - self to show Your praise, We sound Your love a - broad.
Hence - forth, as not our own, but Yours, We fol - low on - ly You.
To new - ness of a life of faith, To new and end - less joys.

TEXT: Anonymous
MUSIC: Robert Jackson

TRENTHAM
S.M.

A higher setting may be found at No. 393

Come, Holy Spirit, Dove Divine 467

Jesus saw the Spirit of God descending like a dove and lighting on Him. Matthew 3:16

1. Come, Ho - ly Spir - it, Dove di - vine, On these bap - tis - mal wa - ters shine,
2. We love Thy name, we love Thy laws, And joy - ful - ly em - brace Thy cause,
3. We sink be - neath the wa - ter's face, And thank Thee for Thy sav - ing grace;
4. And as we rise with Thee to live, O let the Ho - ly Spir - it give

And teach our hearts, in high - est strain, To praise the Lamb for sin - ners slain.
We love Thy cross, the shame, the pain, O Lamb of God for sin - ners slain.
We die to sin and seek a grave With Thee, be - neath the yield - ing wave.
The seal - ing unc - tion from a - bove, The joy of life, the fire of love.

TEXT: Adoniram Judson
MUSIC: H. Percy Smith

MARYTON
L.M.

468 Good Shepherd, Take This Little Child

Jesus took the children in His arms, put His hands on them and blessed them. Mark 10:16

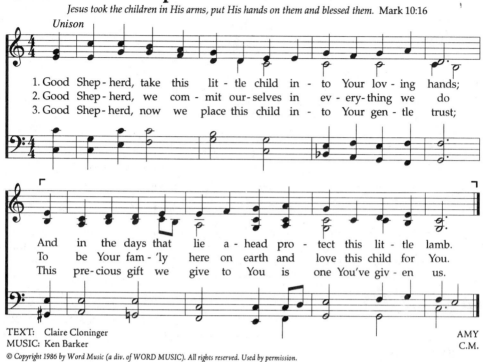

1. Good Shepherd, take this little child into Your loving hands;
2. Good Shepherd, we commit ourselves in everything we do
3. Good Shepherd, now we place this child into Your gentle trust;

And in the days that lie ahead protect this little lamb.
To be Your fam'ly here on earth and love this child for You.
This precious gift we give to You is one You've given us.

TEXT: Claire Cloninger
MUSIC: Ken Barker

AMY
C.M.

469 This Child We Dedicate to Thee

Bring them up in the training and instruction of the Lord. Ephesians 6:4

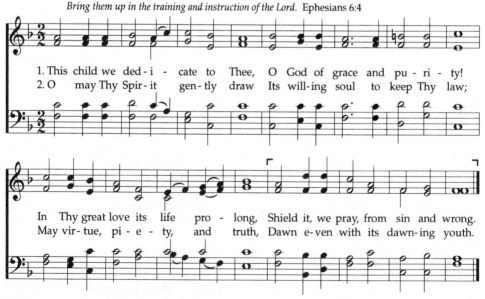

1. This child we dedicate to Thee, O God of grace and purity!
2. O may Thy Spirit gently draw Its willing soul to keep Thy law;

In Thy great love its life prolong, Shield it, we pray, from sin and wrong.
May virtue, piety, and truth, Dawn even with its dawning youth.

TEXT: From the German; translated by Samuel Gilman
MUSIC: Henry K. Oliver

FEDERAL STREET
L.M.

The Blessing Song 470

Little children were brought to Jesus for Him to pray for them. Matthew 19:13

1. May bless-ings be up-on you, pre-cious ba-by. May
2. May bless-ings be up-on your chil-dren's chil-dren. May

fa-vor rest up-on your fam-i-ly. May your fu-ture be a
fa-vor rest up-on your fam-i-ly. May your fu-ture be a

last time rit. Fine

ho-ly leg-a-cy, May bless-ings be up-on you, pre-cious ba-by.
ho-ly leg-a-cy, May bless-ings be up-on your chil-dren's chil-dren.

Solo, choir or congregation

May He bless you in your com-ing; May He bless you in your go-ing;

D.C. al Fine

May your heart be ev-er know-ing the bless-ings of the Lord.

TEXT: Nancy Gordon, Linda Walker and Jamie Harvill
MUSIC: Nancy Gordon, Linda Walker and Jamie Harvill;
arranged by Tom Fettke

THE BLESSING SONG
Irregular meter

471   A GLORIOUS CHURCH

from Matthew 16:15-19; 1 Corinthians 12:12-14;
Ephesians 1:22-23; 2:19-22; 5:25-27 (NKJV)

WORSHIP LEADER
Jesus said to them, "But who do you say that I am?"

EVERYONE
Simon Peter answered and said,
"You are the Christ, the Son of the Living God."

WORSHIP LEADER
Jesus answered and said to him, "Blessed are you, Simon Bar-Jonah,
for flesh and blood has not revealed this to you, but My Father who is in heaven."

MEN
"And I also say to you that you are Peter,
and on this rock I will build My Church,
and the gates of Hades shall not prevail against it."

WORSHIP LEADER
"And I will give you the keys of the kingdom of heaven,
and whatever you bind on earth will be bound in heaven,
and whatever you loose on earth will be loosed in heaven."

WOMEN
For as the body is one and has many members,
but all the members of that one body, being many,
are one body, so also is Christ.

WORSHIP LEADER
For by one Spirit we were all baptized into one body–
whether Jews or Greeks, whether slaves or free–
and have all been made to drink into one Spirit.
For in fact the body is not one member, but many.

EVERYONE
He put all things under His feet,
and gave Him to be head over all things to the church,
which is His body, the fullness of Him who fills all in all.

WORSHIP LEADER
You are no longer strangers and foreigners,
but fellow citizens with the saints and members of the household of God,

EVERYONE
Having been built on the foundation of the apostles and prophets,
Jesus Christ Himself being the chief cornerstone,

WORSHIP LEADER
In whom the whole building, being joined together,
grows into a holy temple in the Lord,

WOMEN
In whom you also are being built together for a dwelling place
of God in the Spirit.

MEN
Husbands, love your wives, just as Christ also loved the Church
and gave Himself for her, that He might sanctify and cleanse her
with the washing of water by the Word,

EVERYONE
That He might present her to Himself a glorious Church,
not having spot or wrinkle or any such thing,
but that she should be holy and without blemish.

A LAMP AND A LIGHT

from Isaiah 40:8; 2 Timothy 3:16-17; Hebrews 4:12; Psalms 19, 119 (NIV)

WORSHIP LEADER and EVERYONE
The grass withers and the flowers fall, but the Word of our God stands forever!

WORSHIP LEADER
All Scripture is God-breathed
and is useful for teaching, rebuking, correcting and training in righteousness,
so that the man of God may be thoroughly equipped for every good work.

EVERYONE
The Word of God is living and active, sharper than any double-edged sword.

WORSHIP LEADER
The law of the Lord is perfect, reviving the soul.

WOMEN
The statutes of the Lord are trustworthy, making wise the simple.

MEN
The precepts of the Lord are right, giving joy to the heart.

WORSHIP LEADER
The commands of the Lord are radiant, giving light to the eyes.

WOMEN
The fear of the Lord is pure, enduring forever.

MEN
The ordinances of the Lord are sure and altogether righteous.

EVERYONE
They are more precious than gold, than much pure gold;
They are sweeter than honey, than honey from the comb.
By them is your servant warned; In keeping them there is great reward.

WOMEN
Teach me knowledge and good judgment,
for I believe in Your commands.

MEN
I am Your servant; give me discernment
that I may understand Your statutes.

EVERYONE
Great peace have they who love Your law,
and nothing can make them stumble.

WORSHIP LEADER
Praise be to You, O Lord; teach me Your decrees.
With my lips I recount all the laws that come from Your mouth.
I rejoice in following Your statutes as one rejoices in great riches.

EVERYONE
My heart is set on keeping Your decrees to the very end.
Open my eyes that I may see wonderful things in Your law.

WOMEN
I meditate on Your precepts.

MEN
I consider Your ways.

WORSHIP LEADER
I delight in Your decrees.

EVERYONE
I have hidden Your Word in my heart that I might not sin against You.
It is a lamp to my feet and a light to my path.

473   GO AND MAKE DISCIPLES

from Matthew 28:16-20; John 4:35; Romans 10:8-15 (NASB)

SOLO 1
The eleven disciples proceeded to Galilee,
to the mountain which Jesus had designated.

SOLO 2
When they saw Him, they worshiped Him,
but some were doubtful.

SOLO 1
And Jesus came up and spoke to them, saying,

EVERYONE
"All authority has been given to Me in heaven and on earth.
Go therefore and make disciples of all the nations,
baptizing them in the name of the Father and the Son and the Holy Spirit,
teaching them to observe all that I commanded you;
And lo, I am with you always, even to the end of the age."

SOLO 1
"Do you not say, 'There are yet four months, and then comes the harvest'?
Behold, I say to you, lift up your eyes,
and look on the fields, that they are white for harvest."

SOLO 2
The Word is near you, in your mouth and in your heart—
that is, the Word of faith which we are preaching;

EVERYONE
That if you confess with your mouth Jesus as Lord,
and believe in your heart that God raised Him from the dead,
you shall be saved.

SOLO 1
For with the heart man believes, resulting in righteousness.

SOLO 2
And with the mouth he confesses, resulting in salvation.

EVERYONE
For the Scripture says, "Whoever believes in Him
will not be disappointed."

SOLO 1
For there is no distinction between Jew and Greek;
for the same Lord is Lord of all,
abounding in riches for all who call upon Him.

EVERYONE
For whoever will call upon the name of the Lord will be saved.

MEN
How then shall they call upon Him in whom they have not believed?

WOMEN
And how shall they believe in Him whom they have not heard?

MEN
And how shall they hear without a preacher?

SOLO 1
And how shall they preach unless they are sent?
Just as it is written,

EVERYONE
"How beautiful are the feet of those who bring glad tidings of good things!"

UNITY OF THE SPIRIT

from Ephesians 4:1-6; Philippians 2:1-5 (NIV)

WORSHIP LEADER or SOLO DRAMATIST
As a prisoner for the Lord, then,
I urge you to live a life worthy of the calling you have received.
Be completely humble and gentle; be patient, bearing with one another in love.
Make every effort to keep the unity of the Spirit through the bond of peace.
There is one body and one Spirit–
just as you were called to one hope when you were called–
One Lord, one faith, one baptism; one God and Father of all,
who is over all and through all and in all.
If you have any encouragement from being united with Christ,
if any comfort from His love, if any fellowship with the Spirit,
if any tenderness and compassion, then make my joy complete by being like-minded,
having the same love, being one in spirit and purpose.
Do nothing out of selfish ambition or vain conceit,
but in humility consider others better than yourselves.
Each of you should look not only to your own interests,
but also to the interests of others.
Your attitude should be the same as that of Christ Jesus.

LOVE NEVER FAILS

475

from 1 Corinthians 13:4-8, 13(NKJV)

WORSHIP LEADER
Love suffers long and is kind.

MEN
Love does not envy.

WOMEN
Love does not parade itself.

YOUTH
Love is not puffed up.

MEN
Love does not behave rudely.

WORSHIP LEADER
Love does not seek its own.

WOMEN
Love is not provoked.

YOUTH
Love thinks no evil.

WORSHIP LEADER
Love does not rejoice in iniquity, but rejoices in the truth.

EVERYONE
Love bears all things. Love believes all things.
Love hopes all things. Love endures all things.

WOMEN and CHILDREN
Love never fails.

WORSHIP LEADER
But whether there are prophecies, they will fail;
whether there is knowledge, it will vanish away.

EVERYONE
And now abide faith, hope, love, these three;
but the greatest of these is love.

476   A MAN OF GOD

from Psalm 119: 9-15 (NIV)
(All participants should be male)

WORSHIP LEADER
How can a young man keep his way pure?

EVERYONE
By living according to Your Word.

SOLO
I seek You with all my heart;
Do not let me stray from Your commands.

YOUNG MEN and BOYS
I have hidden Your Word in my heart that I might not sin against You.

EVERYONE
Praise be to You, O Lord; teach me Your decrees.

SOLO
With my lips I recount all the laws that come from Your mouth.

GRANDFATHERS
I rejoice in following Your statutes as one rejoices in great riches.
I meditate on Your precepts and consider Your ways.

WORSHIP LEADER
How can a man keep his way pure?

EVERYONE
By living according to Your Word.

477   A WOMAN OF GOD

from Psalm 119: 41-48, 55 (NIV)
(All participants should be female)

WORSHIP LEADER
I reach out my hands to Your commandments, which I love,
and I meditate on Your decrees.

EVERYONE
In the night I remember Your name, O Lord, and I will keep Your law.

WORSHIP LEADER
May Your unfailing love come to me, O Lord,
Your salvation according to Your promise.

GRANDMOTHERS
Do not snatch the Word of truth from my mouth,
for I have put my hope in Your laws.

YOUNG WOMEN and GIRLS
I will always obey Your law, forever and ever.

WORSHIP LEADER
I will walk about in freedom, for I have sought out Your precepts.
I will speak of Your statutes before kings and will not be put to shame;

EVERYONE
For I delight in Your commandments, because I love them.

WORSHIP LEADER
In the night I remember Your name, O Lord, and I will keep Your law.

EVERYONE
I reach out my hands to Your commandments, which I love,
and I meditate on Your decrees.

Have You Any Room for Jesus? 478

Now is the time of God's favor, now is the day of salvation. 2 Corinthians 6:2

1. Have you an-y room for Je-sus, He who bore your load of sin?
2. Room for plea-sure, room for busi-ness; But for Christ, the Cru-ci-fied,
3. Room and time now give to Je-sus; Soon will pass God's day of grace—

As He knocks and asks ad-mis-sion, Sin-ner, will you let Him in?
Not a place that He can en-ter In the heart for which He died?
Soon your heart left cold and si-lent And your Sav-ior's plead-ing cease.

Refrain

Room for Je-sus, King of Glo-ry! Has-ten now; His Word o-bey.

Swing the heart's door wide-ly o-pen; Bid Him en-ter while you may.

TEXT: Source unknown; adapted by Daniel W. Whittle
MUSIC: C. C. Williams; Choral ending by Eugene Thomas

ANY ROOM
8.7.8.7. with Refrain

Optional choral ending

Swing the heart's door wide-ly o-pen; Bid Him en-ter while you may, while you may.

479 Softly and Tenderly

Come to Me, all you who are weary and burdened, and I will give you rest. Matthew 11:28

1. Soft - ly and ten - der - ly Je - sus is call - ing,
2. Why should we tar - ry when Je - sus is plead-ing,
3. Time is now fleet - ing; the mo - ments are pass - ing,
4. O for the won - der - ful love He has prom-ised,

Call - ing for you and for me. See, on the por - tals He's
Plead - ing for you and for me? Why should we lin - ger and
Pass - ing from you and from me. Shad - ows are gath - er - ing;
Prom - ised for you and for me! Though we have sinned, He has

wait - ing and watch-ing, Watch-ing for you and for me.
heed not His mer - cies, Mer - cies for you and for me?
death's night is com - ing, Com - ing for you and for me.
mer - cy and par - don, Par - don for you and for me.

Refrain

Come home; come home. You who are wea-ry, come home.
Come home; come home.

TEXT: Will L. Thompson
MUSIC: Will L. Thompson

THOMPSON
11.7.11.7. with Refrain

Ear-nest-ly, ten-der-ly Je-sus is call-ing, Call-ing, "O sin-ner, come home!"

Only Trust Him 480

Believe in the Lord Jesus, and you will be saved. Acts 16:31

1. Come, ev - ery soul by sin op-pressed– There's mer - cy with the Lord,
2. For Je - sus shed His pre - cious blood, Rich bless-ings to be - stow;
3. Yes, Je - sus is the Truth, the Way, That leads you in - to rest;

And He will sure - ly give you rest By trust-ing in His Word.
Plunge now in - to the crim - son flood That wash-es white as snow.
Be - lieve in Him with-out de - lay And you are ful - ly blest.

Refrain

On - ly trust Him; on - ly trust Him. On - ly trust Him now.

He will save you; He will save you. He will save you now.

TEXT: John H. Stockton
MUSIC: John H. Stockton

MINERVA
C.M. with Refrain

481 Come Just as You Are

Come! Let all who wish take the free gift of the water of life. Revelation 22:17

Unison

1. Come just as you are; Hear the Spir - it call.
2. Come just as you are; Hear the Spir - it call.

Come just as you are; Come and see, come, re- ceive;
Come just as you are; Come, re- ceive Christ, the King;

1, 3
Come and live for - ev - er.

2, 4 last time Fine
Come and live for - ev - er - more.

Life ev - er - last - ing, and strength for to - day;

D.C. al Fine
(to stanza one)

Taste the Liv-ing Wa- ter, and nev - er thirst a - gain.

TEXT: Joseph Sabolick
MUSIC: Joseph Sabolick

SABOLICK
Irregular meter

Jesus Is Calling 482

Today, if you hear His voice, do not harden your hearts. Hebrews 4:7

1. Je - sus is ten - der - ly call - ing you home, Call - ing to - day,
2. Je - sus is call - ing the wea - ry to rest, Call - ing to - day,
3. Je - sus is wait - ing, O come to Him now, Wait - ing to - day,
4. Je - sus is plead - ing, O list to His voice, Hear Him to - day,

call - ing to - day. Why from the sun - shine of love will you roam
call - ing to - day. Bring Him your bur - den and you shall be blest;
wait - ing to - day. Come with your sins, at His feet low - ly bow;
hear Him to - day. They who be - lieve on His name shall re - joice;

Refrain

Far - ther and far - ther a - way? Call - ing to -
He will not turn you a - way. Call - ing, call - ing to -
Come and no long - er de - lay.
Quick - ly a - rise and a - way.

day, Call - ing to - day. Je -
day, to - day, Call - ing, call-ing to - day, to - day. Je - sus is

- sus is call - ing, Is ten - der - ly call - ing to - day.
ten - der - ly call - ing to - day,

TEXT: Fanny J. Crosby
MUSIC: George C. Stebbins

CALLING TODAY
10.8.10.7. with Refrain

483 The Savior Is Waiting

Today, if you hear His voice, do not harden your hearts. Hebrews 3:15

1. The Sav-ior is wait-ing to en-ter your heart— Why don't you
2. If you'll take one step toward the Sav-ior, my friend, You'll find His

let Him come in? There's noth-ing in this world to keep you a-
arms o-pen wide. Re-ceive Him and all of your dark-ness will

Refrain

part— What is your an-swer to Him? Time af-ter time He has
end; With-in your heart He'll a-bide.

wait-ed be-fore, And now He is wait-ing a-gain To see if you're

will-ing to o-pen the door— O how He wants to come in.

TEXT: Ralph Carmichael
MUSIC: Ralph Carmichael

CARMICHAEL
11.7.11.7. with Refrain

Optional choral ending

O how He wants to come in, come in.

in.

in.

Come, Let Us Reason 484

Come now, let us reason together. Isaiah 1:18

"Come, let us rea - son to - geth - er," that's what God says.

"Come, let us rea - son to - geth - er," says the Lord. Lord.

1

2, 3 Fine

"Tho' your sins be as scar - let, they shall be as white as snow;

D.C. al Fine

Tho' they be red like crim - son, they shall be as wool."

TEXT: Ken Medema
MUSIC: Ken Medema; arranged by David Allen

COME LET US REASON
Irregular meter

485 Into My Heart

I pray that Christ may dwell in your hearts through faith. Ephesians 3:16-17

In - to my heart, in - to my heart, Come in - to my heart, Lord Je - sus;

Come in to - day, come in to stay, Come in - to my heart, Lord Je - sus.

TEXT: Harry D. Clarke
MUSIC: Harry D. Clarke

INTO MY HEART
L.M.

486 Come, Ye Sinners, Poor and Needy

Come and take the free gift of the water of life. Revelation 22:17

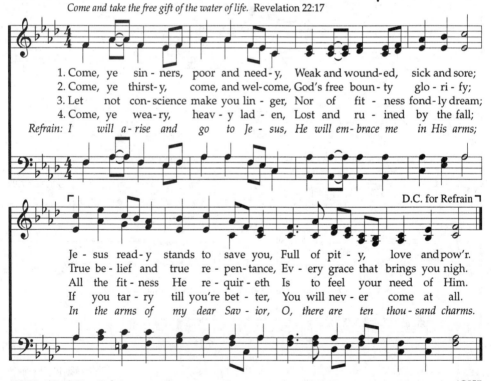

1. Come, ye sin - ners, poor and need - y, Weak and wound - ed, sick and sore;
2. Come, ye thirst - y, come, and wel - come, God's free boun - ty glo - ri - fy;
3. Let not con - science make you lin - ger, Nor of fit - ness fond - ly dream;
4. Come, ye wea - ry, heav - y lad - en, Lost and ru - ined by the fall;

Refrain: I will a - rise and go to Je - sus, He will em - brace me in His arms;

D.C. for Refrain

Je - sus read - y stands to save you, Full of pit - y, love and pow'r.
True be - lief and true re - pen - tance, Ev - ery grace that brings you nigh.
All the fit - ness He re - quir - eth Is to feel your need of Him.
If you tar - ry till you're bet - ter, You will nev - er come at all.
In the arms of my dear Sav - ior, O, there are ten thou - sand charms.

TEXT: Joseph Hart; Refrain, source unknown
MUSIC: Traditional American melody; Walker's *Southern Harmony*, 1835

ARISE
8.7.8.7. with Refrain

Room at the Cross for You 487

There is still room. Luke 14:22

1. The cross up-on which Je-sus died Is a shel-ter in
2. Tho' mil-lions have found Him a friend And have turned from the
3. The hand of my Sav-ior is strong, And the love of my

which we can hide; And its grace so free is suf-fi-cient for me,
sins they have sinned, The Sav-ior still waits to o-pen the gates
Sav-ior is long; Through sun-shine or rain, through loss or in gain,

And deep is its foun-tain– as wide as the sea.
And wel-come a sin-ner be-fore it's too late. There's room at the
The blood flows from Cal-v'ry to cleanse ev-ery stain.

Refrain

cross for you; There's room at the cross for you. Tho' mil-lions have

come, There's still room for one. Yes, there's room at the cross for you.

TEXT: Ira F. Stanphill
MUSIC: Ira F. Stanphill

ROOM AT THE CROSS
Irregular meter

488 Just as I Am

Whoever comes to Me I will never drive away. John 6:37

1. Just as I am, with-out one plea But that Thy
2. Just as I am and wait-ing not To rid my
3. Just as I am, though tossed a-bout With many a
4. Just as I am— Thou wilt re-ceive, Wilt wel-come,

blood was shed for me, And that Thou bidd'st me
soul of one dark blot, To Thee whose blood can
con-flict, many a doubt, Fight-ings and fears with-
par-don, cleanse, re-lieve. Be-cause Thy prom-ise

come to Thee, O Lamb of God, I come! I come!
cleanse each spot, O Lamb of God, I come! I come!
in, with-out, O Lamb of God, I come! I come!
I be-lieve, O Lamb of God, I come! I come!

TEXT: Charlotte Elliott
MUSIC: William B. Bradbury; Last stanza setting and Choral ending by Tom Fettke

WOODWORTH
L.M.

Optional last stanza setting
Unison

4. Just as I am— Thou wilt re-ceive, Wilt wel-come, par-don,

cleanse, re-lieve. Be-cause Thy prom-ise I be-lieve, O

Optional choral ending
Sing harmony

Lamb of God, I come! I come! O Lamb of God, I come!

Pass Me Not 489

He is patient, not wanting anyone to perish, but everyone to come to repentance. 2 Peter 3:9

1. Pass me not, O gen-tle Sav-ior; Hear my hum-ble cry;
2. Let me at the throne of mer-cy Find a sweet re-lief;
3. Trust-ing on-ly in Thy mer-it, Would I seek Thy face.
4. Thou, the Spring of all my com-fort, More than life to me,

While on oth-ers Thou art call-ing, Do not pass me by.
Kneel-ing there in deep con-tri-tion, Help my un-be-lief.
Heal my wound-ed, bro-ken spir-it; Save me by Thy grace.
Whom have I on earth be-side Thee? Whom in heav'n but Thee?

Refrain

Sav-ior, Sav-ior, Hear my hum-ble cry;

While on oth-ers Thou art call-ing, Do not pass me by.

TEXT: Fanny J. Crosby
MUSIC: William H. Doane

PASS ME NOT
8.5.8.5. with Refrain

490 Lord, I'm Coming Home

I will set out and go back to my father and say to him: Father, I have sinned. Luke 15:18

1. I've wan-dered far a - way from God— Now I'm com-ing home.
2. I've wast-ed man - y pre - cious years— Now I'm com-ing home.
3. I've tired of sin and stray - ing, Lord— Now I'm com-ing home.
4. My soul is sick, my heart is sore— Now I'm com-ing home.

The paths of sin too long I've trod— Lord, I'm com-ing home.
I now re-pent with bit - ter tears— Lord, I'm com-ing home.
I'll trust Thy love, be - lieve Thy Word— Lord, I'm com-ing home.
My strength re-new, my hope re - store— Lord, I'm com-ing home.

Refrain

Com-ing home, com-ing home, Nev - er - more to roam.

O - pen now Thine arms of love— Lord, I'm com-ing home.

TEXT: William J. Kirkpatrick
MUSIC: William J. Kirkpatrick

COMING HOME
8.5.8.5. with Refrain

Jesus, I Come 491

He has sent Me to proclaim freedom for the captives. Isaiah 61:1

1. Out of my bond-age, sor-row and night, Je-sus, I come; Je-sus, I come.
2. Out of my shame-ful fail-ure and loss, Je-sus, I come; Je-sus, I come.
3. Out of un-rest and ar-ro-gant pride, Je-sus, I come; Je-sus, I come.
4. Out of the fear and dread of the tomb, Je-sus, I come; Je-sus, I come.

In - to Thy free-dom, glad-ness and light, Je-sus, I come to Thee.
In - to the glo-rious gain of Thy cross, Je-sus, I come to Thee.
In - to Thy bless-ed will to a-bide, Je-sus, I come to Thee.
In - to the joy and light of Thy home, Je-sus, I come to Thee.

Out of my sick-ness in-to Thy health, Out of my want and in-to Thy
Out of earth's sor-rows in-to Thy balm, Out of life's storms and in-to Thy
Out of my-self to dwell in Thy love, Out of de-spair in-to rap-tures a-
Out of the depths of ru-in un-told, In-to the peace of Thy shel-ter-ing

wealth, Out of my sin and in-to Thy-self, Je-sus, I come to Thee.
calm, Out of dis-tress to ju-bi-lant psalm, Je-sus, I come to Thee.
bove, Up-ward for aye on wings like a dove, Je-sus, I come to Thee.
fold, Ev-er Thy glo-rious face to be-hold, Je-sus, I come to Thee.

TEXT: William T. Sleeper
MUSIC: George C. Stebbins

JESUS, I COME
Irregular meter

492 At Calvary

When they came to the place called the Skull, they crucified Him. Luke 23:33

1. Years I spent in van-i-ty and pride, Car-ing not my Lord was
2. By God's Word at last my sin I learned; Then I trem-bled at the
3. Now I've giv'n to Je-sus ev-ery-thing; Now I glad-ly own Him
4. O the love that drew sal-va-tion's plan! O the grace that bro't it

cru-ci-fied, Know-ing not it was for me He died On Cal-va-ry.
law I'd spurned, Till my guilt-y soul im-plor-ing turned To Cal-va-ry.
as my King; Now my rap-tured soul can on-ly sing Of Cal-va-ry.
down to man! O the might-y gulf that God did span At Cal-va-ry!

Refrain

Mer-cy there was great and grace was free; Par-don there was mul-ti-

plied to me; There my bur-dened soul found lib-er-ty, At Cal-va-ry.

TEXT: William R. Newell
MUSIC: Daniel B. Towner

CALVARY
9.9.9.4. with Refrain

Glory to His Name 493

Without the shedding of blood there is no forgiveness. Hebrews 9:22

1. Down at the cross where my Sav - ior died, Down where for
2. I am so won - drous - ly saved from sin, Je - sus so
3. O pre - cious foun - tain that saves from sin, I am so
4. Come to this foun - tain so rich and sweet; Cast thy poor

cleans - ing from sin I cried, There to my heart was the blood ap - plied;
sweet - ly a - bides with - in; There at the cross where He took me in;
glad that I en - tered in; There Je - sus saves me and keeps me clean;
soul at the Sav - ior's feet; Plunge in to - day and be made com - plete;

Refrain

Glo - ry to His name! Glo - ry to His name, Glo - ry to His

name! There to my heart was the blood ap - plied; Glo - ry to His name!

TEXT: Elisha A. Hoffman
MUSIC: John H. Stockton

GLORY TO HIS NAME
9.9.9.5. with Refrain

494 It Took a Miracle

The grace of God that brings salvation has appeared to all. Titus 2:11

1. My Fa - ther is om - nip - o - tent, And that you can't de - ny;
2. Though here His glo - ry has been shown, We still can't ful - ly see
3. The Bi - ble tells us of His pow'r And wis - dom all way through,

A God of might and mir - a - cles— 'Tis writ - ten in the sky.
The won - ders of His might, His throne— 'Twill take e - ter - ni - ty.
And ev - ery lit - tle bird and flow'r Are tes - ti - mo - nies, too.

Refrain

It took a mir - a - cle to put the stars in place; It took a
mir - a - cle to hang the world in space. But when He saved my soul,
Cleansed and made me whole, It took a mir - a - cle of love and grace.

TEXT: John W. Peterson
MUSIC: John W. Peterson

MONTROSE
C. M. with Refrain

Jesus Loves Even Me 495

Christ loved the church and gave Himself up for her. Ephesians 5:25

1. I am so glad that our Fa-ther in heav'n Tells of His love in the Book He has giv'n. Won-der-ful things in the Bi-ble I see— This is the dear-est, that Je-sus loves me.

2. Tho' I for-get Him and wan-der a-way, Still He doth love me wher-ev-er I stray. Back to His dear, lov-ing arms would I flee When I re-mem-ber that Je-sus loves me.

3. O if there's on-ly one song I can sing When in His beau-ty I see the great King, This shall my song in e-ter-ni-ty be: "O what a won-der, that Je-sus loves me!"

Refrain

I am so glad that Je-sus loves me, Je-sus loves me, Je-sus loves me.
I am so glad that Je-sus loves me; Je-sus loves e-ven me!

TEXT: Philip P. Bliss
MUSIC: Philip P. Bliss

GLADNESS
10.10.10.10. with Refrain

496 No One Ever Cared for Me like Jesus

Cast all your anxiety on Him because He cares for you. 1 Peter 5:7

1. I would love to tell you what I think of Je - sus Since I
2. All my life was full of sin when Je - sus found me, All my
3. Ev - ery day He comes to me with new as - sur - ance, More and

found in Him a friend so strong and true; I would tell you how He
heart was full of mis - er - y and woe; Je - sus placed His strong and
more I un - der-stand His words of love; But I'll nev - er know just

changed my life com - plete - ly— He did some-thing that no oth - er friend could do.
lov - ing arms a - round me, And He led me in the way I ought to go.
why He came to save me, Till some-day I see His bless-ed face a - bove.

Refrain

No one ev - er cared for me like Je - sus, There's no

oth - er friend so kind as He; No one else could take the

TEXT: Charles F. Weigle
MUSIC: Charles F. Weigle

WEIGLE
12.11.12.11. with Refrain

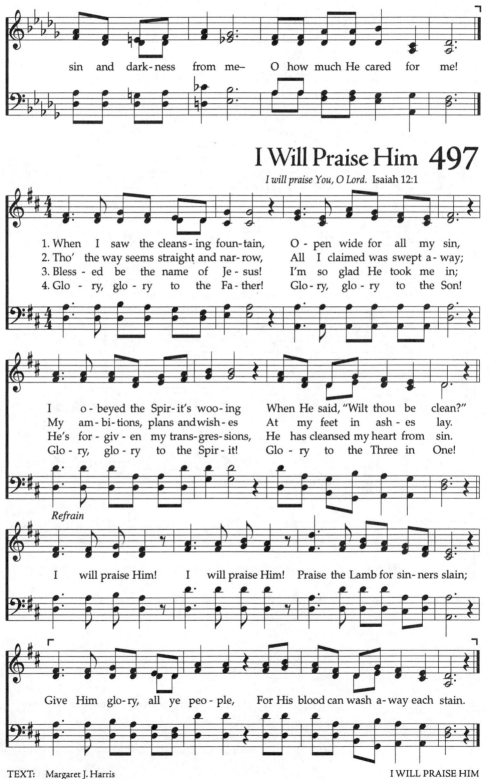

sin and dark-ness from me– O how much He cared for me!

I Will Praise Him 497

I will praise You, O Lord. Isaiah 12:1

1. When I saw the cleans-ing foun-tain, O - pen wide for all my sin,
2. Tho' the way seems straight and nar-row, All I claimed was swept a-way;
3. Bless - ed be the name of Je - sus! I'm so glad He took me in;
4. Glo - ry, glo - ry to the Fa-ther! Glo - ry, glo - ry to the Son!

I o - beyed the Spir-it's woo-ing When He said, "Wilt thou be clean?"
My am - bi - tions, plans and wish-es At my feet in ash-es lay.
He's for - giv - en my trans-gres-sions, He has cleansed my heart from sin.
Glo - ry, glo - ry to the Spir-it! Glo - ry to the Three in One!

Refrain

I will praise Him! I will praise Him! Praise the Lamb for sin-ners slain;

Give Him glo-ry, all ye peo-ple, For His blood can wash a-way each stain.

TEXT: Margaret J. Harris
MUSIC: Margaret J. Harris

I WILL PRAISE HIM
8.7.8.7. with Refrain

498 O Happy Day!

This is the Lord; let us rejoice and be glad in His salvation. Isaiah 25:9

1. O hap-py day that fixed my choice On Thee, my Sav-ior and my God!
2. O hap-py bond that seals my vows To Him who mer-its all my love!
3. 'Tis done, the great trans-ac-tion's done— I am my Lord's and He is mine;
4. Now rest, my long-di-vid-ed heart, Fixed on this bliss-ful cen-ter, rest,

Well may this glow-ing heart re-joice And tell its rap-tures all a-broad.
Let cheer-ful an-thems fill His house, While to that sa-cred shrine I move.
He drew me, and I fol-lowed on, Charmed to con-fess the voice di-vine.
Nor ev-er from my Lord de-part, With Him of ev-ery good pos-sessed.

Refrain

Hap-py day, hap-py day, When Je-sus washed my sins a-way!

He taught me how to watch and pray And live re-joic-ing ev-ery day;

Hap-py day, hap-py day, When Je-sus washed my sins a-way!

TEXT: Philip Doddridge
MUSIC: Attributed to Edward F. Rimbault

HAPPY DAY
L.M. with Refrain

I Will Sing the Wondrous Story 499

They sang the song of the Lamb: "Great and marvelous are Your deeds." Revelation 15:3

1. I will sing the won-drous sto-ry Of the Christ who died for me;
2. I was lost but Je-sus found me– Found the sheep that went a-stray;
3. Days of dark-ness still come o'er me; Sor-row's paths I of-ten tread.
4. He will keep me till the riv-er Rolls its wa-ters at my feet;

How He left His home in glo-ry For the cross of Cal-va-ry.
Threw His lov-ing arms a-round me, Drew me back in-to His way.
But the Sav-ior still is with me; By His hand I'm safe-ly led.
Then He'll bear me safe-ly o-ver, Where the loved ones I shall meet.

Refrain

Yes, I'll sing the won-drous sto-ry Of the Christ who died for me–

Sing it with the saints in glo-ry, Gath-ered by the crys-tal sea.

TEXT: Francis H. Rowley
MUSIC: Peter P. Bilhorn
Alternate tune: HYFRYDOL at No. 309

WONDROUS STORY
8.7.8.7. with Refrain

500 Saved, Saved!

He saved us because of His mercy. Titus 3:5

Unison

1. I've found a Friend who is all to me; His
2. He saves me from ev-ery sin and harm; Se-
3. When poor and need - y and all a - lone, In

love is ev - er true. I love to tell how He
cures my soul each day. I'm lean - ing strong on His
love He said to me, "Come un - to Me and I'll

lift - ed me, And what His grace can do for you.
might - y arm; I know He'll guide me all the way.
lead you home, To live with Me e - ter - nal - ly."

Refrain (harmony optional)

Saved by His pow'r di - vine! Saved to new life sub - lime!
Saved by His pow'r, Saved to new life,

TEXT: Jack P. Scholfield
MUSIC: Jack P. Scholfield

SCHOLFIELD
8.6.8.8. with Refrain

Life now is sweet and my joy is com-plete, For I'm saved, saved, saved!

Now I Belong to Jesus 501

Whether we live or die, we belong to the Lord.   Romans 14:8

1. Je - sus, my Lord, will love me for - ev - er. From Him no pow'r of
2. Once I was lost in sin's deg - ra - da - tion; Je - sus came down to
3. Joy floods my soul, for Je - sus has saved me, Freed me from sin that

e - vil can sev - er. He gave His life to ran - som my soul;
bring me sal - va - tion, Lift - ed me up from sor - row and shame;
long had en - slaved me; His pre - cious blood He gave to re - deem.

Refrain

Now I be - long to Him.
Now I be - long to Him. Now I be - long to Je - sus, Je - sus be - longs to
Now I be - long to Him.

me; Not for the years of time a - lone, But for e - ter - ni - ty.

TEXT: Norman J. Clayton
MUSIC: Norman J. Clayton

ELLSWORTH
10.10.9.6. with Refrain

502 In My Heart There Rings a Melody

Sing with gratitude in your hearts to God. Colossians 3:16

1. I have a song that Je - sus gave me, It was sent from
2. I love the Christ who died on Cal - v'ry, For He washed my
3. 'Twill be my end - less theme in glo - ry, With the an - gels

heav'n a - bove; There nev - er was a sweet - er mel - o - dy,
sins a - way; He put with - in my heart a mel - o - dy,
I will sing; 'Twill be a song with glo - rious har - mo - ny,

Refrain

'Tis a mel - o - dy of love.
And I know it's there to stay. In my heart there rings a mel - o - dy,
When the courts of heav - en ring.

There rings a mel - o - dy with heav - en's har - mo - ny; In my heart there

rings a mel - o - dy, There rings a mel - o - dy of love.

TEXT: Elton M. Roth
MUSIC: Elton M. Roth

HEART MELODY
Irregular meter

Since Jesus Came into My Heart 503

If anyone is in Christ, there is a new creation. 2 Corinthians 5:17

1. What a won-der-ful change in my life has been wrought Since Je-sus came
2. I have ceased from my wan-d'ring and go-ing a-stray Since Je-sus came
3. I shall go there to dwell in that cit-y, I know, Since Je-sus came

in-to my heart! I have light in my soul for which long I had sought,
in-to my heart! And my sins, which were man-y, are all washed a-way,
in-to my heart! And I'm hap-py, so hap-py, as on-ward I go,

Refrain

Since Je-sus came in-to my heart!
Since Je-sus came in-to my heart! Since Je-sus came in-to my
Since Je-sus came in-to my heart!

heart, Since Je-sus came in-to my heart, Floods of joy o'er my

soul like the sea bil-lows roll, Since Je-sus came in-to my heart.

TEXT: Rufus H. McDaniel
MUSIC: Charles H. Gabriel

McDANIEL
12.8.12.8. with Refrain

504 Without Him

Apart from Me you can do nothing. John 15:5

1. With - out Him I could do noth - ing; With - out Him
2. With - out Him I would be dy - ing; With - out Him

I'd sure - ly fail. With - out Him I would be drift - ing
I'd be en - slaved. With - out Him life would be hope - less;

Refrain

Like a ship with - out a sail. Je - sus, O Je -
But with Je - sus, thank God, I'm saved.

sus! Do you know Him to - day? Do not turn Him a - way. O

Je - sus, O Je - sus! With - out Him, how lost I would be.

TEXT: Mylon R. LeFevre
MUSIC: Mylon R. LeFevre

WITHOUT HIM
8.7.8.7. with Refrain

He Touched Me 505

Filled with compassion, Jesus reached out His hand and touched the man. Mark 1:41

1. Shack - led by a heav - y bur - den, 'Neath a load of
2. Since I met this bless - ed Sav - ior, Since He cleansed and

guilt and shame; Then the hand of Je - sus touched me,
made me whole; I will nev - er cease to praise Him—

And now I am no long-er the same.
I'll shout it while e - ter - ni - ty rolls.

Refrain

He touched me, O, He

touched me, And O, the joy that floods my soul! Some - thing

hap-pened, and now I know, He touched me and made me whole.

TEXT: William J. Gaither
MUSIC: William J. Gaither

HE TOUCHED ME
Irregular meter

506 I'd Rather Have Jesus

I consider everything a loss compared to the surpassing greatness of knowing Christ. Philippians 3:8

1. I'd rath-er have Je-sus than sil-ver or gold; I'd
2. I'd rath-er have Je-sus than men's ap-plause; I'd
3. He's fair-er than lil-ies of rar-est bloom; He's

rath-er be His than have rich-es un-told; I'd rath-er
rath-er be faith-ful to His dear cause; I'd rath-er
sweet-er than hon-ey from out the comb; He's all that

have Je-sus than hous-es or lands. I'd rath-er be
have Je-sus than world-wide fame. I'd rath-er be
my hun-ger-ing spir-it needs. I'd rath-er have

Refrain

led by His nail-pierced hand
true to His ho-ly name   Than to be the king of a
Je-sus and let Him lead

TEXT: Rhea F. Miller
MUSIC: George Beverly Shea

I'D RATHER HAVE JESUS
Irregular meter

vast do-main And be held in sin's dread sway. I'd rath-er have

Je-sus than an-y-thing This world af-fords to-day.

Something Beautiful 507

This son of mine was dead and is alive again; he was lost and is found. Luke 15:24

Some-thing beau-ti-ful, some-thing good; All my con-fu-sion

He un-der-stood. All I had to of-fer Him was bro-ken-

ness and strife, But He made some-thing beau-ti-ful of my life.

TEXT: Gloria Gaither
MUSIC: William J. Gaither

SOMETHING BEAUTIFUL
Irregular meter

508 Love Lifted Me

He reached down from on high and drew me out of deep waters. Psalm 18:16

1. I was sink-ing deep in sin, Far from the peace-ful shore, Ver-y
2. All my heart to Him I give; Ev-er to Him I'll cling, In His
3. Souls in dan-ger, look a-bove; Je-sus com-plete-ly saves; He will

deep-ly stained with-in, Sink-ing to rise no more; But the Mas-ter
bless-ed pres-ence live, Ev-er His prais-es sing. Love so might-y
lift you by His love Out of the an-gry waves. He's the Mas-ter

of the sea Heard my de-spair-ing cry, From the wa-ters lift-ed me—
and so true Mer-its my soul's best songs; Faith-ful, lov-ing ser-vice, too,
of the sea, Bil-lows His will o-bey; He your Sav-ior wants to be—

Refrain

Now safe am I.
To Him be-longs. Love lift-ed me! Love lift-ed me!
Be saved to-day. Love lift-ed e-ven me! Love lift-ed e-ven me!

1. When noth-ing else could help, Love lift-ed me!
2. Love lift-ed me!

TEXT: James Rowe
MUSIC: Howard E. Smith

SAFETY
Irregular meter

He Lifted Me 509

He lifted me out of the mud and mire; He set my feet on a rock. Psalm 40:2

1. In loving-kindness Jesus came, My soul in mercy to reclaim; And from the depths of sin and shame, Through grace He lifted me. (He lifted me.)
2. He called me long before I heard, Before my sinful heart was stirred; But when I took Him at His word, Forgiv'n, He lifted me. (He lifted me.)
3. His brow was pierced with many a thorn; His hands by cruel nails were torn When from my guilt and grief, forlorn, In love He lifted me. (He lifted me.)
4. Now on a higher plane I dwell, And with my soul I know 'tis well; Yet how or why, I cannot tell, He should have lifted me. (He lifted me.)

Refrain

From sinking sand He lifted me, With tender hand He lifted me; From shades of night to planes of light, O praise His name, He lifted me!

TEXT: Charles H. Gabriel
MUSIC: Charles H. Gabriel

HE LIFTED ME
8.8.8.6. with Refrain

510 Heaven Came Down

The kindness and love of God our Savior appeared. Titus 3:4

1. O what a won-der-ful, won-der-ful day— Day I will nev-er for-
2. Born of the Spir-it with life from a-bove In-to God's fam-'ly di-
3. Now I've a hope that will sure-ly en-dure Af-ter the pass-ing of

get; Af-ter I'd wan-dered in dark-ness a-way, Je-sus my
vine, Jus-ti-fied ful-ly thro' Cal-va-ry's love, O what a
time; I have a fu-ture in heav-en for sure, There in those

Sav-ior I met. O what a ten-der, com-pas-sion-ate friend—
stand-ing is mine. And the trans-ac-tion so quick-ly was made
man-sions sub-lime. And it's be-cause of that won-der-ful day

He met the need of my heart; Shad-ows dis-pel-ling, With
When as a sin-ner I came; Took of the of-fer Of
When at the cross I be-lieved; Rich-es e-ter-nal And

TEXT: John W. Peterson
MUSIC: John W. Peterson

HEAVEN CAME DOWN
Irregular meter

joy   I am   tell-ing,   He   made all   the dark-ness de - part!
grace He did prof-fer;   He   saved me, O praise His dear   name!
bless-ings su - per - nal   From His pre-cious hand I   re - ceived.

Refrain

Heav-en came down   and glo-ry filled my soul.   (filled my soul.)

When at the cross   the Sav-ior made me whole. (made me whole.)   My

sins were washed a - way,   And my night was turned to day.

Heav-en came down   and glo-ry filled my soul!   (filled my soul.)

511 All That Thrills My Soul

Christ is all, and is in all. Colossians 3:11

1. Who can cheer the heart like Je - sus, By His pres - ence all di - vine?
2. Love of Christ so free - ly giv - en, Grace of God be - yond de - gree,
3. What a won - der - ful re - demp - tion! Nev - er can a mor - tal know
4. Ev - ery need His hand sup - ply - ing, Ev - ery good in Him I see;
5. By the crys - tal, flow - ing riv - er, With the ran - somed I will sing,

True and ten - der, pure and pre - cious, O how blest to call Him mine!
Mer - cy high - er than the heav - en, Deep - er than the deep - est sea!
How my sin, tho' red like crim - son, Can be whit - er than the snow.
On His strength di - vine re - ly - ing, He is All in All to me.
And for - ev - er and for - ev - er Praise and glo - ri - fy the King.

Refrain

All that thrills my soul is Je - sus; He is more than life to me. to me.

And the fair - est of ten thou - sand In my bless - ed Lord I see.

TEXT: Thoro Harris
MUSIC: Thoro Harris

HARRIS
8.7.8.7.D.

Jesus Is All the World to Me 512

For to me, to live is Christ and to die is gain. Philippians 1:21

1. Je - sus is all the world to me, My Life, my Joy, my All;
2. Je - sus is all the world to me, My Friend in tri - als sore;
3. Je - sus is all the world to me, And true to Him I'll be;
4. Je - sus is all the world to me, I want no bet - ter friend;

He is my Strength from day to day, With - out Him I would fall.
I go to Him for bless - ings, and He gives them o'er and o'er.
O how could I this Friend de - ny When He's so true to me?
I trust Him now, I'll trust Him when Life's fleet - ing days shall end.

When I am sad, to Him I go, No oth - er one can cheer me so;
He sends the sun - shine and the rain, He sends the har - vest's gold - en grain;
Fol - low - ing Him, I know I'm right, He watch - es o'er me day and night;
Beau - ti - ful life with such a Friend; Beau - ti - ful life that has no end;

When I am sad, He makes me glad– He's my Friend.
Sun - shine and rain, har - vest of grain– He's my Friend.
Fol - low - ing Him, by day and night– He's my Friend.
E - ter - nal life, e - ter - nal joy– He's my Friend.

TEXT: Will L. Thompson
MUSIC: Will L. Thompson

ELIZABETH
Irregular meter

513 Thank You, Lord

Thanks be to God for His indescribable gift! 2 Corinthians 9:15

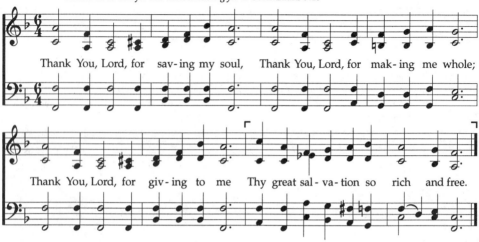

Thank You, Lord, for sav-ing my soul, Thank You, Lord, for mak-ing me whole;

Thank You, Lord, for giv-ing to me Thy great sal-va-tion so rich and free.

TEXT: Seth Sykes
MUSIC: Seth and Bessie Sykes

THANK YOU, LORD
8.8.8.9.

514 I Love to Praise Him

Let me live that I may praise You. Psalm 119:175

Unison

I love to praise Him, I love to praise

Him; I love to praise Him and

lift up His ho-ly name. Sing-ing

TEXT: Jennifer Randolph
MUSIC: Jennifer Randolph

I LOVE TO PRAISE HIM
Irregular meter

515 Since I Have Been Redeemed

Christ redeemed us from the curse of the law by being made a curse for us. Galatians 3:13

1. I have a song I love to sing, Since I have been re-deemed,
2. I have a Christ that sat-is-fies, Since I have been re-deemed.
3. I have a wit-ness bright and clear, Since I have been re-deemed,
4. I have a home pre-pared for me, Since I have been re-deemed,

Of my Re-deem-er, Sav-ior, King, Since I have been re-deemed.
To do His will— my high-est prize, Since I have been re-deemed.
Dis-pel-ling ev-ery doubt and fear, Since I have been re-deemed.
Where I shall live e-ter-nal-ly, Since I have been re-deemed.

Refrain

Since I have been re-deemed, Since I have been re-
Since I have been re-deemed, Since I have been re-deemed, Since I have been re-

deemed, I will glo-ry in His name; Since I have been re-
deemed, I will glo-ry in His name; Since I have been re-deemed, Since

deemed, I will glo-ry in my Sav-ior's name.
I have been re-deemed, I will glo-ry in my Sav-ior's name.

TEXT: Edwin O. Excell
MUSIC: Edwin O. Excell

OTHELLO
C.M. with Refrain

Redeemed 516

You were redeemed with the precious blood of Christ. 1 Peter 1:18-19

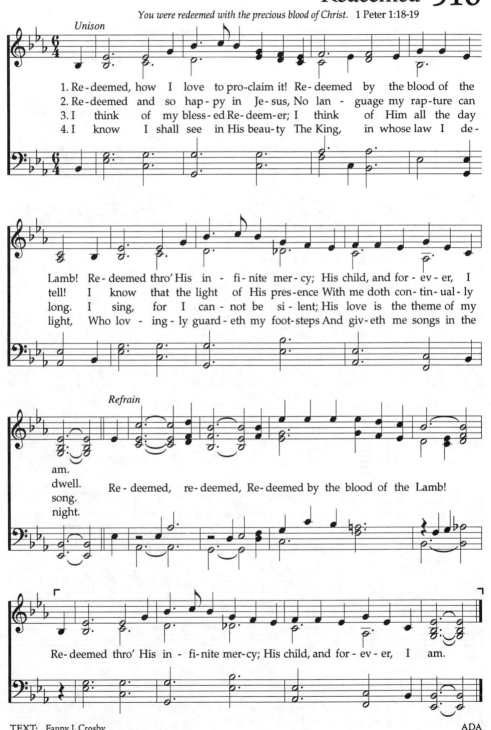

1. Re-deemed, how I love to pro-claim it! Re-deemed by the blood of the Lamb! Re-deemed thro' His in-fi-nite mer-cy; His child, and for-ev-er, I am.
2. Re-deemed and so hap-py in Je-sus, No lan-guage my rap-ture can tell! I know that the light of His pres-ence With me doth con-tin-ual-ly dwell.
3. I think of my bless-ed Re-deem-er; I think of Him all the day long. I sing, for I can-not be si-lent; His love is the theme of my song.
4. I know I shall see in His beau-ty The King, in whose law I de-light, Who lov-ing-ly guard-eth my foot-steps And giv-eth me songs in the night.

Refrain

Re-deemed, re-deemed, Re-deemed by the blood of the Lamb!

Re-deemed thro' His in-fi-nite mer-cy; His child, and for-ev-er, I am.

TEXT: Fanny J. Crosby
MUSIC: Aubrey L. Butler
Alternate tune: REDEEMED at No. 356

ADA
9.8.9.8. with Refrain

517 I Will Sing of My Redeemer

Jesus Christ gave Himself for us to redeem us from all wickedness. Titus 2:13-14

1. I will sing of my Re-deem-er And His won-drous love to me;
2. I will tell the won-drous sto-ry, How my lost es-tate to save;
3. I will praise my dear Re-deem-er, His tri-um-phant pow'r I'll tell,
4. I will sing of my Re-deem-er, And His heav'n-ly love to me;

On the cru-el cross He suf-fered From the curse to set me free.
In His bound-less love and mer-cy, He the ran-som free-ly gave.
How the vic-to-ry He giv-eth O-ver sin and death and hell.
He from death to life hath bro't me, Son of God, with Him to be.

Refrain

Sing, O sing of my Re-deem-er,
Sing, O sing of my Re-deem-er, Sing, O sing of my Re-deem-er,

With His blood He pur-chased me;
With His blood He pur-chased me, With His blood He pur-chased me;

On the cross He sealed my par-don,
On the cross He sealed my par-don, On the cross He sealed my par-don,

TEXT: Philip P. Bliss
MUSIC: James McGranahan

MY REDEEMER
8.7.8.7. with Refrain

Paid the debt and made me free.

Paid the debt and made me free, and made me free, and made me free.

Satisfied 518

He satisfies the thirsty and fills the hungry with good things. Psalm 107:9

1. All my life-long I had pant-ed For a drink from some cool spring
2. Feed-ing on the husks a-round me Till my strength was al-most gone,
3. Poor I was, and sought for rich-es, Some-thing that would sat-is-fy;
4. Well of wa-ter, ev-er spring-ing, Bread of Life, so rich and free;

That I hoped would quench the burn-ing Of the thirst I felt with-in.
Longed my soul for some-thing bet-ter, On-ly still to hun-ger on.
But the dust I gath-ered round me On-ly mocked my soul's sad cry.
Un-told wealth that nev-er fail-eth, My Re-deem-er is to me.

Refrain

Hal-le-lu-jah! I have found Him— Whom my soul so long has craved!

Je-sus sat-is-fies my long-ings; Thro' His blood I now am saved.

TEXT: Clara T. Williams
MUSIC: Ralph E. Hudson

SATISFIED
8.7.8.7. with Refrain

519 Jesus Is Lord of All

God has made this Jesus, whom you crucified, both Lord and Christ. Acts 2:36

1. Je - sus is Sav - ior and Lord of my life,
2. Bless - ed Re - deem - er, all glo - ri - ous King,
3. Will you sur - ren - der your all to Him now?

My hope, my glo - ry, my all. Won - der - ful Mas - ter in
Wor - thy of rev - 'rence I pay. Trib - ute and prais - es I
Fol - low His will and o - bey; Crown Him as Sov - 'reign, be -

joy and in strife, On Him you too may call.
joy - ful - ly bring To Him, the Life, the Way.
fore His throne bow; Give Him your heart to - day.

Refrain

Je - sus is Lord of all. Je - sus is Lord of all— Lord of my

tho'ts and my ser - vice each day. Je - sus is Lord of all.

TEXT: LeRoy McClard
MUSIC: LeRoy McClard

LORDSHIP OF CHRIST
Irregular meter

The Longer I Serve Him 520

I serve with my whole heart in preaching the gospel of His Son. Romans 1:9

1. Since I start-ed for the King-dom, Since my life He con-trols,
2. Ev - ery need He is sup-ply-ing; Plen-teous grace He be-stows.

Since I gave my heart to Je - sus, The long - er I serve Him, the
Ev - ery day my way gets bright-er; The long - er I serve Him, the

Refrain

sweet-er He grows.
sweet-er He grows.
The long - er I serve Him, the sweet-er He grows.

The more that I love Him, more love He be-stows. Each day is like heav-en, my

heart o-ver-flows. The long - er I serve Him, the sweet-er He grows.

TEXT: William J. Gaither
MUSIC: William J. Gaither

THE SWEETER HE GROWS
8.6.8.11. with Refrain

521 A New Name in Glory

Rejoice that your names are written in heaven. Luke 10:20

1. I was once a sin-ner, but I came Par-don to re-ceive from my
2. I was hum-bly kneel-ing at the cross, Fear-ing naught but God's an-gry
3. In the Book 'tis writ-ten, "Saved by grace." O the joy that came to my

Lord. This was free-ly giv-en, and I found That He al-ways kept His
frown, When the heav-ens o-pened and I saw That my name was writ-ten
soul! Now I am for-giv-en, and I know By the blood I am made

Refrain

word.
down. There's a new name writ-ten down in glo-ry, And it's mine,
whole. And it's

O yes, it's mine! And the white-robed an-gels sing the sto-ry,
mine, yes, it's mine!

"A sin-ner has come home." For there's a new name writ-ten down in

home, has come home."

TEXT: C. Austin Miles
MUSIC: C. Austin Miles

NEW NAME
Irregular meter

glo-ry, And it's mine, O yes, it's mine! With my
And it's mine, yes, it's mine!

sins for-giv-en I am bound for heav-en, Nev-er-more to roam.

I'm So Glad, Jesus Lifted Me 522

I will exalt You, O Lord, for You lifted me out of the depths. Psalm 30:1

1. I'm so glad, Je-sus lift-ed me! I'm so glad,
2. I was sink-ing down, Je-sus lift-ed me! I was sink-ing down,
3. Sa-tan had me bound, Je-sus lift-ed me! Sa-tan had me bound,
4. I'm so glad, Je-sus lift-ed me! I'm so glad,

Je-sus lift-ed me! I'm so glad, Je-sus lift-ed me! Sing-ing
Je-sus lift-ed me! I was sink-ing down, Je-sus lift-ed me! Sing-ing
Je-sus lift-ed me! Sa-tan had me bound, Je-sus lift-ed me! Sing-ing
Je-sus lift-ed me! I'm so glad, Je-sus lift-ed me! Sing-ing

Optional extended or choral ending

glo-ry, hal-le-lu-jah! Je-sus lift-ed me!
glo-ry, hal-le-lu-jah! Je-sus lift-ed me!
glo-ry, hal-le-lu-jah! Je-sus lift-ed me! Je-sus lift-ed me!
glo-ry, hal-le-lu-jah! Je-sus lift-ed me!

TEXT: Traditional and Camp Kirkland
MUSIC: Traditional; arranged by Camp Kirkland

I'M SO GLAD
Irregular meter

523   FORGIVENESS

from Isaiah 1:18; 1 John 1: 7-9 (NKJV)

WORSHIP LEADER
"Come now, and let us reason together," says the Lord.

EVERYONE
"Though your sins are like scarlet,
they shall be as white as snow;
though they are red like crimson,
they shall be as wool."

WORSHIP LEADER
If we walk in the light as He is in the light,
we have fellowship with one another,
and the blood of Jesus Christ, His Son, cleanses us from all sin.
If we say we have no sin, we deceive ourselves,
and the truth is not in us.

EVERYONE
If we confess our sins, He is faithful and just
to forgive us our sins and to cleanse us from all unrighteousness.

524   SALVATION BY GRACE

from John 1:17; Ephesians 2:4-9; Titus 2:11; 3:5-7 (NASB)

WORSHIP LEADER
Grace and truth were realized through Jesus Christ.

EVERYONE
God, being rich in mercy, because of His great love with which He loved us,
even when we were dead in our transgressions,
made us alive together with Christ
(by grace you have been saved);

WORSHIP LEADER
And raised us up with Him,
and seated us with Him in the heavenly places in Christ Jesus,
so that in the ages to come He might show the surpassing riches
of His grace in kindness toward us in Christ Jesus.

EVERYONE
For by grace you have been saved through faith;
and that not of yourselves, it is the gift of God;
not as a result of works, so that no one may boast.

WORSHIP LEADER
For the grace of God has appeared,
bringing salvation to all men.

EVERYONE
He saved us, not on the basis of deeds which we have done
in righteousness, but according to His mercy;

WORSHIP LEADER
By the washing of regeneration and renewing by the Holy Spirit,
whom He poured out upon us richly through Jesus Christ our Savior;

EVERYONE
So that being justified by grace
we would be made heirs according to the hope of eternal life.

PRESS ON

Paul's Testimony

from Philippians 3:1-14 (NIV)

WORSHIP LEADER or SOLO DRAMATIST

Finally, my brothers, rejoice in the Lord!
It is no trouble for me to write the same things to you again,
and it is a safeguard for you.

Watch out for those dogs, those men who do evil,
those mutilators of the flesh.
For it is we who are the circumcision,
we who worship by the Spirit of God,
who glory in Christ Jesus,
and who put no confidence in the flesh—
though I myself have reasons for such confidence.

If anyone else thinks he has reasons to put confidence in the flesh,
I have more:
circumcised on the eighth day, of the people of Israel,
of the tribe of Benjamin, a Hebrew of Hebrews;
in regard to the law, a Pharisee;
as for zeal, persecuting the church;
as for legalistic righteousness, faultless.

But whatever was to my profit I now consider loss for the sake of Christ.
What is more, I consider everything a loss
compared to the surpassing greatness of knowing
Christ Jesus my Lord,
for whose sake I have lost all things.
I consider them rubbish, that I may gain Christ
and be found in Him, not having a righteousness of my own
that comes from the law,
but that which is through faith in Christ—
the righteousness that comes from God and is by faith.
I want to know Christ and the power of His resurrection
and the fellowship of sharing in His sufferings,
becoming like Him in His death,
and so, somehow, to attain to the resurrection from the dead.

Not that I have already obtained all this,
or have already been made perfect,
but I press on to take hold of that for which Christ Jesus
took hold of me.
Brothers, I do not consider myself yet to have taken hold of it.

But one thing I do:
Forgetting what is behind and straining toward what is ahead,
I press on toward the goal to win the prize for which
God has called me heavenward in Christ Jesus.

EVERYONE
**Forgetting what is behind and straining toward what is ahead,
we press on toward the goal to win the prize for which
God has called us heavenward in Christ Jesus.**

526 The Solid Rock

No one can lay any foundation other than Jesus Christ. 1 Corinthians 3:11

1. My hope is built on noth-ing less Than Je-sus' blood and
2. When dark-ness veils His love-ly face, I rest on His un-
3. His oath, His cov-e-nant, His blood, Sup-port me in the
4. When He shall come with trum-pet sound, O may I then in

righ-teous-ness; I dare not trust the sweet-est frame, But
chang-ing grace; In ev-ery high and storm-y gale, My
whelm-ing flood; When all a-round my soul gives way, He
Him be found; Dressed in His righ-teous-ness a-lone, Fault-

Refrain

whol-ly lean on Je-sus' name.
an-chor holds with-in the veil.
then is all my hope and stay.   On Christ, the sol-id Rock, I stand; All
less to stand be-fore the throne.

oth-er ground is sink-ing sand, All oth-er ground is sink-ing sand.

TEXT: Edward Mote
MUSIC: William B. Bradbury; Last stanza setting and Choral ending by Doug Holck
Arr. © Copyright 1997 by Integrity's Hosanna! Music and Word Music (a div. of WORD MUSIC). All rights reserved. Used by permission.

SOLID ROCK
L. M. with Refrain

Optional last stanza setting

Unison   **Broader**

rit.

4. When He shall come with trum-pet sound, O

may I then in Him be found; Dressed in His righ-teous-ness a-lone, Fault-

Optional descant

On Christ, the sol - id Rock, I stand; All

less to stand be - fore the throne. On Christ, the sol - id Rock, I stand; All

oth-er ground is sink-ing sand, All oth-er ground is sink-ing sand.

oth-er ground is sink-ing sand, All oth-er ground is sink-ing sand.

Optional choral ending

ff

On Christ, the sol - id Rock, I stand, I stand!

ff

527 I Know Whom I Have Believed

I know whom I have believed. 2 Timothy 1:12

1. I know not why God's won-drous grace To me He hath made known;
2. I know not how this sav-ing faith To me He did im-part;
3. I know not how the Spir-it moves, Con-vinc-ing men of sin;
4. I know not when my Lord may come, At night or noon-day fair;

Nor why, un-wor-thy, Christ in love Re-deemed me for His own.
Nor how be-liev-ing in His Word Wro't peace with-in my heart.
Re-veal-ing Je-sus thro' the Word, Cre-at-ing faith in Him.
Nor if I'll walk the *vale with Him Or "meet Him in the air."

Refrain

But "I know Whom I have be-liev-ed And am per-suad-ed that He is a-ble

To keep that which I've com-mit-ted Un-to Him a-gainst that day."

*vale - Valley of Death

Optional segue to "My Faith Has Found a Resting Place." No transition is needed.

TEXT: Daniel W. Whittle; based on 2 Timothy 1:12
MUSIC: James McGranahan

EL NATHAN
C.M. with Refrain

My Faith Has Found a Resting Place 528

We who have believed enter that rest. Hebrews 4:3

1. My faith has found a rest-ing place— Not in de-vice nor creed:
2. E - nough for me that Je - sus saves— This ends my fear and doubt;
3. My heart is lean-ing on the Word— The writ-ten Word of God:
4. My great Phy - si - cian heals the sick— The lost He came to save;

I trust the Ev - er - liv - ing One— His wounds for me shall plead.
A sin - ful soul, I come to Him— He'll nev - er cast me out.
Sal - va - tion by my Sav - ior's name, Sal - va - tion thro' His blood.
For me His pre - cious blood He shed— For me His life He gave.

Refrain

I need no oth - er ar - gu - ment, I need no oth - er plea;

It is e-nough that Je - sus died, And that He died for me.

TEXT: Lidie H. Edmunds
MUSIC: Norwegian Folk melody; arranged by William J. Kirkpatrick

LANDAS
C.M. with Refrain

529

MY HOPE IS IN THE LORD
A Worship Sequence

I Will Call upon the Lord
Unto Thee, O Lord

WORSHIP LEADER

To You, O Lord, I lift up my soul; in You I trust, O my God.
Guide me in Your truth and teach me, for You are God, my Savior,
and my hope is in You all day long.
I love You, O Lord, my strength.
The Lord is my rock, my fortress and my deliverer;
He is my shield and the horn of my salvation, my stronghold.
I call to the Lord, who is worthy of praise, and I am saved from my enemies.

from Psalms 25:1-2, 5; 18:1-3 (NIV)

530 I Will Call upon the Lord

I call to the Lord, who is worthy of praise. Psalm 18:3

Optional descant

I will call up-on the Lord

Unison

I will call up-on the Lord who is wor-thy to be

who is wor-thy to be praised. So shall I be

praised. So shall I be saved from my en-e-mies.

TEXT: Michael O'Shields, based on Psalm 18:3; 2 Samuel 22:47
MUSIC: Michael O'Shields

O'SHIELDS
Irregular meter

531 Unto Thee, O Lord

To You, O Lord, I lift up my soul. Psalm 25:1

This song may be sung with a swing feeling.

TEXT: Charles F. Monroe, based on Psalm 25:1-2
MUSIC: Charles F. Monroe

UNTO THEE
Irregular meter

God, I trust in Thee; Let me not be a-shamed,

I trust in Thee; Let me not be a-shamed,

let not my en - e - mies tri - umph o - ver me.

let not my en - e - mies tri - umph o - ver me.

The end of MY HOPE IS IN THE LORD - A Worship Sequence

Only Believe 532

Everything is possible for him who believes. Mark 9:23

On - ly be - lieve, on - ly be - lieve; All things are pos - si - ble, on - ly be - lieve.

On - ly be - lieve, on - ly be - lieve; All things are pos - si - ble, on - ly be - lieve.

TEXT: Paul Rader
MUSIC: Paul Rader

ONLY BELIEVE
Irregular meter

533 There Is a Savior

The Father has sent His Son to be the Savior of the world. 1 John 4:14

There is a Sav-ior, What joys ex-press! His eyes are mer-cy; His Word is rest. For each to-mor-row, For yes-ter-day, There is a Sav-ior Who lights our way.

TEXT: Sandi Patty and Phill McHugh
MUSIC: Greg Nelson and Bob Farrell

SAVIOR
5.4.5.4.D.

534 Learning to Lean

Come to Me, and I will give you rest. Matthew 11:28

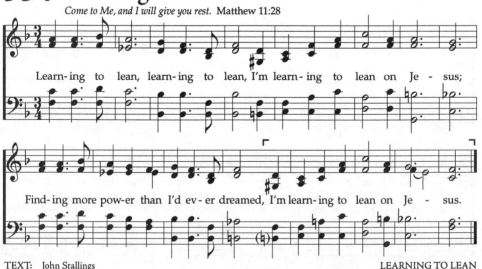

Learn-ing to lean, learn-ing to lean, I'm learn-ing to lean on Je-sus; Find-ing more pow-er than I'd ev-er dreamed, I'm learn-ing to lean on Je-sus.

TEXT: John Stallings
MUSIC: John Stallings

LEARNING TO LEAN
8.8.10.8.

Optional repeat setting

Learn-ing to lean, learn-ing to lean, I'm learn-ing to lean on Je - sus;

Find-ing more pow-er than I'd ev-er dreamed, I'm learn-ing to lean on Je - sus.

Ask Ye What Great Thing I Know 535

I resolved to know nothing except Jesus Christ and Him crucified. 1 Corinthians 2:2

1. Ask ye what great thing I know That de - lights and
2. Who de - feats my fierc - est foes? Who con - soles my
3. Who is life in life to me? Who the death of
4. This is that great thing I know; This de - lights and

stirs me so? What the high re - ward I win? Whose the
sad - dest woes? Who re - vives my faint - ing heart, Heal - ing
death will be? Who will place me on His right With the
stirs me so: Faith in Him who died to save, Him who

name I glo - ry in? Je - sus Christ, the Cru - ci - fied.
all its hid - den smart? Je - sus Christ, the Cru - ci - fied.
count - less hosts of light? Je - sus Christ, the Cru - ci - fied.
tri - umphed o'er the grave: Je - sus Christ, the Cru - ci - fied.

TEXT: Johann C. Schwedler; translated by Benjamin H. Kennedy, altered
MUSIC: H. A. César Malan

HENDON
7.7.7.7.7.

536 Have Faith in God

Have faith in God. Mark 11:22

1. Have faith in God when your path - way is lone - ly; He sees and
2. Have faith in God when your pray'rs are un - an - swered; Your ear - nest
3. Have faith in God in your pain and your sor - row; His heart is
4. Have faith in God tho' all else fail a - bout you. Have faith in

knows all the way you have trod. Nev - er a - lone are the
plea He will nev - er for - get. Wait on the Lord; trust His
touched with your grief and de - spair. Cast all your cares and your
God; He pro - vides for His own. He can - not fail tho' all

least of His chil - dren; Have faith in God, have faith in God.
Word and be pa - tient. Have faith in God; He'll an - swer yet.
bur - dens up - on Him; And leave them there, O leave them there.
king - doms shall per - ish; He rules, He reigns up - on His throne.

Refrain

Have faith in God; He's on His throne. Have faith in God; He watch - es o'er His own.

He can - not fail! He must pre - vail! Have faith in God, have faith in God.

TEXT: B. B. McKinney
MUSIC: B. B. McKinney
MUSKOGEE
11.10.11.8. with Refrain

He Who Began a Good Work in You 537

He who began a good work in you will carry it on to completion. Philippians 1:6

He who be-gan a good work in you,

He who be-gan a good work in you

will be faith - ful to com-plete it,

He'll be faith - ful to com-plete it; He who start-

- ed the work will be faith - ful to com-plete it in you.

TEXT: Jon Mohr
MUSIC: Jon Mohr

A GOOD WORK
Irregular meter

538

MY FAITH, MY HOPE
A Worship Sequence

My Faith Looks Up to Thee; stanzas 1,2
My Hope Is in the Lord; stanzas 1,3,4
Suggested stanzas have been marked with an arrow: ➤

WORSHIP LEADER

Let us fix our eyes on Jesus, the author and perfecter of our faith,
who for the joy set before Him endured the cross, scorning its shame,
and sat down at the right hand of the throne of God.
Praise be to the God and Father of our Lord Jesus Christ!
In His great mercy He has given us new birth into a living hope
through the resurrection of Jesus Christ from the dead.

from Hebrews 12:2; 1 Peter 1:3 (NIV)

539 My Faith Looks Up to Thee

Through faith in Him we may approach God with freedom and confidence. Ephesians 3:12

➤ 1. My faith looks up to Thee, Thou Lamb of Cal - va - ry,
➤ 2. May Thy rich grace im - part Strength to my faint - ing heart,
3. While life's dark maze I tread And griefs a - round me spread,
4. When ends life's pass - ing dream, When death's cold, threat - ening stream

Sav - ior di - vine! Now hear me while I pray, Take all my
My zeal in - spire; As Thou hast died for me, O may my
Be Thou my guide; Bid dark - ness turn to day, Wipe sor - row's
Shall o'er me roll, Blest Sav - ior, then, in love, Fear and dis -

guilt a - way, O let me from this day Be whol - ly Thine!
love to Thee Pure, warm, and change - less be, A liv - ing fire!
tears a - way, Nor let me ev - er stray From Thee a - side.
trust re - move; O lift me safe a - bove, A ran - somed soul!

Optional transition to "My Hope Is in the Lord"

TEXT: Ray Palmer
MUSIC: Lowell Mason

OLIVET
6.6.4.6.6.6.4.

My Hope Is in the Lord 540

Christ in you, the hope of glory. Colossians 1:27

1. My hope is in the Lord Who gave Him-self for me
2. No mer-it of my own His an-ger to sup-press,
3. And now for me He stands Be-fore the Fa-ther's throne;
4. His grace has planned it all, 'Tis mine but to be-lieve

And paid the price of all my sin at Cal-va-ry.
My on-ly hope is found in Je-sus' righ-teous-ness.
He shows His wound-ed hands and names me as His own.
And rec-og-nize His work of love and Christ re-ceive.

Optional descant - sing on last Refrain

For me He died, For me He lives,

Refrain

For me He died; For me He lives,

For me He died; For me He lives,

And ev-er-last-ing life and light He free-ly gives.

And ev-er-last-ing life and light He free-ly gives.

TEXT: Norman J. Clayton
MUSIC: Norman J. Clayton; Descant by Michael James

WAKEFIELD
6.6.12. with Refrain

The end of MY FAITH, MY HOPE - A Worship Sequence

541 The Joy of the Lord

The joy of the Lord is your strength. Nehemiah 8:10

1. The joy of the Lord is my strength, The
2. He heals the bro-ken heart-ed and they cry no more, He
3. He gives me liv-ing wa-ter and I thirst no more, He

joy of the Lord is my strength, The joy of the
heals the bro-ken heart-ed and they cry no more, He heals the bro-ken
gives me liv-ing wa-ter and I thirst no more, He gives me liv-ing

Lord is my strength, The joy of the Lord is my strength.
heart-ed and they cry no more, The joy of the Lord is my strength.
wa-ter and I thirst no more, The joy of the Lord is my strength.

Optional segue to "My Life Is in You, Lord." No transition is needed.

♩ = ♩ a little faster.

TEXT: Alliene G. Vale; based on Nehemiah 8:10
MUSIC: Alliene G. Vale

THE JOY OF THE LORD
Irregular meter

542 My Life Is in You, Lord

For to me, to live is Christ and to die is gain. Philippians 1:21

My life is in You, Lord; My strength is in You, Lord; My

TEXT: Daniel Gardner
MUSIC: Daniel Gardner

MY LIFE
Irregular meter

543 'Til the Storm Passes By

You have been a refuge for the needy in their distress, a shelter from the storm. Isaiah 25:4

1. In the dark of the mid-night Have I oft hid my face,
2. Man-y times Sa-tan whis-pered, "There is no need to try,
3. When the long night has end-ed, And the storms come no more,

While the storm howls a-bove me, And there's no hid-ing place.
For there's no end of sor-row; There's no hope by and by."
Let me stand in Thy pres-ence On that bright, peace-ful shore.

'Mid the crash of the thun-der, Pre-cious Lord, hear my cry,
But I know Thou art with me, And to-mor-row I'll rise
In that land where the tem-pest Nev-er comes, Lord, may I

Refrain

"Keep me safe 'til the storm pass-es by."
Where the storm nev-er dark-ens the skies. 'Til the storm pass-es
Dwell with Thee when the storm pass-es by.

o-ver, 'Til the thun-der sounds no more, 'Til the clouds roll for-

TEXT: Mosie Lister
MUSIC: Mosie Lister

LISTER
7.6.7.6.7.6.9. with Refrain

ev - er from the sky, Hold me fast, let me stand In the
hol - low of Thy hand; Keep me safe 'til the storm pass - es by.

My Faith Still Holds 544

Let us hold firmly to the faith we profess. Hebrews 4:14

My faith still holds on to the Christ of Cal - va - ry; O bless - ed
Rock of A - ges, cleft for me. I glad - ly place my trust in things I
can - not see; My faith still holds on to the Christ of Cal - va - ry!

TEXT: Gloria Gaither and William J. Gaither
MUSIC: William J. Gaither

STRONG FAITH
12.10.12.10.

545 Moment by Moment

Having loved His own, He now showed them the full extent of His love.   John 13:1

1. Dy - ing with Je - sus, by death reck - oned mine; Liv - ing with Je - sus a
2. Nev - er a tri - al that He is not there, Nev - er a bur - den that
3. Nev - er a weak - ness that He doth not feel, Nev - er a sick - ness that

new life di - vine. Look - ing to Je - sus till glo - ry doth shine;
He doth not bear, Nev - er a sor - row that He doth not share;
He can - not heal; Mo - ment by mo - ment, in woe or in weal,

Refrain

Mo - ment by mo - ment, O Lord, I am Thine.
Mo - ment by mo - ment I'm un - der His care. Mo - ment by mo - ment I'm
Je - sus my Sav - ior a - bides with me still.

kept in His love; Mo - ment by mo - ment I've life from a - bove. Look - ing to

Je - sus till glo - ry doth shine; Mo - ment by mo - ment, O Lord, I am Thine.

TEXT: Daniel W. Whittle
MUSIC: May Whittle Moody

WHITTLE
10.10.10.10. with Refrain

THE AUTHOR OF OUR FAITH   546

from Hebrews 11:1-3, 6; 12:1-2 (NIV)

WORSHIP LEADER
Faith is being sure of what we hope for and certain of what we do not see.
By faith we understand that the universe was formed at God's command,
so that what is seen was not made out of what was visible.
Without faith it is impossible to please God, because anyone who comes to Him must
believe that He exists and that He rewards those who earnestly seek Him.
Let us throw off everything that hinders and the sin that so easily entangles,
and let us run with perseverance the race marked out for us.
Let us fix our eyes on Jesus, the author and perfecter of our faith.

HOPE AND TRUST IN GOD   547

from Psalm 25:1-15 (NIV)

WORSHIP LEADER
To You, O Lord, I lift up my soul; in You I trust, O my God.

MEN
Do not let me be put to shame, nor let my enemies triumph over me.

WOMEN
No one whose hope is in You will ever be put to shame.

WORSHIP LEADER
Show me Your ways, O Lord, teach me Your paths; guide me in Your truth
and teach me, for You are God my Savior, and my hope is in You all day long.

MEN
Remember, O Lord, Your great mercy and love,
for they are from of old.

WOMEN
Remember not the sins of my youth and my rebellious ways;

EVERYONE
According to Your love, remember me, for You are good, O Lord.

MEN
All the ways of the Lord are loving and faithful
for those who keep the demands of His covenant.

WOMEN
For the sake of Your name, O Lord, forgive my iniquity, though it is great.

WORSHIP LEADER
Who, then, is the man that fears the Lord?

MEN
He will instruct him in the way chosen for him.

WOMEN
He will spend his days in prosperity,
and his descendants will inherit the land.

WORSHIP LEADER
The Lord confides in those who fear Him;

EVERYONE
He makes His covenant known to them.

WORSHIP LEADER
My eyes are ever on the Lord.

EVERYONE
To You, O Lord, I lift up my soul; in You I trust, O my God.

548 As the Deer

As the deer pants for water, so my soul pants for You. Psalm 42:1

Harmony optional

1. As the deer pant-eth for the wa-ter, So my soul long-eth af - ter Thee.
2. You're my friend and You are my broth-er, E-ven though You are a King.
3. I want You more than gold or sil - ver, On-ly You can sat - is - fy.

You a - lone are my heart's de - sire, And I long to wor - ship Thee.
I love You more than an - y oth-er, So much more than an - y - thing.
You a - lone are the real joy giv-er, And the ap - ple of my eye.

Refrain

You a - lone are my strength, my shield; To You a - lone may my

spir - it yield. You a - lone are my

heart's de - sire, And I long to wor - ship Thee.

TEXT: Martin Nystrom
MUSIC: Martin Nystrom

AS THE DEER
Irregular meter

Higher Ground 549

I press on toward the goal to win the prize. Philippians 3:14

1. I'm press-ing on the up-ward way, New heights I'm
2. My heart has no de-sire to stay Where doubts a-
3. I want to live a-bove the world, Tho' Sa-tan's
4. I want to scale the ut-most height And catch a

gain - ing ev-ery day; Still pray-ing as I'm on-ward
rise and fears dis-may; Tho' some may dwell where these a-
darts at me are hurled; For faith has caught the joy-ful
gleam of glo-ry bright; But still I'll pray till heav'n I've

bound, "Lord, plant my feet on high - er ground."
bound, My prayer, my aim, is high - er ground.
sound, The song of saints on high - er ground.
found, "Lord, lead me on to high - er ground."

Refrain

Lord, lift me up and let me stand By faith on heav-en's ta-ble-land;

A high-er plane than I have found– Lord, plant my feet on high-er ground.

TEXT: Johnson Oatman, Jr.
MUSIC: Charles H. Gabriel

HIGHER GROUND
L.M. with Refrain

550 I Want to Be like Jesus

You become imitators of us and of the Lord. 1 Thessalonians 1:6

1. I have one deep, su-preme de-sire, That I may be like Je-sus.
2. He spent His life in do-ing good; I want to be like Je-sus.
3. A ho-ly, harm-less life He led; I want to be like Je-sus.
4. O per-fect life of Christ, my Lord! I want to be like Je-sus.

To this I fer-vent-ly as-pire, That I may be like Je-sus.
In low-ly paths of ser-vice trod; I want to be like Je-sus.
The Fa-ther's will, His drink and bread; I want to be like Je-sus.
My rec-om-pense and my re-ward, That I may be like Je-sus.

I want my heart His throne to be, So that a watch-ing world may
He sym-pa-thized with hearts dis-tressed; He spoke the words that cheered and
And when at last He comes to die, "For-give them, Fa-ther," hear Him
His Spir-it fill my hun-g'ring soul, His pow-er all my life con-

see His like-ness shin-ing forth in me. I want to be like Je-sus.
blessed; He wel-comed sin-ners to His breast. I want to be like Je-sus.
cry For those who taunt and cru-ci-fy. I want to be like Je-sus.
trol; My deep-est pray'r, my high-est goal, That I may be like Je-sus.

*Optional segue to "O to Be like
Thee!" No transition is needed.*

TEXT: Thomas O. Chisholm
MUSIC: David Livingstone Ives

IVES
8.7.8.7.8.8.8.7.

O to Be like Thee! 551

I am again in the pains of childbirth until Christ is formed in you. Galatians 4:19

1. O to be like Thee! bless-ed Re-deem-er, This is my con-stant
2. O to be like Thee! full of com-pas-sion, Lov-ing, for-giv-ing,
3. O to be like Thee! while I am plead-ing, Pour out Thy Spir-it;

long-ing and prayer. Glad-ly I'll for-feit all of earth's trea-sures,
ten-der and kind; Help-ing the help-less, cheer-ing the faint-ing,
fill with Thy love. Make me a tem-ple meet for Thy dwell-ing;

Refrain

Je - sus, Thy per-fect like-ness to wear.
Seek-ing the wan-d'ring sin-ner to find. O to be like Thee!
Fit me for life and heav-en a-bove.

O to be like Thee, Bless-ed Re-deem-er, pure as Thou art! Come in Thy

sweet-ness, come in Thy full-ness; Stamp Thine own im-age deep on my heart.

TEXT: Thomas O. Chisholm
MUSIC: William J. Kirkpatrick

RONDINELLA
10.9.10.9. with Refrain

552 I Am Thine, O Lord

Let us draw near to God with a sincere heart in full assurance of faith. Hebrews 10:22

1. I am Thine, O Lord; I have heard Thy voice, And it told Thy
2. Con - se - crate me now to Thy ser - vice, Lord, By the pow'r of
3. O the pure de - light of a sin - gle hour That be - fore Thy
4. There are depths of love that I can - not know Till I cross the

love to me. But I long to rise in the arms of faith,
grace di - vine. Let my soul look up with a stead - fast hope,
throne I spend, When I kneel in prayer and with Thee, my God,
nar - row sea; There are heights of joy that I may not reach

Refrain

And be clos - er drawn to Thee.
And my will be lost in Thine.
I com - mune as friend with friend!   Draw me near - er,
Till I rest in peace with Thee.

near - er, bless - ed Lord, To the cross where Thou hast died. Draw me

TEXT: Fanny J. Crosby
MUSIC: William H. Doane

I AM THINE
10.7.10.7. with Refrain

near - er, near - er, near - er, bless - ed Lord, To Thy pre - cious, bleed - ing side.

Nearer, My God, to Thee 553

It is good to be near God. I have made the Sovereign Lord my refuge. Psalm 73:28

1. Near - er, my God, to Thee, Near - er to Thee, E'en though it
2. Though like the wan - der - er, The sun gone down, Dark - ness be
3. *There let the way ap - pear, Steps un - to heav'n; All that Thou
4. Then, with my wak - ing tho'ts Bright with Thy praise, Out of my
5. Or if, on joy - ful wing Cleav - ing the sky, Sun, moon, and

be a cross That rais - eth me! Still all my song shall be:
o - ver me, My rest a stone; Yet in my dreams I'd be
send - est me, In mer - cy giv'n; An - gels to beck - on me
ston - y griefs **Beth - el I'll raise; So by my woes to be
stars for - got, Up - ward I fly, Still all my song shall be:

Near - er, my God, to Thee; Near - er, my God, to Thee, Near - er to Thee.
Near - er, my God, to Thee; Near - er, my God, to Thee, Near - er to Thee.
Near - er, my God, to Thee; Near - er, my God, to Thee, Near - er to Thee.
Near - er, my God, to Thee; Near - er, my God, to Thee, Near - er to Thee.
Near - er, my God, to Thee; Near - er, my God, to Thee, Near - er to Thee.

*Genesis 28:12   **Genesis 35:15

TEXT: Sarah F. Adams; based on Genesis 28:10-22
MUSIC: Lowell Mason

BETHANY
6.4.6.4.6.6.6.4.

554 Give Me Jesus

What good is it for you to gain the whole world, yet forfeit your soul? Mark 8:36

1. Take the world, but give me Je-sus; All its joys are but a name,
2. Take the world, but give me Je-sus, Sweet-est com-fort of my soul.
3. Take the world, but give me Je-sus; Let me view His con-stant smile.
4. Take the world, but give me Je-sus; In His cross my trust shall be,

But His love a-bid-eth ev-er, Thro' e-ter-nal years the same.
With my Sav-ior watch-ing o'er me, I can sing tho' bil-lows roll.
Then thro'-out my pil-grim jour-ney Light will cheer me all the while.
Till, with clear-er, bright-er vi-sion, Face to face my Lord I see.

Refrain

O the height and depth of mer-cy! O the length and breadth of love!

O the full-ness of re-demp-tion, Pledge of end-less life a-bove!

TEXT: Fanny J. Crosby
MUSIC: John R. Sweney

GIVE ME JESUS
8.7.8.7. with Refrain

To Be like Jesus 555

Follow my example, as I follow the example of Christ. 1 Corinthians 11:1

To be like Je - sus, to be like Je - sus, To be the
one I was cre - at - ed to be. To be like Je - sus,
to be like Je - sus; May all who see my heart find Him in me.

TEXT: Dick and Melodie Tunney
MUSIC: Dick and Melodie Tunney

LIKE JESUS
Irregular meter

LET MY LIFE PRAISE HIM 556
A Worship Sequence

Seekers of Your Heart
I Am Crucified with Christ
Praise You

WORSHIP LEADER

I consider everything a loss compared to the surpassing greatness of knowing Christ Jesus
my Lord, for whose sake I have lost all things. I consider them rubbish, that I may gain
Christ. I want to know Christ and the power of His resurrection and the fellowship of
sharing in His sufferings, becoming like Him in His death.

from Philippians 3:8, 10 (NIV)

Optional introduction to "Seekers of Your Heart"

mp

557 Seekers of Your Heart

I keep asking God that you may know Him better. Ephesians 1:17

Lord, we want to know You, Live our lives to show You All the love we owe You— We're seek-ers of Your heart, Seek-ers of Your heart.

Optional transition to "I Am Crucified with Christ"

TEXT: Melodie Tunney, Dick Tunney, Beverly Darnall
MUSIC: Melodie Tunney, Dick Tunney, Beverly Darnall

ISAAC
Irregular meter

558 I Am Crucified with Christ

I have been crucified with Christ and I no longer live, but Christ lives in me. Galatians 2:20

I am cru-ci-fied with Christ, there-fore I no long-er live; Je-sus Christ now lives in me. I am cru-ci-fied with Christ, there-fore

TEXT: John G. Elliott; based on Galatians 2:20
MUSIC: John G. Elliott

CRUCIFIED WITH CHRIST
Irregular meter

I no long-er live; Je-sus Christ now lives in me. I am me.

Je-sus Christ now lives in me.

Optional transition to "Praise You"

Praise You 559

Let me live that I may praise You. Psalm 119:175

Praise You, praise You; Let my life praise You.

Praise You, praise You; Let my life, O Lord, praise

You. Praise You. Let my life, O Lord, praise You.

TEXT: Elizabeth Goodine
MUSIC: Elizabeth Goodine

PRAISE YOU
Irregular meter

The end of LET MY LIFE PRAISE HIM - A Worship Sequence

560 More About Jesus

Grow in the grace and knowledge of our Lord and Savior Jesus Christ. 2 Peter 3:18

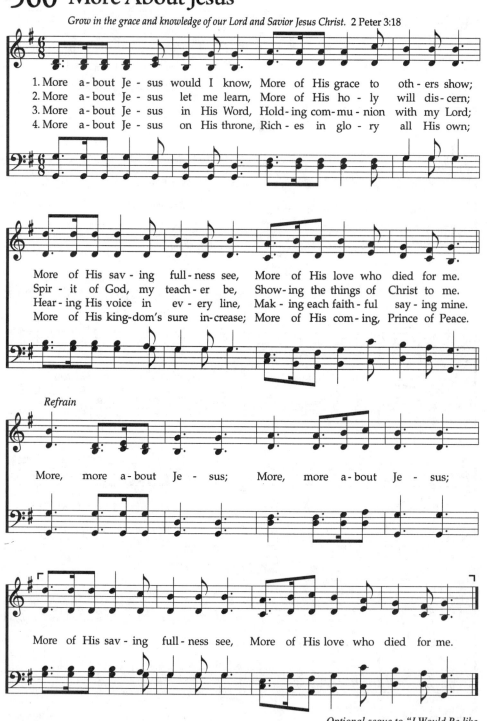

1. More a-bout Je-sus would I know, More of His grace to oth-ers show;
2. More a-bout Je-sus let me learn, More of His ho-ly will dis-cern;
3. More a-bout Je-sus in His Word, Hold-ing com-mu-nion with my Lord;
4. More a-bout Je-sus on His throne, Rich-es in glo-ry all His own;

More of His sav-ing full-ness see, More of His love who died for me.
Spir-it of God, my teach-er be, Show-ing the things of Christ to me.
Hear-ing His voice in ev-ery line, Mak-ing each faith-ful say-ing mine.
More of His king-dom's sure in-crease; More of His com-ing, Prince of Peace.

Refrain

More, more a-bout Je-sus; More, more a-bout Je-sus;

More of His sav-ing full-ness see, More of His love who died for me.

Optional segue to "I Would Be like Jesus." No transition is needed.

TEXT: Eliza E. Hewitt
MUSIC: John R. Sweney

SWENEY
L.M. with Refrain

I Would Be like Jesus 561

Those God foreknew He also predestined to be conformed to His Son. Romans 8:29

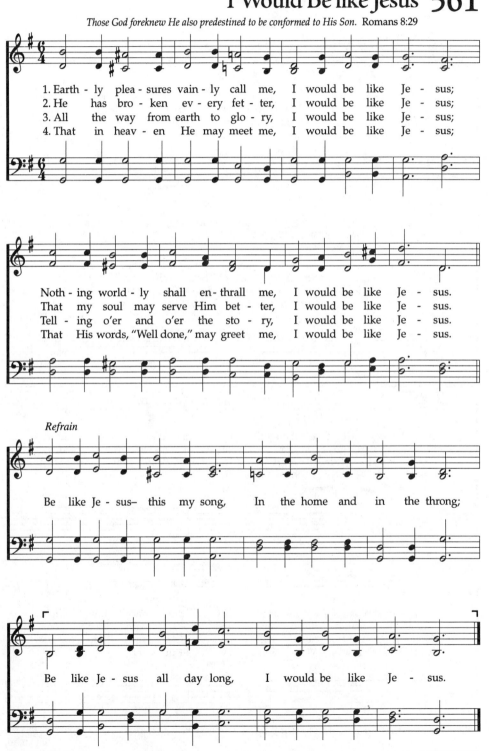

1. Earth - ly plea - sures vain - ly call me, I would be like Je - sus;
2. He has bro - ken ev - ery fet - ter, I would be like Je - sus;
3. All the way from earth to glo - ry, I would be like Je - sus;
4. That in heav - en He may meet me, I would be like Je - sus;

Noth - ing world - ly shall en - thrall me, I would be like Je - sus.
That my soul may serve Him bet - ter, I would be like Je - sus.
Tell - ing o'er and o'er the sto - ry, I would be like Je - sus.
That His words, "Well done," may greet me, I would be like Je - sus.

Refrain

Be like Je - sus— this my song, In the home and in the throng;

Be like Je - sus all day long, I would be like Je - sus.

TEXT: James Rowe
MUSIC: Bentley D. Ackley

SPRING HILL
C.M. with Refrain

562 Be Thou My Vision

Whatever was to my profit I now consider loss for the sake of Christ. Philippians 3:7

Unison

1. Be Thou my Vi-sion, O Lord of my heart;
2. Be Thou my Wis-dom and Thou my true Word;
3. Rich-es I heed not, nor man's emp-ty praise,
4. High King of heav-en, my vic-to-ry won,

Naught be all else to me, save that Thou art—
I ev-er with Thee and Thou with me, Lord;
Thou mine in-her-i-tance, now and al-ways;
May I reach heav-en's joys, bright heav-en's Sun!

Thou my best thought, by day or by night,
Thou my great Fa-ther, I Thy true son,
Thou and Thou on-ly, first in my heart,
Heart of my own heart, what-ev-er be-fall,

Wak-ing or sleep-ing, Thy pres-ence my light.
Thou in me dwell-ing, and I with Thee one.
High King of heav-en, my trea-sure Thou art.
Still be my Vi-sion, O Rul-er of all.

TEXT: Traditional Irish hymn, translated by Mary E. Byrne;
versified by Eleanor H. Hull
MUSIC: Traditional Irish melody; arranged by David Allen

SLANE
10.10.10.10.

Open My Eyes That I May See 563

Open my eyes that I may see wonderful things in Your law. Psalm 119:18

1. O - pen my eyes that I may see Glimp-ses of truth Thou hast for me;
2. O - pen my ears that I may hear Voic - es of truth Thou send-est clear;
3. O - pen my mouth and let me bear Glad - ly the warm truth ev - ery-where;

Place in my hands the won-der-ful key That shall un-clasp and
And while the wave - notes fall on my ear, Ev - ery-thing false will
O - pen my heart, and let me pre - pare Love with Thy chil - dren

Refrain

set me free. Si - lent-ly now I wait for Thee, Read-y, my God, Thy
dis - ap-pear. Si - lent-ly now I wait for Thee, Read-y, my God, Thy
thus to share. Si - lent-ly now I wait for Thee, Read-y, my God, Thy

will to see; O - pen my eyes, il - lu - mine me, Spir - it di - vine.
will to see; O - pen my ears, il - lu - mine me, Spir - it di - vine.
will to see; O - pen my heart, il - lu - mine me, Spir - it di - vine.

TEXT: Clara H. Scott
MUSIC: Clara H. Scott

SCOTT
Irregular meter

564 Just a Closer Walk with Thee

I can do everything through Him who gives me strength. Philippians 4:13

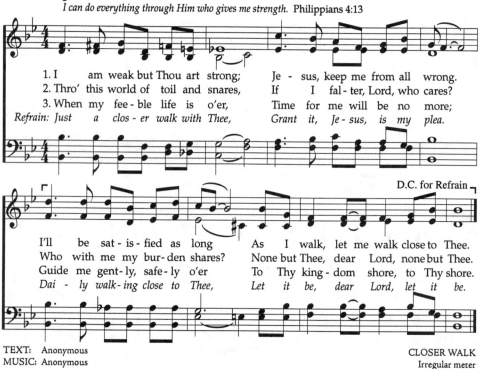

1. I am weak but Thou art strong;   Je - sus, keep me from all wrong.
2. Thro' this world of toil and snares,   If I fal - ter, Lord, who cares?
3. When my fee - ble life is o'er,   Time for me will be no more;

Refrain: Just a clos - er walk with Thee,   Grant it, Je - sus, is my plea.

D.C. for Refrain

I'll be sat - is - fied as long   As I walk, let me walk close to Thee.
Who with me my bur - den shares?   None but Thee, dear Lord, none but Thee.
Guide me gent - ly, safe - ly o'er   To Thy king - dom shore, to Thy shore.
Dai - ly walk - ing close to Thee,   Let it be, dear Lord, let it be.

TEXT: Anonymous
MUSIC: Anonymous

CLOSER WALK
Irregular meter

565 To Be like Jesus

Put on the new self, created to be like God in true righteousness and holiness. Ephesians 4:24

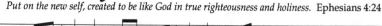

1. To be like Je - sus, to be like Je - sus! My de - sire— to be like Him!
2. To be like Je - sus, to be like Je - sus! How I long to be like Him!

All thro' life's jour - ney from earth to glo - ry, My de - sire— to be like Him.
So meek and low - ly, so pure and ho - ly; How I long to be like Him.

TEXT: Traditional
MUSIC: Traditional

TO BE LIKE JESUS
10.7.10.7.

I Am Resolved 566

I press on toward the goal to win the prize. Philippians 3:14

1. I am re-solved no long-er to ling-er, Charmed by the world's de-light;
2. I am re-solved to go to the Sav-ior, Leav-ing my sin and strife.
3. I am re-solved to fol-low the Sav-ior, Faith-ful and true each day.
4. I am re-solved to en-ter the King-dom, Leav-ing the paths of sin.
5. I am re-solved, and who will go with me? Come, friends with-out de-lay;

Things that are high-er, things that are no-bler— These have al-lured my sight.
He is the true One; He is the just One; He hath the words of life.
Heed what He say-eth, do what He will-eth; He is the Liv-ing Way.
Friends may op-pose me, foes may be-set me; Still will I en-ter in.
Taught by the Bi-ble, led by the Spir-it, We'll walk the heav'n-ly way.

Refrain

I will has-ten to Him, Has-ten so glad and free.
I will has-ten, has-ten to Him, Has-ten so glad and free, has-ten glad and free.

Je-sus, Great-est, High-est, I will come to Thee.
Je-sus, Je-sus, Great-est, High-est, I will come to Thee.

TEXT: Palmer Hartsough
MUSIC: James H. Fillmore

RESOLUTION
10.6.10.6. with Refrain

567 Nearer, Still Nearer

Come near to God and He will come near to you. James 4:8

1. Near - er, still near - er, close to Thy heart, Draw me, my
Sav - ior— so pre - cious Thou art! Fold me, O fold me
close to Thy breast. Shel - ter me safe in that ha - ven of
rest; Shel - ter me safe in that ha - ven of rest.

2. Near - er, still near - er, noth - ing I bring, Naught as an
of - f'ring to Je - sus, my King— On - ly my sin - ful,
now con - trite heart. Grant me the cleans - ing Thy blood doth im -
part; Grant me the cleans - ing Thy blood doth im - part.

3. Near - er, still near - er, Lord, to be Thine! Sin, with its
fol - lies, I glad - ly re - sign, All of its plea - sures,
pomp and its pride. Give me but Je - sus, my Lord, cru - ci -
fied; Give me but Je - sus, my Lord, cru - ci - fied.

4. Near - er, still near - er, while life shall last, Till safe in
glo - ry my an - chor is cast; Thro' end - less a - ges
ev - er to be Near - er, my Sav - ior, still near - er to
Thee; Near - er, my Sav - ior, still near - er to Thee.

TEXT: Lelia N. Morris
MUSIC: Lelia N. Morris

MORRIS
9.10.9.10.10.

May the Mind of Christ, My Savior 568

Your attitude should be the same as that of Christ Jesus. Philippians 2:5

1. May the mind of Christ, my Sav-ior, Live in me from day to day,
2. May the Word of God dwell rich-ly In my heart from hour to hour,
3. May the peace of God my Fa-ther Rule my life in ev-ery-thing,
4. May the love of Je-sus fill me As the wa-ters fill the sea;
5. May I run the race be-fore me, Strong and brave to face the foe,
6. May His beau-ty rest up-on me As I seek the lost to win;

By His love and pow'r con-trol-ling All I do and say.
So that all may see I tri-umph On-ly thro' His pow'r.
That I may be calm to com-fort Sick and sor-row-ing.
Him ex-alt-ing, self a-bas-ing— This is vic-to-ry.
Look-ing on-ly un-to Je-sus As I on-ward go.
And may they for-get the chan-nel, See-ing on-ly Him.

Optional last stanza setting

6. May His beau-ty rest up-on me As I seek the lost to win;

And may they for-get the chan-nel, See-ing on-ly Him.

TEXT: Kate B. Wilkinson
MUSIC: A. Cyril Barham-Gould

ST. LEONARDS
8.7.8.5.

569 THIRSTING FOR GOD

from Psalm 42 (NASB)

WORSHIP LEADER
Why are you in despair, O my soul?
And why have you become disturbed within me?

WORSHIP LEADER and CHOIR (or EVERYONE)
Hope in God, for I shall again praise Him for the help of His presence.

WORSHIP LEADER
Deep calls to deep at the sound of Thy waterfalls;
all Thy breakers and Thy waves have rolled over me.

WORSHIP LEADER and CHOIR (or EVERYONE)
The Lord will command His lovingkindness in the daytime;
and His song will be with me in the night,
a prayer to the God of my life.

WORSHIP LEADER
Why are you in despair, O my soul?
And why have you become disturbed within me?

WORSHIP LEADER and CHOIR (or EVERYONE)
Hope in God, for I shall yet praise Him,
the help of my countenance, and my God.

570 WORDS TO LIVE BY

from Colossians 3 (NIV)

WORSHIP LEADER or SOLO DRAMATIST

Since you have been raised with Christ,
set your hearts on things above, not on earthly things.
For your life is now hidden with Christ in God.
Put to death, therefore, whatever belongs to your earthly nature.
Do not lie to each other, since you have taken off your old self
with its practices and have put on the new self,
which is being renewed in knowledge in the image of its Creator;
Christ is all, and is in all!
Therefore, as God's chosen people, holy and dearly loved,
clothe yourselves with compassion, kindness, humility,
gentleness and patience.
Bear with each other and forgive whatever grievances
you may have against one another.
Forgive as the Lord forgave you.
Over all these virtues put on love,
which binds them all together in perfect unity.
Let the peace of Christ rule in your hearts,
since as members of one Body you were called to peace.
And be thankful.
Let the word of Christ dwell in you richly
as you teach and admonish one another with all wisdom,
and as you sing psalms, hymns and spiritual songs
with gratitude in your hearts to God.
Whatever you do, whether in word or deed,
do it all in the name of the Lord Jesus,
giving thanks to God the Father through Him.

Trust and Obey 571

Now you are the light in the Lord. Live as children of light. Ephesians 5:8

1. When we walk with the Lord In the light of His Word, What a glo-ry He
2. Not a shad-ow can rise, Not a cloud in the skies, But His smile quick-ly
3. Not a bur-den we bear, Not a sor-row we share, But our toil He doth
4. But we nev-er can prove The de-lights of His love Un-til all on the
5. Then in fel-low-ship sweet We will sit at His feet, Or we'll walk by His

sheds on our way! While we do His good will, He a-bides with us still,
drives it a-way; Not a doubt nor a fear, Not a sigh nor a tear,
rich-ly re-pay; Not a grief nor a loss, Not a frown nor a cross
al-tar we lay; For the fa-vor He shows And the joy He be-stows
side in the way; What He says we will do, Where He sends we will go;

Refrain

And with all who will trust and o-bey.
Can a-bide while we trust and o-bey.
But is blest if we trust and o-bey. Trust and o-bey, For there's
Are for them who will trust and o-bey.
Nev-er fear, on-ly trust and o-bey.

no oth-er way To be hap-py in Je-sus, But to trust and o-bey.

TEXT: John H. Sammis
MUSIC: Daniel B. Towner

TRUST AND OBEY
6.6.9.D. with Refrain

572 Blessed Assurance

Let us draw near to God with a sincere heart in full assurance of faith. Hebrews 10:22

1. Bless-ed as-sur-ance, Je-sus is mine! O what a fore-taste of
2. Per-fect sub-mis-sion, per-fect de-light! Vi-sions of rap-ture now
3. Per-fect sub-mis-sion— all is at rest, I in my Sav-ior am

glo-ry di-vine! Heir of sal-va-tion, pur-chase of God,
burst on my sight; An-gels de-scend-ing bring from a-bove
hap-py and blest; Watch-ing and wait-ing, look-ing a-bove,

Optional descant

This is my sto-ry,

Refrain

Born of His Spir-it, washed in His blood.
Ech-oes of mer-cy, whis-pers of love. This is my sto-ry,
Filled with His good-ness, lost in His love.

this is my song, Prais-ing my Sav-ior all the day long; This is my

this is my song, Prais-ing my Sav-ior all the day long; This is my

TEXT: Fanny J. Crosby
MUSIC: Phoebe P. Knapp; Descant by James C. Gibson

ASSURANCE
9.10.9.9. with Refrain

story, this is my song, Prais-ing my Sav - ior all the day long.

story, this is my song, Prais-ing my Sav - ior all the day long.

His Strength Is Perfect 573

My grace is sufficient for you, for My power is made perfect in weakness. 2 Corinthians 12:9

Unison

His strength is per - fect when our strength is gone;

He'll car - ry us when we can't car - ry on.

Raised in His pow - er, the weak be- come strong;

His strength is per - fect, His strength is per - fect.

TEXT: Steven Curtis Chapman and Jerry Salley
MUSIC: Steven Curtis Chapman and Jerry Salley

HIS STRENGTH IS PERFECT
Irregular meter

574 A Child of the King

If we are children, then we are heirs–heirs of God and co-heirs with Christ. Romans 8:16-17

1. My Fa - ther is rich in hous - es and lands; He hold - eth the
2. My Fa - ther's own Son– the Sav - ior of men– Once wan - dered on
3. I once was an out - cast stran - ger on earth, A sin - ner by
4. A tent or a cot - tage, why should I care? They're build - ing a

wealth of the world in His hands. Of ru - bies and dia - monds, of
earth as the poor - est of them. But now He is reign - ing for -
choice and an al - ien by birth. But I've been a - dopt - ed; my
pal - ace for me o - ver there. Tho' ex - iled from home, yet

sil - ver and gold, His cof - fers are full– He has rich - es un - told.
ev - er on high, And will give me a home in heav'n by and by.
name's writ - ten down– An heir to a man - sion, a robe and a crown.
still I may sing: "All glo - ry to God, I'm a child of the King!"

Refrain

I'm a child of the King, A child of the King,

With Je - sus, my Sav - ior, I'm a child of the King.

Optional segue to "Leaning on the Everlasting Arms." No transition is needed.

TEXT: Harriet E. Buell
MUSIC: John B. Sumner

BINGHAMTON
10.11.11.11. with Refrain

Leaning on the Everlasting Arms 575

The eternal God is your refuge, and underneath are the everlasting arms. Deuteronomy 33:27

1. What a fel-low-ship, what a joy di-vine, Lean-ing on the ev-er-
2. O how sweet to walk in this pil-grim way, Lean-ing on the ev-er-
3. What have I to dread, what have I to fear, Lean-ing on the ev-er-

last-ing arms. What a bless-ed-ness, what a peace is mine,
last-ing arms. O how bright the path grows from day to day,
last-ing arms? I have bless-ed peace with my Lord so near,

Refrain

Lean-ing on the ev-er-last-ing arms. Lean - ing,
Lean-ing on the ev-er-last-ing arms. Lean-ing on Je-sus,
Lean-ing on the ev-er-last-ing arms.

lean - ing, Safe and se-cure from all a-larms; Lean -
lean-ing on Je-sus, Lean-ing on

ing, lean - ing, Lean-ing on the ev-er-last-ing arms.
Je-sus, lean-ing on Je-sus,

TEXT: Elisha A. Hoffman
MUSIC: Anthony J. Showalter

SHOWALTER
10.9.10.9. with Refrain

576 The Steadfast Love of the Lord

Because of the Lord's great love we are not consumed. Lamentations 3:22

The stead - fast love of the Lord nev - er ceas - es; His mer - cies nev - er come to an end. They are new ev - ery morn - ing, new ev - ery morn - ing; Great is Thy faith - ful - ness, O Lord, Great is Thy faith - ful - ness.

TEXT: Edith McNeill; based on Lamentations 3:22, 23
MUSIC: Edith McNeill

STEADFAST LOVE
Irregular meter

Optional extended or choral ending

Great is Thy faith - ful - ness.

In Times like These 577

We have this hope as an anchor for the soul, firm and secure. Hebrews 6:19

1. In times like these you need a Sav-ior, In times like these you need an
2. In times like these you need the Bi-ble, In times like these O be not
3. In times like these I have a Sav-ior, In times like these I have an

an-chor; Be ver-y sure, be ver-y sure Your an-chor holds and grips the
i - dle; Be ver-y sure, be ver-y sure Your an-chor holds and grips the
an-chor; I'm ver-y sure, I'm ver-y sure My an-chor holds and grips the

Refrain

Sol - id Rock!
Sol - id Rock! This Rock is Je - sus, Yes, He's the One;
Sol - id Rock!

This Rock is Je - sus, The on - ly One! 1,2. Be ver-y sure, be ver-y
3. I'm ver-y sure, I'm ver-y

sure Your an - chor holds and grips the Sol - id Rock!
sure My an - chor holds and grips the Sol - id Rock!

TEXT: Ruth Caye Jones
MUSIC: Ruth Caye Jones

TIMES LIKE THESE
Irregular meter

578 Trusting Jesus

I delight to see how firm your faith in Christ is. Colossians 2:5

1. Sim - ply trust - ing ev - ery day, Trust - ing thro' a storm - y way;
2. Bright - ly doth His Spir - it shine In - to this poor heart of mine;
3. Sing - ing if my way is clear, Pray - ing if the path be drear;
4. Trust - ing Him while life shall last, Trust - ing Him till earth be past;

E - ven when my faith is small, Trust - ing Je - sus— that is all.
While He leads I can - not fall, Trust - ing Je - sus— that is all.
If in dan - ger, for Him call, Trust - ing Je - sus— that is all.
Till with - in the jas - per wall, Trust - ing Je - sus— that is all.

Refrain

Trust - ing as the mo - ments fly, Trust - ing as the days go by;

Trust - ing Him what - e'er be - fall, Trust - ing Je - sus— that is all.

TEXT: Edgar P. Stites
MUSIC: Ira D. Sankey

TRUSTING JESUS
7.7.7.7. with Refrain

IN GOD I TRUST

579

A Worship Sequence

Through It All; sing twice
'Tis So Sweet to Trust in Jesus; stanzas 1,2,4
Suggested stanzas have been marked with an arrow: ➤

WORSHIP LEADER When you pass through the waters,
I will be with you;

EVERYONE **In God I trust; I will not be afraid.**

WORSHIP LEADER When you pass through the rivers,
they will not sweep over you.

EVERYONE **In God I trust; I will not be afraid.**

WORSHIP LEADER When you walk through the fire,
you will not be burned.

EVERYONE **In God I trust; I will not be afraid.**

WORSHIP LEADER I am the Lord, your God,
the Holy One of Israel, your Savior;
Trust in Me with all your heart.

from Isaiah 43:2-3; Psalm 56:4; Proverbs 3:5 (NIV)

Through It All 580

Trials have come so that your faith may be proved genuine. 1 Peter 1:6-7

Through it all, Through it all, I've learned to trust in Je-sus, I've learned to trust in God; Through it all, Through it all, I've learned to de-pend up-on His Word.

TEXT: Andraé Crouch
MUSIC: Andraé Crouch

THROUGH IT ALL
Irregular meter

*Optional transition to
"'Tis So Sweet to Trust in Jesus"*

581 'Tis So Sweet to Trust in Jesus

Do not let your hearts be troubled. Trust in God; trust also in Me. John 14:1

1. 'Tis so sweet to trust in Je - sus, Just to take Him at His Word,
2. O how sweet to trust in Je - sus, Just to trust His cleans - ing blood,
3. Yes, 'tis sweet to trust in Je - sus, Just from sin and self to cease,
4. I'm so glad I learned to trust Thee, Pre - cious Je - sus, Sav - ior, Friend;

Just to rest up - on His prom - ise, Just to know: "Thus saith the Lord."
Just in sim - ple faith to plunge me 'Neath the heal - ing, cleans - ing flood!
Just from Je - sus sim - ply tak - ing Life and rest, and joy and peace.
And I know that Thou art with me, Wilt be with me to the end.

Refrain

Je - sus, Je - sus, how I trust Him! How I've proved Him o'er and o'er!

Je - sus, Je - sus, pre - cious Je - sus! O for grace to trust Him more!

TEXT: Louisa M. R. Snead
MUSIC: William J. Kirkpatrick

TRUST IN JESUS
8.7.8.7. with Refrain

Optional last refrain setting

no rit.

Je - sus, Je - sus, how I trust Him! How I've proved Him

o'er and o'er! Je - sus, Je - sus, pre - cious Je - sus! O for grace to trust Him more!

Optional choral ending

decresc.   rit.   Word.

Through it all,   I've learned to de - pend up - on His Word, His   Word.
decresc.

Word.

The end of IN GOD I TRUST - A Worship Sequence

I Am Trusting Thee, Lord Jesus 582

Such confidence as this is ours through Christ before God. 2 Corinthians 3:4

1. I   am   trust - ing   Thee,   Lord   Je - sus–   Trust - ing   on - ly
2. I   am   trust - ing   Thee,   to   guide me–   Thou a - lone   shalt
3. I   am   trust - ing   Thee,   for   pow - er–   Thine can   nev - er
4. I   am   trust - ing   Thee,   Lord   Je - sus–   Nev - er   let   me

Thee;   Trust - ing   Thee   for   full   sal - va - tion,   Great   and   free.
lead,   Ev - ery   day   and   hour   sup - ply - ing   All   my   need.
fail;   Words   which   Thou   Thy - self   shalt   give   me   Must   pre - vail.
fall;   I   am   trust - ing   Thee   for - ev - er,   And   for   all.

TEXT: Frances Ridley Havergal
MUSIC: Ethelbert W. Bullinger

BULLINGER
8.5.8.3.

583 You Are My All in All

Christ is all, and is in all. Colossians 3:11

1. You are my strength when I am weak, You are the trea-sure that I
2. Tak-ing my sin, my cross, my shame, Ris-ing a-gain I bless Your

seek; You are my all in all.
name; You are my all in all.

Seek-ing You as a pre-cious
When I fall down, You pick me

jewel, Lord, to give up, I'd be a fool; You are my all in all.
up; When I am dry, You fill my cup; You are my all in all.

Refrain
*Part II Harmony optional

Je - sus, Lamb of God, Wor - thy is Your name!

Je - sus, Lamb of God, Wor - thy is Your name!

The verses (Part I) and the Refrain (Part II) may be sung as a round.

TEXT: Dennis L. Jernigan
MUSIC: Dennis L. Jernigan

JERNIGAN
8.8.5.8.8.5. with Refrain

Optional extended or choral ending   Repeat as desired

Wor-thy is Your   name!   Wor-thy is Your   name!

Yesterday, Today, Forever 584

Jesus Christ is the same yesterday and today and forever. Hebrews 13:8

Yes - ter - day,   to - day,   for - ev - er,   Je - sus is   the   same.

All   may change, but   Je - sus nev - er!   Glo - ry   to   His   name!

Glo - ry   to   His   name!   Glo - ry   to   His   name!

2nd time Fine

All   may change, but   Je - sus nev - er!   Glo - ry   to   His   name!

TEXT: Albert B. Simpson; based on Hebrews 13:8   NYACK
MUSIC: James H. Burke   8.5.8.5.5.5.8.5.

585 Be Still and Know

Be still, and know that I am God. Psalm 46:10

1. Be still and know that I am God. Be still and know that I am God. Be still and know that I am God.
2. I am the Lord that heal - eth thee. I am the Lord that heal - eth thee. I am the Lord that heal - eth thee.
3. My bound - less mer - cy shall en - dure. My bound - less mer - cy shall en - dure. My bound - less mer - cy shall en - dure.
4. I love you with a stead - fast love. I love you with a stead - fast love. I love you with a stead - fast love.
5. In Thee, O Lord, I put my trust. In Thee, O Lord, I put my trust. In Thee, O Lord, I put my trust.

TEXT: Anonymous, stanzas 1, 2, 5; Tom Fettke, stanzas 3, 4
MUSIC: Anonymous; arranged by Lee Herrington

BE STILL AND KNOW
8.8.8.

Optional 4th and 5th stanzas setting

4. I love you with a stead - fast love. I love you with a stead - fast love. I love you with a stead - fast love.

5. In Thee, O Lord, I put my trust. In Thee, O

Lord, I put my trust. In Thee, O Lord, I put my trust.

He's Got the Whole World in His Hands 586

In His hand is the life of every creature. Job 12:10

Unison

1. He's got the whole world in His hands, He's got the
2. He's got the wind and the rain in His hands, He's got the
3. He's got the ti-ny lit-tle ba-by in His hands, He's got the
4. He's got you and me, broth-er, in His hands, He's got

whole world in His hands, He's got the whole
wind and the rain in His hands, He's got the wind and the
ti-ny lit-tle ba-by in His hands, He's got the ti-ny lit-tle
you and me, sis-ter, in His hands, He's got you and me,

world in His hands, He's got the whole world in His hands.
rain in His hands, He's got the whole world in His hands.
ba-by in His hands, He's got the whole world in His hands.
broth-er, in His hands, He's got the whole world in His hands.

TEXT: Traditional Spiritual
MUSIC: Traditional Spiritual; arranged by Eugene Thomas

WHOLE WORLD
Irregular meter

587 BE ASSURED

from Romans 8:28-39 (NASB)

SOLO 1
For we know

EVERYONE
That God causes all things to work together for good to those who love God,
to those who are called according to His purpose.

SOLO 2
For whom He foreknew, He also predestined to become conformed to the image of His Son,
that He might be the first-born among many brethren;

MEN
And whom He predestined, these He also called;

WOMEN
And whom He called, these He also justified;

MEN
And whom He justified, these He also glorified.

SOLO 1
What then shall we say to these things?

EVERYONE
If God is for us, who is against us?

SOLO 2
He who did not spare His own Son,
but delivered Him up for us all,
how will He not also with Him freely give us all things?

SOLO 1
Who will bring a charge against God's elect?

EVERYONE
God is the one who justifies.

SOLO 2
Who is the one who condemns?

EVERYONE
Christ Jesus is He who died, yes, rather who was raised,
who is at the right hand of God, who also intercedes for us.

SOLO 1
Who shall separate us from the love of Christ?

EVERYONE
Shall tribulation, or distress, or persecution, or famine,
or nakedness, or peril, or sword?

SOLO 2
Just as it is written, "for Thy sake we are being put to death all day long;
we were considered as sheep to be slaughtered."

EVERYONE
But in all these things we overwhelmingly conquer through Him who loved us.

MEN
For I am convinced that neither death, nor life, nor angels,

WOMEN
Nor principalities, nor things present, nor things to come, nor powers,

EVERYONE
Nor height, nor depth, nor any other created thing, shall be able to separate us
from the love of God, which is in Christ Jesus our Lord.

All for Jesus 588

Offer your bodies as living sacrifices, holy and pleasing to God. Romans 12:1

1. All for Je - sus! all for Je - sus! All my be - ing's ran-somed pow'rs:
2. Let my hands per - form His bid-ding; Let my feet run in His ways.
3. Since my eyes were fixed on Je - sus, I've lost sight of all be - side;
4. O what won-der! how a - maz-ing! Je - sus, glo-rious King of kings,

All my tho'ts and words and do - ings, All my days and all my hours.
Let my eyes see Je - sus on - ly; Let my lips speak forth His praise.
So en-chained my spir - it's vi - sion, Look-ing at the Cru - ci - fied.
Deigns to call me His be - lov - ed, Lets me rest be - neath His wings.

Refrain

All for Je - sus! all for Je - sus! All my days and all my hours;
All for Je - sus! all for Je - sus! Let my lips speak forth His praise;
All for Je - sus! all for Je - sus! Look-ing at the Cru - ci - fied;
All for Je - sus! all for Je - sus! Rest-ing now be - neath His wings;

All for Je - sus! all for Je - sus! All my days and all my hours.
All for Je - sus! all for Je - sus! Let my lips speak forth His praise.
All for Je - sus! all for Je - sus! Look-ing at the Cru - ci - fied.
All for Je - sus! all for Je - sus! Rest-ing now be - neath His wings.

TEXT: Mary D. James
MUSIC: Source unknown

CONSTANCY
8.7.8.7. with Refrain

589 Here I Am, Lord

"Whom shall I send?" I said, "Here am I. Send me." Isaiah 6:8

1. I, the Lord of sea and sky, I have heard My peo-ple cry.
2. I, the Lord of snow and rain, I have borne My peo-ple's pain.
3. I, the Lord of wind and flame, I will tend the poor and lame.

All who dwell in deep-est sin My hand will save.
I have wept for love of them, They turn a-way.
I will set a feast for them, My hand will save.

I who made the stars of night, I will make their dark-ness bright.
I will break their hearts of stone, Give them hearts for love a-lone.
Fin-est bread I will pro-vide Till their hearts be sat-is-fied.

Who will bear My light to them? Whom shall I send?
I will speak My word to them. Whom shall I send?
I will give My life to them. Whom shall I send?

TEXT: Daniel L. Schutte; based on Isaiah 6:8
MUSIC: Daniel L. Schutte

HERE I AM, LORD
7.7.7.4.D. with Refrain

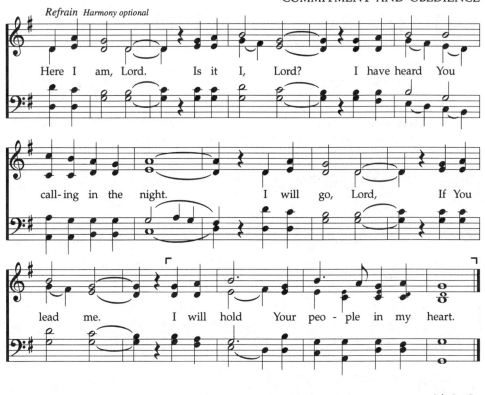

Refrain   Harmony optional

Here I am, Lord. Is it I, Lord? I have heard You

call-ing in the night. I will go, Lord, If You

lead me. I will hold Your peo - ple in my heart.

I'll Live for Him 590

Live self-controlled, upright and godly lives in this present age. Titus 2:12

1. My life, my love I give to Thee, Thou Lamb of God who died for me;
2. I now be-lieve Thou dost re-ceive, For Thou hast died that I might live;
3. O Thou who died on Cal - va - ry, To save my soul and make me free;
Refrain: I'll live for Him who died for me, How hap - py then my life shall be!

O may I ev - er faith - ful be, My Sav - ior and my God!
And now hence-forth I'll trust in Thee, My Sav - ior and my God!
I'll con - se-crate my life to Thee, My Sav - ior and my God!
Ref: I'll live for Him who died for me, My Sav - ior and my God!

D.C. for Refrain

TEXT: Ralph E. Hudson
MUSIC: C. R. Dunbar

DUNBAR
8.8.8.6. with Refrain

591 Have Thine Own Way, Lord

We are the clay, You are the potter. Isaiah 64:8

1. Have Thine own way, Lord! Have Thine own way! Thou art the
2. Have Thine own way, Lord! Have Thine own way! Search me and
3. Have Thine own way, Lord! Have Thine own way! Wound-ed and
4. Have Thine own way, Lord! Have Thine own way! Hold o'er my

Pot - ter; I am the clay. Mold me and make me af - ter Thy
try me, Mas-ter, to - day. Whit - er than snow, Lord, wash me just
wea - ry, help me, I pray. Pow-er— all pow-er— sure - ly is
be - ing ab - so - lute sway! Fill with Thy Spir - it till all shall

will, While I am wait - ing, yield - ed and still.
now, As in Thy pres - ence hum - bly I bow.
Thine! Touch me and heal me, Sav - ior di - vine!
see Christ on - ly, al - ways liv - ing in me!

TEXT: Adelaide A. Pollard
MUSIC: George C. Stebbins

ADELAIDE
5.4.5.4.D.

592 Jesus Calls Us

"Come, follow Me," Jesus said. Matthew 4:19

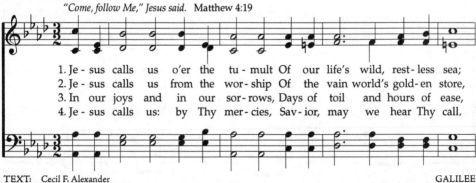

1. Je - sus calls us o'er the tu - mult Of our life's wild, rest - less sea;
2. Je - sus calls us from the wor - ship Of the vain world's gold - en store,
3. In our joys and in our sor - rows, Days of toil and hours of ease,
4. Je - sus calls us: by Thy mer - cies, Sav - ior, may we hear Thy call.

TEXT: Cecil F. Alexander
MUSIC: William H. Jude

GALILEE
8.7.8.7.

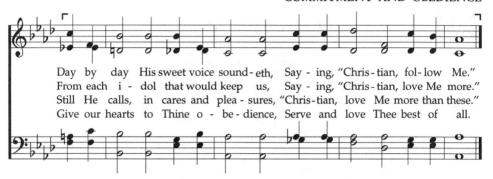

Day by day His sweet voice sound- eth, Say - ing, "Chris - tian, fol - low Me."
From each i - dol that would keep us, Say - ing, "Chris - tian, love Me more."
Still He calls, in cares and plea - sures, "Chris - tian, love Me more than these."
Give our hearts to Thine o - be - dience, Serve and love Thee best of all.

Where He Leads Me 593

My sheep listen to My voice; I know them, and they follow Me. John 10:27

1. I can hear my Sav - ior call - ing; I can
2. I'll go with Him thro' the judg - ment; I'll go
3. He will give me grace and glo - ry; He will

Refrain: Where He leads me I will fol - low; Where He

hear my Sav - ior call - ing; I can hear my Sav - ior
with Him thro' the judg - ment; I'll go with Him thro' the
give me grace and glo - ry; He will give me grace and

leads me I will fol - low; Where He leads me I will

D. C. for Refrain

call - ing, "Take thy cross and fol - low, fol - low Me."
judg - ment, I'll go with Him, with Him all the way.
glo - ry, And go with me, with me all the way.

fol - low, I'll go with Him, with Him all the way.

TEXT: E. W. Blandy
MUSIC: John S. Norris

NORRIS
8.8.8.9. with Refrain

594 LIVING SACRIFICE
A Worship Sequence

I Give All to You; complete
I Surrender All; stanzas 1,4
Take My Life and Let It Be Consecrated; stanzas 1,5,6
Suggested stanzas have been marked with an arrow: ➤

WORSHIP LEADER

Offer yourselves to God, as those who have been brought from death to life.

from Romans 6:13 (NIV)

Optional introduction to "I Give All to You"

595 I Give All to You

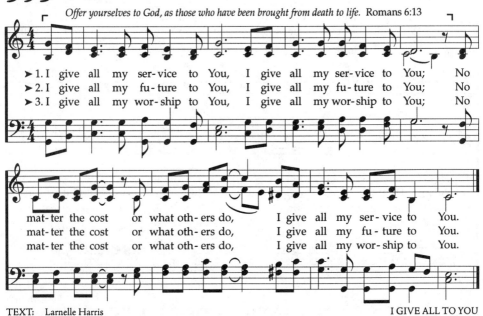

Offer yourselves to God, as those who have been brought from death to life. Romans 6:13

➤ 1. I give all my ser-vice to You, I give all my ser-vice to You; No
➤ 2. I give all my fu-ture to You, I give all my fu-ture to You; No
➤ 3. I give all my wor-ship to You, I give all my wor-ship to You; No

mat-ter the cost or what oth-ers do, I give all my ser-vice to You.
mat-ter the cost or what oth-ers do, I give all my fu-ture to You.
mat-ter the cost or what oth-ers do, I give all my wor-ship to You.

TEXT: Larnelle Harris
MUSIC: Larnelle Harris

I GIVE ALL TO YOU
8.8.10.8.

Optional last stanza setting

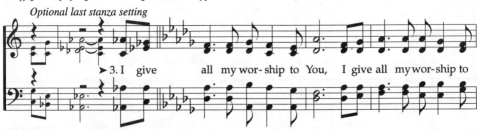

➤ 3. I give all my wor-ship to You, I give all my wor-ship to

LIVING SACRIFICE - A Worship Sequence

You; No mat-ter the cost or what oth-ers do, I give all my wor-ship to You.

Optional segue to "I Surrender All." No transition is needed.

I Surrender All 596

Offer yourselves to God. Romans 6:13

1. All to Je-sus I sur-ren-der, All to Him I free-ly give;
2. All to Je-sus I sur-ren-der, Hum-bly at His feet I bow,
3. All to Je-sus I sur-ren-der, Make me, Sav-ior, whol-ly Thine;
4. All to Je-sus I sur-ren-der, Lord, I give my-self to Thee;

I will ev-er love and trust Him, In His pres-ence dai-ly live.
World-ly pleas-ures all for-sak-en, Take me, Je-sus, take me now.
May Thy Ho-ly Spir-it fill me, May I know Thy pow'r di-vine.
Fill me with Thy love and pow-er, Let Thy bless-ing fall on me.

Refrain

I sur-ren-der all, I sur-ren-der all.
I sur-ren-der all, I sur-ren-der all.

All to Thee, my bless-ed Sav-ior, I sur-ren-der all. *Optional transition to "Take My Life and Let It Be"*

TEXT: Judson W. VanDeVenter
MUSIC: Winfield S. Weeden

SURRENDER
8.7.8.7.with Refrain

597 Take My Life and Let It Be Consecrated

Consecrate yourselves and be holy, because I am holy. Leviticus 11:44

1. Take my life and let it be Con-se-crat-ed, Lord, to Thee; Take my mo-ments and my days— Let them flow in cease-less praise, Let them flow in cease-less praise.
2. Take my hands and let them move At the im-pulse of Thy love; Take my feet and let them be Swift and beau-ti-ful for Thee, Swift and beau-ti-ful for Thee.
3. Take my voice and let me sing Al-ways, on-ly, for my King; Take my lips and let them be Filled with mes-sag-es from Thee, Filled with mes-sag-es from Thee.
4. Take my sil-ver and my gold– Not a mite would I with-hold; Take my in-tel-lect and use Ev-'ry pow'r as Thou shalt choose, Ev-'ry pow'r as Thou shalt choose.
5. Take my love– my Lord, I pour At Thy feet its trea-sure store; Take my-self– and I will be Ev-er, on-ly, all for Thee, Ev-er, on-ly, all for Thee.
6. Take my will and make it Thine– It shall be no long-er mine; Take my heart– it is Thine own, It shall be Thy roy-al throne, It shall be Thy roy-al throne.

TEXT: Frances Ridley Havergal
HENDON
MUSIC: Henry A. César Malan; Last stanza setting, Descant and Choral ending by O. D. Hall, Jr.
7.7.7.7.7.

Optional last stanza setting **Unison**

6. Take my will and make it Thine– It shall be no

The end of LIVING SACRIFICE - A Worship Sequence

598 Wherever He Leads I'll Go

Those who would come after Me must deny themselves and follow Me. Matthew 16:24

1. "Take up thy cross and fol-low Me," I heard my Mas-ter say:
2. He drew me clos-er to His side, I sought His will to know,
3. It may be thro' the shad-ows dim, Or o'er the storm-y sea,
4. My heart, my life, my all I bring To Christ who loves me so;

"I gave My life to ran-som thee, Sur-ren-der your all to-day."
And in that will I now a-bide, Wher-ev-er He leads I'll go.
I take the cross and fol-low Him, Wher-ev-er He lead-eth me.
He is my Mas-ter, Lord, and King, Wher-ev-er He leads I'll go.

Refrain

Wher-ev-er He leads I'll go, Wher-ev-er He leads I'll go;

I'll fol-low my Christ who loves me so, Wher-ev-er He leads I'll go.

TEXT: B. B. McKinney
MUSIC: B. B. McKinney; Choral ending by Ken Barker

FALLS CREEK
8.6.8.7 with Refrain

Optional choral ending   decresc.   rit.

I'll fol-low my Christ who loves me so, Wher-ev-er He leads I'll go.

decresc.

Jesus Is Lord of All 599

No one can serve two masters; You cannot serve both God and money. Matthew 6:24

1. All my to-mor-rows, all my past— Je-sus is Lord of
2. All of my con-flicts, all my thoughts— Je-sus is Lord of
3. All of my long-ings, all my dreams— Je-sus is Lord of

all. I've quit my strug-gles, con-tent-ment at last!
all. His love wins the bat-tles I could not have fought;
all. All of my fail-ures His pow-er re-deems;

Refrain

Je-sus is Lord of all.
Je-sus is Lord of all. King of kings, Lord of
Je-sus is Lord of all.

lords, Je-sus is Lord of all; All my pos-

ses-sions and all my life, Je-sus is Lord of all.

TEXT: Gloria Gaither and William J. Gaither
MUSIC: William J. Gaither

LORD OF ALL
Irregular meter

600 I Pledge Allegiance to the Lamb

They follow the Lamb wherever He goes. Revelation 14:4

I pledge al - le - giance to the Lamb, With all my strength, with all I am;

I will seek to hon - or His com - mands– I pledge al - le - giance to the Lamb.

TEXT: Ray Boltz
MUSIC: Ray Boltz

I PLEDGE ALLEGIANCE
8.8.9.8.

601 Yes, Lord, Yes

Speak, Lord, for Your servant is listening. 1 Samuel 3:9

I'll say yes, Lord, yes to Your will and to Your way.

I'll say yes, Lord, yes; I will trust You and o - bey.

When Your Spir-it speaks to me, With my whole heart I'll a - gree,

TEXT: Lynn Keesecker
MUSIC: Lynn Keesecker

YES, LORD, YES
Irregular meter

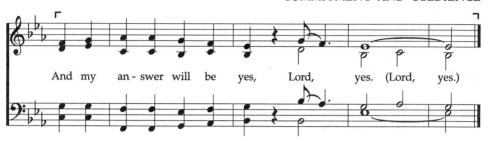

And my an-swer will be yes, Lord, yes. (Lord, yes.)

I Have Decided to Follow Jesus 602

Whoever serves Me must follow Me. John 12:26

1. I have de-cid-ed to fol-low Je-sus, I have de-cid-ed to fol-low Je-sus, I have de-cid-ed to fol-low Je-sus,
2. The world be-hind me, the cross be-fore me; The world be-hind me, the cross be-fore me; The world be-hind me, the cross be-fore me,
3. Tho' none go with me, still I will fol-low, Tho' none go with me, still I will fol-low, Tho' none go with me, still I will fol-low,
4. Will you de-cide now to fol-low Je-sus? Will you de-cide now to fol-low Je-sus? Will you de-cide now to fol-low Je-sus?

No turn-ing

Optional choral ending

back, no turn-ing back. I have de-cid-ed to fol-low Him.

TEXT: Source unknown
MUSIC: Folk melody from India; arranged by Eugene Thomas

ASSAM
Irregular meter

603 Jesus, I My Cross Have Taken

If anyone would come after Me, he must take up his cross daily and follow Me. Luke 9:23

1. Je - sus, I my cross have tak - en, All to leave and fol - low Thee;
2. Let the world de - spise and leave me; They have left my Sav - ior, too.
3. Has - ten on from grace to glo - ry, Armed by faith and winged by prayer;

Des - ti - tute, de - spised, for - sak - en, Thou from hence my all shalt be.
Hu - man hearts and looks de - ceive me; Thou art not, like man, un - true.
Heav'n's e - ter - nal days be - fore me, God's own hand shall guide me there.

Per - ish ev - ery fond am - bi - tion, All I've sought, and hoped and known;
And while Thou shalt smile up - on me, God of wis - dom, love and might,
Soon shall close my earth - ly mis - sion, Swift shall pass my pil - grim days;

Yet how rich is my con - di - tion. God and heav'n are still my own!
Foes may hate and friends may shun me. Show Thy face and all is bright.
Hope shall change to glad fru - i - tion; Faith to sight, and prayer to praise.

TEXT: Henry F. Lyte
MUSIC: Leavitt's *The Christian Lyre*, 1831; attributed to Wolfgang A. Mozart;
arranged by Hubert P. Main

ELLESDIE
8.7.8.7.D.

I Then Shall Live 604

Your kingdom come, Your will be done on earth as it is in heaven. Matthew 6:10

1. I then shall live as one who's been for-giv-en; I'll walk with joy to
2. I then shall live as one who's learned com-pas-sion; I've been so loved that
3. Your king-dom come a-round and thro' and in me, Your pow'r and glo-ry—

know my debts are paid. I know my name is clear be-fore my Fa-ther;
I'll risk lov-ing, too. I know how fear builds walls in-stead of bridg-es;
let them shine thro' me. Your Hal-lowed Name, O may I bear with hon-or,

I am His child, and I am not a-fraid. So great-ly par-doned,
I dare to see an-oth-er's point of view. And when re-la-tion-
And may Your liv-ing King-dom come in me. The Bread of Life, O

I'll for-give my broth-er; The law of love I glad-ly will o-bey.
ships de-mand com-mit-ment, Then I'll be there to care and fol-low through.
may I share with hon-or, And may You feed a hun-gry world thro' me.

TEXT: Gloria Gaither
MUSIC: Jean Sibelius

A higher setting may be found at No. 712

FINLANDIA
11.10.11.10.11.10.

605 Living for Jesus

That you may live a life worthy of the Lord and may please Him in every way. Colossians 1:10

1. Liv-ing for Je-sus a life that is true, Striv-ing to
2. Liv-ing for Je-sus, who died in my place, Bear-ing on
3. Liv-ing for Je-sus wher-ev-er I am, Do-ing each
4. Liv-ing for Je-sus thro' earth's lit-tle while, My dear-est

please Him in all that I do, Yield-ing al-le-giance, glad-
Cal-v'ry my sin and dis-grace— Such love con-strains me to
du-ty in His ho-ly name, Will-ing to suf-fer af-
trea-sure, the light of His smile, Seek-ing the lost ones He

heart-ed and free, This is the path-way of bless-ing for me.
an-swer His call, Fol-low His lead-ing and give Him my all.
flic-tion or loss, Deem-ing each tri-al a part of my cross.
died to re-deem, Bring-ing the wea-ry to find rest in Him.

Refrain

O Je-sus, Lord and Sav-ior, I give my-self to Thee; For Thou, in Thy a-

tone-ment, Didst give Thy-self for me. I own no oth-er mas-ter; My heart shall

TEXT: Thomas O. Chisholm
MUSIC: C. Harold Lowden

LIVING
10.10.10.10. with Refrain

be Thy throne. My life I give, hence-forth to live, O Christ, for Thee a - lone.

O Love That Will Not Let Me Go 606

I have loved you with an everlasting love. Jeremiah 31:3

1. O Love that will not let me go, I rest my wea - ry soul in Thee. I give Thee back the life I owe, That in Thine o - cean depths its flow May rich - er, full - er be.

2. O Light that fol-low'st all my way, I yield my flick-'ring torch to Thee. My heart re - stores its bor-rowed ray, That in Thy sun-shine's blaze its day May bright - er, fair - er be.

3. O Joy that seek - est me thro' pain, I can - not close my heart to Thee. I trace the rain - bow thro' the rain, And feel the prom - ise is not vain That morn shall tear - less be.

4. O cross that lift - est up my head, I dare not ask to fly from thee. I lay in dust life's glo - ry dead, And from the ground there blos - soms red Life that shall end - less be.

TEXT: George Matheson
MUSIC: Albert L. Peace

ST. MARGARET
8.8.8.8.6.

607 Close to Thee

Come near to God and He will come near to you. James 4:8

1. Thou, my ev-er-last-ing por-tion, More than friend or life to me;
2. Not for ease or world-ly plea-sure, Nor for fame my prayer shall be;
3. Lead me thro' the vale of shad-ows, Bear me o'er life's fit-ful sea;

All a-long my pil-grim jour-ney, Sav-ior, let me walk with Thee.
Glad-ly will I toil and suf-fer, On-ly let me walk with Thee.
Then the gate of life e-ter-nal May I en-ter, Lord, with Thee.

Close to Thee, close to Thee, Close to Thee, close to Thee;
Close to Thee, close to Thee, Close to Thee, close to Thee;
Close to Thee, close to Thee, Close to Thee, close to Thee;

All a-long my pil-grim jour-ney, Sav-ior, let me walk with Thee.
Glad-ly will I toil and suf-fer, On-ly let me walk with Thee.
Then the gate of life e-ter-nal May I en-ter, Lord, with Thee.

TEXT: Fanny J. Crosby
MUSIC: Silas J. Vail

CLOSE TO THEE
8.7.8.7.6.6.8.7.

KEEP HIS COMMANDMENTS 608

from Deuteronomy 11:1; 30:11-14; Joshua 1:8;
1 Samuel 15:22; John 14:21, 23; 1 John 2:3 (NASB)

WORSHIP LEADER
You shall therefore love the Lord your God,
and always keep His charge.
His statute which I command you today
is not too difficult for you, nor is it out of reach.
It is not in heaven, that you should say:

MEN
Who will go up to heaven for us
to get it for us and make us hear it,
that we may observe it?

WORSHIP LEADER
Nor is it beyond the sea, that you should say:

WOMEN
Who will cross the sea for us to get it for us
and make us hear it, that we may observe it?

EVERYONE
But the Word is very near you,
in your mouth and in your heart,
that you may observe it.

WORSHIP LEADER
This Book of the Law shall not depart from your mouth,
but you shall meditate on it day and night,
so that you may be careful to do
according to all that is written in it;

EVERYONE
For then you will make your way prosperous,
and then you will have success.

WORSHIP LEADER
Has the Lord as much delight in burnt offerings and sacrifices
as in obeying the voice of the Lord?

EVERYONE
Behold, to obey is better than sacrifice,
and to heed than the fat of rams.

WORSHIP LEADER
"He who has My commandments and keeps them,
he it is who loves Me;

EVERYONE
And he who loves Me shall be loved by My Father,
and I will love him, and will disclose Myself to him."

WORSHIP LEADER
Jesus answered and said to him,
"If anyone loves Me, he will keep My Word;
and My Father will love him,
and We will come to him,
and make Our abode with him."

EVERYONE
And by this we know that we have come to know Him,
if we keep His commandments.

609 No, Not One!

I have called you friends. John 15:15

1. There's not a friend like the low-ly Je-sus— No, not one! No, not one!
2. No friend like Him is so high and ho-ly— No, not one! No, not one!
3. There's not an hour that He is not near us— No, not one! No, not one!
4. Did ev-er saint find this friend for-sake him? No, not one! No, not one!
5. Was e'er a gift like the Sav-ior giv-en? No, not one! No, not one!

None else could heal all our soul's dis-eas-es— No, not one! No, not one!
And yet no friend is so meek and low-ly— No, not one! No, not one!
No night so dark but His love can cheer us— No, not one! No, not one!
Or sin-ner find that He would not take him? No, not one! No, not one!
Will He re-fuse us a home in heav-en? No, not one! No, not one!

Refrain

Je-sus knows all a-bout our strug-gles; He will guide till the day is done.

There's not a friend like the low-ly Je-sus— No, not one! No, not one!

TEXT: Johnson Oatman, Jr.
MUSIC: George C. Hugg

NO NOT ONE
10.6.10.6. with Refrain

No One Understands like Jesus 610

We do not have a High Priest who is unable to sympathize with our weaknesses. Hebrews 4:15

1. No one un-der-stands like Je-sus; He's a Friend be-yond com-pare.
2. No one un-der-stands like Je-sus; Ev-ery woe He sees and feels.
3. No one un-der-stands like Je-sus When the foes of life as-sail.
4. No one un-der-stands like Je-sus When you fal-ter on the way.

Meet Him at the throne of mer-cy; He is wait-ing for you there.
Ten-der-ly He whis-pers com-fort, And the bro-ken heart He heals.
You should nev-er be dis-cour-aged; Je-sus cares and will not fail.
Tho' you fail Him, sad-ly fail Him, He will par-don you to-day.

Refrain

No one un-der-stands like Je-sus When the days are dark and grim.

No one is so near, so dear as Je-sus; Cast your ev-ery care on Him.

TEXT: John W. Peterson
MUSIC: John W. Peterson

NO ONE UNDERSTANDS
8.7.8.7. with Refrain

611 He Hideth My Soul

He will hide me and set me high upon a rock. Psalm 27:5

1. A won - der - ful Sav - ior is Je - sus my Lord, A
2. A won - der - ful Sav - ior is Je - sus my Lord— He
3. With num - ber - less bless - ings each mo - ment He crowns; And,
4. When clothed in His bright-ness, trans - port - ed I rise To

won - der - ful Sav - ior to me; He hid - eth my soul in the
tak - eth my bur-den a - way. He hold - eth me up, and I
filled with His full-ness di - vine, I sing in my rap-ture, "O
meet Him in clouds of the sky; His per - fect sal - va - tion, His

cleft of the rock, Where riv - ers of plea - sure I see.
shall not be moved; He giv - eth me strength as my day.
glo - ry to God For such a Re - deem - er as mine!"
won - der - ful love I'll shout with the mil - lions on high!

Refrain

He hid - eth my soul in the cleft of the rock That shad-ows a

dry, thirst-y land; He hid-eth my life in the depths of His love And

TEXT: Fanny J. Crosby
MUSIC: William J. Kirkpatrick

KIRKPATRICK
11.8.11.8. with Refrain

cov - ers me there with His hand, And cov - ers me there with His hand.

In This Very Room 612

Where two or three come together in My name, there am I. Matthew 18:20

1. In this ver-y room there's quite e-nough love for one like me,
2. In this ver-y room there's quite e-nough love for all of us,
3. In this ver-y room there's quite e-nough love for all the world,

And in this ver-y room there's quite e-nough joy for one like me;
And in this ver-y room there's quite e-nough joy for all of us;
And in this ver-y room there's quite e-nough joy for all the world;

And there's quite e-nough hope and quite e-nough pow'r to chase a-

way an-y gloom, For Je-sus, Lord Je-sus, is in this ver-y room.

TEXT: Ron and Carol Harris
MUSIC: Ron and Carol Harris

IN THIS VERY ROOM
Irregular meter

613 All Your Anxiety

Cast all your anxiety on Him because He cares for you. 1 Peter 5:7

1. Is there a heart o'er-bound by sor-row? Is there a life weighed
2. No oth-er friend so swift to help you; No oth-er friend so
3. Come then at once; de-lay no long-er! Heed His en-treat-y

down by care? Come to the cross, each bur-den bear-ing;
quick to hear. No oth-er place to leave your bur-den;
kind and sweet. You need not fear a dis-ap-point-ment;

Refrain

All your anx-i-e-ty– leave it there.
No oth-er one to hear your prayer. All your anx-i-e-ty,
You shall find peace at the mer-cy seat.

all your care, Bring to the mer-cy seat; leave it there. Nev-er a

bur-den He can-not bear; Nev-er a friend like Je-sus!

TEXT: Edward Henry Joy
MUSIC: Edward Henry Joy

ALL YOUR ANXIETY
Irregular meter

He Is Our Peace 614

He Himself is our peace, who has destroyed the barrier. Ephesians 2:14

He is our peace, who has bro-ken down ev - ery wall.

He is our peace, He is our peace.

He is our peace. Cast all your cares on Him,

for He cares for you. He is our peace,

He is our peace. Cast all your peace.

TEXT: Kandela Groves; based on Ephesians 2:14
MUSIC: Kandela Groves

HE IS OUR PEACE
Irregular meter

615 The Sweetest Name of All

There is no other name under heaven given to people by which we must be saved. Acts 4:12

1. Je - sus, You're the sweet - est name of all; Je - sus, You al - ways
2. Je - sus, how I love to praise Your name; Je - sus, You're still the
3. Je - sus, You're the soon and com - ing King; Je - sus, we need the

hear me when I call. O Je - sus, You pick me up each time I
First, the Last, the same. O Je - sus, You died and took a - way my
love that You can bring. O Je - sus, we lift our voic - es up and

fall; You're the sweet - est, the sweet - est name of all.
shame; You're the sweet - est, the sweet - est name of all.
sing; You're the sweet - est, the sweet - est name of all.

TEXT: Tommy Coomes
MUSIC: Tommy Coomes

SWEETEST NAME
Irregular meter

616 LIVING IN HIS PRESENCE
A Worship Sequence

Near to the Heart of God; complete
In His Presence; complete
Suggested stanzas have been marked with an arrow: ➤

WORSHIP LEADER
I have set the Lord always before me and I will not be shaken.
Therefore my heart is glad.
You have made known to me the path of life;
You will fill me with joy in Your presence,
with eternal pleasures at Your right hand.

from Psalm 16:7-9, 11 (NIV)

Optional introduction to
"Near to the Heart of God"

mp

Near to the Heart of God 617

As for me, it is good to be near God. Psalm 73:28

➤ 1. There is a place of qui - et rest, Near to the heart of God;
➤ 2. There is a place of com - fort sweet, Near to the heart of God;
➤ 3. There is a place of full re - lease, Near to the heart of God;

A place where sin can - not mo - lest, Near to the heart of God.
A place where we our Sav - ior meet, Near to the heart of God.
A place where all is joy and peace, Near to the heart of God.

Refrain

O Je - sus, blest Re - deem - er, Sent from the heart of God, Hold us, who

wait be - fore Thee, Near to the heart of God.

Optional transition to
"In His Presence"

TEXT: Cleland B. McAfee
MUSIC: Cleland B. McAfee

McAFEE
C.M. with Refrain

618 In His Presence

You will fill me with joy in Your presence. Psalm 16:11

1. In His pres - ence there is com - fort,
2. In Your pres - ence there is com - fort,

In His pres - ence, there is peace. When we
In Your pres - ence, there is peace. When we

seek the Fa - ther's heart We will find such blessed as -
seek to know Your heart We will find such blessed as -

sur - ance, In the pres - ence of the Lord.
sur - ance, In Your ho - ly pres - ence, Lord.

TEXT: Dick and Melodie Tunney
MUSIC: Dick and Melodie Tunney

HIS PRESENCE
Irregular meter

Optional choral ending

mp

Hold us who wait be - fore Thee Near to the heart of God.

mp

The end of LIVING IN HIS PRESENCE - A Worship Sequence

Hiding in Thee 619

Lead me to the rock that is higher than I. For You have been my refuge. Psalm 61:2-3

1. O safe to the Rock that is high - er than I,
2. In the calm of the noon - tide, in sor - row's lone hour,
3. How oft in the con - flict, when pressed by the foe,

My soul in its con - flicts and sor - rows would fly. So
In times when temp - ta - tion casts o'er me its pow'r, In the
I have fled to my Ref - uge and breathed out my woe. How

sin - ful, so wea - ry, Thine, Thine would I be; Thou
tem - pests of life, on its wide, heav - ing sea, Thou
of - ten when tri - als like sea bil - lows roll Have I

Refrain

blest Rock of A - ges, I'm hid - ing in Thee.
blest Rock of A - ges, I'm hid - ing in Thee. Hid-ing in Thee,
hid - den in Thee, O Thou Rock of my soul.

Hid - ing in Thee, Thou blest Rock of A - ges, I'm hid - ing in Thee.

TEXT: William O. Cushing
MUSIC: Ira D. Sankey

HIDING IN THEE
11.11.11.11. with Refrain

620 Under His Wings

Under His wings you will find refuge. Psalm 91:4

1. Un - der His wings I am safe - ly a - bid - ing. Tho' the night
2. Un - der His wings— what a ref - uge in sor - row! How the heart
3. Un - der His wings— O what pre - cious en - joy - ment! There will I

deep - ens and tem - pests are wild, Still I can trust Him; I
yearn - ing - ly turns to His rest! Of - ten when earth has no
hide till life's tri - als are o'er; Shel - tered, pro - tect - ed, no

know He will keep me. He has re - deemed me, and I am His child.
balm for my heal - ing, There I find com - fort, and there I am blest.
e - vil can harm me. Rest - ing in Je - sus, I'm safe ev - er - more.

Refrain

Un - der His wings, un - der His wings, Who from His love can sev - er?

Un - der His wings my soul shall a - bide, Safe - ly a - bide for - ev - er.

TEXT: William O. Cushing
MUSIC: Ira D. Sankey

HINGHAM
11.10.11.10. with Refrain

Tell Me the Old, Old Story 621

We love because He first loved us. 1 John 4:19

1. Tell me the old, old sto - ry Of un - seen things a - bove, Of Je - sus
2. Tell me the sto - ry slow - ly, That I may take it in- That won - der -
3. Tell me the same old sto - ry When you have cause to fear That this world's

and His glo - ry, Of Je - sus and His love. Tell me the sto - ry
ful re - demp - tion, God's rem - e - dy for sin. Tell me the sto - ry
emp - ty glo - ry Is cost - ing me too dear. Tell me the sto - ry

sim - ply, As to a lit - tle child; For I am weak and wea - ry,
of - ten, For I for - get so soon; The ear - ly dew of morn - ing
al - ways, If you would real - ly be, In an - y time of trou - ble,

Refrain

And help - less and de - filed.
Has passed a - way at noon. Tell me the old, old sto - ry; Tell me the
A com - fort - er to me.

old, old sto - ry. Tell me the old, old sto - ry Of Je - sus and His love.

TEXT: A. Catherine Hankey
MUSIC: William H. Doane

EVANGEL
7.6.7.6.D. with Refrain

622 Humble Thyself in the Sight of the Lord

Humble yourselves under God's mighty hand, that He may lift you up. 1 Peter 5:6

TEXT: Bob Hudson; based on 1 Peter 5:6
MUSIC: Bob Hudson

HUMBLE THYSELF
Irregular meter

Jesus, Priceless Treasure 623

Now to you who believe, this stone is precious. 1 Peter 2:7

1. Je - sus, price - less trea - sure, Source of pur - est plea - sure, Tru - est
2. In Thy strength I rest me; Foes who would mo - lest me Can - not
3. Ban - ished is our sad - ness! For the Lord of glad - ness, Je - sus,

Friend to me. Long my heart hath pant - ed, 'Til it well - nigh
reach me here. Tho' the earth be shak - ing, Ev - ery heart be
en - ters in. Those who love the Fa - ther, Tho' the storms may

faint - ed, Thirst - ing af - ter Thee. Thine I am, O spot - less Lamb,
quak - ing, God dis - pels our fear. Sin and hell in con - flict fell
gath - er, Still have peace with - in. Yea, what - e'er we here must bear,

I will suf - fer naught to hide Thee, Ask for naught be - side Thee.
With their heav - iest storms as - sail us; Je - sus will not fail us.
Still in Thee lies pur - est plea - sure— Je - sus, price - less trea - sure!

TEXT: Johann Franck; translated by Catherine Winkworth
MUSIC: Traditional German melody; adapted by Johann Crüger

JESU, MEINE FREUDE
6.6.5.6.6.5.7.8.6.

624 His Eye Is on the Sparrow

Are not five sparrows sold for two pennies? Yet not one of them is forgotten by God. Luke 12:6

Solo on stanzas is optional

1. Why should I feel dis-cour-aged? Why should the shad-ows come?
2. "Let not your heart be trou-bled," His ten-der words I hear;
3. When-ev-er I am tempt-ed, When-ev-er clouds a-rise,

Why should my heart be lone-ly And long for heav'n and home When
And rest-ing on His good-ness, I lose my doubt and fear. Tho'
When songs give place to sigh-ing, When hope with-in me dies, I

Je-sus is my por-tion? My con-stant Friend is He: His
by the path He lead-eth But one step I may see: His
draw the clos-er to Him; From care He sets me free: His

eye is on the spar-row, And I know He watch-es me. His
eye is on the spar-row, And I know He watch-es me. His
eye is on the spar-row, And I know He watch-es me. His

eye is on the spar-row, And I know He watch-es me.
eye is on the spar-row, And I know He watch-es me.
eye is on the spar-row, And I know He watch-es me.

TEXT: Civilla D. Martin
MUSIC: Charles H. Gabriel

SPARROW
Irregular meter

Refrain

I sing be-cause I'm hap-py, I sing be-cause I'm free; For His

eye is on the spar-row, And I know He watch-es me.

Sun of My Soul 625

The Lord God is a sun and shield. Psalm 84:11

1. Sun of my soul, Thou Sav - ior dear, It is not night if Thou be near;
2. When the soft dews of kind - ly sleep My wea-ry eye - lids gen - tly steep,
3. A - bide with me from morn till eve, For with-out Thee I can - not live;
4. Be near to bless me when I wake, Ere thro' the world my way I take;

O may no earth - born cloud a - rise To hide Thee from Thy ser - vant's eyes!
Be my last tho't, how sweet to rest For-ev - er on my Sav - ior's breast!
A - bide with me when night is nigh, For with-out Thee I dare not die.
A - bide with me till in Thy love I lose my - self in heav'n a - bove.

TEXT: John Keble
MUSIC: *Katholisches Gesangbuch*, Vienna, c. 1774; Choral ending by Ken Barker

HURSLEY
L.M.

mp **Optional choral ending**

Sun of my soul, Thou Sav - ior dear, It is not night if Thou be near.

mp

626 The Lily of the Valley

I am a rose of Sharon, a lily of the valleys. Song of Songs 2:1

1. I have found a Friend in Je-sus— He's ev-ery-thing to me, He's the
2. He all my griefs has tak-en and all my sor-rows borne. In temp-
3. He will nev-er, nev-er leave me, nor yet for-sake me here, While I

fair-est of ten thou-sand to my soul; The Lil-y of the Val-ley, in
ta-tion He's my strong and might-y Tow'r; I have all for Him for-sak-en, and
live by faith and do His bless-ed will; A wall of fire a-bout me, I've

Him a-lone I see All I need to cleanse and make me ful-ly whole.
all my i-dols torn From my heart, and now He keeps me by His pow'r.
noth-ing now to fear. With His man-na He my hun-gry soul shall fill.

In sor-row He's my com-fort, in trou-ble He's my stay; He
Though all the world for-sake me and Sa-tan tempt me sore, Through
Then sweep-ing up to glo-ry I'll see His bless-ed face, Where

TEXT: Charles W. Fry
MUSIC: William S. Hays

SALVATIONIST
Irregular meter

Refrain

tells me ev-ery care on Him to roll.
Je - sus I shall safe-ly reach the goal.
riv - ers of de-light shall ev - er roll.

He's the Lil-y of the Val-ley,

Hal-le-lu-jah!

the Bright and Morn-ing Star; He's the fair-est of ten thou-sand to my soul.

Cares Chorus 627

Cast your cares on the Lord and He will sustain you. Psalm 55:22

I cast all my cares up-on You. I lay all of my

bur-dens down at Your feet. And an-y time that I don't know

what to do, I will cast all my cares up-on You.

TEXT: Kelly Willard
MUSIC: Kelly Willard

CARES CHORUS
Irregular meter

628   I WILL BE WITH YOU

from Isaiah 43:1-3; 41:10; Jeremiah 29:12-13 (NIV)

WORSHIP LEADER
This is what the Lord says– He who created you:
Fear not, for I have redeemed you; I have summoned you by name;

EVERYONE
You are Mine.

WORSHIP LEADER
When you pass through the waters,

EVERYONE
I will be with you.

WORSHIP LEADER
When you walk through the fire,

EVERYONE
You will not be burned.

WORSHIP LEADER
I am the Lord, your God. So do not fear, for I am with you;
Do not be dismayed, for I am your God.

EVERYONE
I will strengthen you and help you;
I will uphold you with My righteous right hand.

WORSHIP LEADER
When you call upon Me, I will listen to you.

EVERYONE
You will seek Me and find Me when you seek Me with all your heart.

629   THE GOD OF ALL COMFORT

from John 14:1-3, 16, 27; 2 Corinthians 1:3 (NASB)

WORSHIP LEADER
Do not let your heart be troubled; believe in God, believe also in Me.

MEN
In My Father's house are many dwelling places;

WORSHIP LEADER
If it were not so, I would have told you; for I go to prepare a place for you.
If I go and prepare a place for you, I will come again,
and receive you to Myself; that where I am, there you may be also.

MEN
I will ask the Father, and He will give you another Helper,
that He may be with you forever.

WORSHIP LEADER
Peace I leave with you; My peace I give to you;
Not as the world gives, do I give to you.

EVERYONE
Do not let your heart be troubled, nor let it be fearful.

WORSHIP LEADER
Blessed be the God and Father of our Lord Jesus Christ,
the Father of mercies and God of all comfort.

What a Friend We Have in Jesus 630

In everything present your requests to God. Philippians 4:6

1. What a Friend we have in Je - sus, All our sins and griefs to bear!
2. Have we tri - als and temp - ta - tions? Is there trou - ble an - y - where?
3. Are we weak and heav - y - lad - en, Cum - bered with a load of care?

What a priv - i - lege to car - ry Ev - ery - thing to God in prayer!
We should nev - er be dis - cour - aged; Take it to the Lord in prayer.
Pre - cious Sav - ior, still our Ref - uge; Take it to the Lord in prayer.

O what peace we of - ten for - feit, O what need - less pain we bear,
Can we find a friend so faith - ful Who will all our sor - rows share?
Do thy friends de - spise, for - sake thee? Take it to the Lord in prayer.

All be - cause we do not car - ry Ev - ery - thing to God in prayer!
Je - sus knows our ev - ery weak - ness; Take it to the Lord in prayer.
In His arms He'll take and shield thee; Thou wilt find a sol - ace there.

TEXT: Joseph M. Scriven
MUSIC: Charles C. Converse

CONVERSE
8.7.8.7.D.

631 The Lord's Prayer

This, then, is how you should pray. Matthew 6:9

Our Fa - ther, which art in heav - en, Hal - low - ed

be Thy name. Thy king - dom come,

Thy will be done on earth as it is in heav - en.

Give us this day our dai - ly bread, And for - give us our debts, as

TEXT: Matthew 6:9-13
MUSIC: Albert Hay Mallotte; arranged by Donald P. Hustad
© Copyright 1935 (Renewed) by G. Schirmer, Inc. All rights reserved. Used by permission.

MALOTTE
Irregular meter

632

I LOVE YOU, MY LORD
A Worship Sequence

Open Our Eyes, Lord
More Love to Thee; complete
Suggested stanzas have been marked with an arrow: ➤

WORSHIP LEADER

In this you greatly rejoice,
though now, for a little while, you may have had to suffer grief in all kinds of trials.
These have come so that your faith–of greater worth than gold,
which perishes even though refined by fire,
may be proved genuine and may result in praise, glory and honor
when Jesus Christ is revealed.
Though you have not seen Him, you love Him;
and even though you do not see Him now, you believe in Him
and are filled with an inexpressible and glorious joy.

from 1 Peter 1:6-8 (NIV)

633 Open Our Eyes, Lord

Blessed are the pure in heart, for they will see God. Matthew 5:8

O - pen our eyes, Lord, we want to see Je - sus, To
O - pen our ears, Lord, and help us to lis - ten,

reach out and touch Him, and say that we love Him.
O - pen our eyes,

Lord, we want to see Je - sus.
rit.

*Optional transition to
"More Love to Thee"*

TEXT: Robert Cull
MUSIC: Robert Cull; arranged by David Allen

OPEN OUR EYES
11.12.11.11.

I LOVE YOU, MY LORD - A Worship Sequence

More Love to Thee 634

This is my prayer: that your love may abound more and more. Philippians 1:9

1. More love to Thee, O Christ, More love to Thee! Hear Thou the
2. Once earth-ly joy I craved, Sought peace and rest; Now Thee a-
3. Then shall my lat-est breath Whis-per Thy praise; This be the

prayer I make On bend-ed knee. This is my ear-nest plea:
lone I seek; Give what is best. This all my prayer shall be:
part-ing cry My heart shall raise. This still its prayer shall be:

More love, O Christ, to Thee, More love to Thee, More love to Thee!
More love, O Christ, to Thee, More love to Thee, More love to Thee!
More love, O Christ, to Thee, More love to Thee, More love to Thee!

TEXT: Elizabeth P. Prentiss
MUSIC: William H. Doane; Choral ending arranged by Eugene Thomas

MORE LOVE TO THEE
6.4.6.4.6.6.4.

Optional choral ending

mp slowly

rit.   I love You, my Je-sus, I love You, my Lord.

mp

The end of I LOVE YOU, MY LORD - A Worship Sequence

635 In the Garden

The disciples were overjoyed when they saw the Lord. John 20:20

1. I come to the gar-den a-lone, While the dew is
2. He speaks, and the sound of His voice Is so sweet the
3. I'd stay in the gar-den with Him Tho' the night a-

still on the ros-es; And the voice I hear, fall-ing on my ear,
birds hush their sing-ing; And the mel-o-dy that He gave to me
round me be fall-ing; But He bids me go, thro' the voice of woe;

Refrain

The Son of God dis-clos-es.
With-in my heart is ring-ing. And He walks with me, and He
His voice to me is call-ing.

talks with me, And He tells me I am His own; And the joy we

share as we tar-ry there None oth-er has ev-er known.

TEXT: C. Austin Miles
MUSIC: C. Austin Miles

GARDEN
Irregular meter

I Must Tell Jesus 636

Because He Himself suffered, He is able to help those who are being tempted. Hebrews 2:18

1. I must tell Je - sus all of my tri - als; I can-not bear these
2. I must tell Je - sus all of my trou - bles; He is a kind, com -
3. O how the world to e - vil al - lures me! O how my heart is

bur - dens a - lone. In my dis - tress He kind-ly will help me;
pas - sion - ate Friend. If I but ask Him, He will de - liv - er,
tempt-ed to sin! I must tell Je - sus, and He will help me

Refrain

He ev - er loves and cares for His own. I must tell Je - sus!
Make of my trou - bles quick-ly an end.
O - ver the world the vic - t'ry to win.

I must tell Je - sus! I can-not bear my bur-dens a - lone; I must tell

Je - sus! I must tell Je - sus! Je - sus can help me, Je - sus a - lone.

TEXT: Elisha A. Hoffman
MUSIC: Elisha A. Hoffman

ORWIGSBURG
10.9.10.9. with Refrain

637 Instruments of Your Peace

The meek will enjoy great peace. Psalm 37:11

Refrain

Lord, make us in-stru-ments of Your peace; Where there is ha-tred let Your

love in-crease. Lord, make us in-stru-ments of Your peace; Walls of pride and

*Optional last time to CODA

Fine

prej-u-dice shall cease When we are Your in-stru-ments of peace.

**Optional stanzas
a little faster

1. Where there is ha-tred, we will sow His love; Where there is in-ju-ry,
2. Where there is blind-ness, we will pray for sight; Where there is dark-ness,

we will nev-er judge. Where there is striv-ing, we will speak His peace;
we will shine His light. Where there is sad-ness, we will bear their grief;

*Use "Last time to CODA" if optional choral ending is sung.
**Stanzas may be omitted or utilized in the following ways:
  sung by choir, solo, congregation or any combination thereof.

TEXT: Kirk and Deby Dearman; based on a prayer by St. Francis of Assisi, 13th c.
MUSIC: Kirk and Deby Dearman; arranged by Tom Fettke

INSTRUMENTS OF PEACE
Irregular meter

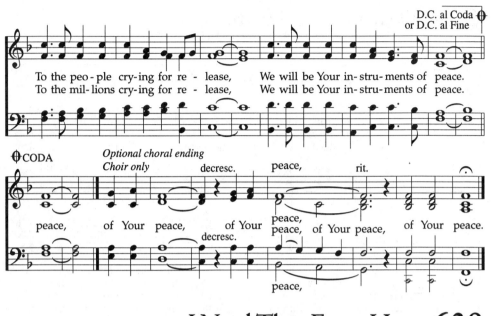

To the peo-ple cry-ing for re - lease, We will be Your in-stru-ments of peace.
To the mil-lions cry-ing for re - lease, We will be Your in-stru-ments of peace.

CODA

Optional choral ending
Choir only decresc. peace, rit.

peace, of Your peace, of Your peace, of Your peace, of Your peace, of Your peace.

peace,

I Need Thee Every Hour 638

Hear, O Lord, and answer me, for I am poor and needy. Psalm 86:1

1. I need Thee ev-ery hour, Most gra - cious Lord; No ten - der
2. I need Thee ev-ery hour, Stay Thou near - by; Temp - ta - tions
3. I need Thee ev-ery hour, In joy or pain; Come quick-ly
4. I need Thee ev-ery hour, Most Ho - ly One; O make me

voice like Thine Can peace af - ford.
lose their pow'r When Thou art nigh.
and a - bide, Or life is vain.
Thine in - deed, Thou bless - ed Son!

Refrain

I need Thee, O I need Thee;

Ev - ery hour I need Thee! O bless me now, my Sav-ior, I come to Thee.

TEXT: Annie S. Hawks; Robert Lowry, Refrain
MUSIC: Robert Lowry

NEED
6.4.6.4. with Refrain

639 Dear Lord and Father of Mankind

Commit your way to the Lord; trust in Him. Psalm 37:5

1. Dear Lord and Father of mankind, Forgive our foolish ways! Re-clothe us in our rightful mind; In purer lives Thy service find, In deeper rev-'rence, praise.
2. In simple trust like theirs who heard, Beside the Syrian sea, The gracious calling of the Lord, Let us, like them, without a word, Rise up and follow Thee.
3. Drop Thy still dews of quietness Till all our strivings cease. Take from our souls the strain and stress, And let our ordered lives confess The beauty of Thy peace.
4. Breathe thro' the heats of our desire Thy coolness and Thy balm. Let sense be dumb, let flesh retire; Speak thro' the earth-quake, wind, and fire, O still small voice of calm!

TEXT: John G. Whittier
MUSIC: Frederick C. Maker

REST
8.6.8.8.6.

640 Sweet Hour of Prayer

Peter and John were going up to the temple at the time of prayer. Acts 3:1

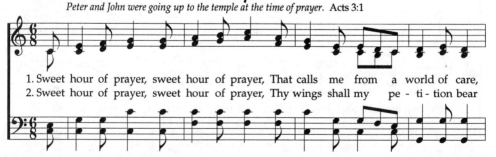

1. Sweet hour of prayer, sweet hour of prayer, That calls me from a world of care,
2. Sweet hour of prayer, sweet hour of prayer, Thy wings shall my petition bear

TEXT: William W. Walford
MUSIC: William B. Bradbury

SWEET HOUR
L.M.D.

And bids me at my Fa-ther's throne Make all my wants and wish-es known:
To Him whose truth and faith-ful-ness En-gage the wait-ing soul to bless:

In sea-sons of dis-tress and grief My soul has of-ten found re-lief
And since He bids me seek His face, Be-lieve His Word, and trust His grace,

And oft es-caped the tempt-er's snare By thy re-turn, sweet hour of prayer.
I'll cast on Him my ev-ery care And wait for thee, sweet hour of prayer.

Hear Our Prayer, O Lord 641

O Lord, hear my prayer, listen to my cry for mercy. Psalm 143:1

Hear our prayer, O Lord, Hear our prayer, O Lord;

In-cline Thine ear to us And grant us Thy peace. A - men.

TEXT: Based on Psalm 143:1
MUSIC: George Whelpton

WHELPTON
Irregular meter

642 Abide with Me

The Lord your God goes with you; He will never leave you nor forsake you. Deuteronomy 31:6

1. A - bide with me; fast falls the e - ven - tide. The dark-ness
2. Swift to its close ebbs out life's lit - tle day. Earth's joys grow
3. I need Thy pres - ence ev - ery pass - ing hour. What but Thy
4. I fear no foe, with Thee at hand to bless; Ills have no
5. Hold Thou Thy cross be - fore my clos - ing eyes; Shine thro' the

deep - ens; Lord, with me a - bide. When oth - er help - ers
dim; its glo - ries pass a - way. Change and de - cay in
grace can foil the tempt - er's pow'r? Who, like Thy - self, my
weight, and tears no bit - ter - ness. Where is death's sting? Where,
gloom and point me to the skies. Heav'n's morn - ing breaks, and

fail and com - forts flee, Help of the help-less, O a - bide with me.
all a - round I see; O Thou who chang-est not, a - bide with me.
Guide and Stay can be? Thro' cloud and sun-shine, O a - bide with me.
grave, thy vic - to - ry? I tri - umph still if Thou a - bide with me.
earth's vain shad-ows flee. In life, in death, O Lord, a - bide with me.

TEXT: Henry F. Lyte
MUSIC: William H. Monk

EVENTIDE
10.10.10.10.

643 O Lord, You're Beautiful

This is what I seek: to gaze upon the beauty of the Lord. Psalm 27:4

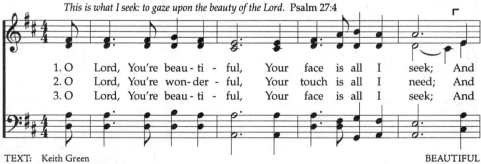

1. O Lord, You're beau - ti - ful, Your face is all I seek; And
2. O Lord, You're won - der - ful, Your touch is all I need; And
3. O Lord, You're beau - ti - ful, Your face is all I seek; And

TEXT: Keith Green
MUSIC: Keith Green

BEAUTIFUL
6.6.8.6.

when Your eyes are on this child, Your grace a-bounds in me.
when Your hand is on this child, Your heal-ing I re-ceive.
when Your eyes are on this child, Your grace a-bounds in me.

The Greatest Thing 644

I consider everything a loss compared to the surpassing greatness of knowing Christ. Philippians 3:8

1. The great-est thing in all my life is know-ing You;
2. The great-est thing in all my life is lov-ing You;
3. The great-est thing in all my life is serv-ing You;

The great-est thing in all my life is know-ing You.
The great-est thing in all my life is lov-ing You.
The great-est thing in all my life is serv-ing You.

I want to know You more, I want to know You more.
I want to love You more, I want to love You more.
I want to serve You more, I want to serve You more.

The great-est thing in all my life is know - ing You.
The great-est thing in all my life is lov - ing You.
The great-est thing in all my life is serv - ing You.

TEXT: Mark Pendergrass
MUSIC: Mark Pendergrass

THE GREATEST THING
Irregular meter

645 THE LORD'S PRAYER

from Matthew 6:5-9 (NKJV); Matthew 6:9-13 (KJV)

WORSHIP LEADER
When you pray, you shall not be like the hypocrites.
For they love to pray standing in the synagogues
and on the corners of the streets, that they may be seen by men.
Assuredly, I say to you, they have their reward.

SOLO
But when you pray, go into your room,
and when you have shut your door, pray to your Father who is in the secret place;
and your Father who sees in secret will reward you openly.

WORSHIP LEADER
When you pray, do not use vain repetitions as the heathen do.
For they think that they will be heard for their many words.

SOLO
Therefore do not be like them.
For your Father knows the things you have need of before you ask Him.

WORSHIP LEADER
In this manner, therefore, pray:

EVERYONE
Our Father which art in heaven, hallowed be Thy name.
Thy kingdom come. Thy will be done in earth, as it is in heaven.
Give us this day our daily bread.
And forgive us our debts, as we forgive our debtors.
And lead us not into temptation, but deliver us from evil:
For Thine is the kingdom, and the power, and the glory, for ever.
Amen.

646 PRESENT YOUR REQUESTS TO GOD

from Philippians 4:4-7, 9 (NIV)

WORSHIP LEADER
Rejoice in the Lord always.
I will say it again: Rejoice!

EVERYONE
Let your gentleness be evident to all.
The Lord is near.

WORSHIP LEADER
Do not be anxious about anything,
but in everything, by prayer and petition, with thanksgiving,
present your requests to God.

EVERYONE
And the peace of God,
which transcends all understanding,
will guard your hearts and your minds in Christ Jesus.

WORSHIP LEADER
Whatever you have learned or received or heard from me,
or seen in me — put it into practice.

EVERYONE
And the God of peace will be with you.

Pure and Holy 647

Be holy because I, the Lord your God, am holy. Leviticus 19:2

1. Pure and ho - ly I would be, Wor - thy of Your love for me.
2. You are great and I am small; You are King and God of all.

Teach me while Your light is clear; Change me while my heart is near.
You are wise in all You do; Lord, I put my trust in You.

Optional descant

Ho - ly, ho - ly, ho - ly Lord.

Refrain

Ho - ly, ho - ly, ho - ly Lord.

Ho - ly, ho - ly, ho - ly Lord.

Ho - ly, ho - ly, ho - ly Lord.

TEXT: Mike Hudson and Bob Farnsworth
MUSIC: Mike Hudson and Bob Farnsworth

PURE AND HOLY
7.7.7.7. with Refrain

648 Love Divine, All Loves Excelling

God is love. Whoever lives in love lives in God, and God in him. 1 John 4:16

1. Love di-vine, all loves ex-cel-ling, Joy of heav'n, to earth come down!
2. Breathe, O breathe Thy lov-ing Spir-it In-to ev-ery trou-bled breast!
3. Come, Al-might-y, to de-liv-er; Let us all Thy life re-ceive.
4. Fin-ish then Thy new cre-a-tion; Pure and spot-less let us be.

Fix in us Thy hum-ble dwell-ing; All Thy faith-ful mer-cies crown.
Let us all in Thee in-her-it; Let us find the prom-ised rest.
Sud-den-ly re-turn, and nev-er, Nev-er-more Thy tem-ples leave.
Let us see Thy great sal-va-tion Per-fect-ly re-stored in Thee:

Je-sus, Thou art all com-pas-sion; Pure, un-bound-ed love Thou art.
Take a-way our bent to sin-ning; Al-pha and O-me-ga be.
Thee we would be al-ways bless-ing, Serve Thee as Thy hosts a-bove,
Changed from glo-ry in-to glo-ry, Till in heav'n we take our place,

Vis-it us with Thy sal-va-tion; En-ter ev-ery trem-bling heart.
End of faith, as its be-gin-ning, Set our hearts at lib-er-ty.
Pray and praise Thee with-out ceas-ing, Glo-ry in Thy per-fect love.
Till we cast our crowns be-fore Thee, Lost in won-der, love and praise.

TEXT: Charles Wesley
MUSIC: John Zundel; Last stanza setting and Choral ending by Bill Wolaver
A higher setting may be found at No. 93

BEECHER
8.7.8.7.D.

Optional last stanza setting

Broader
Unison

rit.

4. Fin - ish then Thy new cre - a - tion;

Pure and spot - less let us be. Let us see Thy great sal - va - tion

Per - fect - ly re - stored in Thee: Changed from glo - ry in - to glo - ry,

Till in heav'n we take our place, Till we cast our crowns be - fore Thee,

Optional choral ending

Lost in won - der, love and praise. Lost in won - der, love and praise.

649 When I Look into Your Holiness

This is what I seek: to gaze upon the beauty of the Lord and to seek Him in His temple. Psalm 27:4

When I look in- to Your ho - li - ness, When I gaze in- to Your love - li -
ness, When all things that sur- round be- come shad- ows in the light of
You; When I've found the joy of reach- ing Your heart, When my
will be- comes en- thralled in Your love, When all things that sur- round be- come
shad- ows in the light of You, I wor- ship You; I wor- ship

TEXT: Wayne and Cathy Perrin
MUSIC: Wayne and Cathy Perrin

PERRIN
Irregular meter

You.

The rea-son I live   is to wor-ship

You.

I wor-ship You;   I wor-ship You.

The rea-son I live   is to wor-ship You.

O for a Heart to Praise My God 650

I will give you a new heart and put a new spirit in you. Ezekiel 36:26

1. O for a heart to praise my God, A heart from sin set free,
2. A heart in ev-ery thought re-newed And full of love di - vine;
3. Thy na-ture, gra-cious Lord, im-part; Come quick-ly from a - bove.

A heart that al-ways feels Thy blood So free-ly shed for me.
Per-fect and right and pure and good, A cop-y, Lord, of Thine!
Write Thy new name up - on my heart, Thy new, best name of Love.

TEXT: Charles Wesley
MUSIC: Carl G. Gläser; arranged by Lowell Mason
A higher setting may be found at No. 21

AZMON
C.M.

651 All That I Need

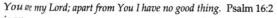
You are my Lord; apart from You I have no good thing. Psalm 16:2

All that is Good, all that is Right; All that is Truth, Jus - tice and Light; All that is Pure, Ho - ly in - deed, All that is You is all that I need.

TEXT: Twila Paris
MUSIC: Twila Paris

ALL THAT I NEED
8.8.8.9.

652 CREATE IN ME A PURE HEART

A Worship Sequence

Whiter than Snow; stanzas 1,4
Change My Heart, O God
Suggested stanzas have been marked with an arrow: ➤

WORSHIP LEADER
Have mercy on me, O God, according to Your unfailing love;
according to Your great compassion blot out my transgressions–
Wash away all my iniquity and I will be whiter than snow.
Create in me a pure heart, O God,
and renew a steadfast spirit within me.

from Psalm 51:1-2, 7, 10 (NIV)

Optional introduction to "Whiter than Snow"

mp

654 Change My Heart, O God

Create in me a pure heart, O God, and renew a steadfast spirit within me. Psalm 51:10

TEXT: Eddie Espinosa
MUSIC: Eddie Espinosa

CHANGE MY HEART
Irregular meter

Whiter than Snow 653

Wash me, and I will be whiter than snow. Psalm 51:7

1. Lord Je - sus, I long to be per - fect - ly whole; I
2. Lord Je - sus, look down from Your throne in the skies, And
3. Lord Je - sus, for this I most hum - bly en - treat; I
4. Lord Je - sus, be - fore You I pa - tient - ly wait; Come

want You for - ev - er to live in my soul. Break down ev - ery
help me to make a com - plete sac - ri - fice. I give up my -
wait, bless - ed Lord, at Your cru - ci - fied feet. By faith, for my
now, and with - in me a new heart cre - ate. To those who have

i - dol; cast out ev - ery foe— Now wash me and I shall be
self, and what - ev - er I know— Now wash me and I shall be
cleans - ing I see Your blood flow— Now wash me and I shall be
sought You, You nev - er said "No"— Now wash me and I shall be

Refrain

whit - er than snow. Whit - er than snow, yes, whit - er than snow;

Now wash me and I shall be whit - er than snow. *Optional transition to "Change My Heart, O God"*

TEXT: James Nicholson
MUSIC: William G. Fischer

FISCHER
11.11.11.11. with Refrain

Mold me and make me, This is what I pray.

Change my heart, O God, Make it ev-er true.

Change my heart, O God, May I be like You. You.

Optional extended or choral ending

Freely *Harmony optional* rit.

Change my heart, O God, May I be like You.

The end of CREATE IN ME A PURE HEART - A Worship Sequence

655 Sanctuary

Your body is a temple of the Holy Spirit. Therefore honor God. 1 Corinthians 6:19-20

Lord, pre - pare me to be a sanc - tu - ar - y, pure and

ho - ly, tried and true; With thanks - giv - ing, I'll be a

Optional repeat chorus setting

liv - ing sanc - tu - ar - y for You. Lord, pre -

pare me to be a sanc - tu - ar - y, pure and ho - ly, tried and true;

With thanks - giv - ing, I'll be a liv - ing sanc - tu - ar - y for

TEXT: John Thompson and Randy Scruggs
MUSIC: John Thompson and Randy Scruggs

SANCTUARY
Irregular meter

You. I'll be a liv-ing sanc-tu-ar-y for You.

Take Time to Be Holy 656

Without holiness no one will see the Lord. Hebrews 12:14

1. Take time to be ho - ly, Speak oft with thy Lord; A - bide in Him al - ways And feed on His Word. Make friends with God's chil- dren, Help those who are weak; For - get-ting in noth-ing His bless-ing to seek.

2. Take time to be ho - ly, The world rush-es on; Spend much time in se - cret With Je - sus a - lone. By look-ing to Je - sus, Like Him thou shalt be; Thy friends in thy con-duct His like-ness shall see.

3. Take time to be ho - ly, Let Him be thy Guide, And run not be- fore Him, What-ev - er be - tide. In joy or in sor - row Still fol - low thy Lord, And, look-ing to Je - sus, Still trust in His Word.

4. Take time to be ho - ly, Be calm in thy soul– Each tho't and each mo - tive Be - neath His con - trol. Thus led by His Spir - it To foun - tains of love, Thou soon shall be fit - ted For ser - vice a - bove.

TEXT: William D. Longstaff
MUSIC: George C. Stebbins

HOLINESS
6.5.6.5.D.

657 Cleanse Me

Search me, O God, and know my heart. Psalm 139:23

Unison

1. Search me, O God, and know my heart to-day;
2. I praise Thee, Lord, for cleans-ing me from sin;
3. Lord, take my life and make it whol-ly Thine;
4. O Ho-ly Ghost, re-viv-al comes from Thee;

Try me, O Sav-ior, know my thoughts, I pray.
Ful-fill Thy Word and make me pure with-in.
Fill my poor heart with Thy great love di-vine.
Send a re-viv-al, start the work in me.

See if there be some wick-ed way in me;
Fill me with fire where once I burned with shame;
Take all my will, my pas-sion, self and pride;
Thy Word de-clares Thou wilt sup-ply our need;

Cleanse me from ev-ery sin and set me free.
Grant my de-sire to mag-ni-fy Thy name.
I now sur-ren-der, Lord– in me a-bide.
For bless-ings now, O Lord, I hum-bly plead.

TEXT: J. Edwin Orr; based on Psalm 139:23
MUSIC: Maori melody; arranged by Robert F. Douglas

MAORI
10.10.10.10.

CHILDREN OF GOD

658

from 1 John 3:1-3, 16-22; Psalm 139:23-24 (NIV)

WORSHIP LEADER
How great is the love the Father has lavished on us,
that we should be called children of God!

EVERYONE
And that is what we are!

WORSHIP LEADER
Dear friends, now we are children of God,
and what we will be has not yet been made known.

EVERYONE
But we know that when He appears, we shall be like Him,
for we shall see Him as He is.

WORSHIP LEADER
Everyone who has this hope in Him purifies himself, just as He is pure.
This is how we know what love is:

EVERYONE
Jesus Christ laid down His life for us.
And we ought to lay down our lives for our brothers.

WORSHIP LEADER
If anyone has material possessions and sees his brother in need
but has no pity on him, how can the love of God be in him?
Dear children, let us not love with words, but with actions and in truth.

EVERYONE
This then is how we know that we belong to the truth, and how we set our hearts
at rest in His presence whenever our hearts condemn us.

WORSHIP LEADER
For God is greater than our hearts, and He knows everything.
Dear friends, if our hearts do not condemn us, we have confidence before God
and receive from Him anything we ask,
because we obey His commands and do what pleases Him.

EVERYONE
Search me, O God, and know my heart;
test me and know my anxious thoughts.
See if there is any offensive way in me
and lead me in the way everlasting.

THE WAY OF THE RIGHTEOUS

659

from Psalm 1 (NASB)

WORSHIP LEADER or SOLO DRAMATIST
How blessed is the man who does not walk in the counsel of the wicked,
Nor stand in the path of sinners, nor sit in the seat of scoffers!
But his delight is in the law of the Lord,
and in His law he meditates day and night.
And he will be like a tree firmly planted by streams of water,
Which yields its fruit in its season, and its leaf does not wither;
And in whatever he does, he prospers.
The wicked are not so, but they are like chaff which the wind drives away.
Therefore the wicked will not stand in the judgment,
Nor sinners in the assembly of the righteous.
For the Lord knows the way of the righteous,
But the way of the wicked will perish.

660 I Will Serve Thee

It is the Lord Christ you are serving. Colossians 3:24

I will serve Thee be-cause I love Thee; You have giv-en life to me. I was noth-ing be-fore You found me; You have giv-en life to me. Heart-aches, bro-ken piec-es, Ru-ined lives are why You died on Cal-v'ry. Your touch was what I longed for; You have giv-en life to me.

SERVING

Irregular meter

Little Is Much When God Is in It 661

God is able to make all grace abound to you. 2 Corinthians 9:8

1. In the har - vest field now rip-ened There's a work for all to do;
2. Does the place you're called to la - bor Seem so small and lit - tle known?
3. When the con - flict here is end - ed And our race on earth is run,

Hark! the voice of God is call - ing To the har - vest call - ing you.
It is great if God is in it, And He'll not for - get His own.
He will say, if we are faith - ful, "Wel - come home, My child, well done!"

Refrain

Lit - tle is much when God is in it, La - bor not for wealth or fame;

There's a crown, and you can win it, If you go in Je - sus' name.

TEXT: Kittie L. Suffield
MUSIC: Kittie L. Suffield

STEWARDSHIP
8.7.8.7. with Refrain

Optional extended or choral ending rit.

There's a crown, and you can win it, If you go in Je - sus' name.

662 With All My Heart

I have sought Your face with all my heart. Psalm 119:58

Unison

With all my heart I want to love You, Lord, And live my life each day to know You more. All that is in me is Yours com - plete - ly; I'll serve You on - ly, with all my heart.

Optional segue to "I Offer My Life." No transition is needed.

TEXT: Babbie Mason
MUSIC: Babbie Mason

MASON
Irregular meter

663 I Offer My Life

Offer your bodies as living sacrifices, holy and pleasing to God. Romans 12:1

Lord, I of-fer my life to You; Ev-ery-thing I've been through, Use it for Your glo - ry. Lord, I of - fer my days to You,

TEXT: Claire Cloninger and Don Moen
MUSIC: Claire Cloninger and Don Moen

I OFFER MY LIFE
Irregular meter

Lift-ing my praise to You As a pleas-ing sac-ri-fice;

1 Repeat optional 2

Lord, I of-fer You my life. life.

Take My Life, Lead Me, Lord 664

Teach me Your way, O Lord; lead me in a straight path. Psalm 27:11

1. Take my life, lead me, Lord; Take my life, lead me, Lord;
2. Take my life, teach me, Lord; Take my life, teach me, Lord;
3. Here am I, send me, Lord; Here am I, send me, Lord;

Make my life use-ful to Thee. Take my life, lead me, Lord;
Make my life use-ful to Thee. Take my life, teach me, Lord;
Make my life use-ful to Thee. Here am I, send me, Lord;

Take my life, lead me, Lord; Make my life use-ful to Thee.
Take my life, teach me, Lord; Make my life use-ful to Thee.
Here am I, send me, Lord; Make my life use-ful to Thee.

TEXT: R. Maines Rawls
MUSIC: R. Maines Rawls

LANGLEY
Irregular meter

665 O Master, Let Me Walk with Thee

Whoever claims to live in Him must walk as Jesus did.   1 John 2:6

1. O Mas - ter, let me walk with Thee In low - ly
2. Help me the slow of heart to move By some clear,
3. Teach me Thy pa - tience; still with Thee In clos - er,
4. In hope that sends a shin - ing ray Far down the

paths of ser - vice free. Tell me Thy se - cret;
win - ning word of love. Teach me the way - ward
dear - er com - pa - ny, In work that keeps faith
fu - ture's broad - 'ning way, In peace that on - ly

help me bear The strain of toil, the fret of care.
feet to stay, And guide them in the home - ward way.
sweet and strong, In trust that tri - umphs o - ver wrong;
Thou canst give, With Thee, O Mas - ter, let me live.

TEXT: Washington Gladden
MUSIC: H. Percy Smith

MARYTON
L.M.

666 A Charge to Keep I Have

Those who have been given a trust must prove faithful.   1 Corinthians 4:2

1. A charge to keep I have, A God to glo - ri - fy,
2. To serve the pres - ent age, My call - ing to ful - fill;
3. Arm me with watch - ful care As in Thy sight to live,
4. Help me to watch and pray, And still on Thee re - ly,

TEXT: Charles Wesley, altered
MUSIC: Lowell Mason

BOYLSTON
S.M.

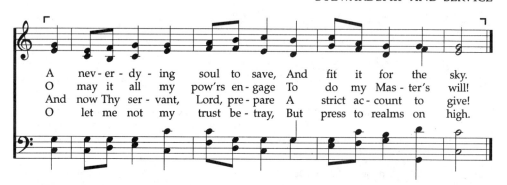

A nev-er-dy-ing soul to save, And fit it for the sky.
O may it all my pow'rs en-gage To do my Mas-ter's will!
And now Thy ser-vant, Lord, pre-pare A strict ac-count to give!
O let me not my trust be-tray, But press to realms on high.

Lord, Speak to Me 667

The things you have heard me say, entrust to reliable people. 2 Timothy 2:2

1. Lord, speak to me, that I may speak In liv-ing
2. O teach me, Lord, that I may teach The pre-cious
3. O fill me with Thy full-ness, Lord, Un-til my
4. O use me, Lord, use e-ven me, Just as Thou

ech-oes of Thy tone; As Thou hast sought, so
things Thou dost im-part; And wing my words that
ver-y heart o'er-flow In kin-dling thought and
wilt, and when, and where, Un-til Thy bless-ed

let me seek Thine err-ing chil-dren lost and lone.
they may reach The hid-den depths of man-y a heart.
glow-ing word, Thy love to tell, Thy praise to show.
face I see— Thy rest, Thy joy, Thy glo-ry share.

TEXT: Frances Ridley Havergal
MUSIC: Robert Schumann

CANONBURY
L.M.

668 I'll Go Where You Want Me to Go

You must go to everyone I send you to and say whatever I command you. Jeremiah 1:7

1. It may not be on the moun-tain's height Or o-ver the storm-y sea;
2. Per - haps to-day there are lov-ing words Which Je-sus would have me speak;
3. There's sure-ly some-where a low - ly place In earth's har-vest fields so wide

It may not be at the bat - tle's front My Lord will have need of me.
There may be now, in the paths of sin, Some wan-d'rer whom I should seek.
Where I may la-bor thro' life's short day For Je - sus, the Cru - ci - fied.

But if by a still, small voice He calls To paths that I do not know,
O Sav - ior, if Thou wilt be my Guide, Tho' dark and rug-ged the way,
So, trust-ing my all to Thy ten - der care, And know-ing Thou lov - est me,

I'll an - swer, dear Lord, with my hand in Thine, "I'll go where You want me to go."
My voice shall ech - o the mes-sage sweet. I'll say what You want me to say.
I'll do Thy will with a heart sin-cere. I'll be what You want me to be.

TEXT: Mary Brown, stanza 1; Charles E. Prior, stanzas 2,3
MUSIC: Carrie E. Rounsefell

MANCHESTER
Irregular meter

Refrain

I'll go where You want me to go, dear Lord, O-ver moun-tain, or plain, or sea.

I'll say what You want me to say, dear Lord. I'll be what You want me to be.

Make Me a Servant 669

Whoever wants to become great among you must be your servant. Matthew 20:26

Make me a ser-vant, hum-ble and meek; Lord, let me lift up those who

are weak. And may the prayer of my heart al-ways be: Make me a

ser-vant, make me a ser-vant, Make me a ser-vant to-day.

TEXT: Kelly Willard
MUSIC: Kelly Willard

SERVANT
Irregular meter

670 Make Me a Blessing

The memory of the righteous will be a blessing.   Proverbs 10:7

1. Out in the high-ways and by-ways of life, Man-y are wea-ry and are
2. Tell the sweet sto-ry of Christ and His love; Tell of His pow'r to for- His
3. Give as 'twas giv-en to you in your need; Love as the Mas-ter loved the

sad. Car-ry the sun-shine where dark-ness is rife, Mak-ing the
wea-ry and sad.
give. Oth-ers will trust Him if on-ly you prove True ev-ery
pow'r to for-give.
you. Be to the help-less a help-er in-deed; Un-to your
Mas-ter loved you.

Refrain

sor-row-ing glad.
mo-ment you live. Make me a bless-ing; make me a bless-ing.
mis-sion be true.

Out of my life may Je-sus shine. Make me a bless-ing, O
Out of my life

TEXT: Ira B. Wilson
MUSIC: George S. Schuler

SCHULER
10.7.10.7 with Refrain

Sav - ior, I pray. Make me a bless - ing to some - one to - day.
I pray Thee, my Sav - ior.

Something for Thee 671

Do your best to present yourself to God as one approved. 2 Timothy 2:15

1. Sav - ior, Thy dy - ing love Thou gav - est me, Nor should I
2. Give me a faith - ful heart, Guid - ed by Thee, That each de -
3. All that I am and have, Thy gifts so free, Ev - er in

aught with - hold, Dear Lord, from Thee; In love my soul would bow, My
part - ing day Hence - forth may see Some work of love be - gun, Some
joy or grief, My Lord, for Thee; And when Thy face I see, My

heart ful - fill its vow, Some of - f'ring bring Thee now, Some - thing for Thee.
deed of kind - ness done, Some wan - d'rer sought and won, Some - thing for Thee.
ran - somed soul shall be, Thro' all e - ter - ni - ty, Some - thing for Thee.

TEXT: Sylvanus D. Phelps
MUSIC: Robert Lowry

SOMETHING FOR JESUS
6.4.6.4.6.6.6.4.

672 What a Mighty God We Serve

Our God, the great, mighty and awesome God. Nehemiah 9:32

TEXT: Anonymous
MUSIC: Anonymous; arranged by Ken Barker and Tom Fettke

MIGHTY GOD
Irregular meter

What a might-y God we serve, What a might-y God we
serve; An-gels bow be-fore Him, Heav-en and earth a-
dore Him, What a might-y God we serve.

Must Jesus Bear the Cross Alone? 673

Those who would come after Me must take up their cross. Mark 8:34

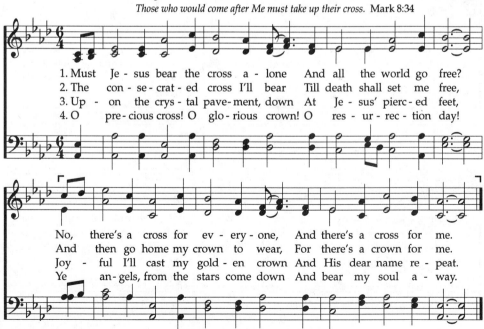

1. Must Je-sus bear the cross a-lone And all the world go free?
2. The con-se-crat-ed cross I'll bear Till death shall set me free,
3. Up-on the crys-tal pave-ment, down At Je-sus' pierc-ed feet,
4. O pre-cious cross! O glo-rious crown! O res-ur-rec-tion day!

No, there's a cross for ev-ery-one, And there's a cross for me.
And then go home my crown to wear, For there's a crown for me.
Joy-ful I'll cast my gold-en crown And His dear name re-peat.
Ye an-gels, from the stars come down And bear my soul a-way.

TEXT: Thomas Shepherd and others
MUSIC: George N. Allen

MAITLAND
C.M.

674 Who Is on the Lord's Side?

Put on the full armor of God, so that you may be able to stand your ground. Ephesians 6:13

1. Who is on the Lord's side? Who will serve the King? Who will be His help-ers, Oth-er lives to bring? Who will leave the world's side? Who will face the foe? Who is on the Lord's side? Who for Him will go? By Thy call of mer-cy,

2. Not for weight of glo-ry, Not for crown and palm, En-ter we the ar-my, Raise the war-rior psalm; But for love that claim-eth Lives for whom He died; He whom Je-sus nam-eth Must be on His side. By Thy love con-strain-ing,

3. Je-sus, Thou hast bought us, Not with gold or gem, But with Thine own life-blood, For Thy di-a-dem. With Thy bless-ing fill-ing Each who comes to Thee, Thou hast made us will-ing, Thou hast made us free. By Thy grand re-demp-tion,

4. Fierce may be the con-flict, Strong may be the foe, But the King's own ar-my None can o-ver-throw. Round His stand-ard rang-ing, Vic-t'ry is se-cure; For His truth un-chang-ing Makes the tri-umph sure. Joy-ful-ly en-list-ing

TEXT: Frances Ridley Havergal
MUSIC: C. Luise Reichardt; arranged by John Goss

ARMAGEDDON
6.5.6.5.D. with Refrain

By Thy grace di - vine, We are on the Lord's side, Sav - ior, we are Thine.
By Thy grace di - vine, We are on the Lord's side, Sav - ior, we are Thine.
By Thy grace di - vine, We are on the Lord's side, Sav - ior, we are Thine.
By Thy grace di - vine, We are on the Lord's side, Sav - ior, we are Thine.

I Gave My Life for Thee 675

Greater love has no one than this, that he lay down his life for his friends. John 15:13

1. I gave My life for thee; My pre - cious blood I shed,
2. My Fa - ther's house of light, My glo - ry - cir - cled throne,
3. I suf - fered much for thee, More than thy tongue can tell,
4. And I have bro't to thee, Down from My home a - bove,

That thou might ran - somed be, And quick - ened from the dead.
I left for earth - ly night, For wan - d'rings sad and lone.
Of bit - t'rest ag - o - ny, To res - cue thee from hell.
Sal - va - tion full and free, My par - don and My love.

I gave, I gave My life for thee. What hast thou giv'n for Me?
I left, I left it all for thee. Hast thou left aught for Me?
I've borne, I've borne it all for thee. What hast thou borne for Me?
I bring, I bring rich gifts to thee. What hast thou bro't to Me?

TEXT: Frances Ridley Havergal
MUSIC: Philip P. Bliss

KENOSIS
Irregular meter

676 O Jesus, I Have Promised

Whoever serves Me must follow Me. John 12:26

1. O Je - sus, I have prom - ised To serve Thee to the end;
2. O let me feel Thee near me, The world is ev - er near;
3. O let me hear Thee speak - ing In ac - cents clear and still,
4. O Je - sus, Thou hast prom - ised To all who fol - low Thee,

Be Thou for - ev - er near me, My Mas - ter and my Friend:
I see the sights that daz - zle, The tempt-ing sounds I hear:
A - bove the storms of pas - sion, The mur - murs of self - will.
That where Thou art in glo - ry, There shall Thy ser - vant be;

I shall not fear the bat - tle If Thou art by my side,
My foes are ev - er near me, A - round me and with - in;
O speak to re - as - sure me, To has - ten or con - trol;
And, Je - sus, I have prom - ised To serve Thee to the end;

Nor wan - der from the path - way If Thou wilt be my guide.
But, Je - sus, draw Thou near - er, And shield my soul from sin.
O speak, and make me lis - ten, Thou guard - ian of my soul.
O give me grace to fol - low, My Mas - ter and my Friend.

TEXT: John E. Bode
MUSIC: Arthur H. Mann

ANGEL'S STORY
7.6.7.6.D.

Glorious Is Thy Name Most Holy 677

Do not forget to do good and to share with others. Hebrews 13:16

1. Glo - rious is Thy name, Most Ho - ly, God and Fa - ther of us all;
2. For our world of need and an - guish We would lift to Thee our prayer.
3. In the midst of time we jour - ney, From Thy hand comes each new day;

We Thy ser - vants bow be - fore Thee, Strive to an - swer ev - ery call.
Faith - ful stew - ards of Thy boun - ty May we with our broth - ers share.
We would use it in Thy ser - vice, Hum - bly, wise - ly, while we may.

Thou with life's great good hast blest us, Cared for us from ear - liest years;
In the name of Christ our Sav - ior, Who re - deems and sets us free,
So to Thee, Lord and Cre - a - tor, Praise and hon - or we ac - cord,

Un - to Thee our thanks we ren - der; Thy deep love o'er - comes all fears.
Gifts we bring of heart and trea - sure, That our lives may wor - thier be.
Thine the earth and Thine the heav - ens, Thro' all the E - ter - nal Word.

TEXT: Ruth Elliott
MUSIC: William Moore

HOLY MANNA
8.7.8.7.D.

678 We Are an Offering

Offer your bodies as living sacrifices, holy and pleasing to God. Romans 12:1

We lift our voic-es, we lift our hands, We lift our lives up to
voic-es; Lord, use our hands; Lord, use our lives, they are

You; We are an of-fer-ing. Lord, use our
Yours; We are an of-fer-ing. All that we have,

all that we are, All that we hope to be, we give to You, we

give to You. We lift our voic-es, we lift our hands, We lift our

lives up to You; We are an of-fer-ing, we are an of-fer-ing.

TEXT: Dwight Liles
MUSIC: Dwight Liles

OFFERING
Irregular meter

YOUR REASONABLE SERVICE 679

from Romans 12:1-5, 9-18, 21 (NKJV)

SOLO 1

I beseech you therefore, brethren, by the mercies of God,
that you present your bodies a living sacrifice,
holy, acceptable to God, which is your reasonable service.

EVERYONE

**And do not be conformed to this world,
but be transformed by the renewing of your mind,
that you may prove what is that good and acceptable
and perfect will of God.**

SOLO 2

For I say, through the grace given to me, to everyone who is among you,
not to think of himself more highly than he ought to think,
but to think soberly, as God has dealt to each one a measure of faith.

EVERYONE

**For as we have many members in one body,
but all the members do not have the same function,
so we, being many, are one body in Christ,
and individually members of one another.**

SOLO 1

Let love be without hypocrisy.
Abhor what is evil.
Cling to what is good.

MEN

**Be kindly affectionate to one another with brotherly love,
in honor giving preference to one another;**

SOLO 2

Not lagging in diligence, fervent in spirit, serving the Lord;

WOMEN

**Rejoicing in hope, patient in tribulation,
continuing steadfastly in prayer;
distributing to the needs of the saints, given to hospitality.**

SOLO 1

Bless those who persecute you; bless and do not curse.
Rejoice with those who rejoice, and weep with those who weep.

EVERYONE

**Be of the same mind toward one another.
Do not set your mind on high things,
but associate with the humble.
Do not be wise in your own opinion.**

SOLO 2

Repay no one evil for evil.
Have regard for good things in the sight of all men.

EVERYONE

**If it is possible, as much as depends on you,
live peaceably with all men.
And do not be overcome by evil,
but overcome evil with good.**

SOLO 1

I beseech you therefore, brethren, by the mercies of God,
that you present your bodies a living sacrifice,
holy, acceptable to God, which is your reasonable service.

680 All the Way My Savior Leads Me

Our God will be our guide even to the end. Psalm 48:14

1. All the way my Sav-ior leads me; What have I to ask be - side?
2. All the way my Sav-ior leads me, Cheers each wind - ing path I tread,
3. All the way my Sav-ior leads me; O the full - ness of His love!

Can I doubt His ten-der mer - cy, Who thro' life has been my Guide?
Gives me grace for ev-ery tri - al, Feeds me with the liv - ing bread.
Per - fect rest to me is prom-ised In my Fa - ther's house a - bove.

Heav'n-ly peace, di - vin-est com - fort, Here by faith in Him to dwell!
Tho' my wea - ry steps may fal - ter, And my soul a - thirst may be,
When my spir - it, clothed, im-mor - tal, Wings its flight to realms of day,

For I know, what-e'er be - fall me, Je - sus do - eth all things well;
Gush-ing from the Rock be - fore me, Lo! a spring of joy I see;
This my song thro' end-less a - ges: "Je - sus led me all the way."

TEXT: Fanny J. Crosby
MUSIC: Robert Lowry

ALL THE WAY
8.7.8.7.D.

For I know, what-e'er be-fall me, Je-sus do-eth all things well.
Gush-ing from the Rock be-fore me, Lo! a spring of joy I see.
This my song thro' end-less a-ges: "Je-sus led me all the way."

In His Time 681

He has made everything beautiful in its time. Ecclesiastes 3:11

1. In His time, (in His time,) In His time; (in His time;)
2. In Your time, (in Your time,) In Your time; (in Your time;)

He makes all things beau-ti-ful in His time. (in His time.)
You make all things beau-ti-ful in Your time. (in Your time.)

Lord, please show me ev-ery day As You're teach-ing me Your way
Lord, my life to You I bring; May each song I have to sing

That You do just what You say In Your time. (in Your time.)
Be to You a love-ly thing In Your time. (in Your time.)

TEXT: Diane Ball
MUSIC: Diane Ball

IN HIS TIME
Irregular meter

682 Guide Me, O Thou Great Jehovah

The Lord will guide you always; He will satisfy your needs. Isaiah 58:11

1. Guide me, O Thou great Je - ho - vah, Pil - grim through this bar - ren land; I am weak, but Thou art might - y; Hold me with Thy pow'r - ful hand; Bread of Heav - en, Bread of Heav - en, Feed me till I want no more, Feed me till I want no more.

2. O - pen now the crys - tal foun - tain, Whence the heal - ing stream doth flow; Let the fire and cloud - y pil - lar Lead me all my jour - ney through; Strong De - liv - 'rer, strong De - liv - 'rer, Be Thou still my strength and shield, Be Thou still my strength and shield.

3. When I tread the verge of Jor - dan, Bid my anx - ious fears sub - side; Bear me through the swell - ing cur - rent, Land me safe on Ca - naan's side; Songs of prais - es, songs of prais - es I will ev - er give to Thee, I will ev - er give to Thee.

TEXT: William Williams; translated by Peter Williams and William Williams
MUSIC: John Hughes; Last stanza setting and Choral ending by Marty Parks

CWM RHONDDA
8.7.8.7.8.7.7.

Optional last stanza setting

a tempo
Unison

rit.

3. When I tread the

verge of Jor - dan, Bid my anx - ious fears sub - side;

Bear me through the swell - ing cur - rent, Land me safe on

Ca - naan's side; Songs of prais - es, songs of prais - es I will

ev - er give to Thee, I will ev - er give to Thee.

Optional choral ending
Sing harmony

Guide me, O Thou great Je - ho - vah, Guide me, Je - ho - vah! A - men.

683 The King of Love My Shepherd Is

The Lord is my shepherd, I shall not be in want. Psalm 23:1

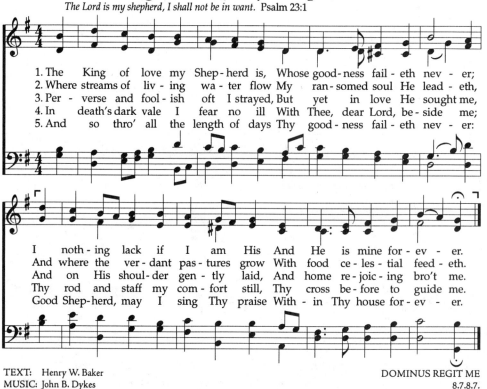

1. The King of love my Shep-herd is, Whose good-ness fail-eth nev - er;
2. Where streams of liv - ing wa - ter flow My ran-somed soul He lead - eth,
3. Per - verse and fool - ish oft I strayed, But yet in love He sought me,
4. In death's dark vale I fear no ill With Thee, dear Lord, be - side me;
5. And so thro' all the length of days Thy good - ness fail - eth nev - er:

I noth - ing lack if I am His And He is mine for - ev - er.
And where the ver - dant pas - tures grow With food ce - les - tial feed - eth.
And on His shoul - der gen - tly laid, And home re - joic - ing bro't me.
Thy rod and staff my com - fort still, Thy cross be - fore to guide me.
Good Shep-herd, may I sing Thy praise With - in Thy house for - ev - er.

TEXT: Henry W. Baker
MUSIC: John B. Dykes

DOMINUS REGIT ME
8.7.8.7.

684 Precious Lord, Take My Hand

I am the Lord, your God, who takes hold of your right hand. Isaiah 41:13

1. Pre - cious Lord, take my hand, Lead me on, help me stand. I am
2. When my way grows drear, Pre - cious Lord, lin - ger near— When my

tired, I am weak, I am worn. Thro' the storm, thro' the night, Lead me
life is al - most gone. Hear my cry, hear my call, Hold my

TEXT: Thomas A. Dorsey
MUSIC: George N. Allen; arranged by Thomas A. Dorsey

PRECIOUS LORD
6.6.9.D.

on to the light. Take my hand, pre-cious Lord; lead me home.
hand lest I fall. Take my hand, pre-cious Lord; lead me home.

Footsteps of Jesus 685

They left everything and followed Him. Luke 5:11

1. Sweet-ly, Lord, have we heard Thee call-ing, "Come, fol-low Me!"
2. Tho' they lead o'er the cold, dark moun-tains, Seek-ing His sheep,
3. If they lead thro' the tem-ple ho-ly, Preach-ing the Word,
4. Then at last, when on high He sees us, Our jour-ney done,

And we see where Thy foot-prints fall-ing, Lead us to Thee.
Or a-long by *Si-lo-am's foun-tains, Help-ing the weak.
Or in homes of the poor and low-ly, Serv-ing the Lord.
We will rest where the steps of Je-sus End at His throne.

Refrain

Foot-prints of Je-sus that make the path-way glow;

We will fol-low the steps of Je-sus wher-e'er they go.

John 9:1-11

TEXT: Mary B. C. Slade
MUSIC: Asa B. Everett

FOOTSTEPS
9.4.9.4. with Refrain

686 O God, Our Help in Ages Past

Lord, You have been our dwelling place throughout all generations. Psalm 90:1

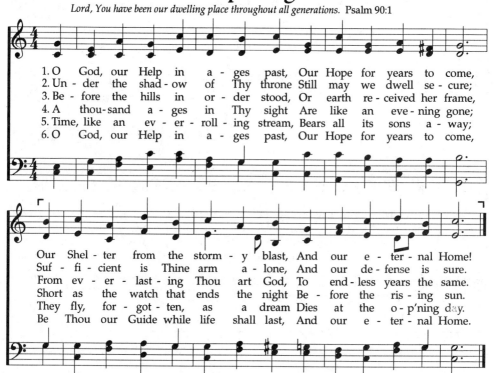

1. O God, our Help in a - ges past, Our Hope for years to come,
2. Un - der the shad - ow of Thy throne Still may we dwell se - cure;
3. Be - fore the hills in or - der stood, Or earth re - ceived her frame,
4. A thou-sand a - ges in Thy sight Are like an eve - ning gone;
5. Time, like an ev - er - roll - ing stream, Bears all its sons a - way;
6. O God, our Help in a - ges past, Our Hope for years to come,

Our Shel - ter from the storm - y blast, And our e - ter - nal Home!
Suf - fi - cient is Thine arm a - lone, And our de - fense is sure.
From ev - er - last - ing Thou art God, To end - less years the same.
Short as the watch that ends the night Be - fore the ris - ing sun.
They fly, for - got - ten, as a dream Dies at the o - p'ning day.
Be Thou our Guide while life shall last, And our e - ter - nal Home.

TEXT: Isaac Watts; based on Psalm 90
MUSIC: William Croft

ST. ANNE
C.M.

687

FOLLOW HIM
A Worship Sequence

Savior, like a Shepherd Lead Us; stanzas 1,2,4
Lead Me, Lord
Suggested stanzas have been marked with an arrow: ➤

WORSHIP LEADER

My sheep hear My voice, and I know them,
and they follow Me.
And I give them eternal life, and they shall never perish;
neither shall anyone snatch them out of My hand.
My Father, who has given them to Me, is greater than all;
and no one is able to snatch them out of My Father's hand.

from John 10:27-29 (NKJV)

Optional introduction to "Savior, like a Shepherd Lead Us"

mf

Savior, like a Shepherd Lead Us 688

He calls His own sheep by name and leads them out. John 10:3

> 1. Sav - ior, like a shep-herd lead us, Much we need Thy ten-der care;
> 2. We are Thine, do Thou be - friend us, Be the Guard-ian of our way;
> 3. Thou hast prom-ised to re - ceive us, Poor and sin-ful tho' we be;
> 4. Ear - ly let us seek Thy fa - vor; Ear - ly let us do Thy will;

In Thy pleas-ant pas-tures feed us, For our use Thy folds pre-pare:
Keep Thy flock, from sin de - fend us, Seek us when we go a - stray:
Thou hast mer - cy to re - lieve us, Grace to cleanse and pow'r to free:
Bless - ed Lord and on - ly Sav - ior, With Thy love our be-ings fill:

Bless - ed Je - sus, bless - ed Je - sus, Thou hast bought us, Thine we are;
Bless - ed Je - sus, bless - ed Je - sus, Hear, O hear us when we pray;
Bless - ed Je - sus, bless - ed Je - sus, Ear - ly let us turn to Thee;
Bless - ed Je - sus, bless - ed Je - sus, Thou hast loved us, love us still;

Bless - ed Je - sus, bless - ed Je - sus, Thou hast bought us, Thine we are.
Bless - ed Je - sus, bless - ed Je - sus, Hear, O hear us when we pray.
Bless - ed Je - sus, bless - ed Je - sus, Ear - ly let us turn to Thee.
Bless - ed Je - sus, bless - ed Je - sus, Thou hast loved us, love us still.

Optional segue to "Lead Me, Lord." No transition
is needed, but tempo will be faster. ♩ = ca. 120

TEXT: *Hymns for the Young,* 1836; attributed to Dorothy A. Thrupp
MUSIC: William B. Bradbury

BRADBURY
8.7.8.7.D.

689 Lead Me, Lord

My sheep listen to My voice; I know them, and they follow Me. John 10:27

Lead me, Lord, I will fol-low; Lead me, Lord, I will go. You have called me— I will an-swer; Lead me, Lord, I will go.

Optional repeat setting

Lead me, Lord, I will fol-low; Lead me, Lord, I will go. You have called me— I will an-swer; Lead me, Lord, I will go, I will go.

TEXT: Wayne and Elizabeth Goodine; based on John 10:27
MUSIC: Wayne and Elizabeth Goodine

GOODINE
Irregular meter

The end of FOLLOW HIM - A Worship Sequence

He Leadeth Me 690

In Your unfailing love You will lead the people You have redeemed. Exodus 15:13

1. He lead-eth me! O bless-ed thought! O words with heav'n-ly com-fort fraught!
2. Lord, I would clasp Thy hand in mine, Nor ev-er mur-mur nor re-pine,
3. And when my task on earth is done, When, by Thy grace, the vic-t'ry's won,

What-e'er I do, wher-e'er I be, Still 'tis God's hand that lead-eth me.
Con-tent, what-ev-er lot I see, Since 'tis Thy hand that lead-eth me.
E'en death's cold wave I will not flee, Since God thro' Jor-dan lead-eth me.

Refrain

He lead-eth me, He lead-eth me; By His own hand He lead-eth me:

His faith-ful fol-l'wer I would be, For by His hand He lead-eth me.

TEXT: Joseph Gilmore
MUSIC: William B. Bradbury

HE LEADETH ME
L.M. with Refrain

Optional extended or choral ending

His faith-ful fol-l'wer I would be, For by His hand He lead-eth me.

691 Surely Goodness and Mercy

Surely goodness and love will follow me all the days of my life. Psalm 23:6

1. A pil-grim was I, and a-wan-d'ring— In the cold night of sin I did roam When Je-sus the kind Shep-herd found me— And now I am on my way home.
2. He re-stor-eth my soul when I'm wea-ry; He giv-eth me strength day by day. He leads me be-side the still wa-ters; He guards me each step of the way.
3. When I walk thro' the dark, lone-some val-ley, My Sav-ior will walk with me there; And safe-ly His great hand will lead me To the man-sions He's gone to pre-pare.

Refrain

Sure-ly good-ness and mer-cy shall fol-low me All the days, all the days of my life; Sure-ly good-ness and mer-cy shall

TEXT: John W. Peterson and Alfred B. Smith; based on Psalm 23
MUSIC: John W. Peterson and Alfred B. Smith

SURELY GOODNESS AND MERCY
Irregular meter

692 God Will Take Care of You

The Lord is good, a refuge in times of trouble. He cares for those who trust in Him. Nahum 1:7

1. Be not dis-mayed what-e'er be-tide; God will take care of you.
2. Thro' days of toil when heart doth fail; God will take care of you.
3. All you may need He will pro-vide; God will take care of you.
4. No mat-ter what may be the test, God will take care of you.

Be-neath His wings of love a-bide; God will take care of you.
When dan-gers fierce your path as-sail; God will take care of you.
Noth-ing you ask will be de-nied; God will take care of you.
Lean, wea-ry one, up-on His breast; God will take care of you.

Refrain

God will take care of you, Thro' ev-ery day, o'er all the way.

He will take care of you; God will take care of you.

TEXT: Civilla D. Martin
MUSIC: W. Stillman Martin

GOD CARES
C.M. with Refrain

A Shelter in the Time of Storm 693

He is my mighty rock, my refuge. Psalm 62:7

1. The Lord's our Rock; in Him we hide, A Shel-ter in the time of storm;
2. A Shade by day, De - fense by night, A Shel-ter in the time of storm;
3. The rag - ing storms may round us beat, A Shel-ter in the time of storm;
4. O Rock di - vine, O Ref - uge dear, A Shel-ter in the time of storm;

Se - cure what-ev - er ill be-tide, A Shel-ter in the time of storm.
No fears a - larm, no foes af-fright, A Shel-ter in the time of storm.
We'll nev - er leave our safe re-treat, A Shel-ter in the time of storm.
Be Thou our Help - er ev - er near, A Shel-ter in the time of storm.

Refrain

O Je-sus is a Rock in a wea-ry land, A wea-ry land, a wea-ry land;

O Je-sus is a Rock in a wea-ry land– A Shel-ter in the time of storm.

TEXT: Vernon J. Charlesworth; adapted by Ira D. Sankey
MUSIC: Ira D. Sankey

SHELTER
L.M. with Refrain

694 The Lord's My Shepherd, I'll Not Want

The Lord is my shepherd, I shall not be in want. Psalm 23:1

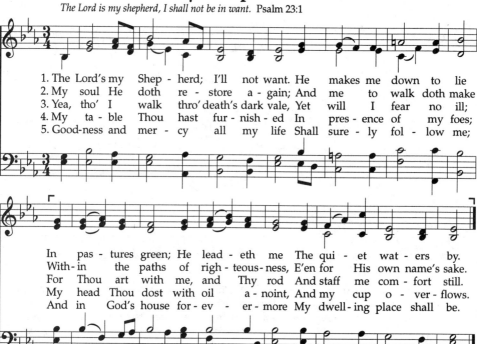

1. The Lord's my Shep - herd; I'll not want. He makes me down to lie
2. My soul He doth re - store a - gain; And me to walk doth make
3. Yea, tho' I walk thro' death's dark vale, Yet will I fear no ill;
4. My ta - ble Thou hast fur - nish - ed In pres - ence of my foes;
5. Good - ness and mer - cy all my life Shall sure - ly fol - low me;

In pas - tures green; He lead - eth me The qui - et wat - ers by.
With - in the paths of righ - teous - ness, E'en for His own name's sake.
For Thou art with me, and Thy rod And staff me com - fort still.
My head Thou dost with oil a - noint, And my cup o - ver - flows.
And in God's house for - ev - er - more My dwell - ing place shall be.

Optional segue to "Lead Me, Lord."
No transition is needed.

TEXT: *Scottish Psalter, 1650;* William Whittingham and others; based on Psalm 23   CRIMOND
MUSIC: Jessie S. Irvine; arranged by David Grant   C.M.

695 Lead Me, Lord

Lead me, O Lord, in Your righteousness–make straight Your way before me. Psalm 5:8

Lead me, Lord, lead me in Your righ - teous - ness;

Make Your way plain be - fore my face. face. Lead me, Lord.

TEXT: Based on Psalm 5:8   LEAD ME, LORD
MUSIC: Samuel S. Wesley   Irregular meter

God Leads Us Along 696

When you pass through the waters, I will be with you. Isaiah 43:2

1. In shad - y, green pas - tures, so rich and so sweet, God leads His dear
2. Some - times on the mount where the sun shines so bright, God leads His dear
3. Though sor - rows be - fall us and Sa - tan op - pose, God leads His dear

chil - dren a - long. Where the wa - ter's cool flow bathes the wea - ry one's feet,
chil - dren a - long. Some - times in the val - ley, in dark - est of night,
chil - dren a - long. Through grace we can con - quer, de - feat all our foes;

God leads His dear chil - dren a - long.
God leads His dear chil - dren a - long.
God leads His dear chil - dren a - long.

Refrain

Some thro' the wa - ters, some thro' the flood, Some thro' the fire, but all thro' the blood. Some thro' great sor - row, but God gives a song In the night sea - son and all the day long.

TEXT: G. A. Young
MUSIC: G. A. Young

GOD LEADS US
11.8.11.8. with Refrain

697 The Way of the Cross Leads Home

There is one God and one mediator between God and human beings: Christ Jesus. 1 Timothy 2:5

1. I must needs go home by the way of the cross; There's no oth-er way but this. I shall ne'er get sight of the Gates of Light If the way of the cross I miss.

2. I must needs go on in the blood-sprin-kled way, The path that the Sav-ior trod, If I ev-er climb to the heights sub-lime, Where the soul is at home with God.

3. Then I bid fare-well to the way of the world, To walk in it nev-er-more; For my Lord says, "Come," and I seek my home Where He waits at the o-pen door.

Refrain

The way of the cross leads home. The way of the cross leads home. It is sweet to know, as I on-ward go, The way of the cross leads home.

TEXT: Jessie B. Pounds
MUSIC: Charles H. Gabriel

WAY OF THE CROSS
Irregular meter

REFUGE UNDER HIS WINGS 698

from Hebrews 10:22; 2 Timothy 2:1; 1:12; Hebrews 4:16;
1 John 5:14-15; 4:16; Psalm 91:1-4; 84:11 (NIV)

WORSHIP LEADER
Let us draw near to God with a sincere heart in full assurance of faith.
Be strong in the grace that is in Christ Jesus.

EVERYONE
I know whom I have believed, and am convinced that He is able
to guard what I have entrusted to Him for that day.

WORSHIP LEADER
Let us then approach the throne of grace with confidence,
so that we may receive mercy
and find grace to help us in our time of need.

EVERYONE
This is the confidence we have in approaching God;
if we ask anything according to His will, He hears us.

WORSHIP LEADER
And if we know that He hears us — whatever we ask —
we know that we have what we asked of Him.
So we know and rely on the love God has for us.

EVERYONE
He who dwells in the shelter of the Most High
will rest in the shadow of the Almighty.

WORSHIP LEADER
I will say of the Lord,

EVERYONE
"He is my refuge and my fortress,
my God, in whom I trust."

WORSHIP LEADER
Surely He will save you from the fowler's snare and from the deadly pestilence.
He will cover you with His feathers, and under His wings you will find refuge.

EVERYONE
For the Lord God is a sun and shield; the Lord bestows favor and honor;
no good thing does He withhold from those whose walk is blameless.

MY HELP COMES FROM THE LORD 699

from Psalm 121 (NASB)

WORSHIP LEADER or SOLO DRAMATIST

I will lift up my eyes to the mountains;
From whence shall my help come?
My help comes from the Lord, who made heaven and earth.
He will not allow your foot to slip;
He who keeps you will not slumber.
Behold, He who keeps Israel will neither slumber nor sleep.
The Lord is your keeper;
The Lord is your shade on your right hand.
The sun will not smite you by day, nor the moon by night.
The Lord will protect you from all evil;
He will keep your soul.
The Lord will guard your going out and your coming in
from this time forth and for ever.

700 You Are My Hiding Place

You are my hiding place; You will protect me from trouble. Psalm 32:7

TEXT: Michael Ledner
MUSIC: Michael Ledner

HIDING PLACE
Irregular meter

God Is My Refuge 701

God is our refuge and strength, an ever-present help in trouble. Psalm 46:1

God is my ref-uge and God is my strength; A ver-y pres-ent help in trou - ble.

God is my ref-uge and God is my strength; A ver-y pres-ent help in trou - ble.

There-fore I will not fear; tho' the earth be re-moved, And

tho' the moun-tains be car-ried in-to the midst of the

1 D.C. 2 *Optional choral ending*

sea.   sea. God is my ref-uge and God is my strength.

TEXT: Judy Horner Montemayor
MUSIC: Judy Horner Montemayor

GOD IS MY REFUGE
Irregular meter

702 Fill My Cup, Lord

Those who drink the water I give them will never thirst. John 4:14

Fill my cup, Lord— I lift it up, Lord! Come and quench this thirst-ing of my soul. Bread of heav-en, feed me till I want no more; Fill my cup, fill it up and make me whole!

TEXT: Richard Blanchard
MUSIC: Richard Blanchard

FILL MY CUP
Irregular meter

703 GOD'S LOVE AND STRENGTH

A Worship Sequence

God Will Make a Way
It Is Well with My Soul; stanzas 1,3,4
Suggested stanzas have been marked with an arrow: ➤

WORSHIP LEADER
I sought the Lord, and He answered me;
He delivered me from all my fears.
Those who look to Him are radiant;
Their faces are never covered with shame.
This poor man called out, and the Lord heard him;
He saved him out of all his troubles.
The angel of the Lord encamps around those who fear Him,
And He delivers them.

EVERYONE
Taste and see that the Lord is good;
Blessed is the man who takes refuge in Him.

from Psalm 34:4-8 (NIV)

*Optional introduction to
"God Will Make a Way"*

God Will Make a Way 704

I am making a way in the desert and streams in the wasteland. Isaiah 43:19

God will make a way where there seems to be no way. He works in ways we

can-not see; He will make a way for me. He will be my guide,

hold me close-ly to His side. With love and strength for each new day;

He will make a way, He will make a way.

*Optional transition to
"It Is Well with My Soul"*

TEXT: Don Moen
MUSIC: Don Moen

HE WILL MAKE A WAY
Irregular meter

705 It Is Well with My Soul

He ransoms me unharmed from the battle waged against me. Psalm 55:18

➤ 1. When peace like a riv-er at-tend-eth my way, When sor-rows like
2. Tho' Sa-tan should buf-fet, tho' tri-als should come, Let this blest as-
➤ 3. My sin— O, the bliss of this glo-ri-ous tho't— My sin— not in
➤ 4. And, Lord, haste the day when the faith shall be sight, The clouds be rolled

sea bil-lows roll; What-ev-er my lot, Thou hast taught me to say,
sur-ance con-trol, That Christ hath re-gard-ed my help-less es-tate,
part, but the whole, Is nailed to the cross, and I bear it no more,
back as a scroll, The trump shall re-sound and the Lord shall de-scend,

Refrain

"It is well, it is well with my soul."
And hath shed His own blood for my soul.
Praise the Lord, praise the Lord, O my soul!
"E-ven so"– it is well with my soul.

It is well with my
It is well

soul, It is well, it is well with my soul.
with my soul,

TEXT: Horatio G. Spafford
MUSIC: Philip P. Bliss

VILLE DU HAVRE
11.8.11.9. with Refrain

Optional repeat refrain setting

mf With confidence

It is well   It is well   with my soul,   with my soul,

cresc.

2nd time *f*

It is   well,   it is   well   with my soul.   It is   soul.

2nd time *f*

The end of GOD'S LOVE AND STRENGTH - A Worship Sequence

Thy Loving Kindness 706

Because Your love is better than life, my lips will glorify You. Psalm 63:3

1. Thy lov-ing kind-ness   is bet-ter than   life,   Thy lov-ing
2. I lift my hands, Lord,   un-to   Thy name,   I   lift my

kind-ness   is bet-ter than life.   My lips shall praise Thee,   thus will I
hands, Lord,   un-to   Thy name.   My lips shall praise Thee,   thus will I

bless Thee: I will   lift   up   my hands un-to   Thy   name.
bless Thee: I will   lift   up   my hands un-to   Thy   name.

TEXT: Hugh Mitchell; based on Psalm 63:3-4
MUSIC: Hugh Mitchell

THY LOVING KINDNESS
10.10.10.10.

707 He Giveth More Grace

He gives strength to the weary and increases the power of the weak. Isaiah 40:29

1. He giv - eth more grace when the bur-dens grow great-er; He send - eth more
2. When we have ex - haust - ed our store of en - dur-ance, When our strength has

strength when the la - bors in-crease. To add - ed af - flic - tion He
failed ere the day is half done, When we reach the end of our

add - eth His mer-cy; To mul - ti - plied tri - als, His mul - ti - plied peace.
hoard-ed re - sourc-es, Our Fa - ther's full giv - ing is on - ly be - gun.

Refrain

His love has no lim - it; His grace has no mea-sure. His pow'r has no

bound - a - ry known un - to men. For out of His in - fi - nite

TEXT: Annie Johnson Flint
MUSIC: Hubert Mitchell

HE GIVETH MORE GRACE
Irregular meter

rich - es in Je - sus, He giv - eth, and giv - eth, and giv - eth a - gain!

Optional segue to "Behold, What Manner of Love." No transition is needed.

Behold, What Manner of Love 708

How great is the love the Father has lavished on us. 1 John 3:1

Be - hold, what man - ner of love the Fa - ther has giv - en un - to us,

Be - hold, what man - ner of love the Fa - ther has giv - en un - to us

That we should be called the sons of God,

That we should be called the sons of God.

May be sung as a 2-part canon. Sing in unison.

TEXT: Patricia Van Tine; based on 1 John 3:1
MUSIC: Patricia Van Tine

MANNER OF LOVE
Irregular meter

709 A Shield About Me

You are a shield around me, O Lord. Psalm 3:3

Thou, O Lord, are a shield a-bout me; You're my glo - ry, You're the lift - er of my head.

head.

Hal - le - lu - jah!

Hal - le - lu - jah! Hal - le - lu - jah! You're the

lift - er of my head. head.

TEXT: Donn Thomas; based on Psalm 3:3
MUSIC: Donn Thomas and Charles Williams

A SHIELD ABOUT ME
Irregular meter

Jesus, Lover of My Soul 710

As the Father has loved Me, so have I loved you. John 15:9

1. Je - sus, lov - er of my soul, Let me to Thy bo - som fly,
2. Oth - er ref - uge have I none; Hangs my help - less soul on Thee;
3. Thou, O Christ, art all I want; More than all in Thee I find:
4. Plen - teous grace with Thee is found, Grace to cov - er all my sin;

While the near - er wa - ters roll, While the tem - pest still is high:
Leave, O leave me not a - lone, Still sup - port and com - fort me:
Raise the fall - en, cheer the faint, Heal the sick and lead the blind:
Let the heal - ing streams a - bound; Make and keep me pure with - in:

Hide me, O my Sav - ior, hide, Till the storm of life is past;
All my trust on Thee is stayed, All my help from Thee I bring;
Just and ho - ly is Thy name, I am all un - righ - teous - ness;
Thou of life the foun - tain art, Free - ly let me take of Thee;

Safe in - to the ha - ven guide; O re - ceive my soul at last.
Cov - er my de - fense - less head With the shad - ow of Thy wing.
False and full of sin I am, Thou art full of truth and grace.
Spring Thou up with - in my heart, Rise to all e - ter - ni - ty.

TEXT: Charles Wesley
MUSIC: Simeon B. Marsh

MARTYN
7.7.7.7.D.

711 Rise and Be Healed

He heals the brokenhearted and binds up their wounds. Psalm 147:3

1. Have fear and doubt come a-gainst your mind? Has your faith been
2. If by faith you reach out to Him, He will meet your

sore - ly tried? Lift up your eyes— here com-eth your help!
ev - ery need; He will re-spond to the cry of your heart;

It is Je - sus— for you He has died!
He will touch you and set you free.

Refrain

Rise and be healed in the name of Je - sus— Let faith a-rise in your soul! Rise and be healed in the name of Je-sus— He will cleanse and make you whole!

TEXT: Milton Bourgeois
MUSIC: Milton Bourgeois

RISE
Irregular meter

Be Still, My Soul 712

Be still, and know that I am God. Psalm 46:10

1. Be still, my soul! the Lord is on thy side; Bear pa-tient-ly the cross of grief or pain. Leave to thy God to or-der and pro-vide; In ev-ery change He faith-ful will re-main. Be still, my soul! thy best, thy heav'n-ly Friend Thro' thorn-y ways leads to a joy-ful end.

2. Be still, my soul! thy God doth un-der-take To guide the fu-ture as He has the past. Thy hope, thy con-fi-dence let noth-ing shake; All now mys-te-rious shall be bright at last. Be still, my soul! the waves and winds still know His voice who ruled them while He dwelt be-low.

3. Be still, my soul! the hour is has-t'ning on When we shall be for-ev-er with the Lord, When dis-ap-point-ment, grief, and fear are gone, Sor-row for-got, love's pur-est joys re-stored. Be still, my soul! when change and tears are past, All safe and bless-ed we shall meet at last.

TEXT: Katharina von Schlegel; translated by Jane L. Borthwick
MUSIC: Jean Sibelius
A lower setting may be found at No. 604

FINLANDIA
10.10.10.10.10.10.

713 Seek Ye First

Seek first His kingdom and His righteousness. Matthew 6:33

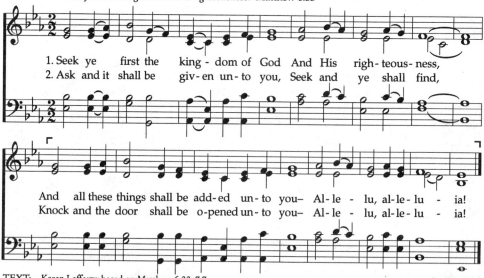

1. Seek ye first the king - dom of God And His righ - teous - ness,
2. Ask and it shall be giv - en un - to you, Seek and ye shall find,

And all these things shall be add - ed un - to you— Al - le - lu, al - le - lu - ia!
Knock and the door shall be o - pened un - to you— Al - le - lu, al - le - lu - ia!

TEXT: Karen Lafferty; based on Matthew 6:33; 7:7
MUSIC: Karen Lafferty

LAFFERTY
Irregular meter

714 GOD WILL PROVIDE

A Worship Sequence

He Is Jehovah; complete
Jehovah Jireh
Suggested stanzas have been marked with an arrow: ➤

WORSHIP LEADER
My God shall supply all your needs
according to His riches in glory.

from Philippians 4:19 (NKJV)

715 He Is Jehovah

The Lord Will Provide. "On the mountain of the Lord it will be provided." Genesis 22:14

Unison

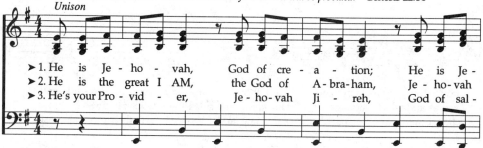

➤ 1. He is Je - ho - vah, God of cre - a - tion; He is Je -
➤ 2. He is the great I AM, the God of A - bra - ham, Je - ho - vah
➤ 3. He's your Pro - vid - er, Je - ho - vah Ji - reh, God of sal -

TEXT: Betty Jean Robinson
MUSIC: Betty Jean Robinson

HE IS JEHOVAH
Irregular meter

GOD WILL PROVIDE - A Worship Sequence

ho - vah,   Lord God Al - might - y,   The Balm of   Gil - e - ad,   the Rock of
Sha - lom,   The God of peace, I AM.   The God of   Is - ra - el,   the Ev - er -
va - tion,   God of Mes - si - ah.   The Son He sent to you,   He tes - ti -

Refrain

A - ges;   He is Je - ho - vah, the God that heal - eth thee.
last - ing One;   He is Je - ho - vah, the God that heal - eth thee.   Sing hal - le -
fied of Him;   He is Je - ho - vah, the God that heal - eth thee.

lu - jah, sing hal - le - lu - jah,   Sing hal - le - lu - jah, sing   hal - le - lu - jah!

He is Je - ho - vah, Lord God Al - might - y;   He is Je - ho - vah, the God that heal - eth

Optional transition to "Jehovah Jireh"

thee.   a little faster

716 Jehovah Jireh

My God will meet all your needs according to His glorious riches in Christ Jesus. Philippians 4:19

Unison

Je-ho-vah Ji-reh, my Pro-vid-er, His grace is suf-fi-cient for

1 me, for me, for me. *2* me. My God shall sup-ply all my

needs ac-cord-ing to His rich-es in glo-ry.

He gives His an-gels charge o-ver me; Je-ho-vah Ji-reh cares for

me, for me, for me; Je-ho-vah Ji-reh cares for me.

TEXT: Merla Watson
MUSIC: Merla Watson

JEHOVAH JIREH
Irregular meter

Optional extended or choral ending
Unison

Je - ho-vah Ji - reh cares for me, for me!

The end of GOD WILL PROVIDE - A Worship Sequence

Optional segue to "I Am the God That Healeth Thee." No transition is needed; but a much slower tempo is necessary.

I Am the God That Healeth Thee 717

I am the Lord, who heals you. Exodus 15:26

Unison

1. I am the God that heal-eth thee, I am the Lord, your
2. You are the God that heal-eth me, You are the Lord, my

heal - er. I sent My Word and healed your dis-ease,
heal - er. You sent Your Word and healed my dis-ease,

1
I am the Lord, your heal - er.
You are the Lord, my

2
heal - er.

slower
You are the Lord, my heal - er.

TEXT: Don Moen
MUSIC: Don Moen

HEALETH THEE
Irregular meter

718 Day by Day

My grace is sufficient for you, for My power is made perfect in weakness. 2 Corinthians 12:9

1. Day by day and with each pass-ing mo-ment, Strength I
2. Ev - ery day the Lord Him-self is near me With a
3. Help me then in ev - ery trib - u - la - tion So to

find to meet my tri - als here. Trust-ing in my Fa - ther's
spe - cial mer - cy for each hour. All my cares He fain would
trust Your prom - is - es, O Lord, That I lose not faith's sweet

wise be - stow - ment, I've no cause for wor - ry or for fear.
bear and cheer me, He whose name is Coun - sel - or and Pow'r.
con - so - la - tion Of - fered me with - in Your ho - ly Word.

He whose heart is kind be - yond all mea - sure Gives un -
The pro - tec - tion of His child and trea - sure Is a
Help me, Lord, when toil and trou - ble meet - ing, E'er to

to each day what He deems best, Lov-ing - ly its part of
charge that on Him-self He laid. "As your days, your strength shall
take, as from a Fa-ther's hand, One by one, the days, the

TEXT: Carolina Sandell Berg; translated by Andrew L. Skoog
MUSIC: Oscar Ahnfelt; Choral ending by Ken Barker

BLOTT EN DAG
Irregular meter

pain and plea - sure, Min - gling toil with peace and rest.
be in mea - sure," This the pledge to me He made.
mo - ments fleet - ing, Till I reach the Prom - ised Land.

Optional choral ending
mp slower

Till I reach the Prom - ised Land, Prom - ised Land, Prom - ised Land.

mp

Children of the Heavenly Father 719

How great is the love the Father has lavished on us. 1 John 3:1

1. Chil - dren of the heav'n - ly Fa - ther Safe - ly in His bos - om gath - er;
2. God His own doth tend and nour - ish; In His ho - ly courts they flour - ish.
3. Nei - ther life nor death shall ev - er From the Lord His chil - dren sev - er;
4. Tho' He giv - eth or He tak - eth, God His chil - dren ne'er for - sak - eth;

Nest - ling bird nor star in heav - en Such a ref - uge e'er was giv - en.
From all e - vil things He spares them; In His might - y arms He bears them.
Un - to them His grace He show - eth, And their sor - rows all He know - eth.
His the lov - ing pur - pose sole - ly To pre - serve them pure and ho - ly.

TEXT: Carolina Sandell Berg; translated by Ernst W. Olson
MUSIC: Traditional Swedish melody

TRYGGARE KAN INGEN VARA
L.M.

720 Come, Every One Who Is Thirsty

Come, all you who are thirsty. Come, buy wine and milk without cost. Isaiah 55:1

1. Come, ev-ery one who is thirst-y in spir-it; Come, ev-ery
2. Child of the world, are you tired of your bond-age? Wea-ry of
3. Child of the King-dom, be filled with the Spir-it! Noth-ing but

one who is wea-ry and sad. Come to the foun-tain; there's
earth-joys, so false, so un-true? Thirst-ing for God and His
full-ness thy long-ing can meet. 'Tis the en-due-ment for

full-ness in Je-sus— All that you're long-ing for; Come and be glad.
full-ness of bless-ing? List to the prom-ise, a mes-sage for you.
life and for ser-vice. Thine is the prom-ise, so cer-tain, so sweet!

Refrain

"I will pour wa-ter on him that is thirst-y; I will pour

floods up-on the dry ground. O-pen your heart for the

TEXT: Lucy J. Rider
MUSIC: Lucy J. Rider; arranged by Lee Herrington

RIDER
11.10.11.10. with Refrain

gift I am bring-ing; While you are seek-ing Me I will be found."

Jesus Never Fails 721

Heaven and earth will pass away, but My words will never pass away. Matthew 24:35

1. Earth - ly friends may prove un - true, Doubts and fears as - sail;
2. Though the sky be dark and drear, Fierce and strong the gale,
3. In life's dark and bit - ter hour Love will still pre - vail.

One still loves and cares for you, One who will not fail.
Just re - mem - ber He is near, And He will not fail.
Trust His ev - er - last - ing pow'r; Je - sus will not fail.

Refrain

Je - sus nev - er fails, Je - sus nev - er fails.

Heav'n and earth may pass a - way, But Je - sus nev - er fails.

TEXT: Arthur A. Luther
MUSIC: Arthur A. Luther

JESUS NEVER FAILS
7.5.7.5. with Refrain

722 THE LORD WILL DELIVER YOU

from Psalm 34 (NIV)

WORSHIP LEADER
I will extol the Lord at all times;
His praise will always be on my lips.
My soul will boast in the Lord;
Let the afflicted hear and rejoice.

EVERYONE
Glorify the Lord with me; let us exalt His name together.

WOMEN
I sought the Lord, and He answered me;
He delivered me from all my fears.
Those who look to Him are radiant;
Their faces are never covered with shame.

MEN
This poor man called, and the Lord heard him;
He saved him out of all his troubles.

EVERYONE
The angel of the Lord encamps around those who fear Him,
And He delivers them.

WOMEN
Taste and see that the Lord is good;
Blessed is the man who takes refuge in Him.

WORSHIP LEADER
Fear the Lord, you His saints,
For those who fear Him lack nothing.

MEN
The lions may grow weak and hungry,
But those who seek the Lord lack no good thing.

WORSHIP LEADER
Come, my children, listen to me; I will teach you the fear of the Lord.
Whoever of you loves life and desires to see many good days,
keep your tongue from evil and your lips from speaking lies.
Turn from evil and do good; seek peace and pursue it.

WOMEN
The eyes of the Lord are on the righteous, and His ears are attentive to their cry.

EVERYONE
Glorify the Lord with me; let us exalt His name together.

WORSHIP LEADER
The righteous cry out, and the Lord hears them;
He delivers them from all their troubles.

EVERYONE
Glorify the Lord with me; let us exalt His name together.

MEN
The Lord is close to the brokenhearted, and saves those who are crushed in spirit.

EVERYONE
Glorify the Lord with me; let us exalt His name together.

WORSHIP LEADER
A righteous man may have many troubles,
But the Lord delivers him from them all.

EVERYONE
Glorify the Lord with me; let us exalt His name together.

Soldiers of Christ, Arise 723

Put on the full armor of God, so that you may be able to stand your ground. Ephesians 6:13

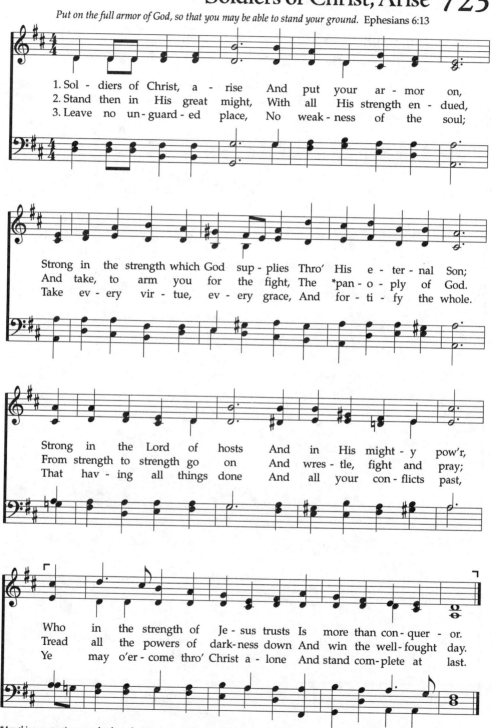

1. Sol - diers of Christ, a - rise And put your ar - mor on,
2. Stand then in His great might, With all His strength en - dued,
3. Leave no un - guard - ed place, No weak - ness of the soul;

Strong in the strength which God sup - plies Thro' His e - ter - nal Son;
And take, to arm you for the fight, The *pan - o - ply of God.
Take ev - ery vir - tue, ev - ery grace, And for - ti - fy the whole.

Strong in the Lord of hosts And in His might - y pow'r,
From strength to strength go on And wres - tle, fight and pray;
That hav - ing all things done And all your con - flicts past,

Who in the strength of Je - sus trusts Is more than con - quer - or.
Tread all the powers of dark - ness down And win the well - fought day.
Ye may o'er - come thro' Christ a - lone And stand com - plete at last.

Anything protecting completely or forming a magnificent covering; especially a full suit of armor; see Ephesians 6:10-18

TEXT: Charles Wesley
MUSIC: George J. Elvey

DIADEMATA
S.M.D.

724 Lead On, O King Eternal

Fight the good fight of the faith. 1 Timothy 6:12

1. Lead on, O King E-ter-nal, The day of march has come;
2. Lead on, O King E-ter-nal, Till sin's fierce war shall cease,
3. Lead on, O King E-ter-nal, We fol-low, not with fears;

Hence-forth in fields of con-quest Thy tents shall be our home.
And ho-li-ness shall whis-per The sweet a-men of peace;
For glad-ness breaks like morn-ing Wher-e'er Thy face ap-pears.

Thro' days of prep-a-ra-tion Thy grace has made us strong;
For not with swords' loud clash-ing, Nor roll of stir-ring drums,
Thy cross is lift-ed o'er us; We jour-ney in its light.

And now, O King E-ter-nal, We lift our bat-tle song.
With deeds of love and mer-cy The heav'n-ly king-dom comes.
The crown a-waits the con-quest; Lead on, O God of might.

TEXT: Ernest W. Shurtleff
MUSIC: Henry T. Smart; Last stanza setting by Bruce Greer

LANCASHIRE
7.6.7.6.D.

725 Mighty Warrior

The Lord is a warrior; the Lord is His name. Exodus 15:3

Unison

Might-y War - rior dressed for bat - tle,

ho- ly Lord of all is He. Com-mand-er- in- Chief,

bring us to at-ten - tion, Lead us in-to bat - tle to crush the en - e-my.

1. Sa- tan has no au-thor- i- ty here in this place; He has no au-thor- i- ty
2. Je- sus has all au-thor- i- ty here in this place; He has all au-thor- i- ty

here. For this hab- i- ta - tion was fash- ioned for the Lord's pres- ence;
here. For this hab- i- ta - tion was fash- ioned for the Lord's pres- ence;

TEXT: Debbye Graafsma
MUSIC: Debbye Graafsma

MIGHTY WARRIOR
Irregular meter

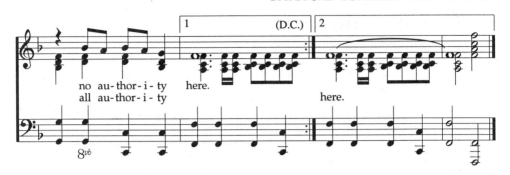

We Will Overcome 726

They overcame him by the blood of the Lamb. Revelation 12:11

TEXT: Carol Cymbala
MUSIC: Carol Cymbala

WE WILL OVERCOME
Irregular meter

727 Faith Is the Victory

This is the victory that has overcome the world, even our faith. 1 John 5:4

1. En-camped a-long the hills of light, Ye Chris-tian sol-diers, rise
2. His ban-ner o-ver us is love, Our sword the Word of God;
3. On ev-ery hand the foe we find Drawn up in dread ar-ray;
4. To him that o-ver-comes the foe White rai-ment shall be giv'n;

And press the bat-tle ere the night Shall veil the glow-ing skies.
We tread the road the saints a-bove With shouts of tri-umph trod.
Let tents of ease be left be-hind And on-ward to the fray.
Be-fore the an-gels he shall know His name con-fessed in heav'n.

A-gainst the foe in vales be-low Let all our strength be hurled;
By faith they, like a whirl-wind's breath, Swept on o'er ev-ery field;
Sal-va-tion's hel-met on each head, With truth all girt a-bout,
Then on-ward from the hills of light, Our hearts with love a-flame,

Faith is the vic-to-ry, we know, That o-ver-comes the world.
The faith by which they con-quered death Is still our shin-ing shield.
The earth shall trem-ble 'neath our tread And ech-o with our shout.
We'll van-quish all the hosts of night In Je-sus' con-qu'ring name.

TEXT: John H. Yates
MUSIC: Ira D. Sankey

SANKEY
C.M.D. with Refrain

Refrain

Faith is the vic-to-ry! Faith is the vic-to-ry!

O glo-ri-ous vic-to-ry That o-ver-comes the world!

Optional segue to "Am I a Soldier of the Cross?" No transition is needed.

Am I a Soldier of the Cross? 728

Endure hardship with us like a good soldier of Christ Jesus. 2 Timothy 2:3

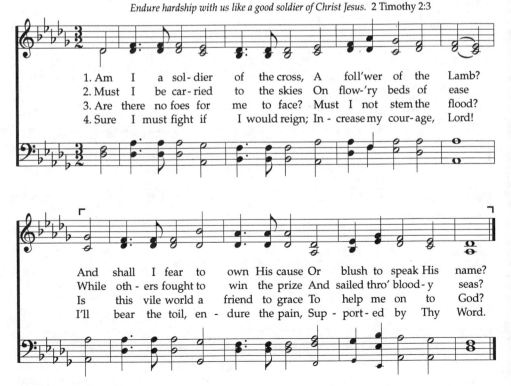

1. Am I a sol-dier of the cross, A foll'wer of the Lamb?
2. Must I be car-ried to the skies On flow-'ry beds of ease
3. Are there no foes for me to face? Must I not stem the flood?
4. Sure I must fight if I would reign; In-crease my cour-age, Lord!

And shall I fear to own His cause Or blush to speak His name?
While oth-ers fought to win the prize And sailed thro' blood-y seas?
Is this vile world a friend to grace To help me on to God?
I'll bear the toil, en-dure the pain, Sup-port-ed by Thy Word.

TEXT: Isaac Watts
MUSIC: Thomas A. Arne

ARLINGTON
C.M.

729 Victory Song (Through Our God)

With God we will gain the victory, and He will trample down our enemies. Psalm 60:12

Through our God we shall do val - iant - ly, It is He who will tread down our en - e-my; We'll sing and shout the vic - to-ry: Christ is King! For God has won the vic - to-ry and set His peo-ple free; His Word has slain the en - e-my. The

TEXT: Dale Garratt
MUSIC: Dale Garratt

VICTORY SONG
Irregular meter

730 Stand Up, Stand Up for Jesus

Stand firm in the faith; be courageous; be strong. 1 Corinthians 16:13

1. Stand up, stand up for Je - sus, Ye sol - diers of the cross; Lift
2. Stand up, stand up for Je - sus, The trum - pet call o - bey; Forth
3. Stand up, stand up for Je - sus, Stand in His strength a - lone; The
4. Stand up, stand up for Je - sus, The strife will not be long; This

high His roy - al ban - ner, It must not suf - fer loss. From vic - t'ry
to the might - y con - flict, In this His glo - rious day. Ye that are
arm of flesh will fail you, Ye dare not trust your own. Put on the
day the noise of bat - tle, The next, the vic - tor's song. To him who

un - to vic - t'ry His ar - my shall He lead, Till ev - ery foe is
men, now serve Him A - gainst un - num - bered foes; Let cour - age rise with
gos - pel ar - mor, Each piece put on with prayer; Where du - ty calls or
o - ver - com - eth A crown of life shall be; He, with the King of

van - quished And Christ is Lord in - deed.
dan - ger And strength to strength op - pose.
dan - ger, Be nev - er want - ing there.
Glo - ry, Shall reign e - ter - nal - ly.

Optional transition to
"Onward, Christian Soldiers"

TEXT: George Duffield, Jr.
MUSIC: George J. Webb

WEBB
7.6.7.6.D.

Onward, Christian Soldiers 731

Endure hardship with us like a good soldier of Christ Jesus. 2 Timothy 2:3

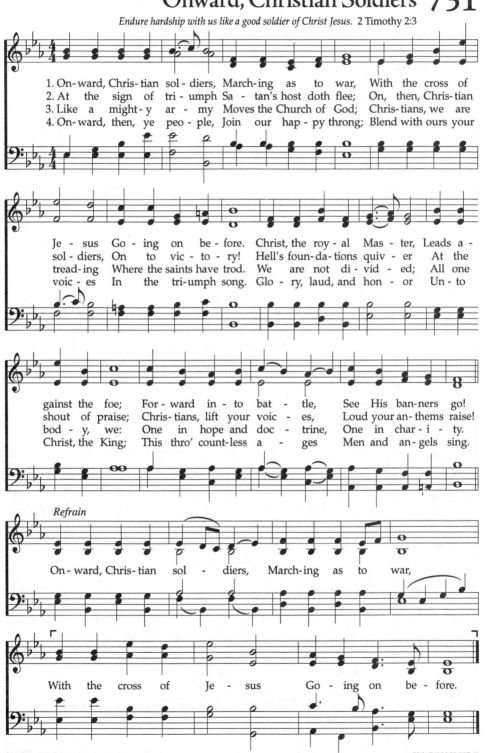

1. On-ward, Chris-tian sol-diers, March-ing as to war, With the cross of Je-sus Go-ing on be-fore. Christ, the roy-al Mas-ter, Leads a-gainst the foe; For-ward in-to bat-tle, See His ban-ners go!

2. At the sign of tri-umph Sa-tan's host doth flee; On, then, Chris-tian sol-diers, On to vic-to-ry! Hell's foun-da-tions quiv-er At the shout of praise; Chris-tians, lift your voic-es, Loud your an-thems raise!

3. Like a might-y ar-my Moves the Church of God; Chris-tians, we are tread-ing Where the saints have trod. We are not di-vid-ed; All one bod-y, we: One in hope and doc-trine, One in char-i-ty.

4. On-ward, then, ye peo-ple, Join our hap-py throng; Blend with ours your voic-es In the tri-umph song. Glo-ry, laud, and hon-or Un-to Christ, the King; This thro' count-less a-ges Men and an-gels sing.

Refrain

On-ward, Chris-tian sol-diers, March-ing as to war, With the cross of Je-sus Go-ing on be-fore.

TEXT: Sabine Baring-Gould
MUSIC: Arthur S. Sullivan

ST. GERTRUDE
6.5.6.5.D. with Refrain

732 The Battle Belongs to the Lord

The battle is not yours, but God's. 2 Chronicles 20:15

Unison

1. In heav-en-ly ar - mor we'll en - ter the land, The
2. When the pow-er of dark - ness comes in like a flood, The
3. When your en-e-my press - es in hard, do not fear, The

bat-tle be-longs to the Lord. No weap-on that's fash - ioned a-gainst
bat-tle be-longs to the Lord. He's raised up a stan-dard, the pow'r
bat-tle be-longs to the Lord. Take cour-age, my friend, your re-demp-

us will stand, The bat-tle be-longs to the Lord.
of His blood, The bat-tle be-longs to the Lord.
- tion is near, The bat-tle be-longs to the Lord. And we sing

Refrain

glo-ry, hon - or, pow-er and strength to the Lord. We sing

glo-ry, hon - or, pow-er and strength to the Lord!

TEXT: Jamie Owens-Collins
MUSIC: Jamie Owens-Collins

THE BATTLE
Irregular meter

Once to Every Man and Nation 733

Choose for yourselves this day whom you will serve. Joshua 24:15

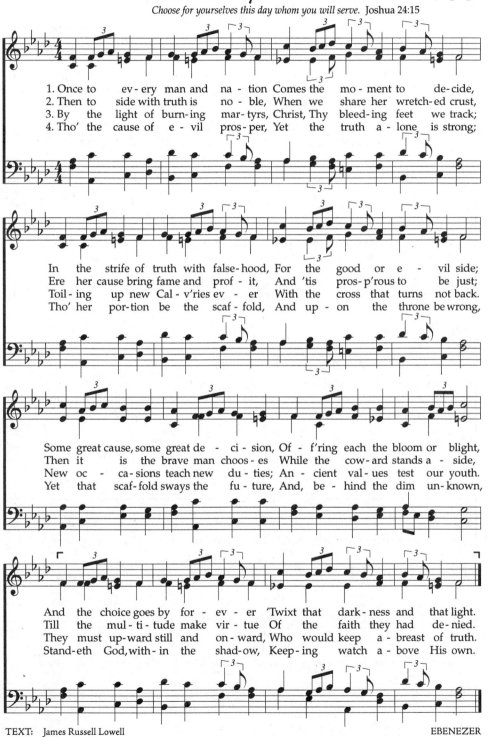

1. Once to every man and nation Comes the moment to decide,
In the strife of truth with falsehood, For the good or evil side;
Some great cause, some great decision, Off'ring each the bloom or blight,
And the choice goes by forever 'Twixt that darkness and that light.

2. Then to side with truth is noble, When we share her wretched crust,
Ere her cause bring fame and profit, And 'tis prosp'rous to be just;
Then it is the brave man chooses While the coward stands aside,
Till the multitude make virtue Of the faith they had denied.

3. By the light of burning martyrs, Christ, Thy bleeding feet we track;
Toiling up new Cal'vries ever With the cross that turns not back.
New occasions teach new duties; Ancient values test our youth.
They must upward still and onward, Who would keep abreast of truth.

4. Tho' the cause of evil prosper, Yet the truth alone is strong;
Tho' her portion be the scaffold, And upon the throne be wrong,
Yet that scaffold sways the future, And, behind the dim unknown,
Standeth God, within the shadow, Keeping watch above His own.

TEXT: James Russell Lowell
MUSIC: Thomas J. Williams

EBENEZER
8.7.8.7.D.

A lower setting may be found at No. 352

734 Be Strong in the Lord

Be strong in the Lord and in His mighty power. Ephesians 6:10

1. Be strong in the Lord, and be of good cour-age; Your might-y De-
2. So put on the ar-mor the Lord has pro-vid-ed, And place your de-
3. Be strong in the Lord, and be of good cour-age; Your might-y Com-

fend-er is al-ways the same. Mount up with wings, as the ea-gle as-
fense in His un-fail-ing care. Trust Him for He will be with you in
mand-er will van-quish the foe. Fear not the bat-tle for the vic-t'ry is

Refrain

cend-ing; Vic-t'ry is sure when you call on His name. Be strong, be
bat-tle, Light-ing your path to a-void ev-ery snare. Be strong, be
al-ways His; He will pro-tect you wher-ev-er you go.

strong, be strong in the Lord; And be of good cour-age, for He is your guide. Be

strong, be strong, be strong in the Lord; And re-joice for the vic-t'ry is yours.

TEXT: Linda Lee Johnson
MUSIC: Tom Fettke

STRENGTH
Irregular meter

THE ARMOR OF GOD   735

from Ephesians 6:10-18 (NASB)

WORSHIP LEADER or SOLO DRAMATIST

Be strong in the Lord, and in the strength of His might.
Put on the full armor of God,
so that you will be able to stand firm against the schemes of the devil.
For our struggle is not against flesh and blood,
but against the rulers, against the powers, against the world forces of this darkness,
against the spiritual forces of wickedness in the heavenly places.
Stand firm therefore, having girded your loins with truth,
and having put on the breastplate of righteousness,
and having shod your feet with the preparation of the gospel of peace;
in addition to all, taking up the shield of faith with which you will be able to
extinguish all the flaming arrows of the evil one.
And take the helmet of salvation, and the sword of the spirit,
which is the Word of God.

THE LORD IS MY LIGHT   736

from Psalm 27 (NIV)

WORSHIP LEADER
The Lord is my light and my salvation — whom shall I fear?

EVERYONE
The Lord is the stronghold of my life — of whom shall I be afraid?

SOLO 1
When evil men advance against me to devour my flesh,

SOLO 2
When my enemies and my foes attack me,

SOLO 1 and 2
They will stumble and fall.

SOLO 1
Though an army beseige me, my heart will not fear;

SOLO 2
Though war break out against me, even then will I be confident.

EVERYONE
The Lord is my light and my salvation — whom shall I fear?
The Lord is the stronghold of my life — of whom shall I be afraid?

WORSHIP LEADER
One thing I ask of the Lord, this is what I seek:
That I may dwell in the house of the Lord all the days of my life,

EVERYONE
To gaze upon the beauty of the Lord and to seek Him in His temple.

SOLO 1
For in the day of trouble He will keep me safe in His dwelling;

SOLO 2
He will hide me in the shelter of His tabernacle and set me high upon a rock.

SOLO 1
Then my head will be exalted above the enemies who surround me;

EVERYONE
At His tabernacle will I sacrifice with shouts of joy;
I will sing and make music to the Lord.

737 Like a River Glorious

Your peace would have been like a river. Isaiah 48:18

1. Like a riv-er glo-rious Is God's per-fect peace, O-ver all vic-to-rious
2. Hid-den in the hol-low Of His bless-ed hand, Nev-er foe can fol-low,
3. Ev-ery joy or tri-al Fall-eth from a-bove, Traced up-on our di-al

In its bright in-crease; Per-fect, yet it flow-eth Full-er ev-ery day.
Nev-er trai-tor stand; Not a surge of wor-ry, Not a shade of care,
By the Sun of Love; We may trust Him ful-ly All for us to do;

Refrain

Per-fect, yet it grow-eth Deep-er all the way.
Not a blast of hur-ry– Touch the Spir-it there. Stayed up-on Je-ho-vah,
They who trust Him whol-ly Find Him whol-ly true.

Hearts are ful-ly blest– Find-ing, as He prom-ised, Per-fect peace and rest.

TEXT: Frances R. Havergal
MUSIC: James Mountain; Choral ending by Ken Barker

WYE VALLEY
6.5.6.5.D. with Refrain

mf **Optional choral ending**   *rit. and dim.*

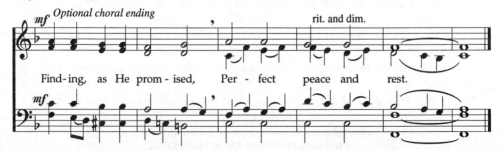

Find-ing, as He prom-ised, Per-fect peace and rest.

mf

The Wonder of It All 738

What is a human being that You care for him? Hebrews 2:6

1. There's the won-der of sun-set at eve-ning, The won-der as
2. There's the won-der of spring-time and har-vest, The sky, the

sun-rise I see; But the won-der of won-ders that thrills my soul
stars, the sun; But the won-der of won-ders that thrills my soul

Is the won-der that God loves me.
Is a won-der that's on-ly be-gun.

Refrain

O the won-der of it all, the won-der of it all— Just to think that God loves me! O the won-der of it all, the won-der of it all— Just to think that God loves me!

TEXT: George Beverly Shea
MUSIC: George Beverly Shea

WONDER OF IT ALL
Irregular meter

WALKING WITH GOD

739 Why Do I Sing About Jesus?

To Him who loves us and has freed us from our sins be glory. Revelation 1:5-6

1. Deep in my heart there's a glad - ness; Je - sus has
2. On - ly a glimpse of His good - ness; That was suf -
3. He is the Fair - est of fair ones; He is the

saved me from sin! Praise to His name, what a Sav - ior!
fi - cient for me. On - ly one look at the Sav - ior—
Lil - y, the Rose. Riv - ers of mer - cy sur - round Him;

Refrain

Cleans - ing with - out and with - in! Why do I sing a - bout
Then was my spir - it set free.
Grace, love and pit - y He shows.

Je - sus? Why is He pre - cious to me? He is my

Lord and my Sav - ior; Dy - ing, He set me free!

TEXT: Albert A. Ketchum
MUSIC: Albert A. Ketchum

KETCHUM
8.7.8.7. with Refrain

Joy Unspeakable 740

You believe in Him and are filled with an inexpressible and glorious joy. 1 Peter 1:8

1. I have found His grace is all com-plete; He sup-pli-eth ev-ery need. While I sit and learn at Je-sus' feet, I am free, yes, free in-deed.
2. I have found the plea-sure I once craved; It is joy and peace with-in. What a won-drous bless-ing! I am saved From the aw-ful gulf of sin.
3. I have found that hope so bright and clear, Liv-ing in the realm of grace. O the Sav-ior's pres-ence is so near; I can see His smil-ing face.
4. I have found the joy no tongue can tell, How its waves of glo-ry roll! It is like a great o'er-flow-ing well Spring-ing up with-in my soul.

Refrain

It is joy un-speak-a-ble and full of glo-ry, Full of glo-ry, full of glo-ry. It is joy un-speak-a-ble and full of glo-ry; O the half has nev-er yet been told!

TEXT: Barney E. Warren
MUSIC: Barney E. Warren

JOY UNSPEAKABLE
9.7.9.7. with Refrain

741 Jesus, I Am Resting, Resting

There remains a Sabbath-rest for the people of God. Hebrews 4:9

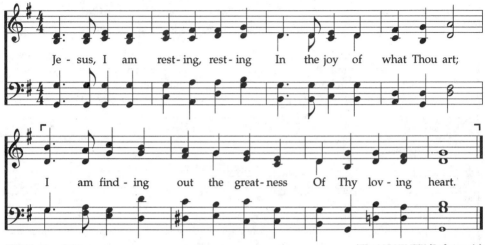

Je - sus, I am rest - ing, rest - ing In the joy of what Thou art;

I am find - ing out the great - ness Of Thy lov - ing heart.

TEXT: Jean S. Pigott
MUSIC: James Mountain

TRANQUILITY (Refrain only)
8.7.8.5.

---

742 GOD OF PEACE

A Worship Sequence

Wonderful Peace; stanzas 1,3
Joy of My Desire
Suggested stanzas have been marked with an arrow: ➤

WORSHIP LEADER

Do not be anxious about anything,
but in everything, by prayer and petition,
with thanksgiving, present your requests to God.
And the peace of God, which transcends all understanding,
will guard your hearts and your minds in Christ Jesus.

from Philippians 4:6-7 (NIV)

---

743 Wonderful Peace

May the Lord of peace Himself give you peace at all times and in every way. 2 Thessalonians 3:16

➤ 1. Far a - way in the depths of my spir - it to - night Rolls a
2. What a trea - sure I have in this won - der - ful peace, Bur - ied
➤ 3. I am rest - ing to - day in this won - der - ful peace, Rest - ing
4. And I know when I rise to that cit - y of peace, Where the
5. O soul, are you here with - out com - fort or rest, Walk - ing

TEXT: W. D. Cornell, altered
MUSIC: W. G. Cooper

WONDERFUL PEACE
12.9.12.9. with Refrain

mel - o - dy sweet-er than psalm; In ce - les - tial-like strains it un -
deep in the heart of my soul; So se - cure that no pow - er can
sweet - ly in Je - sus' con - trol; And I'm kept from all dan - ger by
Au - thor of peace I shall see, That one of the an - thems the
down the rough path-way of time? Make Je - sus your friend ere the

ceas - ing - ly falls O'er my soul like an in - fi - nite calm.
mine it a - way, While the years of e - ter - ni - ty roll.
night and by day, Now His glo - ry is flood-ing my soul.
ran - somed will sing, In that heav - en - ly king-dom shall be:
shad - ows grow dark; O ac - cept this sweet peace so sub - lime.

Refrain

Peace! peace! won-der-ful peace, Com-ing down from the Fa - ther a - bove; Sweep

o - ver my spir - it for - ev - er, I pray, In fath - om-less bil-lows of love.

Optional transition to "Joy of My Desire" ♪ = ♩

744 Joy of My Desire

Earth has nothing I desire besides You. Psalm 73:25

Unison

Joy of my de-sire, All-con-sum-ing Fire,

Lord of Glo-ry, Rose of Shar-on, rare and sweet—

You are now my peace, Com-fort-er and Friend;

Won-der-ful, so beau-ti-ful You are to me.

I wor-ship You in spir-it and in truth;

TEXT: Jennifer Randolph
MUSIC: Jennifer Randolph

JOY OF MY DESIRE
Irregular meter

I wor-ship You in spir-it and in truth. There will nev-er be a friend as dear to me as You. You.

1 *Repeat optional* **2** rit.

The end of GOD OF PEACE - A Worship Sequence

Rejoice in the Lord Always 745

Rejoice in the Lord always. I will say it again: Rejoice! Philippians 4:4

Four-part round (optional)

Re - joice in the Lord al - ways, a - gain I say, re-joice! Rejoice in the Lord al - ways, a - gain I say, re-joice! Re - joice! Re - joice! A-
gain I say, re-joice! Re - joice! Re - joice! A - gain I say, re-joice!

TEXT: Philippians 4:4
MUSIC: Anonymous

REJOICE
Irregular meter

746 He Keeps Me Singing

He put a new song in my mouth, a hymn of praise to our God. Psalm 40:3

1. There's with-in my heart a mel-o-dy; Je-sus whis-pers
2. All my life was wrecked by sin and strife; Dis-cord filled my
3. Feast-ing on the rich-es of His grace, Rest-ing 'neath His
4. Tho' some-times He leads thro' wa-ters deep, Tri-als fall a-
5. Soon He's com-ing back to wel-come me Far be-yond the

sweet and low: "Fear not, I am with thee; peace, be still,"
heart with pain. Je-sus swept a-cross the bro-ken strings,
shel-t'ring wing, Al-ways look-ing on His smil-ing face—
cross the way; Tho' some-times the path seems rough and steep,
star-ry sky. I shall wing my flight to worlds un-known;

Refrain

In all of life's ebb and flow.
Stirred the slum-b'ring chords a-gain.
That is why I shout and sing. Je-sus, Je-sus, Je-sus— Sweet-est
See His foot-prints all the way.
I shall reign with Him on high.

name I know, Fills my ev-er-y long-ing, Keeps me sing-ing as I go.

Optional segue to "Sunshine in My Soul." No transition is needed.

TEXT: Luther B. Bridgers
MUSIC: Luther B. Bridgers

SWEETEST NAME
9.7.9.7. with Refrain

Sunshine in My Soul 747

God made His light shine in our hearts to give us the light. 2 Corinthians 4:6

1. There is sun-shine in my soul to-day— More glo-ri-ous and bright
2. There is mu-sic in my soul to-day— A car-ol to my King;
3. There is mu-sic in my soul to-day, For when the Lord is near
4. There is glad-ness in my soul to-day, And hope and love and praise,

Than glows in an-y earth-ly sky, For Je-sus is my light.
And Je-sus, lis-ten-ing, can hear The songs I can-not sing.
The dove of peace sings in my heart; The flow'rs of grace ap-pear.
For bless-ings which He gives me now, For joys in fu-ture days.

Refrain

O there's sun-shine, bless-ed sun-shine, When the peace-ful, hap-py mo-ments roll; When Je-sus shows His smil-ing face, There is sun-shine in my soul.

TEXT: Eliza E. Hewitt
MUSIC: John R. Sweney

SUNSHINE
9.6.8.6. with Refrain

748 I Am His and He Is Mine

Your life is now hidden with Christ in God. Colossians 3:3

1. Loved with ev - er - last - ing love, Led by grace that love to know;
2. Heav'n a - bove is soft - er blue; Earth a - round is sweet - er green.
3. Things that once were wild a - larms Can - not now dis - turb my rest.
4. His for - ev - er, on - ly His; Who the Lord and me shall part?

Gra - cious Spir - it from a - bove, Thou hast taught me it is so.
Some - thing lives in ev - ery hue Christ - less eyes have nev - er seen.
Closed in ev - er - last - ing arms, Pil - lowed on the lov - ing breast—
Ah, with what a rest of bliss Christ can fill the lov - ing heart!

O this full and per - fect peace! O this trans - port all di - vine!
Birds with glad - der songs o'er - flow; Flow'rs with deep - er beau - ties shine,
O to lie for - ev - er here, Doubt and care and self re - sign
Heav'n and earth may fade and flee; First - born light in gloom de - cline.

In a love which can - not cease, I am His and He is mine. mine.
Since I know, as now I know, I am His and He is mine. mine.
While He whis - pers in my ear, I am His and He is mine. mine.
But while God and I shall be, I am His and He is mine. mine.

TEXT: George W. Robinson
MUSIC: James Mountain

EVERLASTING LOVE
7.7.7.7.D.

Wonderful, Wonderful Jesus 749

You are my hiding place; You will surround me with songs of deliverance. Psalm 32:7

1. There is nev - er a day so drea - ry, There is nev - er a night so
2. There is nev - er a cross so heav - y, There is nev - er a weight of
3. There is nev - er a care or bur - den, There is nev - er a grief or
4. There is nev - er a guilt - y sin - ner, There is nev - er a wan - d'ring

long, But the soul that is trust - ing Je - sus Will some - where
woe, But that Je - sus will help to car - ry Be - cause He
loss, But that Je - sus in love will light - en When car - ried
one, But that God can in mer - cy par - don Thro' Je - sus

Refrain

find a song.
lov - eth so.
to the cross.
Christ, His Son.

Won - der - ful, won - der - ful Je - sus, In the

heart He im - plant - eth a song— A song of de - liv - 'rance, of

cour - age, of strength; In the heart He im - plant - eth a song.

TEXT: Anna B. Russell
MUSIC: Ernest O. Sellers

NEW ORLEANS
Irregular meter

750 Peace like a River

The peace of God will guard your hearts and your minds in Christ Jesus. Philippians 4:7

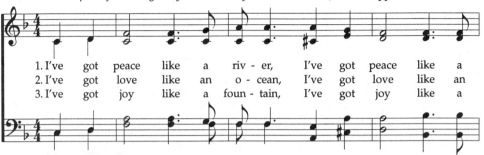

1. I've got peace like a riv-er, I've got peace like a
2. I've got love like an o-cean, I've got love like an
3. I've got joy like a foun-tain, I've got joy like a

riv-er, I've got peace like a riv-er in my soul; I've got
o-cean, I've got love like an o-cean in my soul; I've got
foun-tain, I've got joy like a foun-tain in my soul; I've got

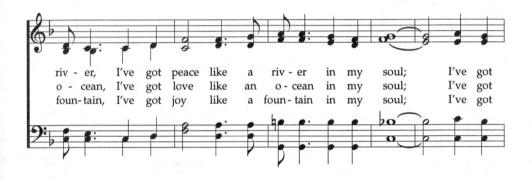

peace like a riv-er, I've got peace like a riv-er,
love like an o-cean, I've got love like an o-cean,
joy like a foun-tain, I've got joy like a foun-tain,

I've got peace like a riv-er in my soul. (my soul.)
I've got love like an o-cean in my soul. (my soul.)
I've got joy like a foun-tain in my soul. (my soul.)

TEXT: Traditional
MUSIC: Traditional

PEACE LIKE A RIVER
7.7.10.D.

PERFECT PEACE

751

from John 14:27; Isaiah 26:3; Psalm 91:1-2; Romans 15:13 (NIV)

WORSHIP LEADER
Peace I leave with you; My peace I give you.
I do not give to you as the world gives.
Do not let your hearts be troubled, and do not be afraid.

EVERYONE
You will keep in perfect peace him whose mind is steadfast,
because he trusts in You.

WORSHIP LEADER
He who dwells in the shelter of the Most High
will rest in the shadow of the Almighty.
I will say of the Lord, "He is my refuge
and my fortress, my God, in whom I trust."
May the God of hope fill you with joy and peace
as you trust in Him.

I SING FOR JOY

752

from Habakkuk 3:18; Psalm 92:1-2, 4; Psalm 113 (NIV)

WORSHIP LEADER
I will rejoice in the Lord;
I will be joyful in God, my Savior.

EVERYONE
It is good to praise the Lord
and make music to Your name, O Most High;
to proclaim Your love in the morning
and Your faithfulness at night.
For You make me glad by Your deeds, O Lord;
I sing for joy at the works of Your hands.

WORSHIP LEADER
Praise the Lord.
Praise, O servants of the Lord.

EVERYONE
Praise the name of the Lord!

WORSHIP LEADER
Let the name of the Lord be praised,
both now and forevermore.

EVERYONE
Praise the name of the Lord!

WORSHIP LEADER
From the rising of the sun to the place where it sets,
The name of the Lord is to be praised.

EVERYONE
Praise the name of the Lord!

WORSHIP LEADER
The Lord is exalted over all the nations,
His glory above the heavens.

EVERYONE
Praise the name of the Lord!

753 Jesus Is Coming Again

If I go and prepare a place for you, I will come back and take you to be with Me. John 14:3

1. Mar - vel - ous mes - sage we bring; Glo - ri - ous car - ol we
2. For - est and flow - er ex - claim, Moun - tain and mead - ow the
3. Stand - ing be - fore Him at last, Tri - al and trou - ble all

sing! Won - der - ful word of the King: Je - sus is
same, All earth and heav - en pro - claim: Je - sus is
past, Crowns at His feet we will cast. Je - sus is

Refrain

com - ing a - gain! Com - ing a - gain, com - ing a - gain!
com - ing a - gain!
com - ing a - gain!

May - be morn - ing, may - be noon, May - be eve - ning and may - be soon!

Com - ing a - gain, com - ing a - gain! O what a

TEXT: John W. Peterson
MUSIC: John W. Peterson

COMING AGAIN
7.7.7.7. with Refrain

won-der-ful day it will be— Je-sus is com-ing a - gain!

Lo, He Comes with Clouds Descending 754

They will see the Son of Man coming with power and great glory. Matthew 24:30

1. Lo, He comes with clouds de-scend-ing, Once for fa-vored sin-ners slain;
2. Ev-ery eye shall now be-hold Him, Robed in dread-ful maj-es-ty!
3. Now the Sav-ior, long-ex-pect-ed, See in sol-emn pomp ap-pear.
4. Yes, a-men! let all a-dore Thee, High on Thine e-ter-nal throne.

Thou-sand thou-sand saints at-tend-ing Swell the tri-umph of His train.
Those who set at naught and sold Him, Pierced and nailed Him to the tree,
All His saints, by man re-ject-ed, Now shall meet Him in the air.
Sav-ior, take the pow'r and glo-ry; Claim the king-dom for Thine own.

Al - le - lu - ia! Al - le - lu - ia! God ap-pears on earth to reign.
Deep-ly wail-ing, deep-ly wail-ing, Shall the true Mes-si-ah see.
Al - le - lu - ia! Al - le - lu - ia! See the day of God ap-pear.
O come quick-ly! O come quick-ly! Ev-er-last-ing God, come down!

TEXT: Charles Wesley and Martin Madan; based on John Cennick
MUSIC: Henry T. Smart

A higher setting may be found at No. 403

REGENT SQUARE
8.7.8.7.8.7.

755 We Shall Behold Him

When He appears, we shall be like Him for we shall see Him as He is. 1 John 3:2

1. The sky shall un-fold, pre-par-ing His en-trance; The stars shall ap-plaud Him with thun-ders of praise. The sweet light in His eyes shall en-hance those a-wait-ing; And we shall be-hold Him then face to face.

2. The an-gel shall sound the shout of His com-ing; The sleep-ing shall rise from their slum-ber-ing place, And those who re-main shall be changed in a mo-ment; And we shall be-hold Him then face to face.

Refrain

And we shall be-hold Him, We shall be-hold Him Face to face in all of His glo-ry. O we shall be-hold Him, We shall be-

TEXT: Dottie Rambo
MUSIC: Dottie Rambo

WE SHALL BEHOLD HIM
Irregular meter

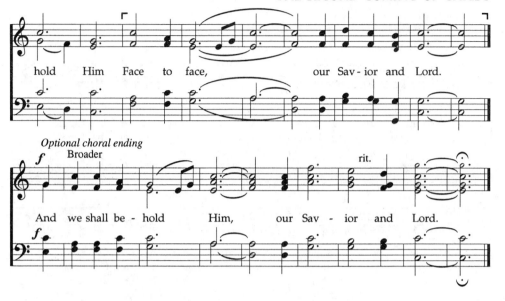

hold Him Face to face, our Sav-ior and Lord.

Optional choral ending

Broader

rit.

And we shall be-hold Him, our Sav-ior and Lord.

THE RETURN OF CHRIST   756

A Worship Sequence

Soon and Very Soon; complete
Lift Up Your Heads
Suggested stanzas have been marked with an arrow: ➤

WORSHIP LEADER

We do not want you to be ignorant about those who fall asleep,
or to grieve like the rest of men, who have no hope.
We believe that Jesus died and rose again
and so we believe that God will bring with Jesus
those who have fallen asleep in Him.
For the Lord Himself will come down from heaven,
with a loud command, with the voice of the archangel
and with the trumpet call of God,
and the dead in Christ will rise first.

EVERYONE

After that, we who are still alive and are left
will be caught up together with them in the clouds
to meet the Lord in the air.
And so we will be with the Lord forever.

from 1 Thessalonians 4:13-14, 16-17 (NIV)

Optional introduction to "Soon and Very Soon"

mf

757 Soon and Very Soon

"Yes, I am coming soon." Amen. Come, Lord Jesus. Revelation 22:20

1,4. Soon and ver - y soon, we are going to see the King!
2. No more cry - ing there– we are going to see the King!
3. No more dy - ing there– we are going to see the King!

Soon and ver - y soon, we are going to see the King!
No more cry - ing there– we are going to see the King!
No more dy - ing there– we are going to see the King!

Soon and ver - y soon, we are going to see the King!
No more cry - ing there– we are going to see the King!
No more dy - ing there– we are going to see the King!

1, 2, 3   *D.C.*

Hal - le - lu - jah! Hal - le - lu - jah! We're going to see the King!

4   *rit.*

going to see the King! Hal - le - lu - jah! Hal - le - lu - jah!

TEXT: Andraé Crouch
MUSIC: Andraé Crouch

SOON AND VERY SOON
Irregular meter

Optional transition to "Lift Up Your Heads"

slight rit.

Lift Up Your Heads 758

Lift up your heads; because your redemption is drawing near. Luke 21:28

Lift up your heads to the com-ing King. Bow be-fore Him
and a-dore Him, sing! To His maj-es-ty, let your prais-es be
Pure and ho-ly, giv-ing glo-ry to the King of kings. kings.

TEXT: Steve Fry
MUSIC: Steve Fry

LIFT UP YOUR HEADS
Irregular meter

Optional choral ending

Praise the King! Praise to the King of kings!

The end of THE RETURN OF CHRIST - A Worship Sequence

759 What If It Were Today?

Lift up your heads, because your redemption is drawing near. Luke 21:28

1. Je - sus is com - ing to earth a - gain– What if it were to - day?
2. Sa - tan's do - min - ion will then be o'er– O that it were to - day!
3. Faith - ful and true would He find us here If He should come to - day?

Com - ing in pow - er and love to reign– What if it were to - day?
Sor - row and sigh - ing shall be no more– O that it were to - day!
Watch - ing in glad - ness and not in fear, If He should come to - day?

Com - ing to claim His cho - sen Bride, All the re - deemed and pu - ri - fied,
Then shall the dead in Christ a - rise, Caught up to meet Him in the skies;
Signs of His com - ing mul - ti - ply, Morn - ing light breaks in east - ern sky;

O - ver this whole earth scat - tered wide– What if it were to - day?
When shall these glo - ries meet our eyes? What if it were to - day?
Watch, for the time is draw - ing nigh– What if it were to - day?

Refrain

Glo - ry, glo - ry! Joy to my heart 'twill bring; Glo - ry, glo - ry!

TEXT: Lelia N. Morris
MUSIC: Lelia N. Morris

SECOND COMING
Irregular meter

When we shall crown Him King. Glo - ry, glo - ry! Haste to pre -

pare the way; Glo - ry, glo - ry! Je - sus will come some - day.

Optional choral ending

Glo - ry, glo - ry! Je - sus will come some - day.

Optional segue to "While We Are Waiting, Come." No transition is needed. A much slower tempo is necessary.

While We Are Waiting, Come 760

Behold, I am coming soon! My reward is with Me. Revelation 22:12

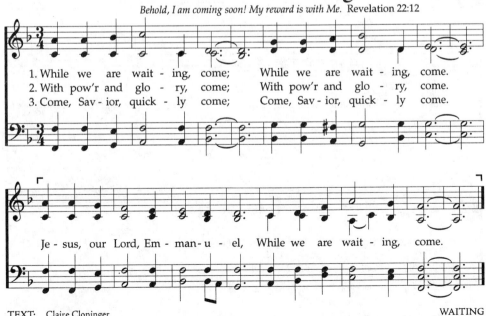

1. While we are wait - ing, come; While we are wait - ing, come.
2. With pow'r and glo - ry, come; With pow'r and glo - ry, come.
3. Come, Sav - ior, quick - ly come; Come, Sav - ior, quick - ly come.

Je - sus, our Lord, Em - man - u - el, While we are wait - ing, come.

TEXT: Claire Cloninger
MUSIC: Don Cason

WAITING
S.M.

761 Therefore the Redeemed of the Lord

The ransomed of the Lord will return. They will enter Zion with singing. Isaiah 51:11

TEXT: Ruth Lake; based on Isaiah 51:11
MUSIC: Ruth Lake

LAKE
Irregular meter

tain   glad-ness and   joy,   And

sor-row   and mourn-ing   shall flee a - way.   There-fore the re-

deemed   of the Lord shall re - turn   and come with sing-ing   un - to

Zi - on,   And ev-er-last-ing joy shall be up - on their heads.

Optional extended or choral ending

And ev-er-last-ing joy shall be up-on their heads.

762 What a Day That Will Be

We shall be like Him, for we shall see Him as He is. 1 John 3:2

1. There is com - ing a day when no heart - aches shall come—
2. There'll be no sor - row there, no more bur - dens to bear,

No more clouds in the sky, no more tears to dim the eye. All is
No more sick - ness, no pain, no more part - ing o - ver there. And for-

peace for - ev - er - more on that hap - py gold - en shore. What a day,
ev - er I will be with the One who died for me. What a day,

glo - ri - ous day that will be!
glo - ri - ous day that will be!

Refrain

What a day that will be when my

Je - sus I shall see, And I look up - on His face— the One who

TEXT: Jim Hill
MUSIC: Jim Hill

WHAT A DAY
Irregular meter

saved me by His grace. When He takes me by the hand and leads me

thro' the Prom-ised Land; What a day, glo-ri-ous day that will be!

Optional segue to "The King Is Coming." No transition is needed.

The King Is Coming 763

The Lord is coming with thousands upon thousands of His holy ones. Jude 14

O the King is com-ing, the King is com-ing! I just

heard the trum-pets sound-ing, And now His face I see. O the King is

com-ing, the King is com-ing! Praise God, He's com-ing for me!

TEXT: Gloria Gaither, William J. Gaither and Charles Millhuff
MUSIC: William J. Gaither

KING IS COMING
Irregular meter

764 The Trees of the Field

You will go out in joy, and all the trees of the field will clap their hands. Isaiah 55:12

Unison

You shall go out with joy and be led forth with peace; The moun- tains and the hills will break forth be - fore you. There'll be shouts of joy and all the trees of the field Will clap, will clap their hands. And all the trees of the field will clap their hands; The trees of the field will clap their hands; The trees of the field will

TEXT: Steffi Geiser Rubin; based on Isaiah 55:12
MUSIC: Stuart Dauermann

THE TREES OF THE FIELD
Irregular meter

Coming Again 765

Look, He is coming with the clouds, and every eye will see Him. Revelation 1:7

1. Je - sus is com - ing; Je - sus is com - ing;
2. In clouds of glo - ry, Bright clouds of glo - ry;
3. We'll rise to meet Him, Rise up to meet Him;
4. We shall be like Him; We shall be like Him;
5. O hal - le - lu - jah! O hal - le - lu - jah!

Je - sus is com - ing, He's com - ing a - gain.
In clouds of glo - ry He's com - ing a - gain.
We'll rise to meet Him, He's com - ing a - gain.
We shall be like Him, He's com - ing a - gain.
O hal - le - lu - jah! He's com - ing a - gain.

Optional last stanza setting

5. O hal - le - lu - jah! O hal - le - lu - jah!

rit. last time

O hal - le - lu - jah! He's com - ing a - gain. gain.

TEXT: Mosie Lister; based on 1 Thessalonians 4:16-17; 1 John 3:2; Revelation 1:7
MUSIC: Mosie Lister

COMING AGAIN
5.5.5.5.

766 At the Name of Jesus

At the name of Jesus every knee should bow. Philippians 2:10

1. At the name of Jesus Ev - ery knee shall bow,
2. Hum - bled for a sea - son To re - ceive a name
3. In your hearts en - throne Him; There let Him re - move
4. Watch, for this Lord Je - sus Shall re - turn a - gain

Ev - ery tongue con - fess Him King of Glo - ry now.
From the lips of sin - ners Un - to whom He came;
All that is not ho - ly, All that is not true.
With His Fa - ther's glo - ry, O'er the earth to reign;

'Tis the Fa - ther's plea - sure We should call Him Lord,
Faith - ful - ly He bore it, Spot - less to the last,
Crown Him as your cap - tain In temp - ta - tion's hour;
For the day is com - ing When each knee shall bow,

Who from the be - gin - ning Was the might - y Word.
Brought it back vic - to - rious When from death He passed.
Let His will en - fold you In its light and pow'r.
All our hearts con - fess Him King of Glo - ry now.

TEXT: Caroline M. Noel
MUSIC: James Mountain

WYE VALLEY (abridged)
6.5.6.5.D.

For All the Saints 767

We are surrounded by such a great cloud of witnesses. Hebrews 12:1

Unison

1. For all the saints who from their la - bors rest,
2. Thou wast their Rock, their For - tress, and their Might;
3. O may Thy sol - diers, faith - ful, true and bold,
4. O blest com - mu - nion, fel - low - ship di - vine!
5. But lo! there breaks a yet more glo - rious day:
6. From earth's wide bounds, from o - cean's far - thest coast,

Who Thee by faith be - fore the world con - fessed, Thy
Thou, Lord, their Cap - tain in the well - fought fight; Thou,
Fight as the saints who no - bly fought of old, And
We fee - bly strug - gle, they in glo - ry shine; Yet
The saints tri - um - phant rise in bright ar - ray; The
Through gates of pearl streams in the count - less host,

name, O Je - sus, be for - ev - er blest.
Thou, in the dark - ness drear, their one true Light.
win with them the vic - tor's crown of gold.
all are one in Thee, for all are Thine.
King of Glo - ry pass - es on His way.
Sing - ing to Fa - ther, Son and Ho - ly Ghost:

Al - le - lu - ia! Al - le - lu - ia!

TEXT: William W. How
MUSIC: Ralph Vaughan Williams

SINE NOMINE
10.10.10. with Alleluias

768 My Savior First of All

We wait for the blessed hope–the glorious appearing of our Savior, Jesus Christ. Titus 2:13

1. When my life-work is end-ed and I cross the swell-ing tide, When the bright and glo-rious morn-ing I shall see; I shall know my Re-deem-er when I reach the oth-er side, And His smile will be the first to wel-come me.

2. O the soul-thrill-ing rap-ture when I view His bless-ed face And the lus-ter of His kind-ly beam-ing eye; How my full heart will praise Him for the mer-cy, love and grace That pre-pare for me a man-sion in the sky.

3. O the dear ones in glo-ry– how they beck-on me to come, And our part-ing at the riv-er I re-call; To the sweet vales of E-den they will sing my wel-come home, But I long to meet my Sav-ior first of all.

4. Thro' the gates to the cit-y in a robe of spot-less white, He will lead me where no tears will ev-er fall; In the glad song of a-ges I shall min-gle with de-light, But I long to meet my Sav-ior first of all.

Refrain

I shall know Him, I shall know Him, And re-deemed by His side I shall stand;
I shall know Him, I shall know Him, I shall know Him By the prints of the nails in His hand.

TEXT: Fanny J. Crosby
MUSIC: John R. Sweney

I SHALL KNOW HIM
14.11.14.11. with Refrain

O That Will Be Glory 769

Our present sufferings are not worth comparing with the glory that will be revealed. Romans 8:18

1. When all my la - bors and tri - als are o'er, And I am safe on that
2. When, by the gift of His in - fi - nite grace, I am ac - cord - ed in
3. Friends will be there I have loved long a - go; Joy like a riv - er a -

beau - ti - ful shore, Just to be near the dear Lord I a - dore
heav - en a place, Just to be there and to look on His face
round me will flow. Yet, just a smile from my Sav - ior, I know,

rit.   *Refrain*

Will thro' the a - ges be glo - ry for me. O that will be

glo - ry for me, Glo - ry for me, glo - ry for me! When by His grace
be glo - ry for me, Glo - ry for me, glo - ry for me!

rit.

I shall look on His face, That will be glo - ry, be glo - ry for me!

TEXT: Charles H. Gabriel
MUSIC: Charles H. Gabriel

GLORY SONG
10.10.10.10. with Refrain

770 DAY OF REJOICING
A Worship Sequence

We'll Understand It Better By and By; stanzas 1,2
When We All Get to Heaven; stanzas 1,3,4
Suggested stanzas have been marked with an arrow: ➤

WORSHIP LEADER

Let not your heart be troubled; you believe in God, believe also in Me.
In My Father's house are many mansions; if it were not so, I would have told you.
I go to prepare a place for you.
And if I go and prepare a place for you, I will come again and receive you to Myself.
And there shall be no more death, nor sorrow, nor crying.
There shall be no more pain,
for the former things have passed away.
Behold, I make all things new.

from John 14:1-3; Revelation 21:4-5 (NKJV)

771 We'll Understand It Better By and By

Faith is being sure of what we hope for and certain of what we do not see. Hebrews 11:1

➤ 1. Tri - als dark on ev - ery hand, And we can - not un - der - stand
➤ 2. Oft our cher - ished plans have failed, Dis - ap - point - ments have pre - vailed,
3. Temp - ta - tions, hid - den snares Of - ten take us un - a - wares,

All the ways that God would lead us to that bless - ed Prom - ised Land;
And we've wan-dered in the dark - ness, heav - y - heart - ed and a - lone;
And our hearts are made to bleed for some tho't - less word or deed,

But He'll guide us with His eye, And we'll fol - low till we die; We will
But we're trust - ing in the Lord, And, ac - cord - ing to His Word, We will
And we won - der why the test When we try to do our best, But we'll

TEXT: Charles A. Tindley
MUSIC: Charles A. Tindley

BY AND BY
Irregular meter

DAY OF REJOICING - A Worship Sequence

Refrain

un-der-stand it bet-ter by and by. By and by, when the morn-ing comes,

When the saints of God are gath-ered home; We will tell the sto - ry

how we've o - ver - come; We will un-der-stand it bet-ter by and by.

Optional repeat refrain setting

By and by, when the morn-ing comes, When the saints of

God are gath-ered home; We will tell the sto - ry how we've o - ver - come;

We will un-der-stand it bet-ter by and by. *Optional transition to*
"When We All Get to Heaven"

772 When We All Get to Heaven

We will be caught up to be with the Lord forever. 1 Thessalonians 4:17

1. Sing the won-drous love of Je-sus, Sing His mer-cy and His grace;
2. While we walk the pil-grim path-way Clouds will o-ver-spread the sky;
3. Let us then be true and faith-ful, Trust-ing, serv-ing ev-ery day;
4. On-ward to the prize be-fore us! Soon His beau-ty we'll be-hold;

In the man-sions bright and bless-ed He'll pre-pare for us a place.
But when trav-'ling days are o-ver, Not a shad-ow, not a sigh.
Just one glimpse of Him in glo-ry Will the toils of life re-pay.
Soon the pearl-y gates will o-pen, We shall tread the streets of gold.

Refrain

When we all get to heav-en, What a day of re-
When we all
What a

joic-ing that will be! When we all see
day of re-joic-ing that will be! When we all

Je-sus, We'll sing and shout the vic-to-ry.
shout, and shout the vic-to-ry.

TEXT: Eliza E. Hewitt
MUSIC: Emily D. Wilson; Choral ending by Ken Barker

HEAVEN
8.7.8.7. with Refrain

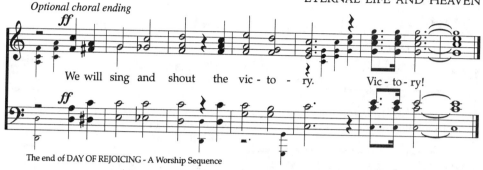

Optional choral ending

We will sing and shout the vic - to - ry. Vic - to - ry!

The end of DAY OF REJOICING - A Worship Sequence

He the Pearly Gates Will Open 773

Those who wash their robes may go through the gates into the city. Revelation 22:14

1. Love di - vine, so great and won - drous, Deep and might-y, pure, sub-lime,
2. Like a dove when hunt-ed, fright-ened, As a wound-ed fawn was I;
3. Love di - vine, so great and won-drous! All my sins He then for-gave;
4. In life's e - ven-tide, at twi - light, At His door I'll knock and wait;

Com - ing from the heart of Je - sus, Just the same thro' tests of time!
Bro - ken-heart-ed, yet He healed me. He will heed the sin-ner's cry.
I will sing His praise for - ev - er, For His blood, His pow'r to save.
By the pre - cious love of Je - sus, I shall en - ter heav-en's gate.

Refrain

He the pearl - y gates will o - pen, So that I may en - ter in;

For He pur-chased my re - demp - tion And for-gave me all my sin.

TEXT: Frederick A. Blom; translated by Nathaniel Carlson
MUSIC: Elsie Ahlwen

PEARLY GATES
8.7.8.7. with Refrain

774 When the Roll Is Called Up Yonder

The Lord Himself will come down with the trumpet call of God. 1 Thessalonians 4:16

1. When the trum-pet of the Lord shall sound, and time shall be no more, And the morn-ing breaks, e-ter-nal, bright and fair; When the saved of earth shall gath-er o-ver on the oth-er shore, And the roll is called up yon-der, I'll be there.

2. On that bright and cloud-less morn-ing when the dead in Christ shall rise, And the glo-ry of His res-ur-rec-tion share; When His cho-sen ones shall gath-er to their home be-yond the skies, And the roll is called up yon-der, I'll be there.

3. Let us la-bor for the Mas-ter from the dawn till set-ting sun; Let us talk of all His won-drous love and care. Then when all of life is o-ver, and our work on earth is done, And the roll is called up yon-der, I'll be there.

Refrain

When the roll is called up yon - der, When the roll is called up yon - der, When the roll is

When the roll is called up yon-der, I'll be there. When the roll is called up yon-der, I'll be there. When the roll is

TEXT: James M. Black
MUSIC: James M. Black; Choral ending by Eugene Thomas

ROLL CALL
Irregular meter

called up yon - der, When the roll is called up yon - der, I'll be there.

Optional choral ending

When the roll is called up yon - der, I'll be there!

Beyond the Sunset 775

There will be no more death or mourning or crying or pain. Revelation 21:4

Unison

1. Be - yond the sun - set, O bliss - ful morn - ing, When with our
2. Be - yond the sun - set no clouds will gath - er, No storms will
3. Be - yond the sun - set a hand will guide me To God the
4. Be - yond the sun - set, O glad re - un - ion, With our dear

Sav - ior, heav'n is be - gun; Earth's toil - ing end - ed, O glo - rious
threat - en, no fears an - noy; O day of glad - ness, O day un -
Fa - ther, whom I a - dore; His glo - rious pres - ence, His words of
loved ones who've gone be - fore; In that fair home - land we'll know no

dawn - ing, Be - yond the sun - set, when day is done.
end - ing, Be - yond the sun - set, e - ter - nal joy!
wel - come Will be my por - tion on that fair shore.
part - ing, Be - yond the sun - set, for - ev - er - more!

TEXT: Virgil P. Brock
MUSIC: Blanche Kerr Brock
© Copyright 1936 by The Rodeheaver Co.
© Renewed 1964 by The Rodeheaver Co. (a div. of WORD·MUSIC). All rights reserved. Used by permission.

SUNSET
10.9.10.9.

776 Sweet Beulah Land

You will be called Hephzibah, and your land Beulah. Isaiah 62:4

1. I'm kind of home-sick for a coun-try To which I've
2. I'm look-ing now a-cross the riv-er Where my
3. I see the lights, I hear the sing-ing; A brand new

nev-er been be-fore; No sad good-byes will there be
faith will end in sight; There's just a few more days to
song of joy di-vine. My soul re-joic-es just in

Refrain

spo-ken, For time won't mat-ter an-y more.
la-bor, Then I will take my heav'n-ly flight. Beu-lah
know-ing That soon these plea-sures will be mine.

land, I am long-ing for you, And some-day
Beu-lah land, And some-

on thee I'll stand; Where my home shall be e-
day Where my home

TEXT: Squire E. Parsons, Jr.
MUSIC: Squire E. Parsons, Jr.

PARSONS
9.8.9.8. with Refrain

ter - nal— Beu-lah land, sweet Beu-lah land.

On Jordan's Stormy Banks 777

They were longing for a better country—a heavenly one. Hebrews 11:16

1. On Jor-dan's storm-y banks I stand, And cast a wish-ful eye
2. All o'er those wide ex-tend-ed plains Shines one e-ter-nal day;
3. No chill-ing winds nor pois'nous breath Can reach that health-ful shore;
4. When shall I reach that hap-py place, And be for-ev-er blest?

To Ca-naan's fair and hap-py land, Where my pos-ses-sions lie.
There God the Son for-ev-er reigns And scat-ters night a-way.
Sick-ness and sor-row, pain and death Are felt and feared no more.
When shall I see my Fa-ther's face, And in His bos-om rest?

Refrain

I am bound for the Prom-ised Land; I am bound for the Prom-ised Land.

O who will come and go with me? I am bound for the Prom-ised Land.

TEXT: Samuel Stennett
MUSIC: Traditional American melody; arranged by Rigdon M. McIntosh

PROMISED LAND
C. M. with Refrain

778 Sweet By and By

Here we do not have an enduring city, but we are looking for the city that is to come. Hebrews 13:14

1. There's a land that is fair-er than day, And by faith we can see it a-far; For the Fa-ther waits o-ver the way To pre-pare us a dwell-ing place there.
2. We shall sing on that beau-ti-ful shore The me-lo-di-ous songs of the blest; And our spir-its shall sor-row no more, Not a sigh for the bless-ing of rest.
3. To our boun-ti-ful Fa-ther a-bove We will of-fer our trib-ute of praise, For the glo-ri-ous gift of His love And the bless-ings that hal-low our days.

Refrain

In the sweet by and by, We shall meet on that beau-ti-ful shore. In the sweet by and by, We shall meet on that beau-ti-ful shore.

TEXT: Sanford F. Bennett
MUSIC: Joseph P. Webster

SWEET BY AND BY
9.9.9.9. with Refrain

I'll Fly Away 779

We would prefer to be away from the body and at home with the Lord. 2 Corinthians 5:8

1. Some glad morn-ing when this life is o'er, I'll fly a-way;
2. When the shad-ows of this life have gone, fly a-way,
3. Just a few more wea-ry days and then, fly a-way,

way; To a home on God's ce-les-tial shore, I'll
fly a-way; Like a bird from pris-on bars has flown, fly a-way,
To a land where joys shall nev-er end, fly a-way,

Refrain

fly a-way. I'll fly a-way, O glo-ry, I'll
fly a-way. fly a-way, fly a-way,

fly a-way; When I die, hal-le-lu-jah, by and by,
in the morn-ing;

Optional choral ending

I'll fly a-way, fly a-way. I'll fly a-way!
fly a-way, fly a-way.

TEXT: Albert E. Brumley
MUSIC: Albert E. Brumley

I'LL FLY AWAY
9.4.9.4. with Refrain

780 Until Then

Be patient and stand firm, because the Lord's coming is near. James 5:8

1. My heart can sing when I pause to re-mem-ber
2. The things of earth will dim and lose their val-ue,
3. This wea-ry world with all its toil and strug-gle

A heart-ache
If we re-
May take its

here is but a step-ping stone A - long a trail that's wind-ing
call, they're bor-rowed for a - while; And things of earth that cause the
toll of mis-er - y and strife; The soul of man is like a

al - ways up-ward— This trou-bled world is not my fi - nal home.
heart to trem-ble, Re - mem-bered there, will on - ly bring a smile.
wait - ing fal-con— When it's re - leased, it's des-tined for the skies.

Refrain

But un - til then my heart will go on sing-ing, Un - til

then with joy I'll car - ry on— Un - til the day my

TEXT: Stuart Hamblen
MUSIC: Stuart Hamblen

UNTIL THEN
Irregular meter

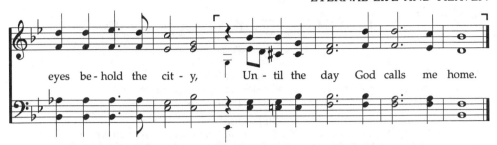

eyes be-hold the cit-y, Un-til the day God calls me home.

Face to Face 781

Now we see but a poor reflection as in a mirror; then we shall see face to face. 1 Corinthians 13:12

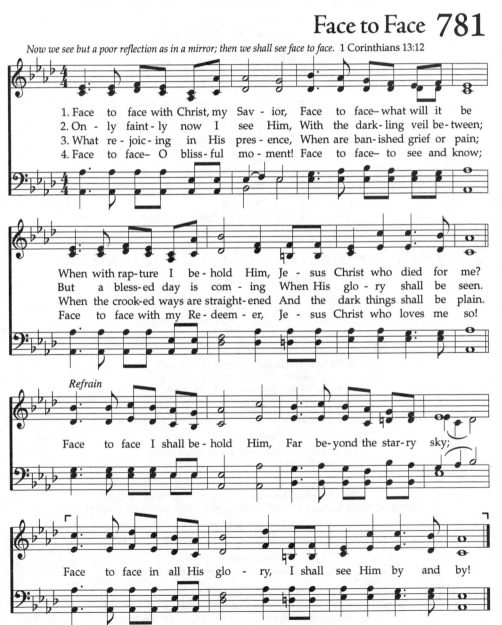

1. Face to face with Christ, my Sav-ior, Face to face—what will it be
2. On-ly faint-ly now I see Him, With the dark-ling veil be-tween;
3. What re-joic-ing in His pres-ence, When are ban-ished grief or pain;
4. Face to face— O bliss-ful mo-ment! Face to face— to see and know;

When with rap-ture I be-hold Him, Je-sus Christ who died for me?
But a bless-ed day is com-ing When His glo-ry shall be seen.
When the crook-ed ways are straight-ened And the dark things shall be plain.
Face to face with my Re-deem-er, Je-sus Christ who loves me so!

Refrain

Face to face I shall be-hold Him, Far be-yond the star-ry sky;

Face to face in all His glo-ry, I shall see Him by and by!

TEXT: Carrie E. Breck
MUSIC: Grant C. Tullar

FACE TO FACE
8.7.8.7. with Refrain

782 THE TRUMPET CALL OF GOD

from 1 Thessalonians 4:13-17 (NIV)

WORSHIP LEADER
Brothers, we do not want you to be ignorant about those who fall asleep,
or to grieve like the rest of men, who have no hope.

EVERYONE
**We believe that Jesus died and rose again, and so we believe
that God will bring with Jesus those who have fallen asleep in Him.**

WORSHIP LEADER
According to the Lord's own Word,
we tell you that we who are still alive,
who are left till the coming of the Lord,
will certainly not precede those who have fallen asleep.

EVERYONE
**For the Lord Himself will come down from heaven,
with a loud command, with the voice of the archangel
and with the trumpet call of God,
and the dead in Christ will rise first.**

WORSHIP LEADER
After that, we who are still alive and are left
will be caught up with them in the clouds to meet the Lord in the air.

EVERYONE
And so we will be with the Lord forever.

783 KING OF KINGS AND LORD OF LORDS

from Revelation 19:11-16 (NIV)

WORSHIP LEADER
I saw heaven standing open, and there before me was a white horse,
whose rider is called Faithful and True.

EVERYONE
**With justice He judges and makes war.
His eyes are like blazing fire,
and on His head are many crowns.**

MEN
He has a name written on Him that no one but He Himself knows.

WOMEN
**He is dressed in a robe dipped in blood,
and His name is the Word of God.**

EVERYONE
**The armies of heaven were following Him,
riding on white horses and dressed in fine linen, white and clean.**

WORSHIP LEADER
Out of His mouth comes a sharp sword with which to strike down the nations.

EVERYONE
He will rule them with an iron scepter.

WORSHIP LEADER
He treads the winepress of the fury of the wrath of God Almighty.
On His robe and on His thigh He has this name written:

EVERYONE
KING OF KINGS AND LORD OF LORDS.

A NEW HEAVEN AND A NEW EARTH 784

from Revelation 21:1-4 (NIV)

WORSHIP LEADER or SOLO DRAMATIST
Then I saw a new heaven and a new earth,
for the first heaven and the first earth had passed away,
and there was no longer any sea.
I saw the Holy City, the New Jerusalem,
coming down out of heaven from God,
prepared as a bride beautifully dressed for her husband.
And I heard a loud voice from the throne saying,
"Now the dwelling of God is with men,
and He will live with them.
They will be His people,
and God Himself will be with them and be their God.
He will wipe every tear from their eyes.
There will be no more death or mourning or crying or pain."

LIFE EVERLASTING 785

from John 3:14-16, 36; 5:24; 10:27-29; 1 John 5:11-13 (NKJV)

WORSHIP LEADER
And as Moses lifted up the serpent in the wilderness,
even so must the Son of Man be lifted up,
that whoever believes in Him should not perish but have eternal life.

EVERYONE
For God so loved the world that He gave His only begotten Son,
that whoever believes in Him should not perish but have everlasting life.

WORSHIP LEADER
He who believes in the Son has everlasting life;
and he who does not believe the Son shall not see life,
but the wrath of God abides on him.

EVERYONE
Most assuredly, I say to you, he who hears My Word
and believes in Him who sent Me has everlasting life,
and shall not come into judgment, but has passed from death into life.

MEN
My sheep hear My voice, and I know them, and they follow Me.
And I give them eternal life, and they shall never perish;
neither shall anyone snatch them out of My hand.

WOMEN
My Father, who has given them to Me, is greater than all;
and no one is able to snatch them out of My Father's hand.

EVERYONE
And this is the testimony: that God has given us eternal life,
and this life is in His Son.

WORSHIP LEADER
He who has the Son has life;
He who does not have the Son of God does not have life.

EVERYONE
These things I have written to you who believe in the name of the Son of God,
that you may know that you have eternal life,
and that you may continue to believe in the name of the Son of God.

786 Count Your Blessings

God has blessed us in the heavenly realms with every spiritual blessing in Christ. Ephesians 1:3

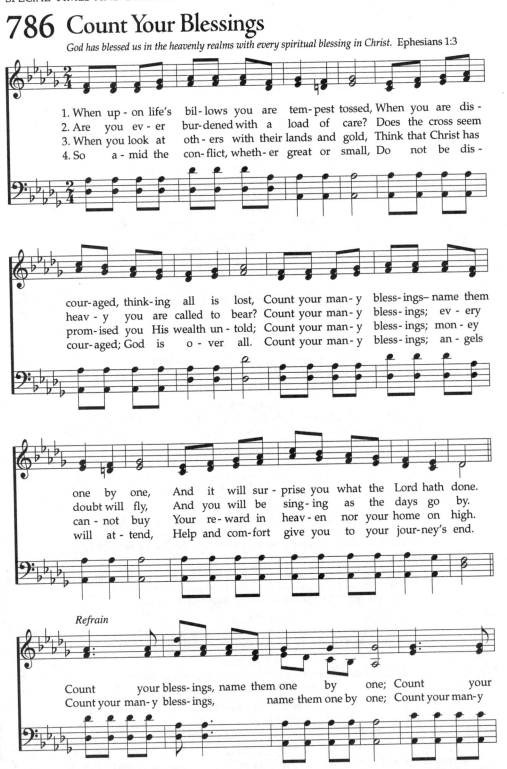

1. When up-on life's bil-lows you are tem-pest tossed, When you are dis-
2. Are you ev-er bur-dened with a load of care? Does the cross seem
3. When you look at oth-ers with their lands and gold, Think that Christ has
4. So a-mid the con-flict, wheth-er great or small, Do not be dis-

cour-aged, think-ing all is lost, Count your man-y bless-ings– name them
heav-y you are called to bear? Count your man-y bless-ings; ev-ery
prom-ised you His wealth un-told; Count your man-y bless-ings; mon-ey
cour-aged; God is o-ver all. Count your man-y bless-ings; an-gels

one by one, And it will sur-prise you what the Lord hath done.
doubt will fly, And you will be sing-ing as the days go by.
can-not buy Your re-ward in heav-en nor your home on high.
will at-tend, Help and com-fort give you to your jour-ney's end.

Refrain

Count your bless-ings, name them one by one; Count your
Count your man-y bless-ings, name them one by one; Count your man-y

TEXT: Johnson Oatman, Jr.
MUSIC: Edwin O. Excell

BLESSINGS
11.11.11.11. with Refrain

bless-ings, see what God hath done. Count your bless-ings,
bless-ings, see what God hath done. Count your man-y bless-ings,

name them one by one; Count your man-y bless-ings, see what God hath done.

GIVE HIM THANKS

A Worship Sequence

787

Now Thank We All Our God; stanzas 1,3
In All Things Give Him Thanks
We Gather Together; complete
Suggested stanzas have been marked with an arrow: ➤

WORSHIP LEADER
You are my God, and I will praise You;

EVERYONE
You are my God, I will exalt You.

WORSHIP LEADER
Oh, give thanks to the Lord, for He is good!
For His mercy endures forever.

EVERYONE
We give thanks to You, O God, we give thanks!
from Psalms 118:28-29; 75:1 (NKJV)

Optional introduction to
"Now Thank We All Our God"

GIVE HIM THANKS - A Worship Sequence
Compilation © Copyright 1997 by Integrity's Hosanna! Music and Word Music (a div. of WORD MUSIC). All rights reserved. Used by permission.

788 Now Thank We All Our God

Give thanks to the Lord; make known what He has done. Isaiah 12:4

1. Now thank we all our God, With heart and hands and voic - es,
2. O may this boun - teous God Through all our life be near us,
3. All praise and thanks to God The Fa - ther now be giv - en,

Who won - drous things hath done, In whom His world re - joic - es;
With ev - er joy - ful hearts And bless - ed peace to cheer us;
The Son, and Him who reigns With them in high - est heav - en,

Who, from our moth - ers' arms, Hath blessed us on our way
And keep us in His grace, And guide us when per - plexed,
The one e - ter - nal God, Whom earth and heav'n a - dore;

With count - less gifts of love, And still is ours to - day.
And free us from all ills In this world and the next.
For thus it was, is now, And shall be ev - er - more.

TEXT: Martin Rinkart; translated by Catherine Winkworth
MUSIC: Johann Crüger; harmonized by Felix Mendelssohn

NUN DANKET
6.7.6.7.6.6.6.6.

Optional transition to
"In All Things Give Him Thanks"

In All Things Give Him Thanks 789

Give thanks in all circumstances, for this is God's will for you. 1 Thessalonians 5:18

And in all things give Him thanks, And in

all things let your grat - i - tude shine through. And in

all things give Him thanks, For He has giv - en

1 *Repeat optional*

all things un - to you. And in

2 *Final ending*

you.

Optional segue to "We Gather
Together." No transition is needed.

TEXT: Claire Cloninger, Andy Cloninger, Ken Barker
MUSIC: Claire Cloninger, Andy Cloninger, Ken Barker

GIVE HIM THANKS
Irregular meter

790 We Gather Together

May God be gracious to us and bless us and make His face shine upon us. Psalm 67:1

1. We gath - er to - geth - er to ask the Lord's bless - ing;
2. Be - side us to guide us, our God with us join - ing,
3. We all do ex - tol Thee, Thou Lead - er tri - um - phant,

He chas - tens and has - tens His will to make known;
Or - dain - ing, main - tain - ing His king - dom di - vine;
And pray that Thou still our De - fend - er wilt be.

The wick - ed op - press - ing now cease from dis - tress - ing:
So from the be - gin - ning the fight we were win - ning:
Let Thy con - gre - ga - tion es - cape trib - u - la - tion:

Sing prais - es to His name; He for - gets not His own.
Thou, Lord, wast at our side— all glo - ry be Thine!
Thy name be ev - er praised; O Lord, make us free!

TEXT: Netherlands Folk hymn; translated by Theodore Baker
MUSIC: Netherlands Folk song; harmonized by Edward Kremser;
Last stanza setting and Choral ending by Ken Barker

KREMSER
12.11.12.11.

Optional last stanza setting   *Unison*   Broader

➤ 3. We all do ex - tol Thee, Thou

Lead - er tri - um - phant, And pray that Thou still our De - fend - er wilt

be. Let Thy con - gre - ga - tion es - cape trib - u - la - tion:

Thy name be ev - er praised; O Lord, make us free!

f Optional choral ending

Thy name be ev - er praised; O Lord, make us free! A - men.

The end of GIVE HIM THANKS - A Worship Sequence

791 Jesus, We Just Want to Thank You

Thanks be to God for His indescribable gift! 2 Corinthians 9:15

1. Je - sus, we just want to thank You, Je - sus, we
2. Je - sus, we just want to praise You, Je - sus, we
3. Sav - ior, we just want to serve You, Sav - ior, we
4. Je - sus, we know You are com - ing, Je - sus, we

just want to thank You, Je - sus, we just want to
just want to praise You, Je - sus, we just want to
just want to serve You, Sav - ior, we just want to
know You are com - ing, Je - sus, we know You are

thank You, Thank You for be - ing so good.
praise You, Praise You for be - ing so good.
serve You, Serve You for be - ing so good.
com - ing, Take us to live in Your home.

TEXT: Gloria Gaither and William J. Gaither
MUSIC: William J. Gaither

THANK YOU
8.8.8.7.

792 For All These Things

Praise be to God, who has blessed us with every spiritual blessing in Christ. Ephesians 1:3

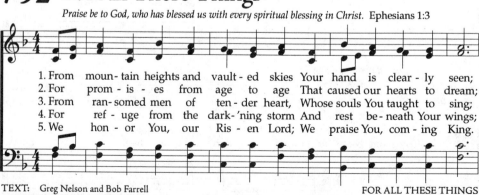

1. From moun - tain heights and vault - ed skies Your hand is clear - ly seen;
2. For prom - is - es from age to age That caused our hearts to dream;
3. From ran - somed men of ten - der heart, Whose souls You taught to sing;
4. For ref - uge from the dark - 'ning storm And rest be - neath Your wings;
5. We hon - or You, our Ris - en Lord; We praise You, com - ing King.

TEXT: Greg Nelson and Bob Farrell
MUSIC: Greg Nelson and Bob Farrell

FOR ALL THESE THINGS
8.6.8.6.

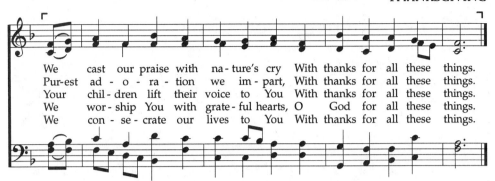

We cast our praise with na-ture's cry With thanks for all these things.
Pur-est ad-o-ra-tion we im-part, With thanks for all these things.
Your chil-dren lift their voice to You With thanks for all these things.
We wor-ship You with grate-ful hearts, O God for all these things.
We con-se-crate our lives to You With thanks for all these things.

For the Beauty of the Earth 793

Give thanks to the Lord for His unfailing love and His wonderful deeds. Psalm 107:8

1. For the beau-ty of the earth, For the glo-ry of the skies,
2. For the won-der of each hour Of the day and of the night,
3. For the joy of hu-man love, Broth-er, sis-ter, par-ent, child,
4. For Thy Church that ev-er-more Lift-eth ho-ly hands a-bove,
5. For Thy-self, best gift di-vine, To our race so free-ly given;

For the love which from our birth O-ver and a-round us lies:
Hill and vale and tree and flower, Sun and moon and stars of light:
Friends on earth and friends a-bove; For all gen-tle thoughts and mild:
Off-ering up on ev-ery shore Her pure sac-ri-fice of love:
For that great, great love of Thine, Peace on earth and joy in heaven:

Lord of all, to Thee we raise This our hymn of grate-ful praise.

TEXT: Folliott S. Pierpoint, altered
MUSIC: Conrad Kocher; arranged by William H. Monk

DIX
7.7.7.7.7.7.

794 Let All Things Now Living

Let everything that has breath praise the Lord. Psalm 150:6

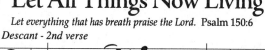

Descant - 2nd verse

2. His law He en - forc - es; The stars in their cours - es And

1. Let all things now liv - ing A song of thanks - giv - ing To
2. His law He en - forc - es; The stars in their cours - es And

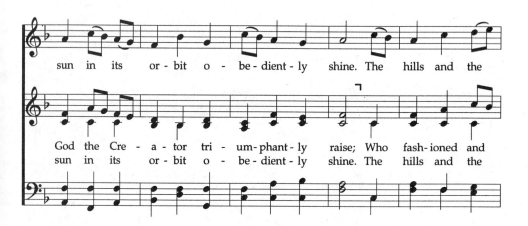

sun in its or - bit o - be - dient - ly shine. The hills and the

God the Cre - a - tor tri - um - phant - ly raise; Who fash - ioned and
sun in its or - bit o - be - dient - ly shine. The hills and the

moun - tains, The riv - ers and foun - tains, The deeps of the

made us, Pro - tect - ed and stayed us, Who still guides us
moun - tains, The riv - ers and foun - tains, The deeps of the

TEXT: Katherine K. Davis

MUSIC: Traditional Welsh Melody; Descant by Tom Fettke

ASH GROVE

6.6.11.6.6.11.D.

o - cean pro - claim Him di - vine. Al - le - lu - ia!

on to the end of our days. God's ban - ners are o'er us; His
o - cean pro - claim Him di - vine. We, too, should be voic - ing Our

Al - le - lu - ia! Al - le - lu - ia, a

light goes be - fore us— A pil - lar of fire shin - ing
love and re - joic - ing; With glad ad - o - ra - tion a

song let us raise Till all things now liv - ing U - nite in thanks-

forth in the night— Till shad - ows have van - ished And dark - ness is
song let us raise Till all things now liv - ing U - nite in thanks-

giv - ing: "To God in the high - est, ho - san - na and praise!"

ban - ished, As for - ward we trav - el from light in - to light.
giv - ing: "To God in the high - est, ho - san - na and praise!"

795 We Are So Blessed

God has blessed us with every spiritual blessing in Christ. Ephesians 1:3

We are so blessed by the gifts from Your hand, I just
so blessed, we just can't find a way Or the

can't un-der-stand Why You've loved us so much. We are
words that can say, Thank You Lord, for Your

touch. When we're emp-ty You fill us 'til we o-ver-

flow, When we're hun-gry You feed us and cause us to

know; We are so blessed, Take what we have to

TEXT: William J. Gaither, Gloria Gaither, Greg Nelson
MUSIC: William J. Gaither, Gloria Gaither, Greg Nelson

SO BLESSED
Irregular meter

bring; Take it all, ev - ery - thing, Lord, we love You so much.

In Thanksgiving, Let Us Praise Him 796

With praise and thanksgiving they sang to the Lord. Ezra 3:11

1. From the first bright light of morn - ing To the last warm glow of dusk;
2. In the sea - son of our plen - ty, In the sea - son of our need;
3. Safe with-in His hand that guides us, Hid-den in His heal - ing wings;

Ev - ery breath we take is sa - cred, For it is God's gift to us.
We will find His grace suf - fi - cient, We will find His love com-plete.
Day by day His love pro - vides us Ev - ery good and per - fect thing.

Refrain

In thanks - giv - ing, let us praise Him; In thanks - giv - ing, let us sing

Songs of praise and ad - o - ra - tion To our gra - cious Lord and King.

TEXT: Claire Cloninger
MUSIC: Franz Joseph Haydn

AUSTRIAN HYMN
8.7.8.7.D.

797 Come, Ye Thankful People, Come

You crown the year with Your bounty. Psalm 65:11

1. Come, ye thank-ful peo-ple, come; Raise the song of har-vest home;
2. All the world is God's own field, Fruit un-to His praise to yield;
3. For the Lord our God shall come, And shall take His har-vest home;
4. E-ven so, Lord, quick-ly come To Thy fi-nal har-vest-home;

All is safe-ly gath-ered in Ere the win-ter storms be-gin.
Wheat and tares to-geth-er sown, Un-to joy or sor-row grown.
From His field shall in that day All of-fens-es purge a-way.
Gath-er Thou Thy peo-ple in, Free from sor-row, free from sin.

God, our Mak-er, doth pro-vide For our wants to be sup-plied.
First the blade, and then the ear, Then the full corn shall ap-pear;
Give His an-gels charge at last In the fire the tares to cast,
There for-ev-er pu-ri-fied, In Thy pres-ence to a-bide.

Come to God's own tem-ple, come; Raise the song of har-vest home.
Lord of har-vest, grant that we Whole-some grain and pure may be.
But the fruit-ful ears to store In His gar-ner ev-er-more.
Come, with all Thine an-gels come; Raise the glo-rious har-vest home.

TEXT: Henry Alford
MUSIC: George J. Elvey

ST. GEORGE'S, WINDSOR
7.7.7.7.D.

HONOR AND THANKSGIVING 798

from Psalms 50:14; 30:4; 97:12; 106:1; 136:1-3, 26; 105:1-7;
Revelation 7:11-12 (NASB)

WORSHIP LEADER
Offer to God a sacrifice of thanksgiving.

EVERYONE
Sing praise to the Lord, you His godly ones,
and give thanks to His holy name.

WOMEN
Be glad in the Lord, you righteous ones,
and give thanks to His holy name.

WORSHIP LEADER
Give thanks to the Lord, for He is good;

EVERYONE
For His lovingkindness is everlasting.

WORSHIP LEADER
Give thanks to the God of gods.

EVERYONE
For His lovingkindness is everlasting.

WORSHIP LEADER
Give thanks to the Lord of lords,

EVERYONE
For His lovingkindness is everlasting.

WORSHIP LEADER
Give thanks to the God of heaven,

EVERYONE
For His lovingkindness is everlasting.

MEN
Oh, give thanks to the Lord, call upon His name;
Make known His deeds among the peoples.

CHOIR (or EVERYONE)
Sing to Him, sing praises to Him;
Speak of all His wonders.
Glory in His holy name;
Let the heart of those who seek the Lord be glad.

WOMEN
Seek the Lord and His strength; seek His face continually.

EVERYONE
Remember His wonders which He has done,
His marvels, and the judgments uttered by His mouth.
He is the Lord our God!

WORSHIP LEADER
And all the angels were standing around the throne,
and around the elders and the four living creatures;
and they fell on their faces before the throne and worshiped God, saying:

EVERYONE
"Amen.
Blessing and glory and wisdom and thanksgiving
and honor and power and might
be to our God, forever and ever!
Amen."

799 America, the Beautiful

The boundary lines have fallen in pleasant places; I have a delightful inheritance. Psalm 16:6

1. O beau - ti - ful for spa - cious skies, For am - ber waves of grain,
2. O beau - ti - ful for pil - grim feet, Whose stern, im - pas - sioned stress
3. O beau - ti - ful for he - roes proved In lib - er - at - ing strife,
4. O beau - ti - ful for pa - triot dream That sees be - yond the years

For pur - ple moun - tain maj - es - ties A - bove the fruit - ed plain!
A thor - ough - fare for free - dom beat A - cross the wil - der - ness!
Who more than self their coun - try loved And mer - cy more than life!
Thine al - a - bas - ter cit - ies gleam, Un - dimmed by hu - man tears!

A - mer - i - ca! A - mer - i - ca! God shed His grace on thee,
A - mer - i - ca! A - mer - i - ca! God mend thine ev - ery flaw,
A - mer - i - ca! A - mer - i - ca! May God thy gold re - fine
A - mer - i - ca! A - mer - i - ca! God shed His grace on thee,

And crown thy good with broth - er - hood From sea to shin - ing sea!
Con - firm thy soul in self - con - trol, Thy lib - er - ty in law!
Till all suc - cess be no - ble - ness, And ev - ery gain di - vine!
And crown thy good with broth - er - hood From sea to shin - ing sea!

TEXT: Katharine Lee Bates
MUSIC: Samuel A. Ward; Last stanza setting and Choral ending by Camp Kirkland

MATERNA
C.M.D.

800 Heal Our Land

He heals the brokenhearted and binds up their wounds. Psalm 147:3

Heal our land, Fa-ther, heal our land; Hear our cry and turn our na-tion back to You. Lord, heal our land, Hear us, O Lord, and heal our land; For-give our sin and heal our bro-ken land. For-give our sin and heal our bro-ken land.

TEXT: Tom and Robin Brooks
MUSIC: Tom and Robin Brooks

HEAL OUR LAND
Irregular meter

King of the Nations 801

All nations will come and worship before You. Revelation 15:4

1. Come, let us wor-ship Je-sus, · King of na-tions, Lord of all;
2. Lav-ish our hearts' af-fec-tion, Deep-est love and high-est praise;
3. Bring trib-utes from the na-tions, Come in joy-ful cav-al-cades;
4. Come, Lord and fill Your tem-ple, Glo-ri-fy Your dwell-ing place
5. Fear God and give Him glo-ry, For His hour of judg-ment comes;

Mag-ni-fi-cent and glo-ri-ous, Just and mer-ci-ful.
Voice, race and lan-guage blend-ing, All the world a-mazed.
One thun-d'rous ac-cla-ma-tion, One ban-ner raised.
'Til na-tions see Your splen-dor And seek Your face.
Cre-a-tor, Lord Al-might-y, Wor-ship Him a-lone.

Refrain

Je-sus, King of the na-tions, Je-sus, Lord of all.

Je-sus, King of the na-tions, Lord of all!

TEXT: Graham Kendrick
MUSIC: Graham Kendrick

KING OF THE NATIONS
7.7.7.5. with Refrain

802 The Star-Spangled Banner

Some trust in chariots and horses, but we trust in God. Psalm 20:7

1. O say, can you see, by the dawn's ear - ly light,
2. O thus be it ev - er, when free men shall stand

What so proud - ly we hailed at the twi - light's last gleam - ing,
Be - tween their loved homes and the war's des - o - la - tion;

Whose broad stripes and bright stars, through the per - il - ous fight,
Blest with vic - t'ry and peace, may the heav'n - res - cued land

O'er the ram - parts we watched, were so gal - lant - ly stream - ing?
Praise the Pow'r that hath made and pre - served us a na - tion!

TEXT: Francis Scott Key
MUSIC: Attributed to John Stafford Smith

NATIONAL ANTHEM
Irregular meter

And the rock - ets' red glare, the bombs burst - ing in air,
Then con - quer we must, when our cause it is just;

Gave proof through the night that our flag was still there.
And this be our mot - to: "In God is our trust!"

O say, does that star - span - gled ban - ner yet
And the star - span - gled ban - ner in tri - umph shall

wave O'er the land of the free and the home of the brave?
wave O'er the land of the free and the home of the brave.

803 If My People Will Pray

If My people will pray and turn from their wicked ways, I will forgive their sin. 2 Chronicles 7:14

TEXT: Adapted from 2 Chronicles 7:14 by Jimmy Owens
MUSIC: Jimmy Owens

OWENS
Irregular meter

Then will I hear and will for-give, for-give their sin. If My

peo-ple, which are called by My name, Shall hum-ble them-selves, shall

hum-ble them-selves and pray; I will for-give their sin, I will for-

give their sin, I will for-give their sin, And heal their land.

Optional choral ending
Unison - hushed

p If My peo-ple, which are called by My name, Shall hum-ble them-selves,

rit. pp *divide

shall hum-ble them-selves, shall hum-ble them-selves and pray.

pp

*a cappella preferred

804 Battle Hymn of the Republic

We are more than conquerors through Him who loved us. Romans 8:37

1. Mine eyes have seen the glo-ry of the com-ing of the Lord,
2. I have seen Him in the watch-fires of a hun-dred cir-cling camps;
3. He has sound-ed forth the trum-pet that shall nev-er call re-treat,
4. In the beau-ty of the lil-ies Christ was born a-cross the sea,
5. We can al-most hear the trum-pet sound, the Lord's re-turn is near;

He is tram-pling out the vin-tage where the grapes of wrath are
They have build-ed Him an al-tar in the eve-ning dews and
He is sift-ing out the hearts of men be-fore His judg-ment
With a glo-ry in His bos-om that trans-fig-ures you and
There are still so man-y peo-ple lost, His mes-sage they must

stored; He hath loosed the fate-ful light-ning of His
damps; I can read His righ-teous sen-tence by the
seat; O be swift, my soul, to an-swer Him! be
me; As He died to make men ho-ly, let us
hear; Fa-ther, give us one more mo-ment, one more

ter-ri-ble, swift sword; His truth is march-ing on.
dim and flar-ing lamps. His day is march-ing on.
ju-bi-lant, my feet! Our God is march-ing on.
live to make men free, While God is march-ing on.
day, just one more year— With God we're march-ing on.

TEXT: Julia Ward Howe, stanzas 1-4; Don Moen, stanza 5
MUSIC: Traditional American melody;
Last stanza setting and Choral ending by Gary Rhodes

BATTLE HYMN
15.15.15.6. with Refrain

Refrain

Glo - ry! glo - ry! Hal - le - lu - jah! Glo - ry! glo - ry! Hal - le - lu - jah!

Glo - ry! glo - ry! Hal - le - lu - jah! His truth is march - ing on.

Optional last stanza setting
mf Unison

5. We can al - most hear the trum - pet sound, the Lord's re - turn is

near; There are still so man - y peo - ple lost, His mes - sage they must hear; Fa - ther,

building

give us one more mo - ment, one more day, just one more year– With God we're march - ing

Continued on next page

Praise Team (or ladies' trio)
f
Glo - ry! Hal - le - lu - jah!
f
on. Glo - ry! glo - ry! Hal - le - lu - jah!
broadening
Glo - ry! Hal - le - lu - jah! Glo - ry! Glo - ry! Hal - le -
Glo - ry! glo - ry! Hal - le - lu - jah! Glo - ry! glo - ry! Hal - le -
lu - jah! His truth is march - ing on.
lu - jah! His truth is march - ing on.
Optional choral ending
Sing harmony
ff
rit.
A - men!
A - men! A - men! A - men!
ff

If My People's Hearts Are Humbled 805

If My people will humble themselves, then will I heal their land. 2 Chronicles 7:14

1. If My peo-ple's hearts are hum-bled, If they pray and seek My face;
2. Then My eyes will see their sor-row, Then My ears will hear their plea.

If they turn a-way from e-vil I will not with-hold My grace.
If My peo-ple's hearts are hum-bled I will set their na-tion free.

I will hear their prayers from heav-en; I will par-don ev-ery sin.
If My peo-ple's hearts are hum-bled, If they pray and seek My face;

If My peo-ple's hearts are hum-bled, I will sure-ly heal their land.
If they turn a-way from e-vil I will not with-hold My grace.

TEXT: Claire Cloninger; based on 2 Chronicles 7:14
MUSIC: John Zundel
A higher setting may be found at No. 93

BEECHER
8.7.8.7.D.

806 O Canada!

It is better to take refuge in the Lord than to trust in princes. Psalm 118:9

1. O Can - a - da! Our home and na - tive land! True pa - triot
2. Al - might - y Love, by Thy mys - te - rious pow'r, In wis - dom

love in all thy sons com - mand. With glow - ing hearts we
guide, with faith and free - dom dow'r; Be ours a na - tion

see thee rise, the true north, strong and free. From far and wide, O
ev - er - more that no op - pres - sion blights, Where jus - tice rules from

Can - a - da, we stand on guard for thee. God keep our land
shore to shore, from lakes to north - ern lights. May love a - lone

glo - rious and free! O Can - a - da, we stand on guard for
for wrong a - tone; Lord of the lands, make Can - a - da Thine

TEXT: Robert S. Weir, stanza 1; Albert C. Watson, stanza 2
MUSIC: Calixa Lavallée; arranged by Frederick C. Silvester

O CANADA
Irregular meter

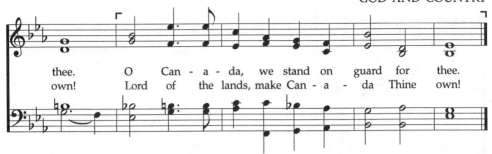

thee.   O Can - a - da, we stand on guard for thee.
own!   Lord of the lands, make Can - a - da Thine own!

My Country, 'Tis of Thee 807

Righteousness exalts a nation, but sin is a disgrace to any people. Proverbs 14:34

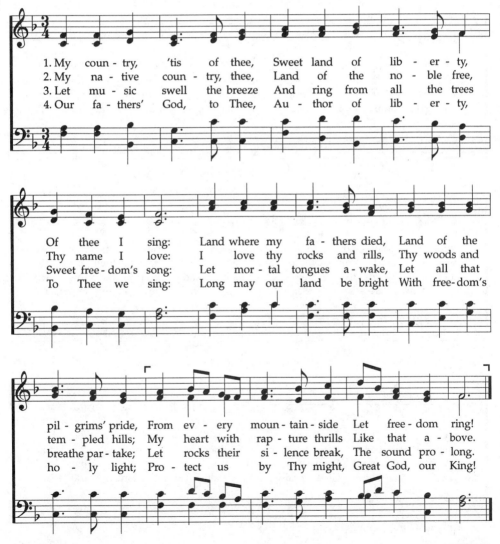

1. My coun - try, 'tis of thee, Sweet land of lib - er - ty,
2. My na - tive coun - try, thee, Land of the no - ble free,
3. Let mu - sic swell the breeze And ring from all the trees
4. Our fa - thers' God, to Thee, Au - thor of lib - er - ty,

Of thee I sing: Land where my fa - thers died, Land of the
Thy name I love: I love thy rocks and rills, Thy woods and
Sweet free - dom's song: Let mor - tal tongues a - wake, Let all that
To Thee we sing: Long may our land be bright With free - dom's

pil - grims' pride, From ev - ery moun - tain - side Let free - dom ring!
tem - pled hills; My heart with rap - ture thrills Like that a - bove.
breathe par - take; Let rocks their si - lence break, The sound pro - long.
ho - ly light; Pro - tect us by Thy might, Great God, our King!

TEXT: Samuel F. Smith
MUSIC: *Thesaurus Musicus*, c. 1745

AMERICA
6.6.4.6.6.6.4.

808 Eternal Father, Strong to Save

He guided them to their desired haven. Let them give thanks to the Lord. Psalm 107:30-31

1. E - ter - nal Fa - ther, strong to save, Whose arm hath bound the
2. O Christ, the Lord of hill and plain O'er which our traf - fic
3. O Spir - it, whom the Fa - ther sent To spread a - broad the
4. O Trin - i - ty of love and pow'r, Our breth - ren shield in

rest - less wave, Who bids the might - y o - cean deep— Its
runs a - main By moun - tain pass or val - ley low; Wher -
fir - ma - ment; O Wind of heav - en, by Thy might Save
dan - ger's hour; From rock and tem - pest, fire and foe, Pro -

own ap - point - ed lim - its keep: O hear us when we
ev - er, Lord, our breth - ren go, Pro - tect them by Thy
all who dare the ea - gle's flight; And keep them by Thy
tect them where - so - e'er they go; Thus ev - er - more shall

cry to Thee For those in per - il on the sea.
guard - ing hand From ev - ery per - il on the land.
watch - ful care From ev - ery per - il in the air.
rise to Thee Glad praise from air and land and sea.

TEXT: William Whiting, stanzas 1,4; Robert Nelson Spencer, stanzas 2, 3
MUSIC: John Bacchus Dykes

MELITA
8.8.8.8.8.8.

God of Our Fathers 809

In You our fathers put their trust; they trusted and You delivered them. Psalm 22:4

*Trumpets before
each stanza*

1. God of our fa - thers, whose al - might - y
2. Thy love di - vine hath led us in the
3. From war's a - larms, from dead - ly pes - ti -
4. Re - fresh Thy peo - ple on their toil - some

hand Leads forth in beau - ty all the star - ry
past, In this free land by Thee our lot is
lence, Be Thy strong arm our ev - er sure de -
way. Lead us from night to nev - er - end - ing

band Of shin - ing worlds in splen - dor through the
cast; Be Thou our Rul - er, Guard - ian, Guide and
fense; Thy true re - li - gion in our hearts in -
day; Fill all our lives with love and grace di -

skies, Our grate - ful songs be - fore Thy throne a - rise.
Stay, Thy Word our law, Thy paths our cho - sen way.
crease, Thy boun - teous good - ness nour - ish us in peace.
vine; And glo - ry, laud and praise be ev - er Thine!

TEXT: Daniel C. Roberts
MUSIC: George W. Warren

NATIONAL HYMN
10.10.10.10.

810 LOVE THE LORD, YOUR GOD

from 2 Chronicles 7:14; Mark 12:29-31; Matthew 7:12;
Romans 13:1-2, 7, 10; 1 Peter 2:13-17 (NKJV)

WORSHIP LEADER
If My people who are called by My name

EVERYONE
Will humble themselves, and pray and seek My face,
and turn from their wicked ways, then I will hear from heaven,
and will forgive their sin and heal their land.

WORSHIP LEADER
Hear, O Israel, the Lord our God, the Lord is one.

EVERYONE
And you shall love the Lord your God with all your heart,
with all your soul, with all your mind, and with all your strength.

WORSHIP LEADER
You shall love your neighbor as yourself.
There is no other commandment greater than these.

EVERYONE
Love does no harm to a neighbor;
Therefore love is the fulfillment of the law.

MEN
Whatever you want men to do to you, do also to them,
for this is the Law and the Prophets.

WORSHIP LEADER
Let every soul be subject to the governing authorities.
For there is no authority except from God,
and the authorities that exist are appointed by God.

EVERYONE
Therefore whoever resists the authority resists the ordinance of God,
and those who resist will bring judgment on themselves.

WORSHIP LEADER
Render therefore to all their due;
taxes to whom taxes are due,
customs to whom customs,
fear to whom fear,
honor to whom honor.

EVERYONE
Submit yourselves to every ordinance of man for the Lord's sake,
whether to the king as supreme, or to governors,
as to those who are sent by him for the punishment of evildoers
and for the praise of those who do good.

WORSHIP LEADER
For this is the will of God,
that by doing good you may put to silence the ignorance of foolish men —
as free, yet not using your liberty as a cloak for vice, but as servants of God.
Honor all people.
Love the brotherhood.
Fear God.
Honor the king.

EVERYONE
Love the Lord your God with all your heart,
with all your soul, with all your mind,
and with all your strength.

Another Year Is Dawning 811

Teach us to number our days aright, that we may gain a heart of wisdom. Psalm 90:12

1. An - oth - er year is dawn - ing: Dear Fa - ther, let it be,
2. An - oth - er year of mer - cies, Of faith - ful - ness and grace;
3. An - oth - er year of ser - vice, Of wit - ness for Thy love;

In work- ing or in wait - ing, An - oth - er year with Thee;
An - oth - er year of glad - ness In the shin - ing of Thy face;
An - oth - er year of train - ing For ho - lier work a - bove.

An - oth - er year of prog - ress, An - oth - er year of praise,
An - oth - er year of lean - ing Up - on Thy lov - ing breast;
An - oth - er year is dawn - ing: Dear Fa - ther, let it be,

An - oth - er year of prov - ing Thy pres - ence all the days.
An - oth - er year of trust - ing, Of qui - et, hap - py rest.
On earth or else in heav - en, An - oth - er year for Thee.

TEXT: Frances Ridley Havergal
MUSIC: Samuel S. Wesley

AURELIA
7.6.7.6.D.

812 Glory Be to the Father

Ascribe to the Lord the glory due His name. Psalm 96:8

Glo - ry be to the Fa - ther, and to the Son, and to the Ho - ly Ghost, As it was in the be - gin - ning, is now and ev - er shall be, world with - out end. A - men, A - men.

TEXT: *Gloria Patri*; Traditional, 2nd century
MUSIC: Christoph Meineke

MEINEKE
Irregular meter

813 Glory Be to the Father

Ascribe to the Lord the glory due His name. Psalm 96:8

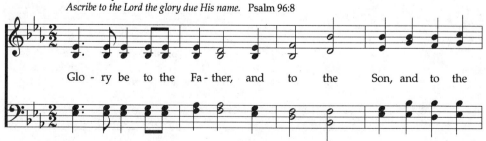

Glo - ry be to the Fa - ther, and to the Son, and to the

TEXT: *Gloria Patri*; Traditional, 2nd century
MUSIC: Henry W. Greatorex

GREATOREX
Irregular meter

Ho - ly Ghost, As it was in the be - gin - ning, is now and

ev - er shall be, world with-out end. A - men, A - men.

Doxology 814

Praise be to the God and Father of our Lord Jesus Christ, who has blessed us. Ephesians 1:3

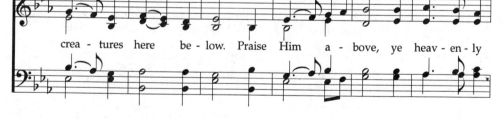

Praise God from whom all bless - ings flow. Praise Him, all

crea - tures here be - low. Praise Him a - bove, ye heav - en - ly

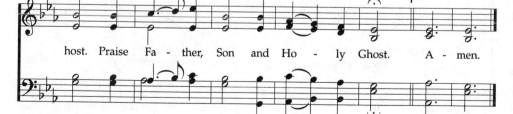

host. Praise Fa - ther, Son and Ho - ly Ghost. A - men.

TEXT: Thomas Ken
MUSIC: Jimmy Owens

FAIRHILL
L. M.

815 Doxology

Praise be to the God and Father of our Lord Jesus Christ, who has blessed us. Ephesians 1:3

Praise God from whom all bless-ings flow. Praise Him, all crea-tures here be-low.

Praise Him a-bove, ye heav'n-ly host. Praise Fa-ther, Son and Ho-ly Ghost. A-men.

TEXT: Thomas Ken
MUSIC: *Genevan Psalter*, 1551; attributed to Louis Bourgeois

OLD HUNDREDTH
L.M.

816 We Give Thee But Thine Own

We have given You only what comes from Your hand. 1 Chronicles 29:14

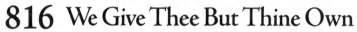

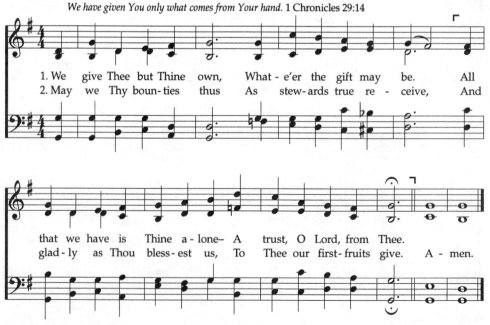

1. We give Thee but Thine own, What-e'er the gift may be. All
2. May we Thy boun-ties thus As stew-ards true re-ceive, And

that we have is Thine a-lone— A trust, O Lord, from Thee.
glad-ly as Thou bless-est us, To Thee our first-fruits give. A-men.

TEXT: William W. How
MUSIC: Mason and Webb's *Cantica Laudis*, 1850

SCHUMANN
S.M.

O Bless the Gifts 817

The gifts you sent are a fragrant offering, pleasing to God. Philippians 4:18

O bless the gifts our hands have brought; And bless the work our hearts have planned. Ours is the faith, the will, the thought; The rest, O God, is in Your hand.

TEXT: Samuel Longfellow, altered
MUSIC: Twila Paris

LAMB OF GOD
8.8.8.8.

We Give These Gifts 818

Freely you have received, freely give. Matthew 10:8

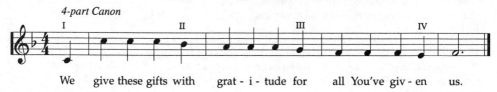

We give these gifts with grat-i-tude for all You've giv-en us.

TEXT: Traditional
MUSIC: Traditional Dutch Folk Song

GRACE
Irregular meter

The Bible Versions Used in *The Celebration Hymnal*

Of the major, standard, committee-produced modern translations of the Bible, the three most popular ones (especially among evangelicals) are the New International Version (NIV), The New King James Version (NKJV), and the New American Standard Bible (NASB). That is the primary reason we chose to use these three.

The NASB represents a more literal, word-for-word approach to the translation task. It has the advantage of being closer to the original Hebrew, Aramaic and Greek in phrasing and word order. The complete Bible was released in 1970 by the Lockman Foundation. Its text was updated in 1995.

The NKJV employs more contemporary English than the NASB, but still follows a generally literal approach to translation. Of the modern versions, it is the closest to the KJV, particularly in the New Testament. The whole Bible was issued by Thomas Nelson Publishers in 1982.

The NIV is a mediating type of translation. The translators wanted to avoid being either woodenly literal or unnecessarily free. To illustrate, the NIV is freer than the NASB and the NKJV but not as free as the Good News Bible (Today's English Version). The result is a balance in translation method. The complete NIV Bible was released in 1978 by the International Bible Society. Its text was updated in 1983.

Why include Scripture readings in a hymnal? It is clear from the Bible itself that three vital elements of worship services are music (both vocal and instrumental), the public reading of Scripture, and preaching or teaching (Neh. 8:3; Ps. 149:1; 150:3-5; Matt. 26:30; 1 Cor. 14:26; 1 Tim. 4:13). According to the end of 1 Cor. 14:26, all parts of Christian worship should be edifying (NIV "strengthening") to the church. We felt that Scripture readings are so important in true, biblical worship that instead of relegating them to the back, we have placed them at the end of each main section of the hymnal. The body of the hymnal also contains Scripture readings for the worship sequences, spoken benedictions and calls to worship, and Scripture verses appearing with song titles.

It is our prayer that the Lord of the Church will be pleased to use all parts of this hymnal (including Scripture) to enhance the worship experience of His people.

Dr. Kenneth L. Barker
Theological Consultant and Scripture Editor

Topical Index of Scripture Readings

TOPICAL INDEX OF SCRIPTURE READINGS

Scripture Readings in Biblical Order

Index of Worship Sequences

INDEX OF WORSHIP SEQUENCES

Creative Worship Resources

TRANSITIONS

From Number   *To Number*

From		To	
8	Come, Thou Almighty King (F)	9	Glorify Thy Name (B♭)
15	No Other Name (D)	16	All Hail the Power of Jesus' Name (A♭/A)
31	I Exalt Thee (F)	32	Be Exalted, O God (B♭)
35	Hallelujah! Our God Reigns (F)	36	He Is Exalted (F)
43	All Hail the Power of Jesus' Name (G)	44	Crown Him King of Kings (A♭/A)
54	My Tribute (B♭)	55	Bless His Holy Name (E♭)
55	Bless His Holy Name (E♭)	56	To God Be the Glory (G/A♭)
62	Blessed Be the Lord God Almighty (B♭/C)	63	All Creatures of Our God and King (D/E♭)
69	Holy, Holy (C/D♭)	70	A Perfect Heart (F)
74	Holy Is He (B♭)	75	Holy Is the Lord (E♭)
87	Fairest Lord Jesus (E♭)	88	More Precious than Silver (F)
91	In Moments like These (D)	92	O How I Love Jesus (G)
103	All Hail King Jesus (E♭/F)	104	O Worship the King (G/A♭)
109	Lamb of Glory (G)	110	Hallelujah! Praise the Lamb (G/A♭)
110	Hallelujah! Praise the Lamb (G/A♭)	111	Glory to the Lamb (C/D♭)
117	His Name Is Life (D)	118	His Name Is Wonderful (F)
121	How Majestic Is Your Name (C)	122	Glorious Is Thy Name (F)
124	O Magnify the Lord (D)	125	How Excellent Is Thy Name (F)
128	I Sing the Mighty Power of God (B♭)	129	Great and Mighty (E♭)
146	I Worship You, Almighty God (F)	147	How Great Thou Art (B♭)
157	The Love of God (D)	158	Think About His Love (E♭)
169	Rejoice, Ye Pure in Heart (F)	170	Give Thanks (F)
181	Everything Was Made by God (D)	182	For the Beauty of the Earth–Family Worship Setting (G)
182	For the Beauty of the Earth-Family Worship Setting(G)	183	Everything Was Made by God–Reprise (E♭)
188	Praise Him, All Ye Little Children (D)	189	Alleluia (G)
189	Alleluia (G)	190	Praise Him, All Ye Little Children–Reprise I (C)
190	Praise Him, All Ye Little Children–Reprise I (C)	191	Father, I Adore You (F)
191	Father, I Adore You (F)	192	Praise Him, All Ye Little Children–Reprise II (D)
192	Praise Him, All Ye Little Children–Reprise II (D)	193	God Is So Good (D/E♭)
213	We Bring the Sacrifice of Praise (D)	214	He Has Made Me Glad (D/E♭)
219	Surely the Presence (of the Lord Is in This Place) (D)	220	He Is Here (D)
224	We Have Come into His House (E♭)	225	Come, Christians, Join to Sing (A♭)
247	Let's Worship and Adore Him (G/A♭)	248	I Extol You (A♭)
248	I Extol You (A♭)	249	O Come, All Ye Faithful (G/A♭)
253	Silent Night! Holy Night! (B♭)	254	Isn't He? (G)
259	Angels, from the Realms of Glory (B♭)	260	Worthy, You Are Worthy–Christmas Setting (E♭/F)
269	How Great Our Joy! (a min.)	270	Joy to the World! (D)
270	Joy to the World (D)	271	Joyful, Joyful, We Adore You (G)
299	In the Name of the Lord (A♭)	300	All Glory, Laud and Honor (B♭)
300	All Glory, Laud and Honor (B♭)	301	We Will Glorify–Palm Sunday Setting (E♭/F)
308	There Is a Redeemer (D)	309	I Will Sing of My Redeemer (E♭/F)
323	At the Cross (E♭/F)	324	When I Survey the Wondrous Cross (F/g min./A♭)
332	I Know a Fount (D♭)	333	O the Blood of Jesus (D/E♭)
333	O the Blood of Jesus (D/E♭)	334	The Blood Will Never Lose Its Power (A♭)
347	And Can It Be? (G)	348	My Savior's Love (A♭)
348	My Savior's Love (A♭)	349	O How He Loves You and Me (A♭)
365	Alleluia! Alleluia! (G)	366	I Live (G/A♭)
366	I Live (G/A♭)	367	Christ the Lord Is Risen Today (C)
384	Spirit Song (D)	385	Where the Spirit of the Lord Is (E♭)
391	Sweet, Sweet Spirit (G)	392	Holy Spirit, Light Divine (A♭)
422	I Love You with the Love of the Lord (F)	423	The Bond of Love (B♭)

TRANSITIONS (continued)

From Number	*To Number*
423 The Bond of Love (B♭)	424 The Servant Song (E♭)
431 Shine, Jesus, Shine (A♭)	432 Revive Us, O Lord (C)
453 Happy Our Home When God Is There (G)	454 The Family Prayer Song (A♭)
530 I Will Call upon the Lord (C)	531 Unto Thee, O Lord (F)
539 My Faith Looks Up to Thee (D)	540 My Hope Is in the Lord (G)
557 Seekers of Your Heart (D♭)	558 I Am Crucified with Christ (D)
558 I Am Crucified with Christ (D)	559 Praise You (B♭)
580 Through It All (E♭)	581 'Tis So Sweet to Trust in Jesus (G/A♭)
596 I Surrender All (D♭)	597 Take My Life and Let It Be Consecrated (F)
633 Open Our Eyes, Lord (D)	634 More Love to Thee (G)
653 Whiter than Snow (G)	654 Change My Heart, O God (C)
704 God Will Make a Way (G)	705 It Is Well with My Soul (C/D♭)
715 He Is Jehovah (e min.)	716 Jehovah Jireh (f min.)
730 Stand Up, Stand Up for Jesus (A♭)	731 Onward, Christian Soldiers (E♭)
743 Wonderful Peace (F)	744 Joy of My Desire (B♭)
757 Soon and Very Soon (F)	758 Lift Up Your Heads (G)
771 We'll Understand It Better By and By (F/G)	772 When We All Get to Heaven (C)
788 Now Thank We All Our God (E♭)	789 In All Things Give Him Thanks (G)

LAST STANZA SETTINGS INCLUDING CHORAL ENDINGS

3 Holy, Holy, Holy! Lord God Almighty	343 Amazing Grace
11 Come, Thou Fount of Every Blessing	367 Christ the Lord Is Risen Today
16 All Hail the Power of Jesus' Name	401 The Church's One Foundation
21 O for a Thousand Tongues to Sing	433 Rise Up, O Church of God
45 Crown Him with Many Crowns	488 Just As I Am
63 All Creatures of Our God and King	526 The Solid Rock
68 We Praise Thee, O God, Our Redeemer	648 Love Divine, All Loves Excelling
79 My Jesus, I Love Thee	682 Guide Me, O Thou Great Jehovah
90 Joyful, Joyful, We Adore Thee	724 Lead On, O King Eternal
104 O Worship the King	790 We Gather Together
151 A Mighty Fortress Is Our God	799 America, the Beautiful
210 Praise to the Lord, the Almighty	804 Battle Hymn of the Republic
309 I Will Sing of My Redeemer	

LAST STANZA SETTINGS

5 I Sing Praises	311 Hallelujah, What a Savior!
69 Holy, Holy	324 When I Survey the Wondrous Cross (3rd and 4th stanzas)
105 We Will Glorify	
106 Worthy, You Are Worthy	333 O the Blood of Jesus
193 God Is So Good	439 Song for the Nations
196 O Come, Let Us Adore Him	568 May the Mind of Christ, My Savior
215 When Morning Gilds the Skies	585 Be Still and Know (4th and 5th stanzas)
247 Let's Worship and Adore Him	595 I Give All to You
260 Worthy, You Are Worthy–Christmas Setting	597 Take My Life and Let It Be Consecrated
	765 Coming Again

REPEAT SETTINGS

5 I Sing Praises	78 I Love You, Lord
20 Let There Be Glory and Honor and Praises	103 All Hail King Jesus
34 He Is Lord	110 Hallelujah! Praise the Lamb
44 Crown Him King of Kings	111 Glory to the Lamb
47 Jesus, Lord to Me	418 Make Us One
58 Bless the Lord, O My Soul	689 Lead Me, Lord

SEGUES

From Number   *To Number*

4	Praise the Savior (G)		5	I Sing Praises (G/A♭)
20	Let There Be Glory and Honor and Praises (G/A♭)		21	O for a Thousand Tongues to Sing (A♭/A)
37	You Are Crowned with Many Crowns (G)		38	Ye Servants of God (G)
40	You Are My God (C)		41	Lift High the Lord, Our Banner (F)
44	Crown Him King of Kings (A♭/A)		45	Crown Him with Many Crowns (D/E♭)
57	Sing unto the Lord (D minor)		58	Bless the Lord, O My Soul (G/A♭)
65	Stand Up and Bless the Lord (G)		66	I Will Celebrate (e min.)
78	I Love You, Lord (E♭/F)		79	My Jesus, I Love Thee (F/G)
86	Jesus, Name Above All Names (E♭)		87	Fairest Lord Jesus (E♭)
99	Thou Art Worthy, Great Jehovah (E♭)		100	Thou Art Worthy (A♭)
170	Give Thanks (F)		171	Come into His Presence (B♭)
220	He Is Here (D)		221	All Praise to Our Redeeming Lord (G)
227	Come, Let Us Worship and Bow Down (D)		228	I Will Come and Bow Down (D)
243	Emmanuel (C)		244	Come, Thou Long-Expected Jesus (F)
258	Go Tell It on the Mountain (F)		259	Angels, from the Realms of Glory (B♭)
277	Hark! the Herald Angels Sing (F)		278	Angels We Have Heard on High (F)
280	One Small Child (e min.)		281	What Child Is This? (e min.)
284	The Birthday of a King (G)		285	O Holy Night (C)
312	Calvary Covers It All (G/A♭)		313	Worthy the Lamb That Was Slain (A♭)
329	There Is Power in the Blood (A♭)		330	Are You Washed in the Blood? (A♭)
340	Turn Your Eyes upon Jesus (F)		341	Jesus, My Jesus (F)
372	Our God Reigns (B♭)		373	To Him Who Sits on the Throne (B♭)
374	Victory Chant (A♭)		375	Jesus Shall Reign (D♭)
382	Come, Holy Spirit (F)		383	Fill Me Now (F)
386	The Comforter Has Come (B♭)		387	Holy Spirit, Thou Art Welcome (B♭)
389	Spirit of the Living God (F)		390	Spirit of God, Descend upon My Heart (B♭)
437	Send the Light (G)		438	Jesus Saves! (G)
440	So Send I You—by Grace Made Strong (F)		441	Rescue the Perishing (B♭)
527	I Know Whom I Have Believed (D)		528	My Faith Has Found a Resting Place (G)
541	The Joy of the Lord (D)		542	My Life Is in You, Lord (G)
550	I Want to Be like Jesus (D♭)		551	O to Be like Thee! (D♭)
560	More About Jesus (G)		561	I Would Be like Jesus (G)
574	A Child of the King (E♭)		575	Leaning on the Everlasting Arms (A♭)
595	I Give All to You (C/D♭)		596	I Surrender All (D♭)
662	With All My Heart (F)		663	I Offer My Life (F)
694	The Lord's My Shepherd, I'll Not Want (E♭)		695	Lead Me, Lord (E♭)
707	He Giveth More Grace (E♭)		708	Behold, What Manner of Love (E♭)
716	Jehovah Jireh (f min.)		717	I Am the God That Healeth Thee (D♭)
727	Faith Is the Victory (D♭)		728	Am I a Soldier of the Cross? (D♭)
746	He Keeps Me Singing (G)		747	Sunshine in My Soul (G)
759	What If It Were Today? (C)		760	While We Are Waiting, Come (F)
762	What a Day That Will Be (A♭)		763	The King Is Coming (A♭)
789	In All Things Give Him Thanks (G)		790	We Gather Together (C/D♭)

DESCANTS

16	All Hail the Power of Jesus' Name		530	I Will Call upon the Lord
56	To God Be the Glory		531	Unto Thee, O Lord
79	My Jesus, I Love Thee		540	My Hope Is in the Lord
186	Lord, Be Glorified		572	Blessed Assurance
198	Sing Hallelujah (to the Lord)		597	Take My Life and Let It Be Consecrated
249	O Come, All Ye Faithful		647	Pure and Holy
439	Song for the Nations		794	Let All Things Now Living
526	The Solid Rock			

CHORAL ENDINGS

17	Our Great Savior	390	Spirit of God, Descend upon My Heart
32	Be Exalted, O God	410	Standing on the Promises
41	Lift High the Lord Our Banner	424	The Servant Song
100	Thou Art Worthy	434	Revive Us Again
111	Glory to the Lamb	478	Have You Any Room for Jesus?
122	Glorious Is Thy Name	483	The Savior Is Waiting
142	Holy, Holy, Holy Is the Lord of Hosts	598	Wherever He Leads I'll Go
147	How Great Thou Art	602	I Have Decided to Follow Jesus
211	Let There Be Praise	618	In His Presence
214	He Has Made Me Glad	625	Sun of My Soul
222	Lord, We Praise You	634	More Love to Thee
225	Come, Christians, Join to Sing	637	Instruments of Your Peace
244	Come, Thou Long-Expected Jesus	701	God Is My Refuge
249	O Come, All Ye Faithful	737	Like a River Glorious
278	Angels We Have Heard on High	755	We Shall Behold Him
294	One Day	758	Lift Up Your Heads
301	We Will Glorify–Palm Sunday Setting	759	What If It Were Today?
310	Lead Me to Calvary	772	When We All Get to Heaven
337	Nothing But the Blood	774	When the Roll Is Called Up Yonder
349	O How He Loves You and Me	779	I'll Fly Away
353	Victory in Jesus	803	If My People Will Pray

EXTENDED OR CHORAL ENDINGS

34	He Is Lord		
59	Our God Is Lifted Up	288	We Three Kings
88	More Precious than Silver	317	O Mighty Cross
92	O How I Love Jesus	334	The Blood Will Never Lose Its Power
96	To Thee We Ascribe Glory	374	Victory Chant
106	Worthy, You Are Worthy	404	Faith of Our Fathers
117	His Name Is Life	459	We Remember You
129	Great and Mighty	522	I'm So Glad, Jesus Lifted Me
138	Holy Ground	576	The Steadfast Love of the Lord
158	Think About His Love	583	You Are My All in All
171	Come into His Presence	597	Take My Life and Let It Be Consecrated
208	Let the Redeemed	654	Change My Heart, O God
217	Holy Ground	661	Little Is Much When God Is in It
259	Angels, from the Realms of Glory	690	He Leadeth Me
260	Worthy, You Are Worthy–Christmas Setting	716	Jehovah Jireh
271	Joyful, Joyful, We Adore You	761	Therefore the Redeemed of the Lord
285	O Holy Night		

REPEAT REFRAINS OR CHORUS SETTINGS

56	To God Be the Glory	410	Standing on the Promises
62	Blessed Be the Lord God Almighty	442	Each One, Reach One
194	We Worship and Adore You	534	Learning to Lean
208	Let the Redeemed	581	'Tis So Sweet to Trust in Jesus
294	One Day	655	Sanctuary
312	Calvary Covers It All	689	Lead Me, Lord
323	At the Cross	705	It Is Well with My Soul
366	I Live	771	We'll Understand It Better By and By

LAST REFRAIN SETTINGS

139	Great Is Thy Faithfulness	353	Victory in Jesus
249	O Come, All Ye Faithful	434	Revive Us Again

Copyright Owners

The use of the valid copyrights of the following publishers and individuals is gratefully acknowledged. In each case, rearranging, photocopying, or reproduction by any other means, as well as the use of the song in performance for profit, is specifically prohibited by law without the written permission of the copyright owner.

ALBERT E. BRUMLEY & SONS, c/o Integrated Copyright Group, PO Box 24149, Nashville, TN 37202: Selections 353, 779
ALL NATIONS MUSIC, c/o Tempo Music Publications, Inc., 3773 West 95th Street, Leawood, KS 66206: Selections 129, 224, 530, 716
ANGEL BAND MUSIC, c/o Gaither Copyright Management, PO Box 737, Alexandria, IN 46001: Selection 504
ANNAMARIE MUSIC (admin. by Maranatha! Music), c/o The Copyright Company, 40 Music Square East, Nashville, TN 37203: Selections 361, 455
ARIOSE MUSIC, c/o EMI Christian Music Publishing, PO Box 5085, Brentwood, TN 37024-5085: Selection 651
BEN L. SPEER, c/o Integrated Copyright Group, PO Box 24149, Nashville, TN 37202: Selection 762
BIRDWING MUSIC, c/o EMI Christian Music Publishing, PO Box 5085, Brentwood, TN 37024-5085: Selections 81, 160, 217, 226, 308, 389, 432, 456, 537, 643, 644, 758
BMG, c/o BMG Music Publishing, 1 Music Circle North, Nashville, TN 37203: Selection 541
BMG SONGS, INC., c/o BMG Music Publishing, 1 Music Circle North, Nashville, TN 37203: Selections 81, 110, 125, 150, 179, 211, 217, 226, 308, 555, 557, 558, 618, 643, 758
BOB FARRELL MUSIC, c/o Integrated Copyright Group, PO Box 24149, Nashville, TN 37202: Selection 792
BOB KILPATRICK MUSIC, Bob Kilpatrick Music, PO Box 2383, Fair Oaks, CA 95628-2383: Selection 186
BRIDGE BUILDING MUSIC (a div. of Brentwood Music Publishing, Inc.) Brentwood Music Publishing, Inc., One Maryland Farms, Suite 200, Brentwood, TN 37027: Selection 208
BROADMAN PRESS, c/o Genevox Music Group, 127 Ninth Avenue North, Nashville, TN 37234: Selections 122, 325, 396, 415, 516, 519, 536, 598, 664
BUD JOHN SONGS, INC, c/o EMI Christian Music Publishing, PO Box 5085, Brentwood, TN 37024-5085: Selections 54, 55, 69, 70, 231, 422, 436, 757, 803, 814
BUG & BEAR MUSIC, c/o LCS Music Group, Inc., 6301 N. O'Connor Blvd., Bldg. 1, Irving, TX 75039: Selections 184, 678
C.A. MUSIC (a div. of C.A. Records), c/o Music Services, 209 Chapelwood Dr., Franklin, TN 37069: Selections 91, 243
CANDLE COMPANY MUSIC, c/o Bridgestone Multimedia Group, 300 North McKemy Ave., Chandler, AZ 85226: Selection 67
CAREERS-BMG MUSIC PUBLISHING CO, c/o BMG Music Publishing, 1 Music Circle North, Nashville, TN 37203: Selections 533, 573, 644
CAROL JOY MUSIC, c/o Integrated Copyright Group, PO Box 24149, Nashville, TN 37202: Selections 341, 418, 726
CELEBRANT MUSIC, Celebrant Music, PO Box 271, Visalia, CA 93279: Selection 96
CELEBRATION, c/o The Copyright Company, 40 Music Square East, Nashville, TN 37203: Selection 576
CHARLES MONROE (admin. by Maranatha! Music), c/o The Copyright Company, 40 Music Square East, Nashville, TN 37203: Selection 531
CHARLIE MONK MUSIC, c/o The Copyright Company, 40 Music Square East, Nashville, TN 37203: Selections 211, 558
COOMSIETUNES (admin. by Maranatha! Music), c/o The Copyright Company, 40 Music Square East, Nashville, TN 37203: Selection 615
CROUCH MUSIC, c/o EMI Christian Music Publishing, PO Box 5085, Brentwood, TN 37024-5085: Selection 757
DANIEL L. SCHUTTE, c/o OCP Publications, 5536 NE Hassalo, Portland, OR 97213: Selection 589
DAYSPRING MUSIC (a div. of WORD MUSIC), WORD MUSIC, 3319 West End Ave., Suite 200, Nashville, TN 37203: Selections 103, 792
DEEP FRYED MUSIC, c/o Music Services, 209 Chapelwood Dr., Franklin, TN 37069: Selection 339
DICK AND MEL MUSIC, c/o BMG Music Publishing, 1 Music Circle North, Nashville, TN 37203: Selections 555, 618
E.C. SCHIRMER MUSIC CO, c/o ECS Publishing, 138 Ipswich St., Boston, MA 02215: Selection 794
EARS TO HEAR MUSIC, c/o EMI Christian Music Publishing, PO Box 5085, Brentwood, TN 37024-5085: Selection 308
EXPRESSIONS OF PRAISE MUSIC, c/o Music Services, 209 Chapelwood Dr., Franklin, TN 37069: Selection 637
F.E.L. PUBLICATIONS, c/o The Lorenz Corp., 501 E. Third St., Dayton, OH 45402: Selection 429
FAIRHILL MUSIC, Fairhill Music, PO Box 6665, Laguna Niguel, CA 92607: Selection 732
FIRST MONDAY MUSIC (a div. of WORD MUSIC), WORD MUSIC, 3319 West End Ave., Suite 200, Nashville, TN 37203: Selection 371
FOURTH DAY PUBLISHING, c/o WORD MUSIC, 3319 West End Ave., Suite 200, Nashville, TN 37203: Selection 28
FOX PUBLICATIONS, c/o Fred Bock Music Company, PO Box 570567, Tarzana, CA 91357: Selection 448
FRED BOCK MUSIC COMPANY, Fred Bock Music Company, PO Box 570567, Tarzana, CA 91357: Selections 100, 399, 462
G. SCHIRMER, INC, G. Schirmer, Inc., 257 Park Avenue South, New York, NY 10010: Selections 1, 631
GAITHER MUSIC COMPANY, c/o Gaither Copyright Management, PO Box 737, Alexandria, IN 46001: Selections 117, 172, 299, 795
GARDEN VALLEY MUSIC, c/o BMG Music Publishing, 1 Music Circle North, Nashville, TN 37203: Selection 644
GENTLE BEN MUSIC, c/o WORD MUSIC, 3319 West End Ave., Suite 200, Nashville, TN 37203: Selection 792
GOSPEL PUBLISHING HOUSE MUSIC, Gospel Publishing House Music, 1445 Boonville Avenue, Springfield, MO 65802-1894: Selection 395
GRACE FELLOWSHIP (admin. by Maranatha! Music), c/o The Copyright Company, 40 Music Square East, Nashville, TN 37203: Selection 66
GREG NELSON MUSIC, c/o EMI Christian Music Publishing, PO Box 5085, Brentwood, TN 37024-5085: Selections 533, 573
HAMBLEN MUSIC CO, c/o Cohen & Cohen Lawyers, 740 North LaBrea Avenue, Second Floor, Los Angeles, CA 90038-3339: Selection 780
HEARTWARMING MUSIC, c/o Benson Music Group, Inc., 365 Great Circle Road, Nashville, TN 37228-1799: Selections 387, 534
HIS EYE MUSIC, c/o EMI Christian Music Publishing, PO Box 5085, Brentwood, TN 37024-5085: Selections 167, 541
HOLLIS MUSIC, c/o The Richmond Organization, 11 West 19th St., New York, NY 10011-4298: Selection 274
HOPE PUBLISHING COMPANY, Hope Publishing Company, 380 South Main Place, Carol Stream, IL 60188: Selections 116, 139, 293, 409, 450, 465, 485, 502, 734, 739
HOUSE OF MERCY (admin. by Maranatha! Music), c/o The Copyright Company, 40 Music Square East, Nashville, TN 37203: Selection 78
INTEGRITY'S ALLELUIA! MUSIC, Integrity Music, Inc., 1000 Cody Road, Mobile, AL 36695: Selection 800
INTEGRITY'S HOSANNA! MUSIC, Integrity Music, Inc., 1000 Cody Road, Mobile, AL 36695: Selections 3, 5, 7, 11, 14, 15, 16, 17, 20, 21, 37, 40, 41, 44, 45, 48, 56, 57, 59, 63, 64,, 68, 79, 88, 90, 99, 104, 106, 146, 151, 158, 170, 171, 201, 207, 210, 218, 225, 228, 234, 247, 248, 249, 256, 258, 260, 271, 275, 278, 294, 309, 310, 313, 317, 324, 337, 343, 362, 367, 373, 390, 401, 410, 411, 433, 439, 447, 452, 453, 464, 470, 478, 488, 514, 522, 542, 597, 625, 634, 648, 649, 663, 682, 701, 704, 717, 718, 720, 725, 737, 744, 772, 774, 790, 794, 799, 800, 804
INTEGRITY'S PRAISE! MUSIC, Integrity Music, Inc., 1000 Cody Road, Mobile, AL 36695: Selections 317, 470
JEHOVAH-JIREH MUSIC, Jehovah-Jireh Music, PO Box 351, Brentwood, TN 37024: Selection 715
JOHN T. BENSON PUBLISHING COMPANY, c/o Benson Music Group, Inc., 365 Great Circle Road, Nashville, TN 37228-1799: Selections 213, 304, 366, 387, 711, 755
JOHN W. PETERSON MUSIC COMPANY, John W. Peterson Music Company, 13610 North Scottsdale Road, Suite 10-221, Scottsdale, AZ 85254: Selections 494, 510, 610, 753
JONATHAN MARK MUSIC, c/o Gaither Copyright Management, PO Box 737, Alexandria, IN 46001: Selections 456, 537
JUNIPER LANDING MUSIC, c/o WORD MUSIC, 3319 West End Ave., Suite 200, Nashville, TN 37203: Selections 411, 452, 663
KAY CHANCE, Kay Chance,Dr. H.-Jasper-Str. 20, D-37581 Bad Gandersheim, Germany: Selection 149
KINGSMEN PUBLISHING CO, c/o Benson Music Group, Inc., 365 Great Circle Road, Nashville, TN 37228-1799: Selection 776

KINGSWAY'S THANKYOU MUSIC, c/o Integrity Music, Inc., 1000 Cody Road, Mobile, AL 36695: Selection 84, 425, 801

KIRK TALLEY MUSIC, c/o Integrated Copyright Group, PO Box 24149, Nashville, TN 37202: Selection 220

L. E. SMITH, JR, New Jerusalem Music, PO Box 225, Pinemill Road, Clarksboro, NJ 08020: Selection 372

LANNY WOLFE MUSIC COMPANY, c/o Integrated Copyright Group, PO Box 24149, Nashville, TN 37202: Selections 219, 394

LATTER RAIN MUSIC, c/o EMI Christian Music Publishing, PO Box 5085, Brentwood, TN 37024-5085: Selection 22

LIFESONG MUSIC PRESS, c/o Benson Music Group, Inc., 365 Great Circle Road, Nashville, TN 37228-1799: Selection 595

LILLENAS PUBLISHING CO, c/o The Copyright Company, 40 Music Square East, Nashville, TN 37203: Selections 222, 271, 423, 543, 550, 707, 764, 765

LINDA STASSEN, New Song Ministries, RR 1 Box 454, Erin, TN 37061: Selection 198

MAGNOLIA HILL MUSIC, c/o Integrated Copyright Group, PO Box 24149, Nashville, TN 37202: Selection 110

MAKANUME MUSIC, c/o EMI Christian Music Publishing, PO Box 5085, Brentwood, TN 37024-5085: Selection 70

MAKE WAY MUSIC, c/o Integrity Music, Inc., 1000 Cody Road, Mobile, AL 36695: Selections 351, 431

MANNA MUSIC, INC., Manna Music, Inc., PO Box 218, Pacific City, OR 97135: Selections 118, 147, 189, 334, 391, 580, 601

MARANATHA! MUSIC, c/o The Copyright Company, 40 Music Square East, Nashville, TN 37203: Selections 9, 66, 107, 119, 133, 159, 191, 199, 214, 227, 339, 454, 459, 481, 531, 548, 614, 622, 627, 633, 669, 681, 700, 708, 713

MARQUIS MUSIC III (a div. of Imperials Music Group), c/o WORD MUSIC, 3319 West End Ave., Suite 200, Nashville, TN 37203: Selection 125

MATERIAL MUSIC, c/o WORD MUSIC, 3319 West End Ave., Suite 200, Nashville, TN 37203: Selection 131

MCKINNEY MUSIC, INC, c/o Genevox Music Group, 127 Ninth Avenue North, Nashville, TN 37234: Selection 153

MEADOWGREEN MUSIC CO., c/o EMI Christian Music Publishing, PO Box 5085, Brentwood, TN 37024-5085: Selections 121, 124, 138, 140, 184

MERCY/VINEYARD PUBLISHING, c/o Music Services, 209 Chapelwood Dr., Franklin, TN 37069: Selections 254, 296, 384, 654

MOUNTAIN SPRING MUSIC, c/o EMI Christian Music Publishing, PO Box 5085, Brentwood, TN 37024-5085: Selections 36, 302, 651, 817

MULTISONGS (A division of Careers-BMG Music Publishing) c/o, BMG Music Publishing, 1 Music Circle North, Nashville, TN 37203: Selections 167, 573

MUSIC BY HUMMINGBIRD/ FARNSWORTH PUBLISHING, Music by Hummingbird/Farnsworth Publishing, 7 Music Square West, Nashville, TN 37203: Selection 647

NAZARENE PUBLISHING HOUSE, c/o The Copyright Company, 40 Music Square East, Nashville, TN 37203: Selection 511

NEW DAWN MUSIC, c/o OCP Publications, 5536 NE Hassalo, Portland, OR 97213: Selection 589

NEW SPRING PUBLISHING (a div. of Brentwood Music Publishing, Inc.), Brentwood Music Publishing, Inc., One Maryland Farms, Suite 200, Brentwood, TN 37027: Selections 559, 689

NOLENE PRINCE, Resource Christian Music, Unit 412 Garden Blvd., Dingley 3172 Victoria, Australia: Selection 142

NORMAN CLAYTON PUBLISHING (a div. of WORD MUSIC), WORD MUSIC, 3319 West End Ave., Suite 200, Nashville, TN 37203: Selections 152, 501, 540

OOH'S AND AH'S MUSIC, c/o EMI Christian Music Publishing, PO Box 5085, Brentwood, TN 37024-5085: Selection 70

PAMELA KAY MUSIC, c/o EMI Christian Music Publishing, PO Box 5085, Brentwood, TN 37024-5085: Selections 125, 211, 555, 557, 618

PEOPLE OF DESTINY INTERNATIONAL, People of Destiny International, 7881 Beechcraft Ave., Suite B, Gaithersburg, MD 20879: Selections 80, 173

PETE SANCHEZ, JR, c/o Gabriel Music, PO Box 840999, Houston, TX 77284-0999: Selection 31

PILOT POINT MUSIC, c/o The Copyright Company, 40 Music Square East, Nashville, TN 37203: Selections 289, 354, 385

PRIESTHOOD PUBLICATIONS, Priesthood Publications, 1894 Rowland Ave., Camarillo, CA 93010: Selection 241

RIVER OAKS MUSIC COMPANY, c/o EMI Christian Music Publishing, PO Box 5085, Brentwood, TN 37024-5085: Selections 47, 109, 175, 299, 445, 795

ROCKSMITH MUSIC, c/o Trust Music Management, Inc., PO Box 9256, Calabasas, CA 91372: Selection 10, 141

RON HARRIS MUSIC, Ron Harris Music Publishing, 22643 Paul Revere Dr, Calabasas, CA 91302-4811: Selection 612

ROYAL TAPESTRY MUSIC, c/o Benson Music Group, Inc., 365 Great Circle Road, Nashville, TN 37228-1799: Selection 74

SACRED SONGS (a div. of WORD MUSIC), WORD MUSIC, 3319 West End Ave., Suite 200, Nashville, TN 37203: Selection 702

SANDI'S SONG MUSIC, c/o Erickson & Baugher, Inc., 114 E. Main Street, Suite 200, Franklin, TN 37064: Selections 299, 533

SCRIPTURE IN SONG (a div. of Integrity Music, Inc.), Integrity Music, Inc., 1000 Cody Road, Mobile, AL 36695: Selections 32, 35, 62, 86, 209, 374, 424, 729, 761

SHEPHERD BOY, c/o WORD MUSIC, 3319 West End Ave., Suite 200, Nashville, TN 37203: Selection 600

SHEPHERD'S FOLD MUSIC, c/o EMI Christian Music Publishing, PO Box 5085, Brentwood, TN 37024-5085: Selections 109, 445

SHEPHERD'S HEART MUSIC, c/o WORD, INC., 3319 West End Ave., Suite 200, Nashville, TN 37203: Selections 376, 583

SINGSPIRATION MUSIC, c/o Benson Music Group, Inc., 365 Great Circle Road, Nashville, TN 37228-1799: Selections 105, 110, 154, 301, 303, 340, 427, 440, 451, 487, 496, 513, 577, 691, 706, 721

SOME-O-DAT MUSIC, c/o WORD MUSIC, 3319 West End Ave., Suite 200, Nashville, TN 37203: Selections 60, 117, 195, 432

SONGCHANNEL MUSIC CO, c/o EMI Christian Music Publishing, PO Box 5085, Brentwood, TN 37024-5085: Selection 138

SOUND III (a div. of All Nations Music), c/o Tempo Music Publications, Inc., 3773 West 95th Street, Leawood, KS 66206: Selections 129, 224, 530, 716

SPARROW SONG, c/o EMI Christian Music Publishing, PO Box 5085, Brentwood, TN 37024-5085: Selection 573

SPIRIT QUEST MUSIC, c/o Gaither Copyright Management, PO Box 737, Alexandria, IN 46001: Selection 483

SPOONE MUSIC, c/o WORD MUSIC, 3319 West End Ave., Suite 200, Nashville, TN 37203: Selection 709

STEADFAST MUSIC, c/o Erickson & Baugher, Inc., 114 E. Main Street, Suite 200, Franklin, TN 37064: Selection 792

STRAIGHTWAY MUSIC, c/o EMI Christian Music Publishing, PO Box 5085, Brentwood, TN 37024-5085: Selections 36, 60, 302, 533, 647, 817

SUMMERDAWN MUSIC, c/o Integrated Copyright Group, PO Box 24149, Nashville, TN 37202: Selections 533, 792

THE HYMN SOCIETY OF AMERICA, c/o Hope Publishing Company, 380 South Main Place, Carol Stream, IL 60188: Selections 407, 677

THE JOY OF THE LORD PUBLISHING, c/o EMI Christian Music Publishing, PO Box 5085, Brentwood, TN 37024-5085: Selection 541

THE RODEHEAVER CO. (a div. of WORD MUSIC), WORD MUSIC, 3319 West End Ave., Suite 200, Nashville, TN 37203: Selections 312, 368, 369, 506, 670, 738, 775

VAN NESS PRESS, INC, c/o Genevox Music Group, 127 Ninth Avenue North, Nashville, TN 37234: Selections 153, 461

WARNER-TAMERLANE PUBLISHING CORP., c/o Warner Bros. Publications U.S. Inc., 15800 NW 48th Ave., Miami, FL 33014: Selection 684

WHOLE ARMOR/FULL ARMOR, TKO Publishers Limited, P.O. Box 130, Hove, East Sussex BN3 6QU England: Selection 655

WILLIAM J. GAITHER, c/o Gaither Copyright Management, PO Box 737, Alexandria, IN 46001: Selections 18, 83, 318, 358, 382, 419, 505, 507, 520, 544, 599, 604, 660, 763, 791

WILLING HEART MUSIC (admin. by Maranatha! Music), c/o The Copyright Company, 40 Music Square East, Nashville, TN 37203: Selection 669

WORD MUSIC (a div. of WORD MUSIC), WORD MUSIC, 3319 West End Ave., Suite 200, Nashville, TN 37203: Selections 3, 7, 11, 14, 16, 17, 21, 28, 34, 45, 46, 56, 63, 68, 74, 79, 90, 104,, 119, 125, 126, 131, 144, 151, 152, 161, 175, 181, 183, 200, 207, 210, 225, 233, 247, 249, 258, 263, 264, 271, 275, 278, 287, 280, 284, 294, 309, 310, 321, 324, 333, 337, 339, 341, 343, 349, 363, 367, 390, 401, 402, 410, 411, 417, 418, 433, 442, 452, 453, 460, 464, 465, 468, 478, 484, 488, 522, 526, 562, 572, 585, 586, 597, 600, 602, 625, 634, 648, 657, 662, 663, 672, 682, 709, 718, 720, 724, 726, 737, 760, 772, 774, 789, 790, 794, 796, 799, 804, 805

WORD OF GOD MUSIC, c/o The Copyright Company, 40 Music Square East, Nashville, TN 37203: Selection 359

YELLOW HOUSE MUSIC, c/o Benson Music Group, Inc., 365 Great Circle Road, Nashville, TN 37228-1799: Selection 47

ZIONSONG MUSIC, ZionSong Music, PO Box 574044, Orlando, FL 32857: Selection 111

Alphabetical Index by Tune Name

Metrical Index of Tunes

*Complete listing of Irregular Meter tunes may be found
in the Worship Resource Edition*

Authors, Composers, Sources, Translators and Arrangers

Topical Index of Songs

At the Name of Jesus (BERRY), 28
Blessed Be the Name, 52
Blessed Be the Name of the Lord, 64
Crown Him King of Kings, 44
Eternal Father, Strong to Save, 808
Freely, Freely, 436
Glorious Is Thy Name, 122
Hallowed Be Thy Name, 200
He Keeps Me Singing, 746
His Glorious Name, 130
His Name Is Life, 117
His Name Is Wonderful, 118
How Majestic Is Your Name, 121
How Sweet the Name of Jesus
   Sounds, 123
I Extol You, 248
In the Name of the Lord, 299
Jesus Is the Sweetest Name I Know, 76
Jesus, Lord to Me, 47
Jesus, Name above All Names, 86
Jesus, Your Name, 119
Join All the Glorious Names, 132
Lift High the Lord Our Banner, 41
Mighty Warrior, 725
Name of All Majesty, 116
No Other Name, 15
Praise Him! Praise Him!, 12
Praise the Name of Jesus, 22
Take the Name of Jesus with You, 235
That Beautiful Name, 266
The Sweetest Name of All, 615
There Is No Name So Sweet on
   Earth, 6
There's Something About That
   Name, 83
Worthy of Worship, 153

CHRIST — Life and Ministry
Come, Thou Long-Expected Jesus, 244
Joy to the World!, 270
O Sing a Song of Bethlehem, 291
One Day, 294
Praise the One Who Breaks the
   Darkness, 293
Tell Me the Story of Jesus, 295
Thou Didst Leave Thy Throne, 292

CHRIST — Lordship and Reign
A Child of the King, 574
Adoration, 289
All Glory, Laud and Honor, 300
All Hail, King Jesus, 103
Alleluia, Alleluia! Give Thanks, 359
Alleluia! Sing to Jesus, 377
Behold the Lamb, 304
Crown Him King of Kings, 44
Crown Him with Many Crowns, 45
Great Is the Lord Almighty!, 376
He Is Exalted, 36
He Is Lord, 34
His Name Is Wonderful, 118
Hosanna, 296
I Am Trusting Thee, Lord Jesus, 582
I Cannot Tell, 354
I Love You, Lord, 78
Jesus Is Lord of All (LORD OF ALL),
   599
Jesus Is Lord of All
   (LORDSHIP OF CHRIST), 519
Jesus Shall Reign, 375
Let's Just Praise the Lord, 18
Lift High the Lord Our Banner, 41

Lord, We Praise You, 222
Majesty, 10
Name of All Majesty, 116
Oh for a Thousand Tongues, 371
Our God Reigns, 372
Praise Him! Praise Him!, 12
Rejoice, the Lord Is King, 370
The Birthday of a King, 284
The Sweetest Name of All, 615
Thou Didst Leave Thy Throne, 292
To Him Who Sits on the Throne, 373
Victory Chant, 374
Victory Song (Through Our God), 729
We Bow Down, 154
What Child Is This?, 281
Worthy of Worship, 153
Worthy, You Are Worthy, 106
Worthy, You Are Worthy-
   Christmas Setting, 260
You Are Crowned with Many
   Crowns, 37
You Are My God, 40

CHRIST — Our Love for
All Hail King Jesus, 103
At the Name of Jesus (WYE VALLEY),
   766
Blessed Redeemer, 326
Close to Thee, 607
I Love You, Lord, 78
I Will Come and Bow Down, 228
I Will Remember Thee (According to
   Thy Gracious Word), 463
Lord, We Praise You, 222
More Love to Thee, 634
My Jesus, I Love Thee, 79
O How I Love Jesus, 92
Shine, Jesus, Shine, 431

CHRIST — Resurrection
Alleluia! Alleluia!, 365
Alleluia, Alleluia! Give Thanks, 359
Be Joyful, 363
Because He Lives, 358
Celebrate Jesus, 362
Christ Arose, 357
Christ the Lord Is Risen Today, 367
Crown Him with Many Crowns, 45
Emmanuel, 243
Hallelujah Chorus, 39
Hallelujah! Praise the Lamb, 110
He Is Lord, 34
He Lives, 368
He Rose Triumphantly, 369
I Cannot Tell, 354
I Live, 366
Jesus Christ Is Risen Today, 360
Lord, I Lift Your Name on High, 107
One Day, 294
Our God Reigns, 372
Were You There?, 315
Worship Christ, the Risen King, 361

CHRIST — Second Coming
At the Name of Jesus (BERRY), 28
Coming Again, 765
Hallelujah, What a Savior!, 311
Jesus Is Coming Again, 753
Jesus, We Just Want to Thank You, 791
Lift Up Your Heads, 758
Lo, He Comes with Clouds
   Descending, 754

One Day, 294
Soon and Very Soon, 757
The King Is Coming, 763
Therefore the Redeemed of the Lord,
   761
We Shall Behold Him, 755
What a Day That Will Be, 762
What If It Were Today?, 759
While We Are Waiting, Come, 760

**CHRIST — The Coming of the
   Wisemen**
Adoration, 289
As with Gladness Men of Old, 290
Break Forth, O Beauteous Heavenly
   Light, 264
Go, Tell It on the Mountain, 258
O Sing a Song of Bethlehem, 291
One Small Child, 280
Sing We Now of Christmas, 275
The First Noel, 265
We Three Kings, 288
What Child Is This?, 281

CHRIST — Triumphal Entry
All Glory, Laud and Honor, 300
Hosanna, 296
Hosanna, Loud Hosanna, 297
In the Name of the Lord, 299
We Will Glorify - Palm Sunday
   Setting, 301

CHURCH — Family of Believers
Bind Us Together, 425
Come, Christians, Join to Sing, 225
Come into His Presence, 171
Good Christian Men, Rejoice, 273
I Love You with the Love of the
   Lord, 422
In Christ There Is No East or West,
   428
Joyful, Joyful, We Adore Thee, 90
Let's Just Praise the Lord, 18
People of God, 427
The Church's One Foundation, 401
The Family of God, 419
The Servant Song, 424
They'll Know We Are Christians by
   Our Love, 429
We Are Called to Be God's People, 415
We Will Stand, 417
We're Marching to Zion, 416

**CHURCH — Nature and
   Foundation**
Christ Is Made the Sure Foundation,
   403
Cornerstone, 402
Find Us Faithful, 456
Glorious Things of Thee Are
   Spoken, 400
How Firm a Foundation, 408
I Love Thy Kingdom, Lord, 405
Lord, Be Glorified, 186
People of God, 427
The Church's One Foundation, 401
We Are God's People, 399

**CLOSING OF WORSHIP —
   Benedictions**
Christ, We Do All Adore Thee, 230
God Be with You, 232

TOPICAL INDEX OF SONGS

INVITATION AND ACCEPTANCE

All Your Anxiety, 613
Are You Washed in the Blood?, 330
Come Just as You Are, 481
Come, Ye Sinners, Poor and Needy, 486
Have Thine Own Way, Lord, 591
Have You Any Room for Jesus?, 478
I Have Decided to Follow Jesus, 602
I Surrender All, 596
Into My Heart, 485
Jesus Calls Us, 592
Jesus, I Come, 491
Jesus Is Calling, 482
Just as I Am, 488
Lord, I'm Coming Home, 490
Only Trust Him, 480
Room at the Cross for You, 487
Softly and Tenderly, 479
Take My Life, Lead Me, Lord, 664
The Savior Is Waiting, 483
Thou Didst Leave Thy Throne, 292
Turn Your Eyes upon Jesus, 340

JOY

Be Joyful, 363
Good Christian Men, Rejoice, 273
He Keeps Me Singing, 746
How Great Our Joy!, 269
In This Very Room, 612
Jesus, I Am Resting, Resting, 741
Joy of My Desire, 744
Joy to the World!, 270
Joy Unspeakable, 740
Joyful, Joyful, We Adore Thee, 90
Joyful, Joyful, We Adore You, 271
Let There Be Praise, 211
Like a River Glorious, 737
Our God Is Lifted Up, 59
Peace like a River, 750
Praise the One Who Breaks the Darkness, 293
Rejoice in the Lord Always, 745
Rejoice, the Lord Is King, 370
Sunshine in My Soul, 747
The Trees of the Field, 764
The Wonder of It All, 738
Therefore the Redeemed of the Lord, 761
'Til the Storm Passes By, 543
Why Do I Sing About Jesus?, 739
Wonderful Peace, 743
Wonderful, Wonderful Jesus, 749

LOVE — God's Love

Children of the Heavenly Father, 719
Father God, 141
God So Loved the World, 350
Hallelujah! Praise the Lamb, 110
I Am His, and He Is Mine, 748
I Will Sing of My Redeemer, 517
Jesus, Lover of My Soul, 710
Jesus Loves Even Me, 495
Jesus Loves Me, 185
Jesus, My Jesus, 341
Joyful, Joyful, We Adore Thee, 90
Joyful, Joyful, We Adore You, 271
Love Divine, All Loves Excelling, 648
Love Has Come!, 256
Love Lifted Me, 508
No One Ever Cared for Me like Jesus, 496
O How He Loves You and Me, 349
O Love That Will Not Let Me Go, 606

O the Deep, Deep Love of Jesus, 352
Of the Father's Love Begotten, 240
Stand Up and Bless the Lord, 65
The Love of God, 157
Think About His Love, 158
Thy Loving Kindness, 706
When I Survey the Wondrous Cross (O WALY WALY), 321
When I Survey the Wondrous Cross (HAMBURG), 324

LOVE — Our Love for God

Abba Father, 81
Bless God, 60
Hosanna, 296
I Offer My Life, 663
I Will Bless Thee, O Lord, 174
In Moments like These, 91
Joyful, Joyful, We Adore Thee, 90
More Love to Thee, 634
My Jesus, I Love Thee, 79
O How I Love Jesus, 92
Seekers of Your Heart, 557
The Greatest Thing, 644
With All My Heart, 662

LOVE — Our Love for Others

Blest Be the Tie that Binds, 426
Each One, Reach One, 442
Here I Am, Lord, 589
I Love You with the Love of the Lord, 422
Make Us One, 418
People Need the Lord, 445
The Bond of Love, 423
The Servant Song, 424
They'll Know We Are Christians by Our Love, 429

LOYALTY AND COURAGE

A Charge to Keep I Have, 666
Faith Is the Victory, 727
Greater Is He That Is in Me, 394
I Must Tell Jesus, 636
I Need Thee Every Hour, 638
Near the Cross, 319
O Jesus, I Have Promised, 676
Take the Name of Jesus with You, 235
Who Is on the Lord's Side?, 674

MEMORIAL DAY

America, the Beautiful, 799
Battle Hymn of the Republic, 804
God of Our Fathers, 809
Once to Every Man and Nation, 733
We Gather Together, 790

MEMORIAL OCCASIONS

Faith of Our Fathers, 404
For All the Saints, 767
God of Our Fathers, 809
O God, Our Help in Ages Past, 686
We Gather Together, 790

MISSIONS AND MINISTRY

All Hail the Power of Jesus' Name (CORONATION), 43
All Hail the Power of Jesus' Name (DIADEM), 16
Each One, Reach One, 442
Freely, Freely, 436
Go, Tell It on the Mountain, 258

I Love to Tell the Story, 444
I'll Go Where You Want Me to Go, 668
I'll Tell the World That I'm a Christian, 448
In Christ There Is No East or West, 428
Jesus Loves the Little Children, 447
Jesus Saves!, 438
Jesus Shall Reign, 375
Lift High the Cross, 450
Little Is Much When God Is in It, 661
Lord, Lay Some Soul upon My Heart, 449
Lord, Speak to Me, 667
Make Me a Blessing, 670
O for a Thousand Tongues to Sing, 21
O Zion, Haste, 443
Open My Eyes, That I May See, 563
Our God Reigns, 372
Our Great Savior, 17
People Need the Lord, 445
Rescue the Perishing, 441
Send the Light, 437
So Send I You- by Grace Made Strong, 440
Song for the Nations, 439
Take the Name of Jesus with You, 235
Tell Me the Story of Jesus, 295
The Church's One Foundation, 401
We've a Story to Tell to the Nations, 446
Wherever He Leads I'll Go, 598
Ye Servants of God, 38

MOTHER'S DAY

For the Beauty of the Earth, 793
Happy Our Home When God Is There, 453
Now Thank We All Our God, 788
O Perfect Love, 458

NEW YEAR

Another Year Is Dawning, 811
Guide Me, O Thou Great Jehovah, 682
Now Thank We All Our God, 788
O God, Our Help in Ages Past, 686
Savior, like a Shepherd Lead Us, 688

OPENING OF WORSHIP — Calls to Worship

Brethren, We Have Met to Worship (see We Have Come to Join in Worship), 207
Cast Thy Burden upon the Lord, 229
Christ, We Do All Adore Thee, 230
Come, Christians, Join to Sing, 225
Come into His Presence, 171
Come into the Holy of Holies, 218
Come, Let Us Worship and Bow Down, 227
He Is Here, 220
Holy Ground, 217
Holy Spirit, Thou Art Welcome, 387
Hosanna, 296
Let the Redeemed, 208
Let There Be Glory and Honor and Praises, 20
Surely the Presence of the Lord Is in This Place, 219
The Lord Is in His Holy Temple, 216
This Is the Day, 209
We Bring the Sacrifice of Praise, 213

TOPICAL INDEX OF SONGS

We Have Come into His House, 224
We Have Come to Join in Worship, 207

OPENING OF WORSHIP —
Hymns and Songs
All Hail King Jesus, 103
All People That on Earth Do Dwell, 101
All Praise to Our Redeeming Lord, 221
At the Name of Jesus (WYE VALLEY), 766
Brethren, We Have Met to Worship (see We Have Come to Join in Worship), 207
Cast Thy Burden upon the Lord, 229
Come, Christians, Join to Sing, 225
Come Holy Spirit, Dove Divine, 467
Come into His Presence (BAIRD) , 171
Come into His Presence (HIS PRESENCE), 420
Come into the Holy of Holies, 218
Come, Let Us Reason, 484
Come, Let Us Worship and Bow Down, 227
Come, Thou Almighty King, 8
He Has Made Me Glad (I Will Enter His Gates), 214
He Is Here, 220
Holy Ground (BEATTY), 217
Holy, Holy, 69
Holy Spirit, Thou Art Welcome, 387
I Will Come and Bow Down, 228
Let the Redeemed, 208
Let There Be Glory and Honor and Praises, 20
Let There Be Praise, 211
Let Us Break Bread Together, 460
Lift High the Lord Our Banner, 41
Lord, We Praise You, 222
Oh the Glory of Your Presence, 226
Open My Eyes, That I May See, 563
Open Our Eyes, Lord, 633
Praise to the Lord, the Almighty, 210
Sing unto the Lord, 46
Sing unto the Lord, 57
Stand Up and Bless the Lord, 65
Surely the Presence of the Lord Is in This Place, 219
This Is the Day, 209
We Bow Down, 154
We Bring the Sacrifice of Praise, 213
We Have Come into His House, 224
We Have Come to Join in Worship, 207
When Morning Gilds the Skies, 215

PEACE
Ask Ye What Great Thing I Know, 535
He Hideth My Soul, 611
He Is Our Peace, 614
He Keeps Me Singing, 746
Heaven Came Down, 510
I Am His, and He Is Mine, 748
In My Heart There Rings a Melody, 502
In This Very Room, 612
It Is Well with My Soul, 705
Jesus, I Am Resting, Resting, 741
Joy of My Desire, 744
Joy Unspeakable, 740
Like a River Glorious, 737
My Faith Has Found a Resting Place, 528
Near to the Heart of God, 617

Now I Belong to Jesus, 501
O Happy Day!, 498
Peace like a River, 750
Rejoice in the Lord Always, 745
Rejoice, Ye Pure in Heart, 169
Saved, Saved!, 500
Since Jesus Came into My Heart, 503
Sunshine in My Soul, 747
The Joy of the Lord, 541
The Wonder of It All, 738
'Til the Storm Passes By, 543
Why Do I Sing about Jesus?, 739
Wonderful Peace, 743
Wonderful, Wonderful Jesus, 749

PRAYER AND DEVOTION
Abide with Me, 642
Change My Heart, O God, 654
Dear Lord and Father of Mankind, 639
Heal Our Land, 800
Hear Our Prayer, O Lord, 641
I Must Tell Jesus, 636
I Need Thee Every Hour, 638
I Will Call upon the Lord, 530
If My People Will Pray, 803
In the Garden, 635
Instruments of Your Peace, 637
Into My Heart, 485
Lord, Be Glorified, 186
Make Me a Servant, 669
Make Us One, 418
More Love to Thee, 634
O Bless the Gifts, 817
O Lord, You're Beautiful, 643
Open Our Eyes, Lord, 633
Sanctuary, 655
Seek Ye First, 713
Song for the Nations, 439
Sweet Hour of Prayer, 640
The Family Prayer Song, 454
The Greatest Thing, 644
The Lord's Prayer, 631
Unto Thee, O Lord, 531
We Give These Gifts, 818
What a Friend We Have in Jesus, 630

PROMISES
God Will Take Care of You, 692
Sanctuary, 655
Seek Ye First, 713
The Joy of the Lord, 541

PROVISION AND DELIVERANCE
A Shield About Me, 709
All That I Need, 651
All the Way My Savior Leads Me, 680
Be Still, My Soul, 712
Behold, What Manner of Love, 708
Children of the Heavenly Father, 719
Come, Every One Who Is Thirsty, 720
Cornerstone, 402
Day by Day, 718
Fill My Cup, Lord, 702
Footsteps of Jesus, 685
God Is My Refuge, 701
God Will Make a Way, 704
Good Shepherd, Take This Little Child, 468
Guide Me, O Thou Great Jehovah, 682
He Giveth More Grace, 707
He Is Jehovah, 715
He Leadeth Me, 690
I Am the God That Healeth Thee, 717

I Believe in a Hill Called Mount Calvary, 318
I Will Call upon the Lord, 530
In His Time, 681
It Is Well with My Soul, 705
Jehovah-Jireh, 716
Jesus, Lover of My Soul, 710
Jesus Never Fails, 721
Lead Me, Lord, 689
O Lord, You're Beautiful, 643
Precious Lord, Take My Hand, 684
Rise and Be Healed, 711
Savior, like a Shepherd Lead Us, 688
The King of Love My Shepherd Is, 683
The Way of the Cross Leads Home, 697
Therefore the Redeemed of the Lord, 761
Thy Loving Kindness, 706
Unto Thee, O Lord, 531
You Are My Hiding Place, 700

PURITY AND HOLINESS
All That I Need, 651
Almighty, 131
Bless God, 60
Bless the Lord, O My Soul, 58
Change My Heart, O God, 654
Cleanse Me, 657
Give Me Jesus, 554
Great Are You, Lord, 159
I Am a Woman, 452
I Live, 366
I Worship You, Almighty God, 146
Love Divine, All Loves Excelling, 648
O for a Heart to Praise My God, 650
Pure and Holy, 647
Revive Us, O Lord, 432
Take Time to Be Holy, 656
Turn Your Eyes upon Jesus, 340
When I Look into Your Holiness, 649
Whiter than Snow, 653
Worthy, You Are Worthy, 106
Worthy, You Are Worthy-Christmas Setting, 260

RENEWAL AND REVIVAL
God of Grace and God of Glory, 435
Revive Us Again, 434
Revive Us, O Lord, 432
Rise Up, O Church of God, 433
Shine, Jesus, Shine, 431
Song for the Nations, 439
There Shall Be Showers of Blessing, 430

REPENTANCE AND FORGIVENESS
At Calvary, 492
Cleanse Me, 657
Come, Ye Sinners, Poor and Needy, 486
Hallelujah! Praise the Lamb, 110
I Am Resolved, 566
If My People Will Pray, 803
If My People's Hearts Are Humbled, 805
Into My Heart, 485
Jesus, I Come, 491
Just as I Am, 488
Lord, I'm Coming Home, 490
O the Blood of Jesus, 333
Pass Me Not, 489
Revive Us, O Lord, 432
Since I Have Been Redeemed, 515

TOPICAL INDEX OF SONGS

Alphabetical Index of Songs

Titles are in regular type; First lines are in *italics*

Many other helpful indexes are available in the Worship Resource Edition (301 0167 369). They include:

Index of Keys
Individual Song Medley Index
Alphabetical Index of Scripture Readings
Biblical Order of Songs Based on or Adapted from Scripture
Non-Scripture Reading
Scripture Appearing beneath Song Titles
Scripture Reference Index of Songs in Alphabetical Order
Scripture Reference Index of Songs in Biblical Order
Scripture Reference Index of Songs in Numerical Order
Spoken Calls to Worship and Benedictions